RISING IN FLAMES

RISING IN
FLAMES

SHERMAN'S MARCH AND
THE FIGHT FOR A NEW NATION

J. D. DICKEY

PEGASUS BOOKS
NEW YORK LONDON

RISING IN FLAMES

Pegasus Books Ltd.
148 W 37th Street, 13th Floor
New York, NY 10018

First Pegasus Books edition June 2018

Interior design by Maria Fernandez

Library of Congress Cataloging-in-Publication Data is available.

ISBN: 978-1-68177-757-3

10 9 8 7 6 5 4 3 2 1

Printed in the United States of America
Distributed by W. W. Norton & Company

To Teresa

CONTENTS

AUTHOR'S NOTE

I spent the majority of my childhood in the South. My father worked for a textile manufacturer and my mother taught school. Typical for the time, my family followed my dad where his job led him, from Birmingham, Alabama, to Greenville, South Carolina. It was an itinerant work life, but a good and productive one, and when it ended, as so many careers in the textile industry did in the 1980s, he moved us to a distant corner of the country to find new opportunities. Yet though I've lived away from the region for decades, I've never forgotten the South, with its deep woods and sublime mountains, its unforgettable food and rich storytelling, and its many legends, ghosts, and phantoms.

One of the earliest field trips I remember was visiting Fort Sumter. It didn't mean much to me as a child—an old fort by the sea guarded by antique cannons—but my schoolteacher couldn't help but remind us students that this was where the Civil War started (or more likely she called it The War Between the States). The fort seemed like a poignant relic from a distant era, and was South Carolina's principal claim to wartime importance, or so it seemed. I learned much later that the state played another significant role during the war, with large parts of it looted, pillaged, and set on fire.

The figure responsible for this violence was, of course, William Sherman. During his Atlanta, Savannah, and Carolinas campaigns, the general ensured he would never be forgotten by the South and would leave a permanent mark on its history, landscape, and psyche. His military actions remain rich and vivid to the Southern mind, despite being more than six generations in the past.

Though I was partly raised in the region, this book is not about Sherman's invasion from the perspective of the South. That view has been covered well and near-exhaustively by onlookers, critics, and aggrieved parties for more than a century now, and anyone with a passing interest in the subject need go no further than a perusal of *Gone with the Wind* to learn the feelings of those who resisted the march of Northern armies and were duly overwhelmed by them. Rather, this volume concerns the perspective of the marchers themselves—the invading troops who did so much to cripple the Confederate economy, damage its landscape, and sap its people of the will to fight and hasten the end of the war.

The effect of William Sherman on the South may be well known, but much less familiar is his effect on the North, and how his invasion of Georgia and the Carolinas helped to transform the Union, and especially the western states, during and after the conflict. From engendering new perspectives on the role of women and African Americans in U.S. society, to helping flower movements for temperance and spiritual revival, Sherman's campaigns had a stark and dramatic effect on long-held social beliefs and political ideologies, as well as what it meant to be an American.

Paradoxically, the general himself wanted none of these things. He was one of the most stubborn reactionaries in the U.S. military, yet ended up as one of its most transformative figures—a looming presence that today still excites angry passions and vigorous debates. And it's easy to understand why. Sherman devastated large swaths of the South, and many of the regions his troops passed over remain impoverished, desolate, demoralized. This book spares none of the violence of his campaigns or their targeted horror. But history like life can be rich with dualities—namely, how something so destructive, so fearsome as a mass invasion can have unplanned consequences for both the invaded and the invaders.

Through journals, letters, and official records, we can learn what it meant to be a part of those brazen Union armies, and how Sherman's marchers (to the sea and elsewhere) were forced to reconcile their firmly held beliefs with the reality of war, and how so many of them ended up reinvented and otherwise changed by it. And it is this transformation this book is about: the alterations to the social and cultural fabric of the North wrought by the damage to the physical landscape of the South. The galvanizing and metamorphic effect of violence on both its perpetrators and its victims. And the way a military genius, unhinged madman, unexpected liberator, and lawless tyrant can all exist in the reputation of the same legendary figure.

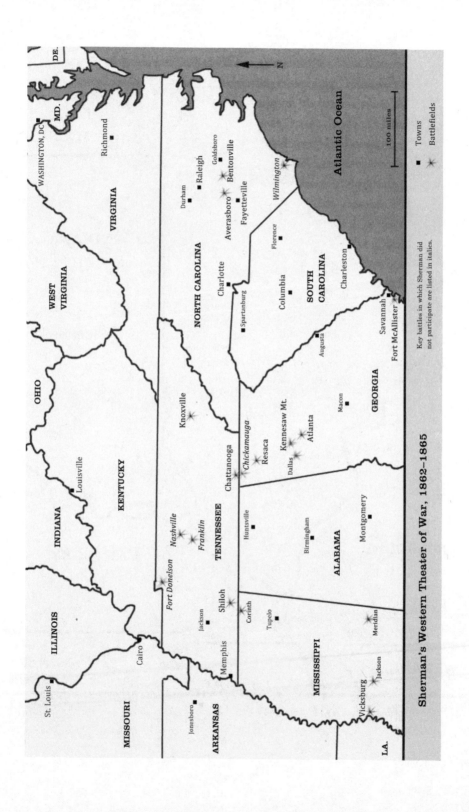

Sherman's Western Theater of War, 1862–1865

Key battles in which Sherman did
not participate are listed in italics.

■ Towns
✦ Battlefields

N

100 miles

Atlantic Ocean

MISSOURI

ILLINOIS

INDIANA

OHIO

WEST VIRGINIA

KENTUCKY

TENNESSEE

VIRGINIA

NORTH CAROLINA

SOUTH CAROLINA

GEORGIA

ALABAMA

MISSISSIPPI

ARKANSAS

LA.

DE.

MD.

St. Louis

Cairo

Jonesboro

Memphis

Jackson

Shiloh

Corinth

Tupelo

Meridian

Vicksburg

Jackson

Louisville

Nashville

Franklin

Fort Donelson

Knoxville

Chattanooga

Chickamauga

Resaca

Dallas

Kennesaw Mt.

Atlanta

Macon

Montgomery

Birmingham

Huntsville

Augusta

Savannah

Fort McAllister

Charleston

Columbia

Florence

Spartanburg

Charlotte

Durham

Raleigh

Goldsboro

Bentonville

Averasboro

Fayetteville

Wilmington

Richmond

WASHINGTON, DC

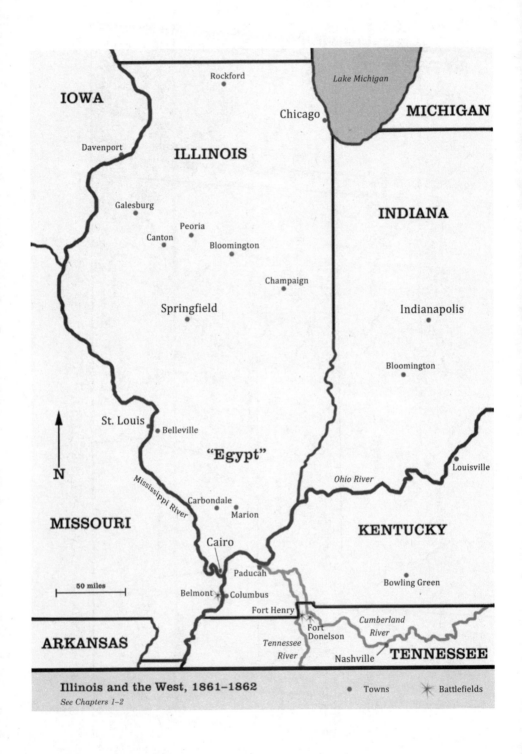

Illinois and the West, 1861–1862
See Chapters 1–2

● Towns   ✴ Battlefields

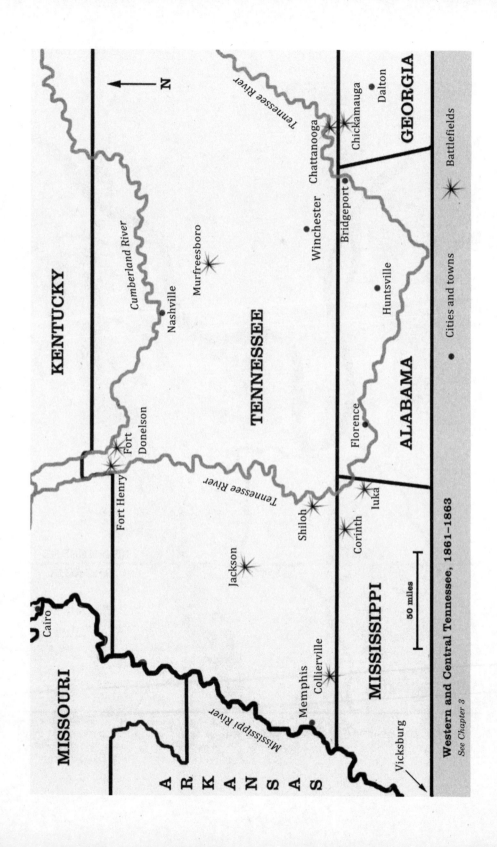

Western and Central Tennessee, 1861–1863
See Chapter 3

✳ Battlefields   • Cities and towns

50 miles

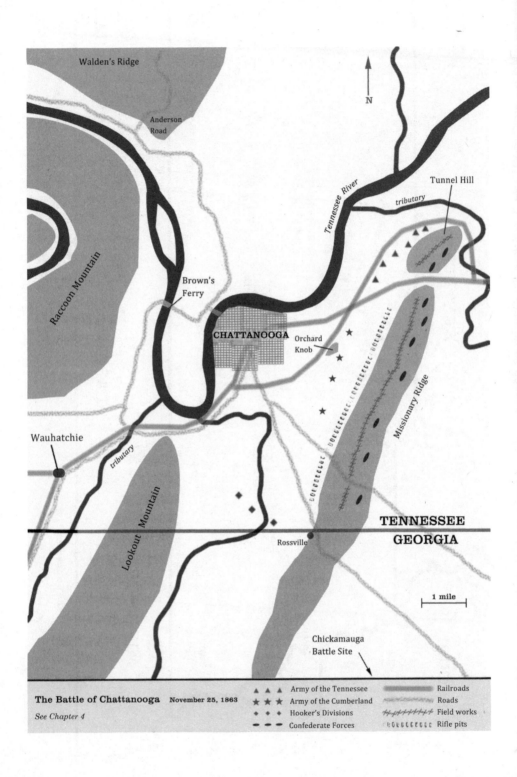

N

Walden's Ridge

Anderson
Road

Tennessee River

tributary

Tunnel Hill

Raccoon Mountain

Brown's
Ferry

CHATTANOOGA

Orchard
Knob

Missionary Ridge

Wauhatchie

tributary

Lookout Mountain

Rossville

TENNESSEE

GEORGIA

1 mile

Chickamauga
Battle Site

The Battle of Chattanooga   November 25, 1863

See Chapter 4

▲ ▲ ▲ Army of the Tennessee
★ ★ ★ Army of the Cumberland
◆ ◆ ◆ Hooker's Divisions
– ◆ – Confederate Forces

Railroads
Roads
Field works
Rifle pits

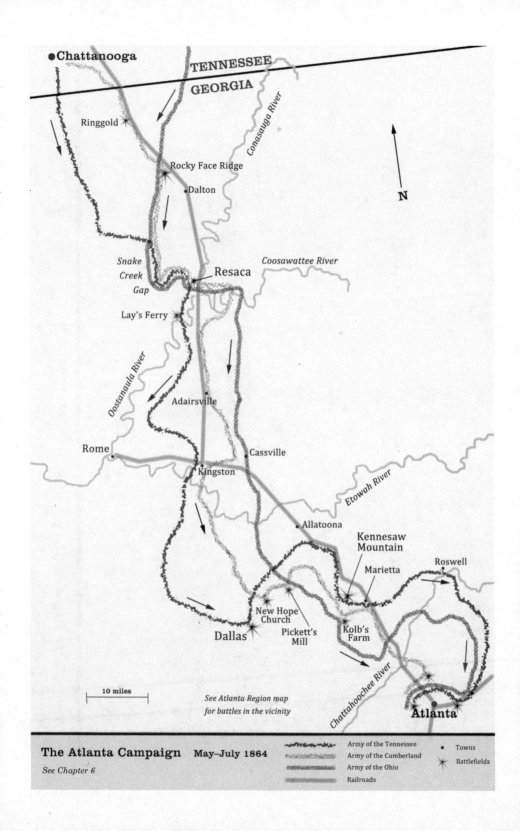

●Chattanooga

TENNESSEE

GEORGIA

Conasauga River

N

Ringgold

Rocky Face Ridge

●Dalton

Snake
Creek
Gap

Coosawattee River

Resaca

Lay's Ferry

Oostanaula River

Adairsville

Rome

Cassville

Kingston

Etowah River

Allatoona

Kennesaw
Mountain

Roswell

Marietta

New Hope
Church

Pickett's
Mill

Kolb's
Farm

Dallas

Chattahoochee River

Atlanta

10 miles

See Atlanta Region map
for battles in the vicinity

The Atlanta Campaign   **May–July 1864**

See Chapter 6

Army of the Tennessee
Army of the Cumberland
Army of the Ohio
Railroads

● Towns
✷ Battlefields

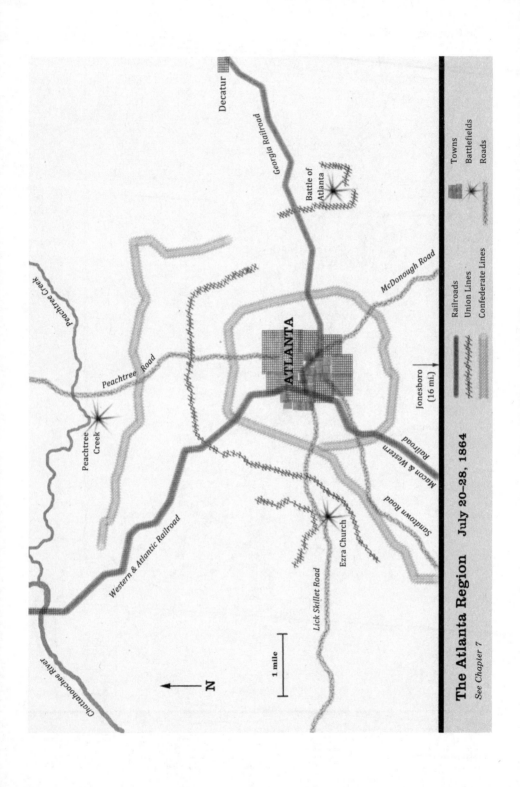

The Atlanta Region   July 20–28, 1864

See Chapter 7

Decatur

Georgia Railroad

Battle of Atlanta

McDonough Road

Peachtree Creek

Peachtree Road

ATLANTA

Jonesboro (16 mi.)

Macon & Western Railroad

Sandtown Road

Peachtree Creek

Ezra Church

Western & Atlantic Railroad

Lick Skillet Road

Chattahoochee River

1 mile

N

Railroads
Union Lines
Confederate Lines

Towns
Battlefields
Roads

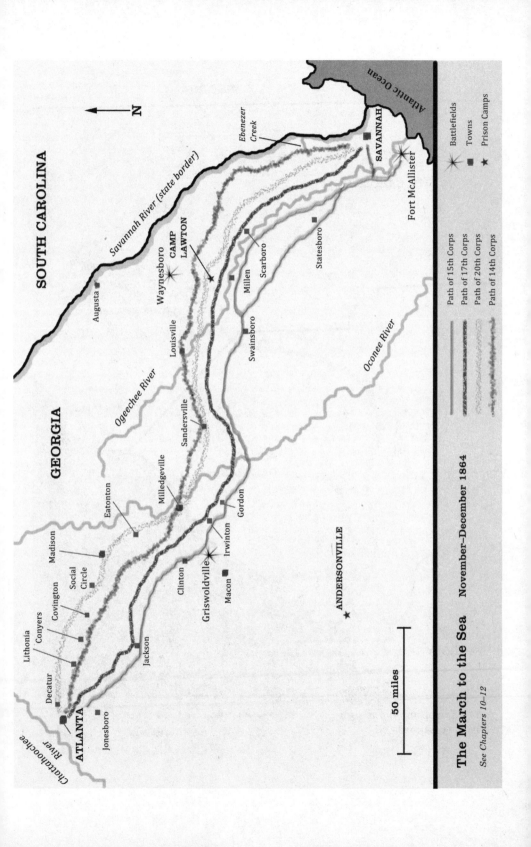

SOUTH CAROLINA

GEORGIA

Chattahoochee River

Savannah River (state border)

Ogeechee River

Oconee River

Ebenezer Creek

Atlantic Ocean

N

Augusta

Waynesboro
CAMP LAWTON

Louisville

Sandersville

Eatonton

Madison

Social Circle

Covington

Lithonia
Conyers

Decatur

ATLANTA

Jonesboro

Jackson

Clinton

Milledgeville

Gordon

Irwinton

Griswoldville

Macon

ANDERSONVILLE

Swainsboro

Millen

Scarboro

Statesboro

SAVANNAH

Fort McAllister

50 miles

The March to the Sea November–December 1864

See Chapters 10–12

Path of 15th Corps
Path of 17th Corps
Path of 20th Corps
Path of 14th Corps

Battlefields

Towns

Prison Camps

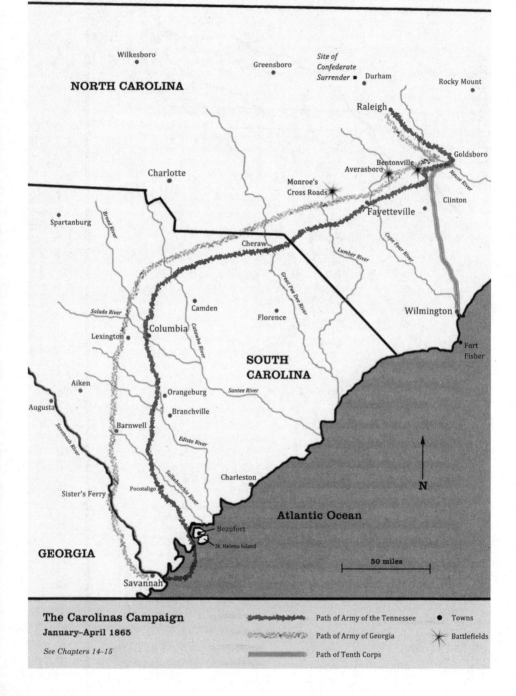

VIRGINIA

NORTH CAROLINA

Wilkesboro

Greensboro

Site of
Confederate
Surrender ■ Durham

Rocky Mount

Raleigh

Charlotte

Bentonville

Averasboro

Goldsboro

Monroe's
Cross Roads

Neuse River

Clinton

Fayetteville

Spartanburg

Broad River

Cheraw

Cape Fear River

Lumber River

Saluda River

Camden

Great Pee Dee River

Florence

Wilmington

Columbia

Catawba River

Lexington

SOUTH
CAROLINA

Fort
Fisher

Aiken

Orangeburg

Santee River

Augusta

Branchville

Savannah River

Barnwell

Edisto River

N

Salkehatchie River

Charleston

Sister's Ferry

Pocotaligo

Atlantic Ocean

GEORGIA

Beaufort

St. Helena Island

50 miles

Savannah

The Carolinas Campaign
January–April 1865

See Chapters 14–15

⟶⟶⟶ Path of Army of the Tennessee   ● Towns

⟶⟶⟶ Path of Army of Georgia   ✳ Battlefields

━━━ Path of Tenth Corps

INTRODUCTION

TWO ARMIES IN WASHINGTON

A t 9 A.M. on May 23, 1865, Washington, D.C., awoke to the roar of a cannon. The blast wasn't an act of aggression, for the great Civil War had concluded a month before. Instead, it marked the start of the Grand Review of the Armies, a colossal military parade that would present 150,000 Union soldiers who had won that war, in all their splendor and glory.

The national capital had been transformed for the event. While much of it was still an eyesore—a hodgepodge of unfinished buildings, rutted dirt roads, ramshackle brothels, and an open sewer—federal leaders had worked for weeks to make the town look its best. Red, white, and blue flags and bunting hung from the public buildings, and black crepe honored the memory of the recently martyred president, Abraham Lincoln. Huge banners offered messages like "The only national debt we can never pay is the debt we owe to the victorious Union soldiers," while other signs recalled federal victories at places like Gettysburg, Shiloh, and Vicksburg. Rousing martial airs echoed through the streets, church choirs sang inspiring hymns, and two thousand children held flowers and sang patriotic songs.

Up to a quarter-million people came for the spectacle—lining the streets, crowding in the parks, watching from the windows of buildings. The capital itself was only home to 61,000 residents, but its population had more than quadrupled in recent days from the masses of visitors arriving in wagons and buggies and on excursion trains. This was well beyond what the town could hold, and anyone who couldn't find space in hotels, private rooms, or boardinghouses just slept in parks or in the open, or stayed up all night carousing or wandering the streets.

The parade began at the U.S. Capitol, where the 90,000 men of the Army of the Potomac, commanded by General George Meade, were first to demonstrate their sharp martial appearance and marching finesse. Traveling along Pennsylvania Avenue on a route that would bring them past thousands of assembled politicians, officials, and reporters, the Potomac troops were familiar to capital residents. These were the soldiers who had captured headlines in the previous four years for their great victories at Antietam and Gettysburg, as well as their huge losses at Fredericksburg and Chancellorsville. Many in the crowd recognized them from their days spent camping near the capital or marching through it to fight the armies of Robert E. Lee and Stonewall Jackson on battlefields in Maryland and Virginia. Some of these troops even had to protect the District of Columbia from Confederate attack—the theater of war was that close.

The men in the Army of the Potomac could not have been prouder. In early April they had conquered the rebel capital of Richmond and forced their longtime nemesis Lee to surrender. And now on the march, they showed all the flair and style of a conquering army. Their boots and belt buckles gleamed, their uniforms and kepis were spotless, their paper collars and white gloves were striking, their swords and bayonets glittered, and their parade step was impeccable—like a machine, as one observer saw. The only unplanned moment occurred when cavalry general George Armstrong Custer's horse, named Don Juan, proved hard to manage among the packed crowds. After regaining control of his steed, the celebrity general received a rousing ovation after getting him to bow in the direction of the new president, Andrew Johnson.

The army concluded its march by passing the reviewing stand near the White House, where President Johnson and Commanding General of the U.S. Army Ulysses S. Grant and other dignitaries watched with approval. Meade dismounted before the president and saluted him, then took his place in the stand next to his counterpart, William Sherman, whose forces would be marching the next day. Impressed by his army's captivating presentation, Sherman said to Meade, "I'm afraid my poor tatterdemalion corps will make a poor appearance tomorrow, when contrasted with yours." But Sherman was being modest: He had no intention of being outperformed.

When the next day dawned, Sherman's 60,000-strong force—recently named the Army of the West—strode across the Long Bridge from Virginia where they had camped, and marched to the U.S. Capitol. But though they followed the same parade route as the soldiers of the Army of the Potomac, they looked nothing like them.

The crowds had heard rumors about these men for years without seeing them. The press would sometimes report on their victories and exploits, but other times the troops would disappear into the wilderness for weeks or months, leaving people to guess their whereabouts. Like their commander, Sherman's troops were unpredictable and elusive on the march, and their reputation had as much to do with rumor and legend as with fact. But they had an unmistakable talent for combat, and that was exactly how Sherman wanted to present them: as the robust, relentless fighters who owned the Southern battlefield and wore the dirt to prove it.

They sported the same uniforms they had fought in—worn and tattered, ripped and frayed, riddled with bullet holes, speckled with mud, and stained with blood. As one eastern soldier saw, they looked "dingy, as if the smoke of numberless battlefields had dyed their garments, and the soil of the insurrectionary states had adhered to them." Their faces and bodies were sunburned and weather-beaten, for they had traveled through swamplands and pine barrens, crossed windy mountain ridges and ravines, and forded countless creeks and bridged scores of rivers in the western campaign. They had marched hundreds or even thousands of miles across the South, and many lacked socks and shoes, with feet bruised and calloused from their journey. But they marched in the Grand Review with an easy swagger that showcased their cavalier confidence.

Marching before them were lines of black men with spades and shovels who had built the roads for the invasion, while behind them were the women and children of those men's families, who had escaped bondage and now marched as free people. And among them were the engineers, pontoniers, ambulance drivers, guardsmen, and signal corpsmen who had helped the soldiers march into the Southern heartland and destroy its material resources, devastate its land, and crush the spirits of its people. They had helped win the war with an invasion force unlike any the world had ever seen.

Some observers thought these western fighters resembled ruffians more than soldiers, a motley collection of bandits instead of an assembly of noble warriors. But for most in the crowd, the sight of these rugged men stunned and delighted them. Finally able to see Sherman's marchers in the flesh, the onlookers realized just how battle-hardened their boys had become, even if they had no idea of what the war had been like or how mercilessly they had waged it. One man who did understand was Confederate general Joseph Johnston, who later said of them, "there had been no such army since the days of Julius Caesar."

Few could have expected the war would end this way. Few could have known that a ragtag collection of farm boys largely untrained and inexperienced in combat before the conflict would become its victors, or that a grizzled, often slovenly, and once-disgraced general like William Sherman would lead them in their triumph. And fewer still could have expected that his method of fighting—a scorched-earth strategy he called "hard war," which generations later would identify as "total war"—would prove to be decisive at a time when Napoleonic battlefield strategies and old-fashioned martial panache still held sway. It caused immense suffering, as students of the war and anyone from the South have long known, and left great swaths of the region as dead zones stripped of food and livestock and riddled with burned-out homes and factories. Yet despite the brutality of this policy, Sherman and his armies found success beyond anyone's measure, crippling the Confederacy's ability to fight the war and hastening the end of it. In so doing, Sherman not only created his own legend as a military genius, he inadvertently gave himself a reputation as a remorseless killer and vandal that still adheres to his name more than 150 years later.

Assembling such legions of homegrown warriors proved to be no easy task. For in the first two years of the war, the Union army had been consistently outfought, outmaneuvered, and outgeneraled by the forces of the Confederacy. Shameful defeats at Fredericksburg and Chancellorsville, among others, tarnished the standing of Northern troops, while causing dismay and disillusion on the home front. A succession of rankly incompetent or slow and dithering Union generals allowed Southern commanders to seize the initiative and press for an advantage that was as much political as it was military. Union victories, such as those at Shiloh and Antietam, had come at a great cost of lives, and the quick and easy victory over the rebels many Northern leaders had promised had, by early 1863, failed to occur. Instead the North got to experience the bloodshed and horror of mechanized warfare, the random killing of grapeshot and canister shot, the thousands of lives lost from cannonades and massed rifle and musket fire, and the amputations and injuries too terrible for even the most fiendish mind to conjure. And in the face of such terrors, many Northerners lost faith—and this became a greater threat to the war effort than any loss on the field of combat. For if their public enthusiasm for the war were to flag, the Confederacy might gain the upper hand and force a settlement to end the conflict. This would give the South its goal of permanent secession, creating a new, battle-born nation that would preserve slavery and possibly even expand it into new territories.

The first transformative victories for the North came around Independence Day 1863, when a colossal loss at Gettysburg ended Robert E. Lee's invasion of the North almost as soon as it began, and a lengthy siege at Vicksburg forced the capitulation of an entire Confederate army, under the command of John Pemberton, giving full control of the Mississippi River to the Union. In the wake of these successes, U.S. Army leaders such as Henry Halleck and Ulysses S. Grant and President Lincoln considered several plans for striking into the heart of the South, the key option being an advance into Middle Tennessee and from there into Georgia, the industrial and agricultural heart of the region.

The troops of this invasion force would be drawn largely from the western states (a region known as the Old Northwest and in modern parlance as the Midwest). These were vast former territories of the United States once known for their hunting, trapping, and fishing outposts that, in the three decades before the war, had begun to emerge as economic powerhouses—thick with wheat and corn farms, hog and cattle pens, burgeoning towns and cities, and an expanding lattice of railroads to tie them all together.

States like Ohio, Indiana, Wisconsin, Michigan, Minnesota, Missouri, Iowa, and especially Illinois raised the greatest share of troops that would be deployed in the force, as well as its most enterprising generals. Among these troops were teenage boys fresh from their labors on the farm, small-time merchants and businessmen who knew little of warfare, ministers and preachers who followed their congregations into battle, and local and national politicians who fashioned themselves as colonels, provided they could raise a regiment and regardless of whether they had ever fought in battle. Newcomers to America also populated the ranks, some from far-flung places like Russia, Spain, and Norway, yet most from Ireland and the German states. They had largely been merchants and farmers before the war, some having fled the Old World in their youth, others barely fluent in the English language. Regardless of their background, the majority decided to take up arms for their adopted country. They would prove their loyalty to it by leaving their blood on its soil, and their names on its headstones.

Amid these forces were more unexpected figures, whose role in support of the war was at first surprising, but soon became essential to the success of Union armies. These included countless thousands of women on the home front who, in the absence of men in combat, learned to run businesses and farmsteads, buy supplies and machinery, sell goods in the marketplace, and contribute massive amounts of relief supplies for soldiers on the front lines. They became not only the economic backbone of the western states, but delivered tons of food, clothing, and medicine to the U.S. Army through commissions and aid societies. This work ultimately fed and clothed the very troops who would come to conquer the Confederacy, among them their fathers, sons, brothers, neighbors, and fellow parishioners. Many also served on the front lines as nurses, matrons, and staff operating field kitchens, serving in hospital wards, caring for the wounded, curing the sick, and giving comfort to the dying. Some women even followed the army into the bleakest and most fearsome fields of combat, and saw the face of battle in a way few people did outside of the military.

Other participants in the invasion had been enslaved before or during the war, and used their newfound freedom as an opportunity to aid the army in its advance. Black men and women—the freedmen, as they were known—assisted Union troops, conveyed supplies, led horse and mule teams, and acted as messengers and spies. Later in the war, many African American men fought in uniform at a number of key battles, especially in the eastern theater in Virginia. William Sherman, plagued by racist notions, prohibited them from fighting in his armies of the west, so the freedmen instead built roads and bridges through forbidding wilderness, and aided the troops as they sacked plantations, seized cotton and food stores, and freed thousands more slaves.

All these forces—black and white, men and women, military and civilian—coalesced on the march through the South. Following their commander's lead, they helped destroy the rebellion and eradicated slavery on the ground well before it was forbidden by national law. They triumphed in the most violent conflict ever fought on American soil, and took the lessons they had learned to transform its politics and society when the war ended—changing its outlook on slavery and racial equality, women's rights, and evangelical religion, and giving new power to movements for temperance and westward expansion. Thus, their campaign didn't end when the war did in 1865. They would continue their march in the decades to come.

RISING IN FLAMES

HOME FRONT

ONE

THE WESTERN EDGE

I t began with a scream. A wild, terrifying roar that echoed out through the great hall and forced hundreds of people to cover their ears in pain. An unearthly noise that rang out like the call of untamed beasts or primitive warriors—"the banner cry of Hell." Then a black swarm of hats flew overhead like hornets, seeming to rise ever higher as the clamor reached earsplitting decibels. As a show of furious enthusiasm and political force, the demonstration was unprecedented, even in a town like Chicago known for its spectacles. That made it official: Senator William Seward was a contender to be the Republican nominee for president.

The Lincoln men knew they would have to do better. So after their candidate's name was seconded for the nomination, they created their own uproar. It was, some said, like the clamor of a hog slaughter, or the Illinois Central passing by, or dozens of steam whistles pealing in unison. It impressed many of the delegates, but it wasn't enough. So, after a brief pause to gather their collective breath, the hometown crowd let loose again, this time with pandemonium—a collective and terrifying shriek mixed with infernal stomping that made the entire building quiver and shake. The monumental outburst did the job, and helped the Illinois contingent win the battle of the noise. Soon they would win the nomination, too, making Abraham Lincoln the official Republican candidate in the American election of 1860.

The Republican Party had gathered at the great wooden Wigwam building not only to nominate a presidential candidate, but to make itself whole. For the Wigwam was a lot like the party itself: hastily put together, built from clashing elements that might only be temporary, featuring an impressive silhouette from a distance but a much flimsier façade up close. And so, when the committed Unionists, fervent abolitionists, orphaned Whigs, and ardent nationalists all gathered in the crowded and claustrophobia-inducing hall to choose a candidate for president, they were looking for a suture as much as a savior.

Down on the convention floor, where the high-stakes horse trading took place, political operatives jockeyed for delegates while campaign directors counted votes from committee rooms at the edge of the stage. It should have been easy to get lost in the sound of pounding feet and bellowing voices, to get swept up in the drama, to disappear amid the hubbub. At least that's what Mary Livermore hoped—she knew she wasn't supposed to be there.

Amid this "gigantic pantomime," as she called it, women were barred from the closely guarded floor, "which was sacred to men exclusively." Instead, they had to find a male chaperone to accompany them to the raked galleries high above the floor, and try to glimpse the activity from up in the rafters. But Mary had little patience for such rules. Dressed in black to appear less conspicuous, she snuck in and found a spot where she could follow the action. Her role as a journalist demanded it.

Despite her efforts, the convention marshal spotted her. Barking at Mary in aggressive tones, he tried to sic the security police on her—since women were strictly forbidden in an area where the serious business of politicking took place. At first she began to leave, but her fellow reporters prevented it. As the convention hall cops moved in to grab her, the rowdy scribblers fought back, screaming at the marshal and demanding he back down and "dry up!" Finally, in a surge of bodies and voices, they rose up and kept him from arresting her. Mary had never seen anything like it.

Growing up on the much more genteel East Coast, she had seen men protect women from physical harm even as they lorded over them. But here in the West it was different. These professional journalists were also tribal combatants, animated not by patrician gentility but by vigorous and sometimes violent emotions, and they were more than ready to defend one of their own, even if she was a woman.

So Mary stayed on the floor. And it was a good thing: She was in a perfect position to see Lincoln nominated after three ballots—and to see her colleagues embrace and cheer for their native son with great passion, reduced to "laughing, crying and talking incoherently" in an "insanity of gladness."

Gustave Koerner looked into the abyss of the great hall and heard only screaming. He could see nothing of the audience thanks to the glare of the footlights illuminating him and the other dignitaries on stage, but he could certainly hear the delegates in their guttural bellowing joy. Yet it was joy tinged with rage—the pleasure of seeing their own country lawyer crowned as party nominee fused with vengeance against the slave power that had divided the nation and mocked the idea of liberty itself. For Lincoln, there were cheers of hope and passion; for the Democratic enemy, angry cries of political combat. Koerner was pleased. Everything had turned out exactly as he had planned.

Political conventions were political theater, and those who made the best showing—the splashiest parades, the wittiest signboards, the most gallant singing, the most powerful lungs—commanded the hearts of onlookers and the press. But Koerner knew there was more to getting a candidate nominated than just songs and pageantry, and he had planned accordingly.

While the Seward boosters had spent their days marching through Chicago singing and roaring, Koerner's men swarmed into the Wigwam when the doors opened, using their free tickets to occupy the choicest turf in the building. While rival forces were out drinking whiskey, swearing a blue streak, and howling at top volume, Koerner kept track of the delegates and what they were up to around town. And on the second night of the convention, while Seward's men were cheering their expected victory the next day, the Lincoln men were making sure it would never happen. Without a raised voice or a hurled hat, they consolidated the opposition and ensured Lincoln would become the nominee before any of the delegates ever opened their mouths to vote.

It was a hard-won victory, but Koerner had the skill to pull it off, honed by years of practice in the Prairie State. He had assembled a life as rich with honor and accomplishment as anyone in Illinois—state legislator, supreme court justice, lieutenant governor—but engineering the Republican nomination for Lincoln might have been his greatest achievement. He had come a long way in three decades.

An ocean, and most of a lifetime, separated Koerner from his former homeland. As a young man, he had tried to start a revolution in Frankfurt against the confederation of German states, and had failed in spectacular fashion, only avoiding a possible death sentence by fleeing to France. He later exiled himself to America, not to an established city like New York or Philadelphia, but to a state on its western edge—a place bereft of great libraries and universities, legendary artists and poets, and impeccable restaurants and grand hotels. Illinois in 1834 was hardly a place for a civilized American, let alone a European sophisticate. It had become a state less than a generation before, and the land still seemed raw and uncut, peopled with grizzled frontiersmen and rangy old trappers who increasingly shared space with pioneer farmers from the East and South. Despite the obstacles, Koerner knew this had to be the place, *his* place. For in the rich wet soil of this new American landscape, he could reinvent himself and prosper. Like any good German, he laid out a meticulous strategy for realizing his goals; and like any good immigrant, he began executing it as soon as he arrived.

These days, he told stories of his background to marshal votes for Lincoln. And he could adapt his approach and style depending on which Germans he was speaking to. In northern Illinois, the churchgoing, politically active Germans divided their loyalties between Lutheran and Catholic, Republican and Democrat, but they all enjoyed hearing him lavish praise on their small but productive farms. In Chicago, the working-class Germans on the city's "Nord Seite" worked in factories, ran their own breweries and newspapers, and fought vigorously for their communities, and they cheered the loudest when he condemned the nativists and xenophobes who tried to make life difficult for them. Finally, to the south, the Germans were a strange mix of pious but hardworking farmers with conservative leanings, peppered with restive expats who dreamed of revolution. No rhetorical trickery could convince both groups, so he focused on converting the farmers to the cause and placating the radicals. Ultimately, he found both support and hostility to the Republican Party almost everywhere he went, and had been to every corner of the state in his three decades living in it. Now that the convention was over, he made yet another journey—this time to Springfield on the Illinois Central to inform Lincoln of his status as the party's new nominee.

Koerner had known the rail-splitter for many years now, from his early days in state politics as a Democrat when Lincoln was a Whig, to his time on the state bench hearing him argue cases before the court with a certain droll humor, to the current era when he considered him a key political ally. Although they were never close friends, Koerner considered Lincoln "one of the most just, kind and indulgent of men, who intentionally I believe never did an unkind thing to anyone." For such a decent fellow, he was also one of the most canny political operators Koerner had ever known, with great ambition not only for himself but for the region he called home. As a young legislator in the 1830s, Lincoln had helped bring the state capital to Springfield, and ever since, as a politician and lawyer, he had worked ceaselessly to transform this once lonely and remote prairie into a place of limitless commercial and industrial progress.

As the landscape of Illinois rapidly sped past, Koerner found it hard to believe this was the same state that seemed so rustic, so primitive, when he had first set foot here as an immigrant. Now the noise of progress was everywhere: the throbbing industrial drone of rail cars shipping tons of beef to the East Coast and thousands of pigs to Chicago slaughterhouses, the slash and whirr of McCormick reapers cutting grain on huge farmsteads, the bracing din of land auctions and the eager cries of speculators. Once he reached town, the sound of the state capital took over: the clamor of lawyers and politicians, the bustle of merchants, the whinny of teamed horses. It didn't take long to hear the ring of a foreign accent, either, as scores of migrants arrived from western Europe with names like Fitzpatrick, Schmidt, and Magnuson. The success of Springfield mirrored the success of Illinois itself, which had pulled the nation's political and economic gravity to its western edge and become an engine of industry that the rest of America couldn't help but admire, or at least envy.

Despite the breathless changes in store for the state and its people, Koerner resisted becoming overly excited about such things. The consummate pol, he was known for his cool reason and intellectual dispassion, and he had a reputation to uphold. Considering the amount of work it would take to get Lincoln elected, he'd need to keep his passion and emotions in check. It would be a long campaign.

Koerner entered the parlor of Lincoln's home, and he scarcely had time to inform the new nominee of his status before the official Republican delegation arrived to do the same thing. It didn't matter—Lincoln already knew. He'd learned of his nomination almost the moment it happened, by a wire he had received in the Springfield telegraph office. Now that he had time to consider what it meant, he chose his words carefully in accepting the honor. But instead of expressing joy or relief, he spoke with a serious, even troubled, tone. Everyone in the room then had "a foreboding of the eventfulness of the moment," and what lay in store for the nation. Although they could have used a stiff drink, the only beverage served was ice water.

Mary Livermore returned from the Wigwam with a touch of ambivalence. She was happy to remember the great sights of the convention—the passions, the tears, the brush with violence—but she wished she could be more confident in the outcome. Mary wavered on Lincoln. Was he really a trailblazer for justice, or was he just using the anti-slavery cause to fuel his ambition? Hadn't he resisted the abolitionist label, and avoided calling for the overthrow of the slaveocracy? Her doubts were nettlesome and constant. Even during the convention, she had wondered aloud to her fellow reporters, "Is it certain Mr. Lincoln is an uncompromising slavery man? . . . There is no humbug about it?"

Despite her doubts, she knew there could be no middle ground. Not in this time of ferment, not with the country on the edge of collapse. She would promote Lincoln in her writing and firmly support the Republican position, no matter how her conscience nagged at her.

In any case, her readers expected unyielding praise for the Republican platform, and she would deliver it in her *New Covenant* newspaper. She wrote that the Republicans had made history as the first major party to explicitly demand the end of slavery's expansion into the territories, and would stop the federal government's corrupt deals to aid the slave barons. Even though the party didn't specifically call for the abolition of the immoral institution or the promotion of universal rights, it would do—for now.

The paper took up a lot of her time: writing for it, publishing it, and keeping it in the black. Its daily demands were considerable, especially now that she was expanding its readership beyond its core group of adherents of the Universalist church, of which she was a committed member. To her work on the paper she added a huge number of other tasks: raising three children, hosting numerous political and religious gatherings, forcing herself to learn "feminine arts" like cooking and sewing, running charities like the Hospital for Women and Children, the Home for Aged Women, and the Chicago Home of the Friendless (caring for homeless women and kids), persuading politicians to back her causes, using their allegiance as a tool to garner even greater public support, and, of course, attending political conventions.

Even though she had left behind her father's fire-and-brimstone brand of Protestantism decades before, she never forgot his dire Calvinist warning about idleness. If anything, she had overdone it. She had set about to do so many tasks, and to accomplish so many goals, that she scarcely had time to rest. Luckily, her enterprising spirit solved the problem, as she acquired an ability to "hold sleep in abeyance" and work at all hours of the day, if needed.

It had been this way since she and her husband, Daniel, had moved from Auburn, New York, three years before, following his itinerant career as a Universalist minister. As with most other Christian denominations, spreading the gospel was key to their sect, and Mary and Daniel frequently found themselves on the move, sharing a message of universal salvation. Although far from zealots, they were deeply engaged by the tenets of their faith, which above all stressed the idea of a benevolent, loving God who lifted up souls instead of condemning them to hell, and offered grace to anyone regardless of their beliefs. The tide of church liberalism, Daniel believed, would soon rise throughout the nation and "the days of Orthodoxy are fast being numbered!"

The spiritual trail eventually led them away from the East to the foreign world of the West. Daniel had caught "Western fever" and imagined a pioneer life for his family on the Great Plains. Though she remained skeptical of their prospects as trailblazers, Mary agreed to the relocation. They intended Chicago to be no more than a stopover on their way to Kansas, to spread the gospel as they understood it, to set up new religious colonies, and to speak against slavery and other sins. However, with a sick daughter requiring the kind of medical care not found on the frontier, and with Kansas mired in a storm of pro- and anti-slavery violence, they decided to make their home in Illinois.

Unlike the charming antique streets and homes of New England where Mary had grown up, she saw Chicago as a brazen, loud, and "somewhat astonishing city, in which mud, dust, dirt and smoke seemed to predominate." Hardly any of the streets were paved, rough boards doubled as sidewalks (through which "green and black slime oozed up between the cracks in wet weather"), the drinking water pumped from the lake was polluted, and there was no sewer system aside from ditches on both sides of the road. Not surprisingly, disease ran rampant and public cleanliness was largely unknown, and a traveler taking a simple walk had to resort to "compulsory gymnastics" to avoid being entombed in all the mud.

Daniel never remained home for long, and frequently left town to set up new churches and colonies, while Mary remained in Chicago teaching Sunday school and writing stories with uplifting messages. However, she was anything but a stereotypical minister's wife, discreet and docile. When they were married in 1845, her vows pointedly did not include the duty to "obey," and ever since they had formed an effective, respectful partnership in which he spread the gospel on the road and she ran the paper and managed their household.

Yet despite their apparent tranquility, they had been immersed in controversy for almost as long as Daniel had been preaching. Universalism was hardly a mainstream doctrine, and while it had many adherents in upper-middle-class and elite circles, many traditional and nearly all fundamentalist Christians saw it as heretical. Mary grew frustrated at constantly having to battle theological enemies who subscribed to notions of "endless punishment" and maintained "utter ignorance" of her church. It reminded her of the vigorous battles she used to wage with her father over ideas of grace and salvation. The arguments were so passionate and often bitter, she suspected he was trying to win her soul as much as win the argument, and to save her from hell if she died a heretic. The thought made her sad, since she had no doubt he would someday find his way to heaven.

Despite the peace and optimism of their beliefs, Daniel and Mary had countless foes outside their church, and even within it they could be a magnet for controversy. A few years before, when they lived in Stafford, Connecticut, their efforts to pass a law to ban the sale and manufacture of alcohol aroused the hostility of their neighbors, many of them fellow church members. Opponents of the ban denounced Daniel as someone who "dragged the white ermine of his profession into the dirty pool of politics," many of Daniel and Mary's closest friends rejected them, and the pews of his church began to empty on Sunday. Threatened with violence, Daniel eventually became subject to such verbal abuse that Mary had to accompany him to the polls on Election Day—with the idea that a mob would be less likely to attack a woman. Although the law did pass, Daniel had to resign his position and find a new one in another town. This dramatic episode haunted the Livermores for years afterward, but instead of learning to avoid conflict, they continued to seek it out, regardless of the trouble it might bring.

In this election season, no cause was more controversial than the fight against slavery. Unlike many Northerners, Mary was well acquainted with the "peculiar institution" ever since she had worked as a governess on a Virginia farmstead as a young woman. From slave auctioneers buying and selling human beings like cattle, to white children slapping and abusing black adults, to an overseer nearly whipping a man to death, the specter of brutality was vivid and unavoidable. And the experience marked her for life, turning her into a committed abolitionist who had been "steeped to the lips in horrors on the Virginia plantation."

Not everyone in Illinois was quite so committed to fighting slavery. The greatest divide was between upstaters, who if not always supportive were at least tolerant of anti-slavery activists, and downstaters, who despised them. In fact, southern Illinois was distinct enough from its northern counterpart that it had a peculiar nickname—Egypt. So when traveling to such a foreign place, the Livermores often found themselves on dangerous ground, advancing a political agenda that many saw as incendiary, while promoting a theology that others saw as heresy.

They found themselves on somewhat safer ground advocating for Lincoln, who had spent much of the campaign casting an image of himself as a sensible, down-home country lawyer. He didn't want slavery to expand, but also didn't want to eradicate it where it had long existed, in the South. Although such platitudes appealed to a certain type of moderate voter and allowed Lincoln to dampen controversy in the North, they didn't engage the more radical elements in the party. Indeed, these half-measures were exactly what Mary had feared about Lincoln, and having to praise such milquetoast policies in her newspaper troubled her to no end. Despite her private doubts, though, Mary continued to hold out hope that Lincoln might rise above his campaign rhetoric and, upon taking the oath of office, resolve to smash the system of human oppression once and for all.

Friedrich Hecker was running out of adjectives to describe the slave masters. He had condemned them in his writing and in his speeches as depraved, as repugnant, as barbaric, as tyrannical, but with each new abomination they foisted upon the nation, he reached for an adjective that would be even more damning and explosive. He could easily pull the words from German—*schrecklich, grässlich, widerlich*—but even now, after a dozen years in this country, he still had trouble finding the right translation.

He wavered on whether his adopted country was truly devoted to democratic liberty or hopelessly hidebound to slavery. To many of his neighbors in Belleville, Illinois, there was no contradiction. They saw the concepts of freedom and slavery being in perfect alignment, as the natural order of human relations, as an essential part of the economy, as something enshrined in the Constitution. To him, these were pathetic excuses for barbarism and intellectual dishonesty.

He couldn't say any of this on the stump. He knew he would have to hone his rhetoric if he were to go out on the road in support of the Republican Party's platform and its presidential candidate. He couldn't just promote the righteousness of the cause with his brilliant and strident invective; he would have to appeal to the heart as well as the mind to convince other Germans of it, too.

He agreed to this great election tour at the behest of Gustave Koerner, who along with other members of the Republican state committee had sent him a letter asking for his help. Party leaders from Lincoln down knew the German immigrant vote would be the linchpin of the election, and catering to it was essential if they had any hope of winning in November. Hecker was one of the biggest names in the community ("the most influential German in America," according to a Chicago newspaper), so of course he received a letter.

But while Hecker agreed to the tour, he didn't want to be tied into a straitjacket of party rhetoric, either—offering generic platitudes in support of the Union and moderate, inoffensive policies. This was a historic election, he knew, and he couldn't just talk about slavery without talking about free labor, or talk about racial justice without talking about class conflict, or talk about civil rights without talking about universal human rights.

But this was also what exhausted people about him. He never knew when to stop. He could preach about all these things until his voice gave out, but might offend as many people as he persuaded. So Hecker would have to find a new way to convince his audience, and sway their votes by using his fame to the party's advantage.

He was so well known because he had flourished in America, a true immigrant success story, drawing the admiration of his neighbors and awestruck reporters from the German-language press. At his Belleville home, he had settled into the life of a gentleman farmer, trying out innovative technologies, writing impassioned articles, and corresponding with politicians. Despite his influence among elected officials, though, he had no interest in getting elected himself, deriding the "humiliation incumbent on chasing offices," and remaining above the fray. But this refusal to debase himself only grew his reputation even more, and made his farm a major draw for visitors from the German states.

They came to share a smoke, enjoy a belt of whiskey, and hear the famous refugee talk politics, tell witty jokes, and regale them with stories of his colorful life and adventures. These tales often involved his youth, when he tried to lead a rebellion in Baden-Württemberg and, after its failure, fled to the United States. Upon his arrival on a steamer in New York Harbor, thousands of German immigrants had turned out to greet him, offering any sympathy, assistance, and money they could for this brilliant yet star-crossed firebrand from the Fatherland.

A dozen years later, none of his youthful pride and passion had diminished, and Hecker was just as committed to promoting freedom and liberty now as he had been then—breaking the bonds of slavery, recommitting to the ideals of the founding fathers, and fighting against entrenched capital and political corruption. His exiled peers shared many of the same beliefs, and were known as 48ers, after the year in which most of them had left Europe. Many considered Hecker a leader of the community, or even a sort of messiah. Carl Köhler described how a visit to his farm made him feel "like a pilgrim at Golgotha" as he stood in awe of his icon.

Surprisingly, one person whom Hecker didn't impress was Gustave Koerner. Although he respected Hecker's celebrity and status as a political refugee like himself, Koerner also had a long memory. And his memories of Hecker were not good.

It had started when they met at a Munich university in the early 1830s, as young men preparing for a career in law and politics. Both clever and opinionated, they were quick to find uncommon ground and debate each other. Heated words became insults, and Hecker challenged Koerner to a duel. Koerner easily won the contest and left a permanent mark on Hecker—a slash to his hand that required stitches to heal. By contrast, not only did Hecker fail to leave a scratch on his rival, nothing he had done since had provided a more favorable impression.

Koerner didn't trust Hecker's judgment or self-control, and he paid careful attention to critics in Belleville who complained about Hecker's radical politics and called him "a devilish rascal who easily seizes those who have no understanding, as blind as they are, with his rhetorical talent and his enthusiasm." Koerner knew that, despite appearances, Hecker and the 48ers had little in common with other German immigrants.

While the 48ers were obsessed with politics and revolutionary ideals, most other immigrants focused on making a living. Whereas the 48ers trumpeted social radicalism, labor reform, and universal suffrage, the other immigrants remained conservative and wary of change. And even as the 48ers promoted freethinking, the taxation of church property, and the removal of the Bible from classrooms, many other Germans saw such ideas as sacrilege. Koerner had even warned Lincoln to avoid appearing with Hecker on the stump, for he not only saw him as an overly zealous public speaker, but among Catholics and orthodox Protestants, "he is considered the very Anti-Christ."

But Hecker had a great deal of followers, too, and had skillfully convinced the English-language press that German immigrants and 48ers traveled in the same circles and believed the same things. This was quite a rhetorical feat because, while one million Germans had come to the U.S. after 1848, only 4,000 to 6,000 of them were 48ers. Despite their small numbers, they did what they could to transplant the failed revolution in Europe to the new soil of America, where it still had a chance to prosper.

Though an elitist, Hecker knew this would be no ivory-tower revolution. So the 48ers traveled the region and set up "Dutch meetings" to engage the German immigrants, even if they firmly or angrily rejected their messages. In small groups their speakers (known as "moustaches" for their pronounced facial hair) would brazenly advocate for an immediate end to slavery as well as even more radical propositions on capital, labor, and private property. After the speakers ran through the major themes, a party atmosphere might break out, with an ox roasted on a spit, a barrel of beer tapped for guzzling, and lively singing echoing well into the night. Such spectacles gave the moustaches quite a reputation, and slowly but surely, their message began to take hold among their listeners.

For good reason, then, Koerner saw Hecker as a threat to the stability of the party, and to the reputation of the community itself. But despite his misgivings, he had no choice but to ask for Hecker's help in getting Lincoln elected, given his rival's undeniable popularity and his knack for drawing attention to himself. Koerner did so even though he knew such a campaign role might add to Hecker's allure and enable him to further spread his radical ideas and deviations from party orthodoxy.

Hecker realized Koerner had given him the perfect opportunity—he had the chance to influence the nation at the most critical time in its modern history. So he would have to decide: Did he want to elect a president or start a revolution?

By the summer Koerner was at a loss. He had managed to convince renegades like Hecker to stump for the party by appealing to national duty and the glories of Abraham Lincoln, but he still hadn't locked down the German vote. And the Democratic nominee for president, Stephen Douglas, was working feverishly to exploit the weaknesses Republicans had with such voters. To rile up the traditional, conservatively minded immigrants, Douglas depicted native-born Republicans as a source of division and chaos for threatening to undermine the nation's Constitutionally protected practice of slavery. And if abolitionism held sway, it would mean nothing less than "revolution—undisguised revolution."

Koerner simply couldn't believe any respectable immigrant, having firsthand knowledge of the brutal oppression and rigid hierarchies of Europe, would ever want to be associated with the party of the South. He had helped change the Republican party platform to support greater immigration to the country, and to oppose any change to the naturalization laws that would impede it. That wasn't enough, and he knew why.

For nearly a decade, a certain political group had been sowing mistrust and hatred of immigrants. In their vicious cartoons and acerbic rhetoric, they depicted the Germans as either subversives aiming to undermine the capitalist system or drunken buffoons marinating in their own beer. Even worse, they claimed immigrants were nothing less than threats to the unity and values of the white, Protestant, Anglo-Saxon people of the

United States. Although this group called itself the American Party, the public knew it better as the Know-Nothings.

Named for their blithe refusal to reveal anything about their organization when asked, they reached their peak in the previous election, when doddering ex-president Millard Fillmore ran at the head of their ticket. Four years later, a rigid minority of Republicans still maintained loyalty to the Know-Nothings, to Koerner's embarrassment. For good reason, then, many immigrant voters feared they might be deported or imprisoned or otherwise mistreated if the Know-Nothings rode the Republicans to victory as a stalking horse, and they refused to vote for the party of Lincoln until it purged all remnants of the party of Fillmore.

Even social reformers dallied with the xenophobes. Mary Livermore, for one, was far from a Know-Nothing, but she maintained a strong allegiance to the temperance movement, which to the Germans was little more than a smoke screen for nativist aggression. Its members seized on any opportunity to advance their Sunday laws (banning liquor sales on the Sabbath) and raise the tax on booze to astronomical levels, hoping to drive brewers and saloon keepers out of business. The teetotalers targeted German immigrants in particular for their rowdy and colorful celebrations on Sunday, their carefree social imbibing, and the many breweries they owned or ran. Mary wasn't exactly a bigot, but she wasn't free from bias, either, and in her writing she sometimes described her political enemies as including "the low and the foreign born." This was just the type of nonsense that plagued Koerner and drove him to distraction.

Koerner knew stodgy rhetoric and policy proposals alone would not do in this era of brash theatrics and eye-popping spectacles. So he and other members of the party's "Foreign Department" desperately searched for a way to attract the votes of newcomers and make them forget about the attacks of the nativists. He knew how successful the 48ers had been in transforming their gatherings into wild celebrations, so he decided to follow the cue of his adversaries. Henceforth, the Republican Party would delight its voters with mass rallies and grand spectacles.

The party had to organize vast numbers of people in a short amount of time, but with Koerner in the lead, it did so with great verve and skill. At one huge event in Springfield, 60,000 people turned out to listen to impassioned speeches, march in torchlight parades, and shout their enthusiasm. Koerner led a company of some 300 Wide Awakes, young men bedecked in black capes with red, white, and blue ribbons, as part of a larger national organization that he claimed numbered up to a half-million. It was essentially a paramilitary force, not only taking part in rallies, but acting as a self-described "political police" to protect Republican candidates, especially in hostile regions like Egypt.

Friedrich Hecker had his chance to join the fray in Belleville, where a mass demonstration gave him an opportunity to prove he could give a more traditional speech that could sway votes for Lincoln—instead of a sharp harangue that might repel as many listeners as it would attract. Actually, Hecker hadn't planned on speaking at all, but after a splendid evening torchlight parade, the crowd became restive and excited to see their hometown hero, demanding he make an appearance and offer his wholehearted support of Honest Abe.

It wasn't hard for him to muster the enthusiasm. Hecker remembered a traumatic event just a few years before, in the early 1850s, when a fire had destroyed his home and nearly ruined his life. He suspected his political enemies of causing the blaze, but never found the culprits. He received countless offers of help from German Americans, as he expected, but one offer stood out for its sincerity and kindness. Former representative and Springfield lawyer Abraham Lincoln asked if he could do anything at all to help out the German émigré, whom he hadn't yet met and knew only by reputation. Although he was too proud to accept the assistance, Hecker was humbled by his entreaty and began a correspondence with Lincoln that never flagged in its graciousness. Lincoln seemed to be a rare specimen in this growing region—an ambitious and clever dealmaker who was nonetheless one of the most down-to-earth and, indeed, salt-of-the-earth individuals anyone could meet. Hecker felt honored to have known the rail-splitter and would now do everything he could to elevate him to his proper stature as leader of all Americans.

Speaking with great passion and control, Hecker implored his listeners to fight for the Republicans and resist the siren call of the slavery-beholden Democrats. He spoke until late in the evening, and the crowd never lost interest or enthusiasm. The success of his oratory gave him the chance to be invited to speak in increasingly prominent venues like the St. Louis Opera House. But while his campaign speeches focused on partisan politics instead of, say, the evils of private property and entrenched capital, he still resembled the Hecker of old. To spellbound crowds of rural farmers, he brought the shared experience of a fellow rustic; to small-town merchants and tradesmen, he brought the fire and drama of a skilled orator; and to everyone, he celebrated a humble backwoods lawyer as a champion they could all believe in. *Ein Held von heute*—a modern-day hero.

On Election Day, the country lawyer won in magnificent fashion. Koerner received the news in the Springfield telegraph office, as state after state in the North went into the Republican column and Lincoln garnered all the electoral votes he needed to become the nation's sixteenth president. Surprisingly, Lincoln and Koerner's grand coalition of contradictions—drinkers and teetotalers, churchgoers and freethinkers, radicals and conservatives, Protestants and Catholics, natives and newcomers—held together and triumphed at the ballot box. And thanks to Koerner's help, enough foreign-born German Americans voted for the ticket in Illinois that they may have been the difference in the outcome. And so all the effort bringing in figures like Hecker, and burying the influence of the Know-Nothings, and stumping throughout the state *auf Deutsch*— it had all worked, and Koerner now had a president-elect to show for it. Even Lincoln acknowledged as much, and knew he owed the German immigrants a real debt.

But even in victory, the Republican Party scarcely had time to celebrate. Three days after the election, the South Carolina legislature declared the victory of Lincoln a "hostile act" and laid the groundwork for a convention to consider secession from the United States. Six weeks later, the convention adopted an ordinance to secede and began the process of the dissolution of the country, with other Southern states to follow in short order. All the while, the feckless President James Buchanan did nothing to prevent it.

The sympathies of the North demanded a strong federal response to secession, to bind the union together once again, and by force if necessary.

Most of the strongest advocates for war had never experienced such a conflict directly, let alone a civil war that would bring the bloodshed to the front door of the nation. Still, the Northern rallies, the newspaper editorials, the torchlight parades, and the angry speeches all demanded revenge against the enemy. Radicals like Friedrich Hecker and reformers like Mary Livermore, despite their disagreements, called for martial action to battle the breakaway states. Even Koerner, for all his careful deliberation, knew that secession had to be countered with federal troops.

Mary feared for the Union's survival, but she knew the greatest danger could also provide the greatest opportunity. She had improved Chicago with her charity work and journalism, but what of the larger nation? This monumental contest could bring dramatic change to the United States as a whole, which so desperately needed it—to galvanize social reform, to bring about a new spiritual awakening, to destroy the practice of human bondage. As soon as the crisis began, she quoted approvingly from the sermons of ministers who announced "the real contest [is] between slavery and freedom. . . . Better that the land should be drenched with fraternal blood than any further concessions shall be made to the slaveocracy." The threat of war would test Mary's deep and abiding disgust for violence, as well as her view that all men and women were equal before the eyes of God. The secessionists had become the enemy—including those she knew intimately as a young woman in Virginia. She would now work to fight "the insult offered the nation" by the South, even if it meant violating her convictions for charity, humility and peace. As she said, "Conservative and peaceful counsel was shrivelled in a blaze of belligerent excitement . . . . The Union was not to be destroyed without a struggle that would deluge the land with blood."

Hecker also welcomed the prospect of war as a means of overthrowing the institution of slavery, which he saw as no different from the autocratic regime he had fled a dozen years before. Although far from a military man, he knew his commitment to the Union had to be proven by his actions, and he looked to raise troops for the conflict, to fight the enemy in the field, to stand for his ideals at the risk of his own life. He had been preparing for this opportunity ever since he had come to America, awaiting a chance to crush the hereditary plantation system just as he had tried, and failed, to do against the oppressive nobility of Baden-Württemberg. Tyranny must fall for democracy to rise, and "Southern aristocracy be broken . . . for liberty to flourish." His moment had come.

For Koerner the prospect of social revolution did not come so easily, for he had settled into the comforts and habits of a solid, middle-class immigrant for many decades after he had fled Frankfurt. But the call to war was a clarion one, and it shook him out of his old habits. Despite being a counsel of moderation in Illinois politics and despite warning against wild-eyed radicals and demagogues, he abandoned his usual reserve and seemed to welcome the specter of war, no matter the bloodshed or the horrors it might bring. Now echoing the zealous style of Hecker, he summoned his old rebellious spirit, and praised "the feeling of enthusiasm which pervaded the whole North. . . . There was but one cry: 'To arms!—To arms!'"

TWO

TIP OF THE SWORD

John Logan was mad.

This was nothing new, of course. John Logan was often mad. But this time was different. The downstate Illinois Democrat had turned away from his friends, his allies, even his mentor Stephen Douglas, in the fullest expression of his latest rage. He had good reason to be angry.

His enemies were tearing the country to pieces and he couldn't do anything about it. He condemned the press, the Northerners, the Republicans, the state politicians, the federal politicians, and the damned secessionist "fire-eaters"—those miscreants who were trying to dissolve the nation's bonds and reveling in its potential collapse. During the campaign, they had invaded Democratic Party strongholds like the Illinois towns of Marion and Carbondale and unfurled banners praising U.S. Vice President John Breckinridge, the rogue who had split the party and launched his own quest for the White House. The Breckinridge men had lied to the voters, claimed Stephen Douglas was no better than Abe Lincoln, and even heckled Logan on the stump—in his own district!

The "abolitionist black Republicans" were nearly as bad. Not only did Logan attack their plans to end slavery as part of a misguided political agenda, for years he had had repeated run-ins with them, sometimes to the point of violence. Most recently, he insinuated on the floor of the House of Representatives that a fellow congressman from Illinois was as cowardly as a spaniel dog. The two nearly came to blows, resulting in a melee in the House, after which Logan dusted himself off and announced, "God knows that I have differed from the other side from my childhood, and with that side I will never affiliate so long as I have breath in my body."

He had taken a proud and ardent stand against the Republicans, and for his efforts, his fellow Democrats had deserted him. As 1861 began, they allied with their former adversaries and stranded him as a rare voice of opposition to the war fever afflicting the North. He felt trapped, corralled into either supporting an insurgency he opposed or a rival party he despised. In short order he became a fat target for newspapers like the *Chicago Tribune*, which dared to criticize him for his "semi-secessionist" views in not joining the martial bandwagon. If they only knew the falsehood they had printed! In fact, pro-Southern forces in Illinois had tried to enlist him to their side for months now, and he had always resisted. Secession was no nobler a pursuit than anarchy, and those who stood for it promoted nothing less than treason. The *Tribune*, like all his other enemies in Illinois, had misunderstood his intentions and made a parody of his beliefs.

To lay out his views, he'd been preparing to give a definitive speech in the House of Representatives, to announce his sympathies in the conflict and warn of the madness he saw gripping the nation. But despite his earnest pleas, his fellow Congressmen didn't want to hear him speak; they knew how incendiary he could be, and how volatile the political climate was. So the Speaker of the House thwarted Logan's attempt to take the floor—repeatedly.

His fellow legislators didn't understand him, and they didn't understand the people of his district—the people of Egypt. The press, the

Republicans, the Northerners, they could never appreciate the region or what made it unique. Yes, it was part of Illinois, but as the southernmost part of the state, it was closer to Mississippi than to Chicago. And it inspired him in ways the North never could. When he visited Cairo, the symbolic capital of Egypt, he would stand at the conflux of the Ohio and Mississippi rivers, and marvel at the levees and constant flow of riverboat traffic.

Logan saw Cairo as a gateway between South and North, and a potential boomtown for the commerce of a nation. But the warmongers wanted to strip away all of its life and energy and future greatness. They only saw it as a military target: the tip of the sword pointing into the heart of the Confederacy, or a valuable foothold on the Union home front, depending on which side got there first. It would come to ruin if either got their way.

The Egyptians had better sense than to trust anyone from the North. They were crafty and resourceful, and knew how to pilot a steamboat, ride out the flood season, grow good crops in bad farmland, and build an entire world from the plains and prairie. They did not cotton to upstaters who came here with patronizing "advice" that only belittled them and mocked their culture and beliefs—especially if they were from Chicago, whose banks, creditors, and land agents they uniformly blamed for their mediocre economy and exorbitant debts. Logan understood. He knew all about his people's fears and frustrations, and the best ways to appeal to their hearts or fan their resentments, depending on his own political needs.

By far the easiest way to stir them up was to talk about race. Egyptians had a hostile view of anyone from the North, especially if they weren't white. They would chase blacks from town on horses or force them to leave by railcar or riverboat. Failing that, they might trick them into being sold into slavery across the river in Kentucky, or make their life a living hell if they tried to linger. They greeted illicit slave traders with a wink and abolitionists with a cudgel. They favored deporting any black residents in the state, and widely supported an 1853 state law that banned any such migrants from even setting foot in Illinois. Its author was John Logan.

Strongly influenced by the pro-slavery attitudes of his parents, Logan as a young legislator in Springfield inveighed against blacks with great passion, calling them "not suited to be placed upon a level with white men." His actions matched his words, and his law became known as one of the most severe in the region against black visitors, imposing fifty-dollar fines on them if they stayed in the state longer than ten days, and if they could not pay, selling them as veritable slaves at public auction. It soon acquired the name "Logan's Black Law."

Logan had no shame about this, or whether it gained him fame or infamy. He was a fierce defender of the act, as well as one of the most controversial bills of the age, the Fugitive Slave Act. Proudly proclaiming Illinois to be a western—not a northern—state, he asserted Democrats would be more than willing to "perform that dirty work" of hunting down fugitive slaves and returning them to bondage if no one else would. For this, the *Tribune* labeled him "Dirty Work" Logan. The moniker stuck and, depending on his audience, brought him either praise or enmity for his actions—his fierce oratory against black citizens, his hell-raising style of politicking, his defamation of his political rivals, his raising a mob to attack a newspaper that had endorsed Lincoln for president.

In the campaign against racial equality, Logan saw himself as a foot soldier. He would do anything it took for his side to triumph: He championed the party line on popular sovereignty, which would bring slavery to any corner of the nation that wanted it. He railed against the "radical proclivities" of Republicans for their support of abolition, and castigated them with great enthusiasm. He even bought out the newspaper he attacked, flipped its editorial position, and took to writing jeremiads against his increasing number of enemies.

Logan accomplished much work, clean and dirty, in the recent campaign, but nothing he did could save the Democrats. Months before the election, Stephen Douglas knew he would lose, and gave a speech vowing to help Lincoln defeat any attempt at secession or rebellion. Logan smelled an air of defeatism, and blamed Douglas for lacking the passion to win at all costs. He knew the power of Douglas's words would enflame the South, ensure the sectional divide of the party, and usher in a new Republican era. He was right: Lincoln destroyed Douglas in November, and would take the oath of office on March 4.

Unlike some Democrats, Logan continued to see the president-elect as more nemesis than ally, thinking he harbored the secret views of an abolitionist and would try to impose his will on the nation after his inauguration. Yet despite being the target of Logan's criticism, Lincoln had high hopes for him. During the winter, he informed a confidante that if he had his way, his cabinet would be formed solely of Illinois politicians, including those of the rival party. Incredulously, the confidante asked if that would include an adversary like Logan. Lincoln replied, "Yes, I would. . . . I know Logan. He's [against] me now and that's all right. You can count on Logan to do the right thing by the country, and that's the kind of men I want."

On February 5, Logan finally had a chance to give his speech in the House, to outline the views of his people and preach sanity to the increasingly bellicose factions. With expectations high, he took to the floor of the House, dispensing with decorum to get to his main point: Abolitionists and secessionists were equally to blame for the recent turmoil and the South should be guaranteed protection for slavery. This was a familiar position for him and one that wouldn't surprise anyone who knew anything about his politics. From there they expected he would grudgingly endorse Lincoln's policies, dismiss the fire-eaters as troublemakers or malcontents, and praise the eternal unity of the nation.

But instead of providing a firm affirmation, he made a shocking accusation: Republicans of 1861 were no different than King George III in 1776, and, by implication, stood to oppress the South with coercion and tyranny. And his constituents and those from border states were like "noble Spartans standing in the breach" between hostile forces. While the secessionists should be shown mercy, if the North were to "let slip the dogs of war," they would never return to the Union—"never, never!"

Logan's hostile tone and uncompromising message had an immediate effect, winning him applause and admiration in Egypt and points farther south, and open derision and contempt in the North. Some Republicans said he harbored the views of a traitor, and had been secretly encouraging people to fight for the rebels. The speech added fuel to the anti-government fire in southern Illinois. Now louder demands for insurrection echoed in the streets, along with talk of resistance, rebellion, and warfare against the tyrannical Republican power.

But this had not been his intention. He spoke out against war to prevent secession, not to cause it. Did his people even understand what he meant? Struck by the baleful impact of his speech, Logan had no choice but to retreat into public silence on the subject of secession. However, many of his fellow Illinois Democrats, like John McClernand, took the opposite course, choosing to uphold the Union and malign the "compromisers"— including Logan himself. The most dramatic blow came when Stephen Douglas parted company with Logan, too. The occasion came two weeks after the federal garrison at Fort Sumter surrendered to Confederate forces, the first step to open warfare. Douglas made his way to Springfield and, in clear and powerful language, excoriated the secessionist states and demanded the U.S. government quash the rebellion. It was as dramatic and influential a stand in favor of the Lincoln administration's policy as any Democrat had yet made, and it won Douglas praise in Illinois and beyond. But to Logan it was unforgivable.

John Logan's temper rose as he read how Douglas had endorsed the Republican war policy; it expanded into wrath as he learned how his onetime ally had "sold out the Democratic Party"; and it finally exploded into fury when he discovered Douglas had singled out Logan himself as unpatriotic. A few days later, when Logan encountered Douglas on the streets of Springfield, he refused to shake his hand; and when they later found themselves on the same train and one of Douglas's men tried to encourage him to give a speech in support of the Union, Logan was sharp and dismissive: "I'll be damned if I will. I'm a traitor and I will not speak."

Soon after, Illinois Governor Richard Yates sent four thousand militiamen to occupy Cairo. They quickly seized control of the town despite the hostility they encountered from the locals, many of whom openly mocked the Union and cheered for the Confederacy. Logan saw the quaint riverside community turned into a garrison. He expected to see it destroyed in short order.

The news from April and May only got worse: Lincoln called for 75,000 volunteers to fight the rebels, Illinois alone responded with

10,000 men, and war fever reached its peak. Northerners raised toasts, sang martial songs, and threw great parades as new army enlistees left for training camps around the state. Logan greeted such sights warily but could say nothing about the conflict, for fear of being arrested like others who had been charged as Confederate sympathizers, spies, or traitors.

He found himself in a vise of his own making. Though he stood as Egypt's champion, giving voice to its rage and resistance, the people who most ardently followed his words were those who didn't understand them. On the side of rebellion stood many of his constituents and even some of his family members; on the side of the Union stood a president-elect he didn't trust and a party he despised. By the unfortunate fact of geography, his home region stood squarely, helplessly in the path of Northern and Southern armies. Like Egypt itself, Logan would soon have to decide what side he was on, and whether he could ever stomach fighting under the banner of his nemesis, Abraham Lincoln.

Logan wasn't the only one caught between competing loyalties. Many other Northerners who had found comfort in being agreeably pro-peace and pro-Union in 1860 found themselves labeled as suspicious or even treasonous in 1861. The election of Lincoln and especially the advent of war had changed the energy of the nation's politics, as militant factions were rewarded for their zeal and peace proponents were punished for their supposed lack of patriotism. The political whiplash that ensued only furthered the sense of disintegration in the country, as former friends and allies found themselves at odds, and old alliances fell into angry schism.

The new ideological landscape favored those most in favor of pounding the South into submission, and many of these loyalists quickly joined the army. No draft was even necessary in Illinois at the war's outset, as volunteer recruits provided more than enough men to fill the ranks, and a lively spirit of free enterprise animated the recruiting process. State and federal governments offered cash bounties for enlistment ($100 and up), which attracted a variety of recruits, from former militiamen who knew how to fire a musket to bumbling greenhorns who would last no more than three months in uniform and never see a battle.

Though the U.S. military still maintained many professional units in the regular army, sixteen hundred regiments in the war were run by colonels who came from civilian, not military, life. Many attained their position through a vote of the regiments they mustered, but many others gained it through political patronage, with state leaders like Governor Yates deciding who got the plum positions and who didn't. Officers could organize regiments around any groupings imaginable: geography, politics, neighborhood, ethnicity, and so on. There were regiments for teachers, preachers, and miners, as well as for temperance advocates, committed Christians, and even tall men.

With war fever high in the months after Fort Sumter, state regiments formed and filled in a few days or weeks, and the towns and cities of Illinois couldn't seem to wait to send their boys off to fight. Often, their family members thought they might only be away for a short time, until a few quick battles decided matters, the South was sufficiently whipped, and the entire business of secession quickly forgotten.

Still, for all the passion and patriotism the war unleashed, the economic strain showed immediately. Whether it was a farmstead that no longer had enough workers to plant the seeds or reap the harvest, or a factory that had to retool for the newly militarized economy, building a war machine became a costly endeavor. The state arsenal still didn't have enough weapons for the new armies to use, and the state itself was sinking into debt trying to produce them. What's more, the weapons not only weren't sufficient, the inventories were paltry. The arsenal boasted just 362 muskets and 297 pistols. Some regiments had to make do with antiquated flintlock muskets, others with nothing more than bayonets, while still others had to deal with faulty or obsolete weapons that offered a greater threat to the person firing them than the person aimed at.

Even worse, bureaucratic disorganization and lack of funds and oversight led to wasted resources, corruption, and downright incompetence in providing basic food and shelter for the men—and reports of the mismanagement and mistreatment of soldiers couldn't remain hidden for long. As the stories of their hardship began to circulate around the state, more than a few citizens resolved to do something about it.

The Reverend Edward Beecher held in his hand a letter from a doctor in Egypt. Its author was one Doctor Benjamin Woodward, a former member of his First Congregational Church in Galesburg, Illinois, presently assigned to Camp Defiance, the army base at Cairo. Beecher's parishioners watched him in silence, knowing the letter had to be important, for he had made it the centerpiece of his Sunday sermon. Yet the topic was not the evils of slavery or the blessed cause of abolition, but something a bit more unfamiliar—camp life in the U.S. army.

He told them that, despite what they might have read in the news, the troops at the base were in deep distress. Not only did they suffer from debilitating diseases like dysentery and cholera, they scarcely had enough weapons to fight the rebels or enough food to keep from starving. Adequate medical care was nowhere to be found, doctors were thin on the ground, and old shirts and rags doubled as gauze and bandages. Some of the men had to be housed in cattle stalls, while others were reduced to sleeping on bare wooden floors or lodging in filthy barracks. If conditions weren't improved soon, more of the men would sicken and some might perish, before they even had the chance to face the enemy on the battlefield. And so, could the worshippers please consider sending any supplies or assistance they could muster? The troops could use food, medicine, clothing, even the congregation's own labors if anyone was interested in going there in person.

The reverend thought his words had gone over well. If they didn't quite ring with the oratory of his brother Henry Ward Beecher or the elegant prose of his sister Harriet Beecher Stowe, they would at least be enough to rile up the crowd and stir their passions. But he was wrong. Only one person stood up—a stout, middle-aged woman in a handmade dress with a calico bonnet.

Her name was Mary Ann Bickerdyke, and the townsfolk knew her as a sharp-tongued, somewhat eccentric figure who called herself a "botanic physician," or something close to a naturopath. Her husband and daughter had both died recently and she had two sons to look after, along with her regular duties prescribing herbal tea, hot compresses, and other treatments to anyone who might have need of them. But despite her current duties, without hesitation she agreed to make the 350-mile journey downstate to Cairo.

A few days later the Illinois Central sent her on her way, as an agent of her church delivering much-needed aid to the troops. She took along four packages of homemade meals, two trunks of clothing, eleven dollars in cash and $360 worth of medical supplies, all donated by parishioners. The churchgoers knew these pickled vegetables, fruit pies, hand-sewn socks, and assorted hats and shirts wouldn't be enough to solve all the boys' problems, but might be enough to get them back into fighting shape and brighten their spirits a long way from home.

Yet when Mary Ann got off the train in Cairo, what she saw shocked her. The small river town had been transformed into a muddy and toxic hellhole. Dead dogs and garbage littered the streets, basic sanitation seemed to be nonexistent, and stagnant pools of black, filthy water pockmarked the landscape. Even worse were the "hospitals" in town—anything from hotels to saloons, given over to the care of sick and desperate men, who had to sleep on the ground on sacks filled with corn husks, without sheets or pillows. Properly trained doctors and nurses were absent, the state of disorganization was total, and dirt, grease, and excrement made for an environment better suited to spreading disease than to stopping it.

Although she had only planned a short visit, Mary Ann knew she couldn't leave until things were set right and proper. How could the Union allow its boys to suffer like draft animals, or force them to eat scraps and leavings that wouldn't be fit for a goat or a pig? The problem began with the hospitals, which were in profane and shameful condition. None was more of an affront to human decency than the general hospital, a ramshackle wreck of a converted hotel that was lacking in cleanliness and hygiene but abundant with foul odors and unchecked filth. She took it all in, and it soon became clear to her. She realized the best way for her to help would not be delivering donations from Galesburg, but working right here in Cairo—getting her hands dirty in the wards, eating terrible food, scrubbing, cleaning, toiling, anything to help out those poor enlisted boys.

She took to the work quickly, but the hospital was a forbidding place for a nurse. Though she accomplished many things, from making bandages to sanitizing the bathrooms to concocting meals in the staff kitchen, no one appreciated her labors. Worse, because of the soldiers' hostility to women working in the wards, they took great pleasure in trying to insult and intimidate her. Shouting out catcalls and taunting her, they tried to make her work experience as dismal as the hospital itself. But she would not be daunted.

In short order, Mary Ann established a tireless regimen to get the hospital in shape. She cooked palatable meals from the dreadful army rations, washed the soldiers' fetid clothing, helped bathe even the most diseased men, and provided them a fair ration of whiskey, which she saw as valuable tonic, despite being a firm supporter of temperance. Finally, she put herself in charge of all the nurses in the ward, giving orders to the male ones, and generally browbeating or pushing aside anyone who got in her way, regardless of their rank. All the while, she had no formal authority whatsoever to do any of this. When questioned about who had given her license to take such action, she simply replied, "From the Lord God Almighty. Do you have anything that ranks higher than that?"

The doctors at the hospital didn't see the Lord on their protocol chart, and hated having their authority threatened, and they let Mary Ann know it. To them she was an untamed "cyclone in calico." The men, however, had a different name for her. Dispensing with their usual insults, they began to call her "Mother."

Mary Ann was also the actual mother of two young boys, whom she had left behind in Galesburg. She knew her neighbors would take them in for a spell while she did her work down south. That left her with no family, no finances, no home in the hinterland of southern Illinois. The abrupt change would have disturbed anyone's life, but to Mary Ann it was all part of the Lord's plan. She was now free to set things right as she saw fit, to spread her wings after being caged up for years.

Most of her early adult life had been spent with Robert Bickerdyke, a first-generation English immigrant who had chosen Cincinnati to start a life in the 1840s. He was a widower with children when they met, as well as a skilled musician who played the bass viol. He had enough talent that amateur orchestras regularly hired him and he hoped to bring his music to a wider audience. But success was fleeting, and when opportunities did arise—such as a chance to go on a national tour with celebrity soprano Jenny Lind—he inexplicably passed them up. This left him reduced to scrambling for jobs, usually as a house painter or a mechanic.

Mary Ann and Robert married in 1847, then drifted around the region for a decade, as he looked for a creative spark as well as a paycheck, and she ran the household and raised their three children and a pair of stepsons from his earlier marriage. A decade later they settled in Galesburg, a quaint little place in upstate Illinois founded by anti-slavery New York Presbyterians. Mary Ann fit in well there, for she believed firmly in abolition as well as Christianity—though she wasn't too dogmatic about it. As she said, "I worship with the Methodists, the Congregationalists or the Episcopals, as I happen to light on 'em." Around town she became known for her charity work, gathering and selling secondhand clothes to pay for fabric to sew clothes for those in need. As Reverend Beecher said, "No one could stretch a dime or a yard of calico so far as Sister Bickerdyke."

Just as she began to make a name for herself in charity circles, though, Robert struggled to find work and make enough money to support the family. He managed to practice his art as the unpaid director of a local symphony and choir, but never had enough time or resources to go further than that. Because of his penury, the symphony and choir decided to throw a benefit concert for him, but on that very night he died of apoplexy. He left behind almost no savings and children from two marriages to care for. These obligations now fell to Mary Ann.

The townsfolk were stunned that their music director had passed on so soon, after they had just honored him. But to Mary Ann it was no surprise. She thought he could have lived longer if he hadn't been so domineering. As she said, "He wanted me to do everything his way, and just as he did. But his way was too slow, and I just couldn't stand it." His death gave her the chance to find her own way. Within a few weeks of his passing, she acted quickly to hang up her shingle on the little cottage where she lived—"M.A. Bickerdyke, Botanic Physician."

By late 1861, almost everyone who knew Mary Ann in Camp Defiance called her Mother Bickerdyke. She cut a striking figure for a woman who in other circles might have inspired pity for being a widow, isolated from her children, and impoverished. Here in Cairo, though, she inspired awe. As Doctor Woodward said, she was "strong as a man, muscles of iron, nerves of finest steel—sensitive, but self-reliant, kind, and tender, seeking all for others, for herself, nothing." She wore a weather-beaten sun bonnet and rode an old white mule, cutting an indelible image everywhere she went.

Not everyone was happy to see her. She had special contempt for army officers, those "pesky ossifiers" who routinely got in the way of her work and challenged her authority—or lack of it. They didn't dislike her, exactly; they just didn't know what to make of her. She gathered her power without any source of patronage, or means of support, or elite defenders in the wings. She only had the support of the enlisted men, who knew Mother Bickerdyke to be their greatest champion.

Soon she was running all six military hospitals around Cairo. To get them into shape, her regimen was brisk and thorough: She inspected each one; condemned their lack of hygiene and medical supplies; forced the nurses to make improvements; cleaned and sanitized the wards; reorganized the hospitals' staff; removed the nurses who were convalescent soldiers and replaced them with healthy men; and tackled the worst case of the lot—the filthy regimental hospital in Bird's Point, Missouri. When she located the doctor in charge, she gave her anger free rein and delivered a shocking tirade against him in front of the staff and patients.

Thoroughly humiliated, the doctor expressed his anger to the brigadier general in charge of Cairo, Benjamin Prentiss. Like other generals, Prentiss was a politician who had used his connections to get a plum assignment; unlike those generals, however, he actually had military experience, as well as a proper respect for rules and order—of which Mary Ann seemed ignorant and dismissive. After hearing reports of her actions, Prentiss reacted coolly: "The matter is easily disposed of." Women were not allowed to enter camp without a pass from a relative, and then only at certain times. Open and shut.

Mary Ann caught wind of the trouble she had caused from Dr. Woodward, and when General Prentiss summoned him to a meeting to discuss the matter, she came along, too, though she hadn't been invited. The conversation didn't take long.

Although no one recorded the exact words Mary Ann used with the general, he emerged from the meeting convinced of the value of her work and the importance of her staying put. He also gave her a new job: running a central kitchen for all local military hospitals and coordinating their care. Against all convention and expectation, Mary Ann had been officially promoted—not dismissed.

As she said, "I talked sense to him."

Fifty miles north in the town of Marion, Congressman John Logan stood waiting to give a long-awaited speech about the war and his views on it. He was nervous. The day before, his train was late and he had to put off the speech. A crowd of four thousand, already sweltering in the summer heat, took exception to the delay by breaking out in a riot. Today the atmosphere in the town square was again charged with potential violence, as angry feelings about the war boiled over and the streets seemed to be filled with brutes and miscreants. Mary Logan feared for her husband's safety: "I felt sure I could at least scream should they move toward him with evil intent. . . . I trembled in every limb, my head swam, and I dared not speak to any one."

Ever since his last major speech in February, Logan had tried to be silent on the subject of secession, but his reticence only brought more charges of disloyalty. The *Tribune* especially delighted in hinting he was a traitor, using ever more creative language. Meanwhile, his mentor, Stephen Douglas, had died in June, a victim of typhoid fever, and Logan never had a chance to repair his bond with a political legend who had once been his friend and champion. It was a deep and sudden loss, and it motivated him to clearly state his position on the war. He hoped the crowd would forgive him for it.

With some hesitation, Logan stepped up on a horse wagon and began to speak. Secession, he said, has already made America pay a terrible cost in violence and disunity. Logan looked out and saw the crowd had settled into "a deathlike stillness," listening intently to his words. He continued:

> The time has come when a man must be for or against his country, not for or against his State. How long could one State stand up against another, or two or three States against others? The Union once dissolved, we should have innumerable confederacies and rebellions. I, for one, shall stand or fall for this Union, and shall this day enroll for the war! I want as many of you as will to come with me.

The crowd paused for a moment in shock. Then it gave him a rousing cheer, as people applauded him with passion, clapped him on the back, and shook his hand so hard it hurt. He was stunned and delighted.

Logan remained a hero to them, even as he openly supported the war. With their beloved congressman's approval, they could now support it too, and could join army regiments with their friends and neighbors, and battle the turncoats who had left Egypt to become graycoats. With much relief, Logan thanked them for their enthusiasm, and realized it would go far in helping him fill the 1,100 positions of his new 31st Illinois Volunteer Infantry Regiment, which he would command as a colonel.

The change in Logan had been months in the making. Over the summer, his anger had become increasingly directed at the secessionists, who destroyed property in Egypt and tried to threaten anyone who didn't join the Confederacy. Just as his sentiments began to turn, in Virginia he witnessed a skirmish in the Battle of Bull Run and came away shocked at the scale of the Union disaster, making him realize just how much help the army needed. While he still harbored intense anger at abolitionists, he was now ready to stand with the Unionists, even if they were Republicans. He met with Colonel Ulysses S. Grant, and came away impressed that this army veteran had so many enterprising notions to beat the rebels. And when he met with President Lincoln, the rail-splitter offered him kind words, and gave him sanction to enter the war as an officer and resign his seat in Congress. But while persuading the president that he supported the war was easy for Logan, convincing his family was a much more difficult task.

The conflict had caused a rift among his relatives. One of his brothers-in-law now fought for the South, and another had been arrested for treasonous activity. Only his youngest brother, James, agreed to fight against the Confederacy, while two other brothers remained hostile to his plans. His mother was even more intransigent. When he visited the family home to explain himself, she refused him entrance, saying "Go away from my house, John Logan . . . I never want to see your face." But as much as her words wounded him, his wife suffered even more from the family division. After his sister Annie openly wished he would die in the war, Mary Logan slapped her, and the two women got into a bare-knuckle brawl "complete with punching, scratching, and hair pulling. Mary ended the fight by picking up a chair and smacking her sister-in-law over the head with it."

The war may have tattered his family bonds, but Logan forged new ones with young men from southern Illinois who joined his ranks. He had picked out many of them personally. At Camp Dunlap in central Illinois, he watched them marching in formation, practicing drills, preparing for combat like men of war. They would soon become known as the "Dirty-First" regiment, "the 'hardest' swearers in the army," and they were determined to transform themselves into soldiers, even though the army could not match their enthusiasm with adequate training, uniforms, or weapons. They would go into battle untested.

Despite their lack of experience, newly appointed Brigadier General Ulysses S. Grant had a bold stroke for them planned downriver. Grant—who now commanded the District of Southeast Missouri, with headquarters in Cairo—planned an attack on the village of Belmont, Missouri, to secure a foothold against the rebel-held bluffs across the river at Columbus, Kentucky. He picked Logan's regiment and five others to make the journey down the Mississippi to make the demonstration. They would show the Union would not be cowed into accepting Confederate control of the great river, and would seize control of the "Father of Waters," as Lincoln called it, with martial pride and determination.

The evening came to embark. Logan's riverboat rode the current under a dark sky, the lights of Cairo dimming on the horizon. The boys of the 31st were quiet as they went, determined not to betray their movement to the rebels or their fears to themselves. To a man, they had spoiled for a fight, suffered through training camp, and cursed the damned Johnny Rebs just like Logan did. They were green and naive and brave and strong and innocent, and he loved them all.

The next day, the battle ended with Logan's troops clambering aboard the riverboats, their mud-soaked uniforms and flooded muskets sharing space with haversacks and cartridge boxes in a great wet pile of troops in desperate retreat. Some of them sported flesh wounds, others broken arms and bloody jaws, but they had been the lucky ones. The unlucky had been left in the wooded ravine behind them, cloaked in gun smoke and cannon fire. Logan brought aboard all the men and arms the transport could hold.

He clenched his ribs, recalling how his horse had thrown him early in the battle. His chest didn't hurt then, not when victory looked so clearly in sight—when they raided the enemy camp at dawn and sent its defenders to flight. But the triumph vanished when the untrained Union troops looted the rebel camp and incurred the wrath of General Grant. He had the entire camped burned, which made for an easy target for the guns of Columbus. The rebels counterattacked, and sent them scrambling back to the river.

And now they had escaped, and the battle was lost. Logan took one last look back at Belmont as the transport moved up the river. Then he turned to the north, where the lights of Cairo had just become visible over the horizon.

There were six hundred Union casualties in the Belmont expedition. Ninety of them were Logan's own. He had talked many of the troops into joining him on the ill-fated mission, and his guilt was strong over their deaths and injuries. He thought of them as family, his relatives in spirit since so many members of his own family now fought for the enemy—people like his brother-in-law, Hybert Cunningham, who had attacked his regiment at Belmont as a lieutenant for the Confederacy.

He had lost almost one-tenth of his recruits. To avoid a similar fate next time, his men would need much more training, much better weapons, and a much improved strategy, but Logan knew they would get none of it. Grant had already planned their next foray into the South, and this time it would be no mere demonstration but a strategic strike into the rebel homeland.

A few days after Belmont, under a flag of truce, Logan scoured the battlefield to identify the men missing or killed in action and recover their remains if he could. He moved slowly and looked for any hint of life or breath from the fallen soldiers, but found none.

He was abruptly jolted from his labors by a Missouri farmer, who saw his Northern uniform and confronted him with blunt and vile language. The battle had destroyed the farmer's crops and his land, and Union colonels like Logan were to blame. He even damned Logan as a "nigger thief" for allowing his slaves to run away during the chaos. For once, Logan chose to hold his tongue and take the abuse, not once mentioning his nickname, "Dirty Work," or that he had written the Black Law, or that he was an old-line Democrat. He knew that in his uniform he looked every bit the Unionist, the Yankee invader, the enemy of the South. For all the farmer knew, he could have even been an abolitionist.

Up in Cairo, Mary Ann Bickerdyke stood inspecting the latest haul of goods that had just come in for her boys, in wooden crates stamped CHICAGO SANITARY COMMISSION. It was a huge stash: thousands of fresh linens and pillows, bandages and rags, clean clothes and undergarments, and food and drink from brandy, crackers, and eggs to 200 pounds of dried fruit. She checked the shipment—it was everything she had asked for—then commanded a nurse to secure the crates to keep them away from the prying fingers of the surgeons and their lackeys.

She had battled with the doctors ever since her meeting with General Prentiss. Now he was gone and the recently promoted General Ulysses S. Grant was the commander, so the medical officers thought it might be a fine idea to challenge her authority again. She challenged them back, accusing them of theft and dereliction of duty and other malfeasance, and for good measure took up the matter with Grant himself—and won. He gave her even more power to hire staff members and coordinate nursing care, and distribute the massive shipments of food and supplies any way she saw fit.

The surgeons were furious, but Mary Ann hardly cared. Her duty to the troops came first, and she would raise any hell she needed to make sure her boys were properly fed and cared for. She had a firm ally too in the Chicago Sanitary Commission, which had marshaled the support of countless Illinois women to cook the food and sew the garments that ended up in these crates. Mary Ann offered a little prayer to their grace and charity, then ordered her staff to seal the boxes with massive iron locks.

Several months later, on a bleak winter morning in 1862, Mary Ann set sail on the hospital ship *The City of Memphis*. It was headed for the wilds of central Tennessee on the Cumberland River, in support of Grant's attack against the forts that guarded the heart of the Confederacy and could open the door to an invasion of the South. The first, Fort Henry, had fallen, but the other, Fort Donelson, remained a forbidding objective. Mary Ann knew the battle would bring great carnage, and suspected many of the wounded might die before they reached the hospitals in Cairo, so she and her staff brought the hospital to them.

Although this was a Sanitary Commission ship, Mary Ann held sway over it. Her voice echoed throughout the ship, from the boiler deck to the pilothouse, shouting commands at the doctors and nurses until the staff became tired of her incessant demands. To onlookers she seemed to be running the entire ship, even though she had not been invited, held no official title, and received no pay for her labors. Nonetheless, she turned the *Memphis* into the very model of what a floating hospital should look like, even though no one had ever seen or imagined such a thing before.

She didn't mean to be a martinet, but knew everything had to be ready when the wounded arrived. She remembered her nursing work in Cincinnati during the cholera epidemic of 1849. The doctors thought they were ready, but no one imagined how bad it could get: the shortages of food and medicine, the lack of hospital beds, the failure of doctors to soothe

the pains of plague victims, the coffins stacked in the hospital basement. The sights were almost too much to bear.

She had the memory of Cincinnati to guide her, and resolved not to be blindsided again. She had prepared the crew, organized the supplies, made the beds, cleaned the decks, and sanitized the operating rooms. Then the *Memphis* arrived at Fort Donelson and lowered its ramp for the ambulance carts and wagons. Only then did the full horror of war emerge, in more inventive and extreme ways than she could have ever imagined.

The damage was unique to each man: Some bore the gaping wounds of artillery, with their torsos and limbs torn apart by grape and canister shot. Others arrived with the fevers of disease, the ravages of dysentery and typhoid fever, or the scourge of madness, driven to deafness or insanity by the roar of shell fire and the terror of combat. Still others were lucky to lose only a leg or an arm—the unlucky lost a jaw, or part of a face. And then came the men who lay as pale as ghosts, the victims of frostbite and hypothermia, who had spent an entire evening or even several days suffering on the battlefield. The armies on the move had left them behind, frozen in the mud, until nurses and orderlies could arrive to hack them out and deliver them to safety. Many of their companions, though, would never arrive at the *Memphis*. They still lay on the field of combat, perforated by lead, crushed by fallen trees, or drowned in shallow streams, their final resting place a cold and pitiless Tennessee battlefield.

Many of the dead included the men of twenty different Illinois infantry regiments—including the 31st, whose commander, Colonel John Logan, newspapers said had been killed in action. The last his men had seen of him, he lay motionless and bloody with lead in his hip, wood from a shattered pistol in his ribs, and even more lead in his shoulder. A doctor detected no pulse in his pallid and icy body.

Mary Ann heard gruesome stories of such men who still lay bleeding and broken on the battlefield of Fort Donelson. She imagined their fears, their isolation, their quiet deaths so many miles from home. She still had plenty of work to do on the hospital ship, but couldn't get the vision of those men frozen on the battlefield out of her mind. At midnight she ventured out to see if she could find anyone to rescue, or give comfort to a soldier in his last moments of life.

Her journey was harrowing. Teams of horses lay dead on the field, tied in pairs, threes, and fours; pools of blood pockmarked the rutted ground; and random clothing and belongings were scattered across the terrain, from hats and coats to cartridge boxes and bayonets—and everywhere the shrapnel of exploded shells, and the men who had absorbed that shrapnel. Some bodies lay still on the ground, while others showed only a hand or foot or head, the rest hidden and entombed in the ice. Mary Ann did not cower. She steeled herself, and with her lantern carefully looked at each fallen soldier to see if she could find any signs of life.

After some time, the glare of her lamp attracted the attention of a shadowy figure who approached her. It was an orderly, sent to find whatever fiend might be desecrating the bodies of the dead. He discovered Mary Ann inspecting the bodies to check for any hint of breath or a pulse. She told him what she was doing, and he summoned her to a field hospital that had been set up near the battlefield.

He led her to a tent where a bloodied and bandaged Union colonel lay. Stricken with an infection, he burned with fever, and his injuries were so severe his doctor had even demanded his entire left arm be amputated. But John Logan would hear nothing of it. He had cheated death, despite what the newspapers said, and wanted to emerge from this war intact. He looked at the sturdy, calico-clad woman in front of him.

He asked her what she was doing on the battlefield at midnight. He had sent out his orderly to apprehend what looked to be a grave robber.

Mary Ann explained her mission, and before the colonel could reprimand her, she thanked him for sending out his orderly to assist with her work. With that, she swiftly gathered her lantern and belongings and went out to find more abandoned souls on the field of battle.

She would soon return to Cairo, but for John Logan the battle was only beginning—grievously injured, he was one of the 2,700 Union casualties from the assault on Fort Donelson. His condition seemed to worsen in the field hospital, with fever and infection threatening his life, so the medical staff transferred him to the *New Uncle Sam*, a riverboat that contained hospital facilities as well as an office for General Grant.

Grant had known Logan from southern Illinois, and was interested in how well the colonel had performed in the field, and why he had been injured. Reports described his conduct during the attack: how he had led his regiment in battling a Confederate surge of 10,000 men; had been shot in the thigh but refused to give up command; had been bruised in the ribs and shot in the shoulder but still held on; and had finally dropped from his horse and blacked out. He had even been left for dead—the Confederates overran his position, and rebel soldiers assumed he was a corpse. If not for a timely Union counter-surge, he would have never survived.

In respect of his service, Grant wrote to Congressman Elihu Washburne recommending John Logan's promotion to brigadier general, for among the colonels leading regiments in his army, "a braver or more gallant man is not to be found." His wife, Mary, would soon arrive and nurse him back to health, but it would be months before he would see action in the field again.

Recommending Logan's promotion was one of Grant's easier tasks in the days after Fort Donelson. With the great Union victory, he now had to contend with a flood of dispatches from Washington, D.C., from fellow generals and superior officers, and from the press, which wanted to know all about the battle and how "Unconditional Surrender" Grant had won it—his new nickname referring to the terms he had given the rebels before their defeat. Amid all the requests and messages, one stuck out.

It was from a fellow general who outranked him. Grant recognized him as the new commander of the District of Cairo, one of his former positions. Grant recalled him as a down-on-his-luck officer from Ohio— someone who had failed repeatedly in civilian life before the war, just as he had. The general had been a banker, a lawyer, a businessman, but nothing seemed to fit. His reputation was checkered due to a failed attempt to command the Department of the Cumberland a few months before, and rival officers called him a lunatic just as they called Grant a drunk.

Grant didn't care. Men of war were a hard-bitten lot, tarnished with failure as often as they were crowned with laurels. This Ohio general had merely lived a hard life, with the scars to prove it. The army could use more bold and relentless soldiers like him, and fewer "political generals" who never risked anything but always stole credit for victories.

The final words of the letter spoke to him. The general congratulated Grant on his recent victories and offered his services to the army, even in a subordinate role. "I . . . have faith in you," the letter said. "Command me in any way."

Grant did not hesitate. He wrote back to William Sherman immediately.

INVASION

THREE

ECHOES OF CHICKAMAUGA

At first it sounded like the wind, a high whistle that echoed through the oak forest and grew louder in volume and pitch until the branches seemed to quiver and bend around it. Then the boughs shattered as hundreds of shells split the trees in a hail of lead and bark and leaves and smoke. The high keening peaked into a shrieking roar, the kind the Union boys had heard far too many times not to fear. As one young soldier, Ambrose Bierce, said, it was "the ugliest noise that any mortal ever heard"—the rebel yell of Southern soldiers on the attack.

Their screams chased the Northern soldiers off the ridgeline, down the hillside, and scattered them in fits of chaos and terror. As one observer wrote, "our broken columns were flying, in utter demoralization. There were men, horses without riders, sections of artillery" all rushing to safety, trying to flee from the massive Confederate onslaught as well as the Union guns the rebels had seized and now turned on their former owners. "Shot and shell, and canister, screamed and shrieked over the flying fugitives, making a scene, and causing sounds in which the very demons of the infernal regions might well find delight."

The once-promising day of Sunday, September 20, 1863, had turned into a nightmare. The first step in the Northern invasion of Georgia, intended to bring the South to its knees, had become a disaster beyond any expectation or imagination. Even the name of the battle site seemed to mock and disparage the hopes of the North. According to legend, the Cherokee called it "Chickamauga"—River of Death.

The disaster unfolded because of a single error. The commanding general of the Army of the Cumberland, William Rosecrans, had a reputation as a skilled tactician, and in recent months had maneuvered his army in Tennessee from Murfreesboro to Chattanooga with a combination of bold moves, clever advances, and simple good fortune. But his luck ran out across the Georgia state line at Chickamauga when he mistakenly pulled several brigades from a key defensive line—and opened up a half-mile gap in the process. The Union troops could only watch in horror as a timely Southern attack exploited the error and broke their force in two, destroying the entire right wing of the army. This sent Rosecrans into a panic, and he fled with two of his corps leaders to the safer confines of Chattanooga. The enlisted men and lower-ranking officers, however, had to fend for themselves.

Countless troops scattered in confusion, without proper orders or guidance. Others mounted a last-ditch fight against their attackers. The brigade that Colonel George Buell commanded had it especially bad, as one of the units Rosecrans had mistakenly removed from the defensive line. The brigade's regiments had to contend not only with the rebel onslaught, but with retreating Northern soldiers charging off the battlefield "in the wildest disorder and most shameful confusion." They faced bedlam in every direction:

- The 26th Ohio pushed through the Union stragglers and tried to mount a charge, only to face the stabbing bayonets of a regiment of enraged rebel Texans.

- The 100th Illinois tried to counterattack, only to face the wrath of those same Texans, who saw how they "ran like turkeys" to get away from their knives.
- The 58th Indiana got trampled when terrified horses from Union batteries set loose their limbers and caissons carrying artillery and ammunition boxes, and the Indianans got crushed under the wheels of the gun carriages.
- Throughout the melee, the Union boys heard one sound clearly: the deafening cry of the rebel yell.

Despite the chaos, some of Buell's men managed to regroup. They relocated to Snodgrass Hill and joined the remnants of the 14th Corps and its commander George Thomas. Through the afternoon and early evening, this remaining force fought off countless rounds of Confederate attacks and saved what remained of the army, many of them literally fighting to their last round of ammunition. They withdrew under cover of darkness and kept a defeat on the battlefield from becoming a catastrophe for the Union cause.

Into the night and the next morning, the cohesion of the rest of the Army of the Cumberland splintered into fragments. Troops lost in the fog of battle found themselves outnumbered, running into the dark forest, firing at an unseen enemy. While some escaped to the north, others ran into a pocket of Southern soldiers and faced capture or death. Many of those who fell died in the woods.

The injured soldiers who managed to be rescued found themselves at hospitals like the one near Crawfish Springs, where Reverend John Hight, the chaplain of the 58th Indiana, tended to the spiritual needs of troops in their most desperate hours. Like most field hospitals, it was little more than a temporary facility, a way station for broken men who needed immediate attention before they could be transported back to the main facilities in Chattanooga. Yet this one was a bit too close to the site of the day's violence.

Hight wanted to stay and do what he could to aid the troops, but with the battlefield rout still unfolding, the Confederates had surged uncomfortably near to the hospital. He had no choice but to leave with the rest of the staff and the less injured patients on the wagon train north. The bedridden men who remained, however, had no such opportunity; they would become lost to wounds or disease, or captured and sent into captivity.

Hight felt uneasy about leaving, and anxious about the journey. The wagon train moved slowly as it snaked through the mountain redoubts and hollers of northwestern Georgia, and every creeping shadow and unknown sound foretold an attack in the minds of the shaken troops. As Hight saw it, the rebels could have lobbed a few artillery shells at them and "some of the panic stricken would have plunged headlong into the river."

The reverend himself was no less afraid. He had served in some of the hottest conflicts of the war, but rarely had he seen such a stunning defeat. He knew his rank wouldn't protect him from retribution either, for "the rebels utterly despise Yankee preachers." If caught he would be sent to a prison camp just like any other hapless soldier, and subjected to untold devilment that his wary mind preferred not to conjure.

Hours later the wagon train reached Chattanooga, now a scene of utter disarray. Thousands of men searched to find the members of their shattered regiments and sought out their close friends and colleagues, if any had survived. Among them traveled the horse-drawn ambulances—150 by one count—conveying the injured, dying, and near-dead to hospitals and makeshift tents that served as hospitals. And then there were the generals, some too ashamed to look their men in the eye, others maintaining a brave face despite the losses. Hidden among them was William Rosecrans in his private quarters, kneeling before a minister and desperately seeking spiritual guidance for all the pandemonium he had unleashed.

Hight had a difficult night upon his arrival in town. For once he had avoided the carnage of battle as it unfolded—the brutal assaults, the shocking casualties, the scenes of horror and loss—but he knew the result would be just as difficult to bear. He continued to wonder whether he should have stayed with the wounded at the hospital near Crawfish Springs, and thought of what had become of the troops in his care, the "men suffering untold agony," whose faces he couldn't forget. He remembered one sergeant asking for an ambulance that would never come, and another captain who broke his silence to ask, "You are not going to leave us, are you?" Hight knew the answer: "I never expected to see either of them again."

It had been more than a year and a half since he had begun serving the boys of the 58th Indiana, and this was only the latest chapter in the saga of human sorrow and destruction he had witnessed. It was a martial conflict that played out over the great rivers, swamps, and mountain ranges of the South, and was a world away from the bucolic, small-town travels in the West of his earlier years. But he had ridden this epic circuit with a full heart and a knotted stomach, knowing that God must have a plan for him. Otherwise he would never have accepted Colonel Buell's offer for him to become the minister for the regiment, starting in March of 1862.

Hight's service began even before he first joined up with the troops stationed in Tennessee. On his way to meet them, he tramped across the Fort Donelson battlefield after the battle there had ended. He saw the shocking remnants of the carnage and realized the war had become bloodier and more devastating than anyone at home had yet realized. As he wrote, "It was my first sight of a real battlefield and it made a deep impression."

From there he made his way to Nashville, and introduced himself to the 58th Indiana. He packed bundles of amenities and provisions he thought he would need, and had two tailors make a fancy chaplain's suit for him, expecting to be lauded and esteemed when he set foot in camp.

But as soon as he arrived, he wanted to escape his new life in the army. He remembered how hard and cold his bed was, and how unimaginative the rations—crackers, bacon, and coffee. He endured sleepless nights and could not find support or comfort. The army camp was bleak and inhospitable to his sensibilities, made even more forbidding by its location in the occupied territory of the South. He found it hard to make friends and find allies, even among the younger soldiers. At first they "seemed glad to see me, yet had a distrust of my ability to fill the place of Chaplain. I could not blame them, since I was filled with the same distrust of myself."

He resolved to endure the doubt and privation, however, reasoning that it must be part of God's plan, however mysterious it might be.

In a year's time since Nashville, much had changed: Hight had stuck with the army and learned its ways. He had traveled throughout the western theater of war with the Army of the Ohio and the Army of the Cumberland, experienced glory and misery, ingratiated himself with the men, cheered their triumphs and mourned their losses, and came to command a fair deal of respect in his regiment. Still, despite the well-earned esteem of his position, he continued to feel isolated, distant. This wasn't a new feeling, and had been with him throughout his adult life, wherever he had ministered.

Although married and a longtime servant of the Methodist faith, Hight had experienced a strangely rootless life. Born in Bloomington, he graduated from the state university at nineteen, then spent the next eight years on the road for the church. He preached the gospel in wayside hamlets and little chapels, spread the word of God to help parishioners find a personal connection to their savior, and tried to inspire his fellow believers and uplift their souls. He represented the Indiana Conference, an evangelical group attempting to rekindle the fires of faith in places where only its ashes remained, whether that was a village tavern, or a gambling hall, or in his case, an army camp.

This suited him, for even if his work for the Army of the Cumberland could be challenging, or even horrifying, he preferred being on the road. He found the idea of home uncomfortable and elusive. While he loved his friends and family in Bloomington, he also kept his distance:

> I have become cosmopolitan. The attachments of early days
> have to some extent been severed, but not forgotten. For near
> ten years I have been a wanderer on the face of the earth. I
> have traveled much in my own land. I have been amongst the
> good and bad, the high and low. I have gazed upon many of
> the grand scenes of art and nature. I have been present in the
> din of battle. . . . I am not unmindful of relatives or friends,
> nor forgetful of the scenes and circumstances of other years.
> But I hurry on, hoping to meet the loved and lost in Heaven.

And so this man who encouraged the communion of worshippers, who pleaded with them to seek out and support their fellow brothers and sisters in Christ, could not find comfort among them on earth. He would wait for that in the afterlife.

As with their chaplain John Hight, the boys of the 58th Indiana Volunteer Infantry had traveled far across the landscape of the war. They had seen some of its worst episodes and had persevered despite their struggles. Fighting alongside the 58th in Colonel Buell's brigade at Chickamauga, another regiment fought just as tirelessly and suffered just as greatly—the 13th Michigan. Its commander Joshua Culver had even lost his hearing when a shell exploded over his head during the rebel attack, but his troops continued to battle until nightfall. When they retreated to Chattanooga, many returned with their heads bandaged and arms in slings as they staggered back on foot, while teams of ambulances carried those who couldn't. Among them was a young man who was not a soldier himself, did not hail from Michigan, and wasn't white like the other boys in the regiment. He hadn't signed up for the army. Instead he had made a run for it, risking death to join the cause.

His name was John McCline, and he wasn't even of legal age to be a solider. Not more than 11 years old, he was an escaped slave from a Tennessee plantation east of Nashville, and had made a place for himself in the regiment despite the threat to his safety. Freedmen were brutalized by Southern armies if they were caught, especially if they were part of an invading Northern army. Still, compared to his former life on the plantation, a war zone seemed like a better place.

Usually it was. But September 21 was different, a dark day after the battle in which the names of the wounded and killed in action began to be known. Among the fallen of the 13th Michigan were a number of friends and allies he had made in the past year. Perhaps the greatest loss was Frank Murray, who had suffered grievous wounds and died earlier that day. John would always remember him as the dashing soldier with the knapsack and musket across his back, the young man from Company C who saw him herding cows and provided the means for his escape.

John recalled life on the plantation as ceaseless work. He not only tended to livestock, he plowed the fields and harvested crops from corn to millet; he caught fish in the river and cultivated plants in the garden; he even helped grind the grain at the mill and milk cows in the barn. He knew if he didn't do these things, well and efficiently, there would be consequences.

He had a grandmother and three older brothers who also toiled on the plantation, and a father who was owned by a different family a short distance away. His mother and sister had died years earlier. Long before, the planters had divided his family up, trading and bargaining for his relatives as if they were livestock. However, none of them could protest the injustice, for fear of the retribution that would surely come—in the form of a three-foot-long rawhide whip.

Despite its pleasant name of Clover Bottoms, the farmstead had been rife with violence and brutality, even murder on several occasions. The overseer Phillips was the worst offender, but the mistress of the house, Mrs. Hoggatt, was almost as bad. She carried the rawhide in her skirts, and she would use it to savage any slave for the slightest infraction, belting them across the shoulders or back of the neck and always leaving a painful, bloody mark.

John would never forget that cold but hopeful December day in 1862. The Union infantry had appeared on the pike marching in rows of four, bringing with them a large covered ambulance. He watched as they got closer and closer, and the ambulance pulled up beside him. The soldiers greeted him, some seeming not much older than he was. They were on their way to Nashville. Private Frank Murray approached him and said, "Come on, Johnny, and go with us up North, and we will set you free."

How had he known his name? John was surprised and impressed, only later finding out "Johnny" was an all-purpose moniker the soldiers gave to Southerners, as in "Johnny Reb." Private Murray meant it as a friendly joke.

John set loose the favorite cow he was tending, Nell, who trotted away over the fields, offering a last snort before disappearing. He followed the ambulance and began to march alongside these curious soldiers from the North, with their sharp uniforms, precise movements, and odd sense of humor.

He almost didn't make it out. As the regiment went through a local toll gate, two young miscreants—the Blankenship boys—were waiting there to cause trouble. He knew them all too well, and fought them often. They spotted him and figured out he had escaped. They threatened to inform his master, who would no doubt give him the kind of remorseless beating reserved for disobedient slaves.

John knew these young men were not to be trifled with. They were the kind of boys who, free from conscience or remorse, could engage in the most vicious behavior with a laugh and a smile. Just two years before, he had seen their kind attack an old man on a country road. First they shot and killed his horse, then gutted the creature, stuffed and sewed the man inside, buried him in gore up to his neck, and left him by the roadside for an hour until they had had their fun. Such mayhem was not unheard of in these parts.

Luckily, John's former master never appeared after his escape. He could fiercely attack a young boy with a whip, but confronting an actual army was a different story. This removed the immediate threat of violence, and John had a moment of peace as the troops marched over the rolling Tennessee hills and away from the place that had caused him so much hardship. At least now that he was in the army John wouldn't have to face the lash. At least here he could fight back against his tormentors, and with a weapon if need be. As a reminder of this, on his escape he brought with him the whip he had used to corral the cows. He had always treated them more humanely than he and his family had ever been treated by the Hoggatt clan.

But while he felt a sense of liberation, another sensation soon began to rise in him: loneliness. He missed his family deeply, and he felt a gnawing sense of loss, wondering if he'd ever see them again or whether they would survive the war. He cried thinking about them, still trapped on the plantation, facing untold dangers. They even risked facing the master's wrath for his untimely departure.

His first night away was dark, the stars were out, the air was cold and frosty. He tried to take stock of the new adventure he was on, the places he would see, the friends he would make, marching to new and unseen destinations. The soldiers were kind to him, fed him and treated him well, but he couldn't get over how strange this world was. It was a hard night and he cried again, but at last fell asleep.

He awoke to the sound of bugles, and a fire warming the tent where he had slept. He left his bunk as light broke, and stepped out into camp. There he stood amazed at the thousands of men before him, in dozens of infantry and cavalry regiments, and the masses of teamsters, wagoners, grooms, nurses, cooks, engineers, carpenters, laundresses, blacksmiths, guides, servants, laborers, and telegraphers, all making up a giant city on wooden wheels—his new and unexpected home. But to him, it was most impressive as "a world of tents. Clean and white, they seemed to cover the earth for miles around; and, as far as the eye could trace."

Resolving to clean up, he washed his face and hands, combed his hair and put on a pair of glasses. Now it was clear: "I looked like a real Yankee soldier."

John McCline hadn't become a soldier yet, though. Instead he found paid work as one of the regiment's muleteers, driving a half-dozen animals and a wagon loaded with supplies of salt pork, hardtack, coffee, and other provisions. Used to rustling cattle on the farm, he had no trouble getting the mules in line. And compared to some of the other teamsters—who made frequent and aggressive use of the whip—he was kind to the animals, offering plenty of feed and rest if possible.

In nine months he had been with the same team across Tennessee and into Alabama, over mountain passes and valleys, following narrow creeks and stream banks, and even crossing mighty rivers like the Tennessee on perilous pontoon bridges. More than once he thought the team might lose its footing or that a wagon wheel would catch a sharp edge and they would all fall off a cliff or be drowned in a river. But his luck and skill held and they averted danger on many occasions. However, crossing open country made him nervous, as rebel sharpshooters could lurk in the trees and take aim at the Yankee wagon trains passing by. He remembered how a few months before a band of guerrillas had opened fire on the wagons and killed seven of the mules before they were driven off. It almost made him want to carry a gun himself.

John had never wanted to kill anyone, though. He didn't have the nerve or the martial spirit. But he couldn't forget the words of his "superior officer," Aron, a friend who had also escaped captivity and now worked for the regiment. John was a citizen now, he said, and a citizen had a duty to serve his country, even if it meant laying down his life. And these days, serving your country meant fighting rebels.

Even so, John felt a lot of fear at the prospect of facing enemy guns and risking his neck. Aron told him a story. He had been at Shiloh and seen Union troops move against a ridgeline held by Confederate troops. After they readied their rifles and fixed their bayonets, in one great surge they charged forward and drove the rebels off the ridge. The Yankee boys were screaming the whole time. "Why did they yell like that?" John wondered aloud. Aron said, "It gives you courage and you forget yourself and all about being afraid." Once he wore the blue, he would feel the same way.

A few months after Chickamauga John came upon one of the new "colored infantry regiments" that President Lincoln had supported, which had been quite successful in enlisting young black men—many of them former bondsmen—as Union troops. He was struck by the precision of their drills, the neatness of their uniforms, and the cleanliness of their camp, so unlike the workaday appearance of the 13th Michigan. A minister was teaching some of them to read and write, while others were busy writing reports and letters home. They greeted him kindly and asked many questions, including whether he would like to join their regiment. Since he was still a few years too young, he turned them down. But he held out hope that eventually he could take up arms and commit to the Union in body and spirit, to fight for the cause of uniting the nation and destroying slavery.

The Union began enlisting the first black troops to fight the Confederacy in the spring of 1863, with the formation of regiments given the name United States Colored Troops. President Lincoln and General Grant both endorsed the policy as one of military necessity. The rebels would no longer be able to depend on people they considered their "property" to aid the martial effort, and the Union would benefit from a motivated group of free blacks and ex-slaves to fight for freedom in some of the greatest conflicts of the war. To many Northern generals, especially of the abolitionist stripe, the recruitment of black troops was the inevitable, and greatly welcomed, result of the Emancipation Proclamation. To others, like General William Sherman, it was a disgrace.

"I won't trust niggers to fight yet," he said. While he welcomed them serving as railway laborers, trench diggers, fort builders, and water haulers, it was all to support the aim of bringing glory to white soldiers. By autumn 1863, well after the Union had recruited black troops for many of its armies, Sherman still refused to back down. He imagined a triumphant Union cause "vindicating its just and rightful authority, independent of niggers, cotton, money, or any earthly interest."

In fact, there were a lot of people General Sherman didn't like or trust. These included Jews, whom he saw as mercenary speculators and arms dealers who traveled in "swarms." They included American Indians, who if not under control of whites might be inclined to rise up against them in guerrilla bands to attack and murder them. And they included Mexicans, whose embrace of "general equality and amalgamation" for different races and peoples led only to anarchy, race mixing, and a collapse of civilization.

He didn't stop there. In his fouler moods, especially at the outset of the war, he sprayed his spleen onto just about every corner of society. So many people were ruining the country as he saw it, and for that they merited his deep and unmitigated scorn. The "old women and grannies of New England" and their permissive politicians had subverted the Constitution and allowed the rampage of uncontrolled democracy over the law. The Southerners had destroyed the nation with secession and enveloped it in what he would later call useless debates over "the political nonsense of Slave Rights, State Rights, uncontrolled freedom of conscience, License of the press and such other trash." The urban capitalists had enriched themselves at the expense of the economy. And the great mass of people themselves had delighted in violence and chaos for their own depraved ends, because from "California to Maine, any man could do murder, robbery or arson if the people's prejudices lay in that direction." He had contempt for himself as well, writing, "I look upon myself as a dead cock in the pit, not worthy of further notice and will take the chances as they come." About the only thing Sherman did trust or value was the U.S. military. As he wrote at the beginning of the war, "My only hope for the salvation of the Constitution of the country is in the army."

By late September 1863, he was getting his wish. The massive armies of the North were indeed the only things preventing the permanent dissolution of the nation. And Sherman commanded a key section of one of them, as the head of the 15th Corps of General Grant's Army of the Tennessee. He had helped them win the critical siege of Vicksburg in July, and now just a few months later, Grant needed his help again—to relieve the foundering Army of the Cumberland and rescue William Rosecrans from disaster after Chickamauga. The Confederates under Braxton Bragg had cut off most of that army's supply lines in Chattanooga for food, equipment, and medicine, and were trying to starve it to death.

The rescue mission would be no easy task. Sherman would have to move his 17,000 men some three hundred miles east over steep ridges and rolling hills, deep streams and wide rivers, and around violent bands of guerrillas who were all too happy to pick off and kill any groups of Yankees they could take aim at. They were also given the additional duty of guarding the Memphis and Charleston Railroad from attack, which would be difficult since the track of the railway ran parallel to the great mass of territory held by the rebels, who regularly destroyed sections of it to slow down the rescue operation and increase their chance of strangling Rosecrans's army.

Sherman thought he was up for the task. The business of war came second nature to him as a longtime military man, and he had few doubts about the strength of his battle-hardened veterans or their tenacity to fight their way through Tennessee mostly on foot. He made careful plans for the journey, alerted his subordinates to its hazards, and prepared himself for his corps' next heroic endeavor. Then his son died.

Young Willy, named after his dad, had contracted typhoid fever while the Shermans were camped in Mississippi, and he died a few days later in Memphis. The general was shocked and crushed by the weight of the loss, and expressed his feelings publicly—unlike many military men who suppressed their grief with steely resolve.

To General Grant, he wrote, "this is the only death I have ever had in my family, and falling as it has so suddenly and unexpectedly on the one I most prised on earth has affected me more than any other misfortune would."

To members of his guard battalion: "The child who bore my name . . . now floats as a mere corpse, seeking a grave in a distant land."

To his wife Ellen: "Why oh Why should that child be taken from us? leaving us full of trembling & reproaches. . . . I will try and make Poor Willys memory the cure for the defects which have sullied my character."

He was plagued by images of his lost son returning to his Ohio hometown as a corpse, as well as visions of Willy "moaning in death in this Hotel" in Memphis; women and children playing in the room where he died; and the boy's haunting face drained of color and life. Sherman blamed himself for bringing his family to the Deep South and its humid, subtropical climate, and asked Ellen "Why was I not killed at Vicksburg and left Willy to grow up to care for you?"

This was a perilous place for Sherman to be in. On the cusp of a momentous march to rally the Union cause, he threatened to sink into a terrible depression laced with guilt and self-loathing. The danger was that he could slip further, and return to the Sherman of old—the version of himself who had almost ruined his life and career.

This was the Sherman who ranted and raved about the collapse of civilization. The Sherman whose anger and bigotry bloomed to its full dark flower. The Sherman who fixated on the slightest insult and obsessed over his own failings. The Sherman whose faith in himself had faltered. The Sherman who many said was crazy, unhinged, a madman.

Less than two years before, in the autumn of the first year of the war, Sherman had nearly let his dark side overwhelm him. Memories of the time continued to trouble him, and reminded him of the fragile state of his ego, and perhaps sanity. He had at that time acquired a checkered reputation in private life and a middling one in public service. He had failed as a banker and businessman in San Francisco and New York, as a lawyer in Kansas, and as a streetcar president in St. Louis; he had succeeded as a college president in Louisiana until the outbreak of secession, which forced his resignation; and he had been in and out of the U.S. army and militia forces for years, with varying results.

The last thing he wanted was more public responsibility, such as a major Union military command. He would be happy to serve the nation in a background role but would do nothing that would elevate his stature—or elevate his fears, anxieties, and paranoia. He had told President Lincoln as much in August 1861 and the president had agreed.

Just two months later the promise was broken. By October he found himself in charge of the Department of the Cumberland in Tennessee and Kentucky, chiefly trying to keep the latter state in the Union and defeat its attempts at secession and insurrection.

It was a tall order, and too much so for Sherman. As he saw it, the only troops willing to defend the state from rebellion were from Ohio and Indiana. Young Kentuckians agitated for rebellion while the older, Unionist Kentuckians were too apathetic to stop them. His own forces comprised a smattering of green volunteers, not the hardened military veterans who could have kept the state in line. He had no confidence in his inexperienced troops, and expected them to run or panic at the first sound of gunfire.

To him, saboteurs, spies, and guerrillas were everywhere; his soldiers were vastly outnumbered by a cunning and tireless enemy; and the locals who smiled at his troops during the day prepared to stab their backs at night. He especially despised the press, which printed too many details of his troop movements, questioned his decisions constantly, and made him a target of abuse and mockery. He attempted to exclude all reporters from accessing his forces, and even threatened to hang one who disobeyed. But his collective fears and grievances only made him a larger target for criticism, even within the army itself.

Many of Sherman's fellow officers, as well as his wife, were increasingly concerned about his erratic and self-destructive behavior, which often occurred in full view of reporters and guests while he stayed at the Galt House hotel in Louisville. He chain-smoked, he stayed up all night, he fidgeted with his hair and coat buttons, he paced obsessively, he fell victim to headaches and wild swings of emotion, and he talked nonstop, giving voice to a full range of delusions and terrors—his men were doomed, they were surrounded by enemies, the cause was hopeless, he was a figure of disgrace, and worse. As he wrote to Ellen, "I find myself riding a whirlwind unable to guide the storm. . . . The idea of going down to History with a fame such as threatens me [i.e., failure] nearly makes me crazy—indeed I may be so now."

Word began to spread that the commander of the Department of the Cumberland had lost control of his army and his mind. His subordinates feared for his safety; his superiors weakened his authority; and his wife rushed to be by his side. By November the pressure he had put himself under became too great, and he tendered his resignation from the department.

In the weeks that followed, he recovered his bearings somewhat, but stories leaked out to the press that caricatured him as a dangerous lunatic or a hysterical fool. His rivals delighted in his misfortunes and spread an exaggerated portrait of him as a raving buffoon. An army doctor pronounced him as prone to "such nervousness as he was unfit for command," and a Cincinnati newspaper announced on its front page "GENERAL WM. T. SHERMAN INSANE."

Though many generals had been the target of ire and mockery (Grant, for one, had been widely disparaged as a drunk), Sherman became a target of particular abuse, both from the press and himself. He had shamed the army and his family, and harbored tremendous guilt over damaging the national cause. In only a few months, he had fallen into a deep pit of public humiliation, and found himself trapped there.

Soon, however, his closest family members began to dig him out of it. Ellen Sherman and her powerful father-in-law, Thomas Ewing, contacted influential figures in Washington and provided a ringing defense of his sound military judgment and temper. Indeed, in their telling, he had not so much failed in his mission as his various enemies had plotted to destroy him in a grand conspiracy. These malefactors included senior western commander Henry Halleck, who undermined him at every turn, and Army of the Potomac head George McClellan, whom they claimed to be in league with secessionist traitors. Indeed, the nefarious plot against Sherman was designed to cripple the power of one of the North's most talented men and, by implication, ensure the demise of the war effort.

Surprisingly, their angry words had an effect, and within weeks had restored some of the general's lost luster. Despite being a target of their criticism, Halleck assisted Sherman and eased him back into key roles in the military hierarchy. Lincoln gave his endorsement too, with effusive praise for the beleaguered Ohioan. Finally, with a measure of growing confidence, Sherman wrote to Grant after his victory at Fort Donelson offering his services, and the general welcomed him back to the fold.

He had succeeded in the field ever since. It began at Shiloh, where he had been injured and yet rallied his troops to victory, and culminated at Vicksburg, where he had been a key element of Grant's successful siege of the town and subsequent Union control of the Mississippi River. Indeed, two years had passed since Sherman's breakdown, and he had done much to erase lingering memories of himself as an unstable commander with a broken mind. But Willy's death threatened all of his progress, and easily could have overwhelmed him with the blackest despair and imperiled his ability to lead his troops into combat.

Again, Ellen helped him find a way out. In a series of letters, she reminded her husband of their lost child's purity and noble spirit. She convinced him Willy should be exalted to the highest degree, as a boy whose existence had power and meaning beyond that of any mere child. Sherman welcomed this idea of his son as a redeeming spirit, worthy of sacrifice: "I believe hundreds would have freely died could they have saved his life. I know I would, & occasionally indulge the wish that some of those bullets that searched for my life at Vicksburg had been successful."

In short order, the Shermans canonized Willy to their friends and correspondents and made him into an icon of grace and courage. Far from a simple child who died a tragic death, Willy became something larger, a heroic soul who was both "brave and manly" and "utterly fearless" as well as Sherman's own "alter ego"—the kind and benevolent force in heaven who stood at odds with the general's own increasingly brutal tactics on earth. This made it easier for Sherman to accept Willy's passing and to justify his conduct in the landscape of war.

Willy's death set loose a change in his mind. Far from restraining him with grief and mourning, the tragedy fueled Sherman's energy to fight the war. For in the absence of his son, he said, "I must work on purely and exclusively for love of country and Professional Pride." That sense of ambition drove him even harder to crush the rebels, and made his 15th Corps a relentless and unforgiving foe of anything that stood in its way.

He had set the template that summer when his troops destroyed Jackson, Mississippi. In a series of messages to General Grant, he boasted of setting it ablaze with constant shelling and "absolutely stripping the country of corn, cattle, hogs, sheep, poultry, everything" and ensuring "the inhabitants are subjugated. They cry aloud for mercy. The land is devastated for 30 miles around." Pleased with the results of his soldiers' work, he announced "Jackson is utterly destroyed as a military point."

No community wanted to face the same fate as Jackson. With that in mind, by the fall of 1863, Sherman laid out unofficial rules that demanded several things of Southern civilians: They would submit to federal authority when commanded; they would turn over known saboteurs and guerrillas to federal armies; and they would provide comfort and aid to federal troops as needed. If they failed to do these things, their land and property could be confiscated or destroyed, their towns could be burned, and they could be subject to collective punishment—in which an entire community could face retribution for the actions of a few individuals. In short, brutal army actions that would have been considered out of bounds just a year before were now standard policy. Sherman sent messages to his subordinates to ensure they understood the new approach:

- To a garrison commander in Memphis: "If any enemy of good government or manners insult or offend any of the Union people, the whole town will be held responsible, and the chief men banished and their property destroyed."

- To his brigade leaders in Pulaski, Tennessee: "Show them no mercy, and if the people don't suppress guerrillas, tell them your orders are to treat the community as enemies."
- To recently promoted General John A. Logan: "To secure the safety of the navigation of the Mississippi, I would slay Millions. On that point I am not only insane, but mad. . . . For every bullet shot at a Steam-boat I would shoot a thousand [cannons] into even helpless Towns . . . wherever a Boat can float or a Soldier march."

He called his ruthless strategy "hard war," and it worked. General Grant saw how Sherman's tactics led to undeniable results, if not exactly Southern submission to federal authority, then at least a string of victories for the Union. Grant and President Lincoln respected Sherman as a man of action, sometimes untethered but also unafraid, which gave him a boldness and resolve all too lacking in other Northern generals. So many of them had been plagued by "the slows"—and here was one who wasn't, who acted fast and aggressively, and was the ideal choice to assume command of an entire army group. This would be the Army of the Tennessee itself, Grant's own prized force, which had whipped the Confederates at Vicksburg and now promised to do the same at Chattanooga. All it needed was the right man to command it. One who had little patience for delay or for dallying, who could take the fight to the enemy, and use all the resources he had to fight this brutally hard war with an increasingly hard spirit.

FOUR

THREE VIEWS OF CHATTANOOGA

t wasn't that Charles Wills was angry—he was not. It wasn't that he had regrets—he did not. But after three weeks back in the field with the 103rd Illinois Volunteer Infantry, his patience had grown thin. He wanted the fall campaign to begin readily, to fight under the banner of William Sherman, and attack the rebels in their home country. But instead he was bogged down on one of the most tedious and exhausting marches of the war—450 miles from Vicksburg to Memphis to Chattanooga. It was all to relieve the beleaguered Army of the Cumberland, which had either suffered a minor defeat or been annihilated, depending on which rumor you believed. Wills had no idea himself; he just wanted to get there and get on with the invasion.

For now he had to deal with the miseries of Mississippi, especially Vicksburg, "a miserable hole [that] was never anything better." The weather was wet, humid, and dismal, and the army had packed two regiments onto one steamboat for transit upriver. Not only were the boats good at "capturing sandbars," forcing the troops to portage over sodden ground with all their gear, they also faced the threat of guerrillas and arsonists, who were well known for torching any boats they could ignite and shooting the survivors who swam away. Mississippi was the graveyard of his pleasures.

This was deep enemy country. What had formerly been just another region in the U.S. had since the beginning of the war become part of the Confederate States of America. And he was in the heart of it, just upstream from the plantation house of rebel president Jefferson Davis. The master secessionist was much loved in these parts, and the Union troops much hated.

The Southerners despised them for the ruin of their homes and property and the liberation of their slaves. Captain Wills distrusted these "secesh" locals, and knew to keep his guard up and his rifle handy. Any one of them could smile and nod at you during the day and take a few shots at you at night. And while he and the boys were happy to accept any hospitality they could get from the locals, what they couldn't get with their charm they stole and looted. In the absence of an effective Confederate force to counter them, they could not be stopped. This was the Army of the Tennessee, after all.

They weren't too far off the trail of their new army commander General Sherman in early October 1863 when they reached Mount Pleasant, Tennessee. The general had stumbled into a skirmish with cavalrymen a dozen miles away at Collierville, and the 103rd faced its own diversion when a few snipers took aim at them in town. In response, "the citizens were required to take the 'Oath of Allegiance,' to the United States or have their houses burned. Many declined to take the oath, and the consequences followed." Most of the forty houses in Mount Pleasant went up in flames.

This was nothing new. He and the 103rd, as part of Sherman's 15th Corps, had been foraging in rebel country and burning property for more than a year. The previous December, he had worried "The army is becoming awfully depraved. . . . If we don't degenerate into a nation of thieves, 'twill not be for lack of the example set by a fair sized portion of our army."

Though he could have easily stolen $500 in less than a week, he had no interest in giving in to "such devilish, pointless wickedness." But the foraging and looting continued apace, sometimes to feed the soldiers in the field, sometimes out of spite. It targeted everyone from plantation owners to the poorest of poor whites—and blacks. It was indiscriminate, and it troubled him greatly. As he wrote when arriving in Lagrange, Tennessee, "the marks of the 'Vandal Yankees' are visible." They had desecrated the cemetery, and stripped other parts of town threadbare:

> This town has been most shamefully abused since we left here with the Grand Army last December. There are only about three houses which have a vestige of a fence left around them. All the once beautiful evergreens look as though three or four tornadoes had visited them. . . . Not a chicken is left to crow or cackle, not a pig to squeal, and only such milch cows as were composed entirely of bone and cuticle.

While army policy approved of foraging, it forbade looting—if only in name—and required official permission for arson. Still, "it is pretty well understood in this army now that burning Rebel property is not much of a crime." But looting and arson hadn't been what Charles Wills had signed up for.

These days, it wasn't quite clear what he had signed up for. He had started as a private in the 8th Illinois Volunteer Infantry, rejoined as a captain the 103rd, but still hadn't witnessed a major battle. He had seen plenty of garrison duty, and watched troops strip the countryside and scorch assorted houses, but the actual practice of soldiery—fighting behind breastworks, attacking the enemy, taking prisoners—eluded him. He owed this to a certain general.

Even though he was part of a different army corps than Captain Wills, General Richard Oglesby had taken a liking to him, and earlier that summer had "gobbled" him for his staff at 16th Army Corps headquarters in Lagrange. This took him away from the 103rd and its endless marching and foraging, and he enjoyed it, at least for a while. To Wills, the general was "the very ideal of a chivalric, honorable, gallant, modest, high-spirited, dignified, practical, common-sense, gentleman" with "a big rolling river of fun and humor in his conversation." His communion with the general was matched with the pleasures of his position, which included meeting high society in Union-friendly towns, eating well and never wanting for supper, meeting comely young women and enjoying a nightly dance, and other frolics.

His cozy assignment should have deeply satisfied him, but somehow it didn't. Wills, for all his easy manner and wry humor, at heart wanted to be a soldier, and he didn't want to miss out on the fall campaign. He wanted to engage in the kind of wartime experience they called "seeing the elephant" for the size and drama and thrill of the experience. He knew he would have to leave the general—by his own choice. And so he became the rare soldier who could claim "girls, fun, etc., have lost their charm, and I've made up my mind to go back to my regiment."

He couldn't have imagined making such a choice at the outset of the war, two years before. As a private in the 8th Illinois, he had seen the conflict as a jolly boys' adventure, a break from his life in Canton, where he had grown up, and an opportunity to visit new places not too far from home. How different life had been then, during his idylls in Missouri, when he lived a comfortable life in what rival soldiers called "the featherbed regiment." They tramped around the countryside, skirmishing with the occasional rebel band, but were also healthy and enjoyed plenty of biscuits and coffee, and foraged for roasted corn, pumpkins, and pawpaw nuts. And they encountered "lots of pretty girls . . . that smile very sweetly on shoulder-strapped soldiers, but well, you understand me." He had never spent nine months more pleasantly than he did in those good old days of the war.

He didn't think too much about the reasons for the war then. He didn't care for secession, but was indifferent to slavery. Even when black men wandered into camp bruised and bloody from terrible beatings, he was callous to them, even hostile. In a letter to his sister, he complained, "You have no idea what a miserable, horrible-looking, degraded set of brutes these plantation hands are" and decried the sight of "46 of the ugliest, dirtiest niggers I ever saw, dressed in dirty white cotton. Awful nasty!"

The farther into rebel territory he traveled, though, the more he grew up, and the more his mind changed. He not only saw black men and women with deep scars of torture and abuse, he saw the wealthy plantations that profited from it. He met escaped slaves who supported the Union and white Southerners who undermined it. He met elegant black women who spoke in lovely cadences, played the piano and sang beautifully, and could mix an excellent cocktail—and white women who chewed a quid of tobacco "the size of my stone inkstand, and if they didn't make the extract fly worse than I ever saw it in a country grocery, shoot me." It confused and puzzled him. It also made him quit using tobacco.

More than anything, Captain Wills's mind changed because of Abraham Lincoln, who in 1863 demanded that black men be armed to fight the secessionists. Like a number of his fellow soldiers in the 103rd, he initially resisted but soon came around to the idea. By that summer he vowed to "go down the Mississippi and forage for mules, horses and negroes and put muskets in the hands of the latter." A month later he became even more convinced, and even a bit chastened:

> An honest confession is good for the soul. I never thought I would, but I am getting strongly in favor of arming them, and am be coming so blind that I can't see why they will not make soldiers. How queer. A year ago last January I didn't like to hear anything of emancipation. Last fall accepted confiscation of Rebel's negroes quietly. In January took to emancipation readily, and now believe in arming the negroes. The only objection I have to it is a matter of pride. I almost begin to think of applying for a position in a regiment myself.

However, there would be no such positions in black regiments in the Army of the Tennessee any time soon, because there would be no black regiments serving under Sherman. The free blacks and former slaves mostly enlisted and fought in the eastern theater, outside Sherman's jurisdiction, and Wills and the 103rd fought in the west—although fighting may not have been the right word for it.

—⁓—

Instead they marched. On their way to Chattanooga, the railroad took them as far as Corinth, Mississippi, but after that they were on foot. With their mule wagons and light artillery and cavalry units, they marched. Regardless of weather or road conditions or hardship, they marched. And even if a soldier had once served in a featherbed regiment, in Sherman's 15th Corps he marched. They averaged twenty-five miles a day.

At the outset of their trek the weather was seasonable, but after a few weeks it turned bad. The troops stepped into "bottomless" mud, and slogged through the rain and traversed hundreds of miles over dirt and rock, past limestone springs, and through dense woods. They ferried 200 wagons and 1,200 horses across the Tennessee River, and stood astounded at the wild bluffs and cliffs and ravines of the uncut countryside. Closer to central Tennessee they reached the edge of the Cumberland Plateau, where they had to pick up their wagons by hand and carry them up rocky ledges two or three feet high, because the rocks were too slippery for the mules.

This soldiering was arduous work, but Wills didn't mind, and couldn't help but find pleasure in the rustic foreign world of Tennessee and Alabama. He hunted for wild turkey and other game, which seemed to be plentiful, and he saw new birds and insects and creatures that he could not have imagined back in Illinois, including a chameleon that he kept as a pet for a while. The journey had been hard and exhausting and strange and magnificent and he wouldn't soon forget it.

Near Winchester, Tennessee, the captain's company came upon a wagon route to Chattanooga. This was one of the few lifelines to the city, a narrow artery that allowed a thin stream of food and supplies to reach the soldiers of the Army of the Cumberland and keep them from starving. Looking at the wagon road, Captain Wills knew that only one brigade had ever crossed the rocky and eroded stretch on foot, so his Company C would go by horses—which of course they had found through foraging. Once again he would have to detach from the rest of his regiment, and hope they wouldn't find martial glory while he was sent on a reconnaissance mission, or garrison duty, or a wild-goose chase.

After feeding their horses for the trip, he was ready. His last duty was to unhitch a mule for one of his men—and it bolted "like lightning." It knocked over a fence rail, which "struck me on the calves of my legs and elevated my boots five feet," as he wrote to his sister. "The attraction of gravitation brought me down to the globe and I landed with a great deal of vim on a rock about the size of our parlor floor."

His wrist was now badly injured, and the sharp jolts of the trip to come would make it hard to sit in the saddle or even in a wagon without a great deal of torment. This was his first major injury of the war, and not a shot had been fired. It would be a long, painful trip to Chattanooga.

About forty miles southeast of Winchester, a different army camped in Bridgeport, Alabama. They were also on their way to Chattanooga and had come by train over 1,200 miles from Virginia—a record distance in only a week's time. They had seen brutal fighting in the eastern theater and had been decimated by the carnage, until their divisions now stood depleted of men and short of quality provisions, weapons, and horses. Their leader General Joseph Hooker had been reduced in status, too. Once the head of the Army of the Potomac at Chancellorsville, he now led a much smaller detachment of three divisions from that same army, two from the 11th Corps and one from the 12th. A total of 15,000 men to beat back the rebel siege.

Among them was Friedrich Hecker, who had just been elevated to commander of the third brigade of the third division of the 11th Corps. The promotion should have gratified him, but it didn't—it was long overdue, and came without a promotion in rank. It was a hollow victory, and it did not surprise him. Hecker had come to distrust the army and its politics, from General-in-Chief Henry Halleck to Joseph Hooker and corps leader Oliver Howard to the division commanders under them and even some of his fellow brigade leaders.

Hecker and the other commanders had been briefed on the situation in Chattanooga, and it was nothing less than mortifying. Braxton Bragg had severed four of the city's supply routes by rail and road along the Tennessee River, and the army's coffers of fresh meat, crackers, medicine, clothing, and equipment had become depleted. The soldiers were reduced to half or even quarter rations—as little as three crackers a day and the occasional strip of near-inedible meat. Hunger bred theft, and the men of the Cumberland paid outrageous costs on the black market for a slice of cow muscle or an organ. Rumor had it that a beef liver commanded ten dollars.

The situation was intolerable, and Hecker and his troops had come to the region to open up a new supply route—the so-called Cracker Line—to resupply the miserable souls of Chattanooga. Otherwise, there was only one route for getting provisions to the city: the Anderson Road, the dreaded wagon route that tumbled into town over the rocky, broken shelf of Walden's Ridge. Field reports claimed its landscape had been stripped of forage for animals and humans, and the rocky terrain turned every errant step into a near-fatal hazard, made worse by the regular torrents of rain and mud. Its conditions were brutal, and its waysides stood littered with the corpses of mules and horses, festering and becoming food for vultures.

The salvation of the city appealed to the romantic in Hecker, however. He understood the stakes involved in the rescue, as well as the peril of the operation. Only a few weeks before, rebel general Joseph Wheeler had attacked a ten-mile-long wagon train of 800 Union wagons containing food, medicine, clothing, and ammunition, as well as liquor. The cavalrymen shot and stabbed the mules, raided the wagons, then set fire to them, and robbed or beat any teamsters, officers, and sutlers they rounded up. The rebels celebrated by guzzling the wagon train's whiskey, updated their shabby wardrobes with new Union attire, and escaped with their loot before federal pursuers could give proper chase.

The shameful episode helped lead Grant to dismiss William Rosecrans as the head of the Army of the Cumberland and replace him with George Thomas. Grant also took control over most of the west with a new federal entity called the Military Division of the Mississippi. Hecker approved of the much-needed reorganization, as well as the next step: the opening of the Cracker Line to resupply the starving men of the Cumberland.

On the night of October 27, Hecker's brigade and the rest of Joseph Hooker's forces moved out of Bridgeport on their way to Brown's Ferry. This was a critical link across the Tennessee River, and a Cumberland brigade had just recaptured it. The 11th Corps needed to hold the ferry crossing, so George Thomas's troops would once again be able to eat decent meals, enjoy a change of clothes and a belt of whiskey, and feed their near-dead horses and mules. Hecker girded himself for the battle sure to come.

But the conflict did not come at Brown's Ferry. Instead, the rebels targeted Wauhatchie Station, a railway crossing to the south, which General John Geary's single division of the 12th Corps occupied. On October 28, in a risky nighttime attack, successive waves of Confederate troops attacked the station, and though low on ammunition, the thinly spread troops of the 12th Corps held on.

Hooker ordered the 11th Corps to relieve Geary's men. If Hecker's brigade and four others could drive off the rebels, they could secure the Cracker Line and contribute greatly to the esteem of the corps. It would mark Hecker as a man of courage and resolve, and justify his recent promotion to brigade leader. He hastened his troops from Brown's Ferry. Five miles down the pike they would find Wauhatchie, and perhaps glory.

It didn't take long for the 11th Corps to march into disarray. The quick march south led directly into a thick fog. General Hooker gave confusing orders, the division leaders couldn't tell which units were meant to be in the lead, the regiments marched in random directions, and officers became separated from their men. Some brigades were ordered to halt for no clear reason, and those that advanced walked into merciless picket fire from rebel troops.

Hecker fulminated over the corps' bumbling movement. He wanted only to move against the Confederates, drive them away from Wauhatchie, and force them back into the hills. But it was hard enough even knowing where Wauhatchie was, or where he could find enemy troops to attack.

By the time the 11th Corps did find Wauhatchie at 4 A.M., Geary's men were in a terrible state, nearly out of ammunition, with more than 400 having been wounded or killed. Geary's own son, a lieutenant, had died in his father's arms. The 11th Corps only showed up after the battle was over and Geary's men had survived the onslaught—and single-handedly secured the Cracker Line.

Although the Union technically won the skirmish, it was the ugliest of victories. To Hecker it showed the mismanagement and incompetence of Joseph Hooker. However, Hooker refused to accept responsibility, and blamed division leader Carl Schurz for the debacle.

This sort of scapegoating had become common in Hooker's ranks, because the 11th Corps was an easy target. It was thick with immigrants, especially German soldiers, who often enlisted together and elected their own colonels from their ranks. The corps commander Oliver Howard was native-born—and a teetotaler to boot—but division leaders Schurz and Adolph von Steinwehr were German, many of the regimental commanders were first-generation immigrants, and the brigade leaders had names like Buschbeck and Krzyzanowski.

Hecker condemned the criticism of immigrant soldiers that had percolated through the army and surfaced in the rhetoric of nativist newspapers and politicians. To them, the Germans were forever the political radicals who spoke vigorous words, yet shrank away when asked to put their lives on the line in the field of combat. They called them the "flying Dutchmen" and claimed their one talent in war was to skedaddle away from the sound of gunfire. This was a blatant lie, but one nativists were quick to spread. The Germans had become an easy target, especially with men like Hecker in command. He had attracted controversy from the start.

When the war began, prominent immigrants helped him raise his first regiment, the 24th Illinois Volunteer Infantry, with the aim of making him colonel. He accepted the role, with the understanding the regiment would be run according to his dictates without interference. But just a few months after it began recruiting soldiers, the 24th became embroiled in controversy when Hecker tried to fire seven of its officers—one of whom he called a "whoremonger." Unfortunately, this decision was contrary to military law and the wishes of the army brass. Weeks of intrigue and a power struggle followed, figures like John C. Fremont and William Sherman were pulled into the fray, and in the end Hecker lost his fight. The army reinstated the men, Hecker quit the regiment he had led, and he retreated back to his Belleville farm almost as quickly as he had left it.

But as the months passed, he again hungered for a chance at wartime glory. He had a chance in 1862 to lead a second regiment, and seized it. Several politicians and businessmen in Chicago had organized a new regiment to be called the 82nd Illinois Volunteer Infantry, with city alderman Edward Salomon doing the recruiting. Salomon, like a few other allies, had followed Hecker out of the 24th Illinois when he quit, and had since emerged as an invaluable ally. Not only was he the regiment's second in command, he was Hecker's friend and correspondent, and a reliable officer as well. The colonel also found much-needed friends among junior officers like Lieutenant Eugene Weigel, the son of a prominent Unionist who had helped save Hecker's career after the 24th Illinois imploded, and Lieutenant Rudolph Mueller, a dry-goods clerk from Peoria who had developed a real attachment to him—sharing many of Hecker's revolutionary ideas and incendiary rhetoric.

With this cast of Germans at the core of the regiment, along with a handful of others, the 82nd Illinois drilled, trained, and took the field in the eastern theater under Hecker's leadership. This time, he had done everything he could to become a model officer: He cut a bold figure in his dress and manner, he promoted himself and his cause to the press, he tried to recruit new immigrants to his ranks, and he commanded his troops in the most gallant manner he could, with close attention to rules and detail. Yet somehow he could never win.

One problem: The enlisted men didn't love, or even particularly like, him. Even the German immigrants called him "the old man" and saw him as a stern, uncompromising martinet, someone who routinely pilloried his subordinates for small infractions and insisted on his own rectitude even when the facts suggested otherwise. He forbade any officers from bringing their wives into camp, dressed them down in front of their troops for minor transgressions, and waged fierce campaigns against anyone drinking without authorization or smuggling in alcohol—under penalty of imprisonment.

He had trouble beyond the regiment, too. The Union's commanding generals proved to be foolish or incompetent and cast blame for their setbacks upon Germans like himself. Even among capable generals like Grant and Sherman, he had few allies, and also lacked powerful friends in Washington to help him navigate the military bureaucracy. But more than anything, he suffered a terrible run of bad luck, fighting in some of the Union's worst losses and its most checkered victories.

Most of the trouble stemmed from the battle of Chancellorsville, in May of 1863. In the worst defeat for the Union army in the war, Robert E. Lee and Stonewall Jackson successfully outfought and outmaneuvered the federal troops led by none other than Joseph Hooker. This time the feckless general had left his extreme right flank "in the air," untethered to the rest of the Army of the Potomac. Despite being outnumbered, the rebels attacked the federals and caught them by surprise. This sent the Yankee troops into a panic. Hecker's regiment, as part of Carl Schurz's division, did what it could to fight the swarms of rebels on the attack, dodge the terrified front-line Union infantrymen retreating through their ranks, and beat back the chaos enveloping them in the woods of Virginia. Hecker grabbed the flag of his regiment, rallied his troops on horseback, charged into the face of enemy fire on the front lines—and got shot in the leg and fell off his horse.

Though he and many other German regiments had battled bravely, their efforts failed. Lee won a signature victory and pressed forward into the North, Joseph Hooker was humiliated and lost command of the Army of the Potomac, and the Germans became ready-made scapegoats for an angry press looking to point fingers. General Hooker encouraged the abuse, and singled out the 11th Corps for blame while absolving himself. Schurz lauded his immigrant-heavy division, writing in a report, "These men are no cowards!" And Hecker defended himself vigorously in print: "No one says of me, nor can say of me, that I did not hold my ground." It didn't matter. To much of the public, the "Dutch corps," as Hooker called them, were simply cowards who spoke a different language.

Since then the troops of the 11th Corps looked for opportunities to prove themselves beyond any doubt. They did so at Gettysburg, fiercely holding off Confederate attacks on Cemetery Hill despite losing many men to death and injury. Yet the press seized upon the corps' withdrawal from the center of town on the first, indecisive day of the battle as a shameful embarrassment, compounded by the rebels taking scores of German prisoners. It didn't help that one division leader, Alexander

Schimmelfennig, had to avoid capture by hiding for three days in a woodshed—which the press errantly called a "pigsty." After that, the German troops again came in for public mockery, even though they had ultimately emerged victorious and had done nothing to merit such treatment. Their reward for Gettysburg was to be once again assigned to the command of Joseph Hooker, who brought them west and led them again into a fiasco, this time at Wauhatchie.

Hecker became wary, even cynical, after all these struggles, but still nursed hopes of finding success on the battlefield and perhaps promotion to brigadier or even major general. He had help from the foreign-language newspapers back home, which praised his battlefield exploits and excoriated his critics. Because of their pressure, he knew Lincoln would soon have to pay attention to him and his sway over the Germans—after all, they would again be critical votes in next year's election. Even better, there was no longer any competition from his occasional rival Gustave Koerner, who after raising the 43rd Illinois regiment and barely participating in the war had left for Europe to become Lincoln's envoy to Spain. Hecker now could command the loyalty of 48ers back in Belleville and German immigrants throughout Illinois without worrying about Koerner contradicting or undermining him. Perhaps with enough public enthusiasm, the president would have to give in and allow him to rise in rank and fulfill his purpose: to command a division, perhaps even a corps.

His next major opportunity was coming, one that could redeem all the missed chances and fiascos: the assault against the Confederate army surrounding Chattanooga.

On November 23, Hecker took the first steps to his goal, literally. Along with 25,000 men from Howard's 11th Corps and the Army of the Cumberland, he took part in a massive parade on the field outside Union lines surrounding Chattanooga. Dressed in their Union best, Hecker and the rest of his brigade and others marched with bayonets gleaming, regimental flags flying, drums beating, and bugles blaring. The Confederates watched this sprightly display of martial spirit from their strongpoint of Orchard Knob, a 100-foot mound between Chattanooga and the range of Missionary Ridge they held to the southeast. Many rebels stood transfixed at the spectacle, thinking it was in honor of the new commander of the western theater, Ulysses S. Grant. Indeed, the grizzled general was only too happy to watch his troops proudly display their colors and reinvigorated spirit. He was even prouder when one soldier shouted "Forward!" and the Union troops broke rank, turned, and charged up Orchard Knob in a frenzy.

It became an unexpected melee—and the Confederates watched in shock for a moment. Some readied their defenses, some scampered down the Knob in a panic. Hecker's brigade and the rest of Schurz's division gave chase, trying to run down the rebels in flight. Still, they had trouble keeping up with the lightning progress of Thomas Wood's division to their right, which captured Orchard Knob and drove its defenders back.

By the end of the day, the 11th Corps had come up short again. Some brigades never tried to pursue the enemy or ended up out of place. Schurz's division came to an abrupt halt under rebel fire, and failed to advance on the retreating Confederates even though they outnumbered them. It took Wood's own troops to sweep the last rebel pickets from the field. This made it an ideal day for Wood's division, which not only captured the enemy's position, but got a bit of revenge for being routed at Chickamauga.

Hecker, however, was denied an opportunity for redemption. The 11th Corps troops fought bravely but again their leaders let them down. During the thick of the Orchard Knob fight, Oliver Howard scuttled off the field and took his place behind Union siege lines. Once there, he had to be reminded his troops were still in action and needed his leadership! When he returned it was too late, and Thomas Wood had seized the glory for himself.

Because Hecker's brigade saw action at Orchard Knob, it wouldn't have to fight the next day at Lookout Mountain. This may have been a relief to Hecker, because the commander leading the fight up to the 1,500-foot summit would be Joseph Hooker. The general had planned an audacious and possibly foolish gambit: He would direct 12,000 troops in three divisions up the mountainside in the face of fierce artillery fire and determined resistance. They set off on the morning of November 24 and soon disappeared into the thick fog enveloping the peak. Union observers could only watch and wait for the "Battle Above the Clouds"—which was actually in the clouds—to come to a dramatic conclusion.

The next morning, the conclusion was clear. General Hooker had won, the Union had triumphed, and the U.S. flag fluttered at the summit. Displaying unexpected talent, Hooker had driven the defenders off the mountain—again with the courage of John Geary's division of the 12th Corps. Also essential to the attack was General "Peter Joe" Osterhaus, a 48er and German exile Hecker may have known from Belleville, who had started the war as a private and was well on his way to being promoted to major general. Yet Hecker himself had no role on Lookout Mountain, and could not claim any credit in the victory. Nor could he stand upon it on the morning of November 25, when the mountain rose free above the clouds to become one of the indelible images of the war.

Instead, Hecker found himself on that morning in the ranks of what many considered the best fighting force in the U.S. military: the Army of the Tennessee. William Sherman had finished his march with the 15th Corps some weeks before, and now readied his attack along the northern end of Missionary Ridge, at the far left of Union forces. Friedrich Hecker's Third Brigade, with Schurz's Third Division, stood ready to assist Sherman in his bold, aggressive action to roll up Braxton Bragg's rebel army, which stood scattered on a six-mile front along the ridgeline. This could be his best chance to prove himself in action.

The reputation of Sherman's men preceded them. These were the battle-hardened, steel-tempered group of warriors who had beaten back the Confederates at Shiloh at a high cost in lives, surrounded the enemy at Vicksburg and forced it to capitulate, and come west with their former commander Grant to take the main role in the fight to smash the Confederates and send them fleeing into Georgia. This would open the door to a proper invasion of that state—unlike the disastrous attempt mounted by William Rosecrans two months before. Ever since his return to power in 1862, Sherman had proven himself time and again, scorching the Southern earth and issuing no quarter to those who stood in his way. Bragg was next.

Sherman surveyed the line of attack in person; he gathered reports on the enemy in detail; he chose some of his toughest brigades to lead the fight. He brought a rousing attitude and great inspiration for his men. And yet, uncharacteristically and unexpectedly, he failed.

He had scouted Goat Hill and led his forces there the day before, assuming it offered gradual terrain that connected smoothly to the main crest of Missionary Ridge. But when the clouds dissolved atop Goat Hill, Sherman realized his error: He was faced with a solid line of Confederate cannons and infantrymen who were ready for him. Also, Goat Hill wasn't directly connected to Missionary Ridge. Instead, it was cut off from the ridge by sharp ravines and steep inclines, and a large, deep saddle stood between it and the Confederates on Tunnel Hill. The assault on the rebel line would be a bloody and tortuous affair over broken ground in the face of hellish artillery fire.

Brigade by brigade, Sherman sent his forces against the division of Patrick Cleburne, an Irish immigrant who fought for the Confederates after previously serving in the British army. He may have been the best officer in Bragg's army, and fought ferociously to keep Tunnel Hill from Sherman's grasp. He succeeded because the Union general never committed all of his troops at once, but threw them piecemeal against the rebel works. This strategy served to stymie the Union attackers, even though they outnumbered the Confederates four to one.

By the afternoon Sherman's troops had made no headway against Cleburne's wall of resistance, and had not taken Tunnel Hill or in any way threatened the Confederate hold over Missionary Ridge. Worse, the Ohio general vacillated over his options, and didn't even use all the divisions he had in reserve.

One of them was Carl Schurz's Third Division of the 11th Corps, and within it Friedrich Hecker's Third Brigade. However much they demanded a role in the fight, Sherman held them back. They waited for their turn near the railroad tracks adjacent to Goat Hill, and their turn never came.

It began to look like Friedrich Hecker was star-crossed. Perhaps the gods had decided he was never meant for battlefield glory; perhaps he had some small, indefinable flaw that prevented him from succeeding. For amid all the tumult of recent months, amid the high hopes and dashed opportunities, in the end even William Sherman couldn't provide Hecker the victory he was desperate for. Instead, he got to watch the general they called "Uncle Billy" get pummeled from the safety of a railroad crossing.

Perhaps no one understood him. Perhaps he hadn't made it plain. He was ready to lay down his life and commit his body and spirit to the Union cause. He was prepared to sacrifice himself to the struggle. *He was no coward.*

But still, no matter how great his effort, Hecker could do nothing to erase the stain of Chancellorsville from his reputation and that of his troops, and could not risk his life for his adopted country when army leaders didn't give him the opportunity.

He didn't know what was worse: to be shamed in battle even though he had fought bravely, or to be ignored and never have the chance to fight at all.

Fifty miles from Chattanooga, in the wilds of the Cumberland Mountains, Captain Charles Wills was enjoying a day out with his Company C. It was a leisurely afternoon, his wrist had healed, and he was relaxed and satisfied. Ever since the Cracker Line had reopened, he had been dining on pork and cornbread, of which he could "destroy immense quantities." If anything, he had enjoyed too much hoecake and spareribs in recent days. He thought he should be fighting with the rest of his regiment, but wondered if he'd ever see a battle. "Being shot by a guerrilla is as good as I will probably get."

His unit had put him in charge of rounding up horses and sheep, and he had gotten quite good at it. He swiped the animals from the "poor miserable citizen devils" for the use of the federal army, and was beginning to have fewer qualms about it, though he still had a fair measure of guilt. "Can't look an honest man in the face," he wrote. "Fortunately there are no honest men in this command, so I am spared the mortification of turning my eyes."

He was near Paint Rock when he heard the sound of cannons, far off in the distance. He knew they must be from Chattanooga, and he thought his regiment must be in action. Doubtless his friends in the 15th Corps would be engaged, and would probably have many glorious stories to tell when he returned. He might be a bit jealous, but could at least say he had done his part. Sherman would now have plenty of new horses to go with his next conquest.

Back in Chattanooga, from the heights of Missionary Ridge, the artillery barrage opened up at 3:30 P.M. The Confederate guns unleashed shot and shell from the heights of the ridge crest in a display of fire and thunder the likes of which had never been heard in these parts. The clamor of the cannons echoed across the valley over and over, until the sequence of blasts overlapped and made for one giant, continuous *BOOM*.

The boys of the Army of the Cumberland moved at quick time—some at double-quick time—out of the trees and across the plain between the city of Chattanooga and the ridge. Some were even running, trying to hold their regiments close and their muskets closer. John Hight moved along with them, in the 58th Indiana Volunteer Infantry Regiment.

It was a mile to the rifle pits at the base of Missionary Ridge, and the last few hundred yards lay exposed to gunfire from below and shot and shell from the crest above. Avoiding the smoke and shrapnel, Hight followed the 58th Indiana as it moved in formation. He watched some boys fall, but the great mass of the troops crossed the field intact. The rebel cannons had aimed too high.

It was a commanding show of force from the Union army, a display of power and strength and resolve. But it wasn't a formal attack. The charge of the Cumberland boys was only a demonstration, a way to distract the rebels from reinforcing their right flank and to give Sherman more time to figure out what he was doing at Tunnel Hill. If anything the demonstration was too convincing, and made the rebels in the rifle pits panic and scurry up the ridge to safety.

The Union soldiers collapsed into the pits gasping, exhausted from the quick-time run with all their gear, sweaty and disheveled and packed in tight. Disorder ruled. Crossing the field the Indiana boys had been in the second line of battle. Now they were in the first, and the regiments tried to re-sort themselves amid the tumult.

It got worse when the cannoneers retargeted their weapons.

The rebels switched from shot and shell to grape and canister, trading their great bursting bombs for lead balls and pellets. These were much more effective, and ideal for tearing through human flesh with the grace and precision of a shotgun blast.

The metallic spray ripped through the Union boys with ease, and there was no defense from it. The deadly hail of lead rained down upon them "in shovelfuls," as one soldier put it. Occupying the rifle pits had been a mistake—they were now sitting ducks.

But they couldn't go any farther. Grant had given the order to occupy the pits and the pits alone. They had to remember: It was only a diversion from the battle at Tunnel Hill. Except the diversion had consequences— namely, the possible crippling of an entire army exposed to cannon fire. An army that had already been routed at Chickamauga.

Reverend Hight was in the middle of this chaos, this turkey shoot. Some of the canister shot passed right by him, close enough to maim or kill. He huddled close with the troops, knowing there was "hot work" ahead. But what kind of work?

Headquarters had no answer to the potential slaughter playing out in the pits. Grant and Cumberland commander George Thomas watched from Orchard Knob, spectators to the mayhem.

In the weeks prior, many of the troops of the Cumberland thought Grant had treated them like a second-rate army, like second-class soldiers. Even when he had arrived in Chattanooga a month before, word had gotten out that he had little respect for this fighting force, thought them inferior to the battle-hardened heroes of William Sherman's Army of the Tennessee, and would assign a secondary role to the Cumberland boys when the day of attack arrived.

And sure enough—here they were, a giant diversionary squad, a *side show* to Sherman's main event. And unlike some armies in the field, they were exhausted, they were hungry, and they hadn't been given proper supplies or rations. Hight wrote just a few days before that food was "exceedingly scarce; relief must come soon, or we will be starved out." Their bellies still rumbled in the rifle pits.

Many of the brigade leaders on the front line didn't understand—were these the correct orders? Would Grant really allow them to be slaughtered in the rifle pits? They couldn't imagine it. So they decided on a different plan.

The headstrong German immigrant August Willich was the first. Not only was he a bona fide revolutionary from the uprising of 1848, he was an actual Communist, an enemy of capitalism who, at this very strange moment, was also an enemy of the rebels and a foe of whatever ridiculous nightmarish order Grant had given. So he took his brigade and he started up the ridge. Because to stay in the pits would be "certain destruction and final defeat; every soldier felt the necessity of saving the day and the campaign by conquering . . . the enemy's works on the crest of the ridge."

Without authorization from headquarters, Willich's boys advanced. They headed straight for a terrifying horseshoe formation, riddled with rifle and cannon fire from two sides. They slipped into ravines and crawled over rocky spurs and hid in the dense brush, anything to get away from the guns and closer to the heights.

Other brigade leaders followed, some inspired by Willich, some unable to see anything through the smoke and confusion, just trying to escape the pits. The 58th Indiana and Reverend Hight were among them.

As part of George Wagner's brigade, the Indiana troops were on the first line of battle, where, as Hight saw it, "an enfilading fire was poured upon our columns from right and left, and it was here that many of our brave men fell." But they kept coming, advancing up the slope, where the unexpected dips and crags of the mottled terrain protected them. Paradoxically, this was the same kind of terrain that had ruined Sherman's battle plan on Tunnel Hill.

About halfway up, an order from headquarters reached their brigade—they had gone beyond their objective and now must retreat.

How could this be? After all their effort, they had to scurry downhill again? Many paused, bewildered. Then some retreated, some advanced, and others were caught in between, descending first, then ascending, then trying to hide in a ravine or thicket. Were they really meant to go back to the rifle pits?

As they were trying to decide, showers of grape and canister shot ripped them apart.

A corrected order came fifteen minutes later, but only after more soldiers from Wagner's brigade had been hit. The bloodletting in this brigade—and in Philip Sheridan's larger division—was gruesome, and much worse than in other units.

Reverend Hight left the field to attend to the wounded, who were increasing in number farther down the hill. But the rest of the 58th Indiana continued up, to the place and the moment many dreaded: making a frontal assault against a fortified position.

They scrambled up near the breastworks, to the log piles, the abatis at the crest—the jagged wooden landscape the Confederates had erected to defend their position and shoot down any Yankees who had the temerity to venture that close. There were four rebel divisions and 16,000 men behind all that lumber.

The boys feared it would be like Gettysburg—like Pickett's Charge—when the Union guns opened up and destroyed the Confederate troops who had almost reached their objective. Wagner's brigade was that close to the 1,100-foot crest, panting and gasping and hungry and battle-weary, and ready for the final lunge. Except this time there was no division leader like General Pickett in sight. The boys would have to make their own charge.

They couldn't see how many defenders the Confederates had arrayed behind their field works. They had no idea how much death by cannon, rifle, and bayonet might await them.

It didn't matter. They attacked the works anyway. Screaming: "Chicka-mauga!" "Chickamauga!" "*Chickamauga!*"

It was their own Yankee rebel yell, and it echoed out across the crest. Federal attacker after attacker climbed the works and shot or stabbed the defenders.

Many like the troops from Mississippi surrendered wholesale, while others fought desperately. Some Union boys seized cannons, then wheeled them around to point squarely at the rebel artillery down the line. Those cannoneers responded in kind, and for a few bloody, eerie, and horrible minutes the top of the ridge was blasting itself to bits, edge to edge, in a relentless cannonade.

Meanwhile the federals kept coming, destroying the rebel defensive line that was much thinner than anyone could have predicted or known.

And there were no troops in reserve. Braxton Bragg had earlier sent them on a fool's errand to east Tennessee to attack a different Union force. They were gone from the field.

First in the dozens, then in the hundreds, then in full regiments and brigades, the Union soldiers seized the ridge. As Hight saw, "To my left, long lines of men in blue were going up, and up the ridge, and over them the stars and stripes waved gloriously." The celebration was as immense as it was shocking.

Hundreds of Southern soldiers surrendered and became prisoners, dragged to Union lines in a miserable parade of defeat. Others escaped down the eastern slope of the ridge, dropping their rifles and costing the Confederacy thousands of weapons it could not afford to lose. The rebel leaders were nowhere to be seen; the enlisted men took the punishment.

At Orchard Knob, the Union army brass could do little but watch. Ulysses S. Grant, George Thomas, and many of the division heads had been bystanders to the assault and capture of the mountain. As Hight wrote, "The taking of Missionary Ridge, therefore, was inaugurated not so much by the genius of commanders, or the bravery of soldiers, as by mistake . . . what was commenced by mistake was completed most gloriously by courage."

The reverend felt happy for the troops, and encouraged the 58th Indiana had played such a critical role in the battle and this key victory. Yet his spirit was dampened.

After the battle he walked over the crest of the ridge and saw the items the rebels had left behind when they fled, "anything from a siege gun to a lousy shirt"—mementos and keepsakes that would never find their owners. He also saw a darker element, the vultures of war, "the parties of thieves prowling . . . who remain behind to rob the honored dead."

As the day ended, Hight returned to tend to the wounded and the dying, who were light in the Cumberland army overall but heavy in his brigade. "The scene of suffering at the foot of the ridge, in the old camp, was terrible. In every direction could be seen fires which had been kindled, and about them was collected the wounded, trying to keep warm. The night was cold and many perished from suffering and exposure."

He got to know many of these boys by name, and would attend to their wishes in their final hours. It had become a forlorn and familiar ritual for the clergyman. This time, 730 of them had fallen—one-third of the brigade.

At midnight he finally lay down to rest. He and his horse were spent, drained of energy and reserve after the pandemonium and unplanned assault and shocking victory. It wasn't an unusual feeling. He had felt it before at Shiloh and Stones River and Chickamauga and all the other battlefields where he had been. It was the feeling of life condensed, sped up and made unrecognizable in a fiery blur. The blinding comet of war. As he wrote, "It seemed as if the experience of a month had been crowded into a day."

He only had a few hours of sleep before he rose to start the next one.

FIVE

HEROES IN THE FIELD

O n October 28, 1863, the city of Chicago awoke to a blaze of Confederate flags—from secessionist states like Texas and Virginia, from artillery batteries to cavalry units, from the Stars and Bars to the black flag of no surrender. One flag signified Braxton Bragg's army in Tennessee; others were stained in blood. The great crowd lining the streets applauded joyfully for the spectacle, and the flag bearers were only too happy to hold these banners of secession. For these were the spoils of war, and many of the troops on parade had ripped the flags out of the hands of rebels they had shot or captured. And now they held pride of place at the head of one of Chicago's greatest events, the first North-Western Soldiers' Fair.

After the soldiers came the ranks of men of the city's benevolent societies and brotherhoods, and clergymen, judges, and politicians, and seamstresses, butchers, and blacksmiths, and a crowd of children singing "John Brown's Body." Last were the farmers from Lake County, hauling a mighty bounty of produce in their wagons: massive piles of potatoes, onions, squashes, beets, turnips, and cabbages. They brought all this largesse to the offices of the Chicago Sanitary Commission, whose storerooms already overflowed with huge quantities of produce, codfish, and smoked salmon, pickles and sauerkraut, ginger, whiskey, tobacco, and hundreds of homemade and hand-sewn clothes—all to support the boys on the Union front from Mississippi to Tennessee. The Commission oversaw everything from the planning of the parade to the great commercial and cultural fair yet to come. And overseeing the Commission itself was Mary Livermore.

The entire event was her idea. She had envisioned it earlier in 1863, convinced her colleague Jane Hoge to go along with it, and made a forceful case to the Commission leaders for it, claiming it would inspire mass donations and enthusiasm for their organization, and for the cause of the Union.

The men who led the Commission didn't agree. They didn't believe that such an enterprise run by women could ever turn a profit, much less the $25,000 Livermore promised it would make. Ultimately, they "barely tolerated it" and "were doubtful of its success," as she wrote.

This was how the United States Sanitary Commission operated: Big-name men like Henry Bellows and George Templeton Strong occupied the national positions of power, while the women in the branches did the work and ran the show. And at the Chicago branch, associate managers Mary Livermore and Jane Hoge were definitely in charge.

The Soldiers' Fair they created was unique, and Chicago had never seen anything like it. At Bryan Hall, where the event took place, Jane and Mary designed a dining hall that served 1,500 people daily, stuffing them with roast turkeys and ducks, pies and puddings, milk and coffee, and countless cans of oysters, all for the price of a fifty-cent ticket. Tickets to the exhibit halls were half that cost, and exposed up to six thousand visitors a day to the latest farm equipment for sale—everything from corn shellers and straw cutters to oil funnels and millstones. In the Curiosity Shop, war held center stage, from the battle flags of home-state regiments and their Confederate adversaries, to an array of fearsome weapons like bowie knives, scimitars, swords, shells, and, of course, guns. Also on view was the "Southern necklace," the tortuous iron collar a Louisiana slave had been forced to wear before Union troops had removed it and freed him from bondage.

In Metropolitan Hall, Mary created wildly different diversions for visitors' attention, from a charming children's concert in which youngsters sang patriotic songs, to elaborate theatrical tableaux in which actors staged "living pictures"—anything from a gloomy procession of monks, to prison and execution scenes, to visions of the murdered wives of Bluebeard. Even more of a spectacle was the presence of spellbinding orator Anna Dickinson, who though barely twenty-one, gave two commanding speeches to an awestruck crowd, fervently defending the Union and excoriating secessionists and their fellow travelers in the North. The undeniable highlight, though, was the auctioning of an original copy of the Emancipation Proclamation, which Mary had persuaded President Lincoln to donate to the fair. A Chicago jeweler bought it for $3,000 and promptly gave it to the charitable Home for Illinois Soldiers.

The results were stunning: In two weeks the fair earned $86,000, well above the expectations of its organizers and far beyond the imagination of the commissioners. It led the way for a spate of successful fund-raising fairs throughout the nation, and raised the name of Mary Livermore from a local patron of charity to a nationally known champion of the Union, the war, and abolition.

How things had changed in a year. At the outset of the war, Mary was still juggling her charity work with her church duties and writing for *The New Covenant*. After the Chicago Sanitary Commission took over the local soldiers' aid society she ran, her new role in the Commission expanded rapidly, and the work consumed her utterly. Within months she became the face of war relief in Chicago, and took much of the credit and blame that went with it.

Newspapers like the Democratic *Chicago Times* derided her, portraying her as a bluestocking ninny who shamelessly promoted abolition through the Commission and had an "overbearing and unladylike" character. They said she hadn't done enough to prevent the theft or misuse of relief supplies, or to make sure every last dollar was accounted for. And besides, she was a woman, and women were better off in the shadows, quietly baking pies and darning socks for the boys instead of hamming it up in the public arena. She even got a salary from the Commission, and no respectable woman would ever do that!

She had heard these complaints so often she no longer deigned to respond. She didn't have enough time, and besides, there was too much work to do. And in any case, she dealt with far worse things than newspaper critics. She had "seen the elephant" of combat in the field, or at least had come close.

Mary had gotten her first taste of the horror of war after Fort Donelson, when the Commission sent her and Jane to inspect the hospitals of St. Louis. Her genteel background and proper middle-class upbringing did nothing to prepare her for the sights and sounds she found there. Amid the noxious odors and suppurating wounds and ghastly amputations, she came upon a boy whose tongue and jaw had been shot off, in obvious agony.

Mary became sick to her stomach, and overwhelmed by the gruesome injuries and immense suffering of the boys. Nauseated and in tears, Mary fled from the ward. It crushed her spirit and affected her beyond description, to see the bodies God had created in His own image reduced to bleeding and shattered fragments. She questioned her commitment to the cause, and wondered if others were better suited to work that seemed so abhorrent, so tragic, so revolting.

But after she left, she became even more sickened at her own inability to bear the truth of what the war was all about. So with an "iron control," she went back to the hospital ward and resolved to stay and help.

In November 1862 she attended a Women's Council in Washington, D.C., and demanded more latitude for her Commission branch in Chicago. It needed more independence from the edicts sent from the national headquarters, and a more creative approach to drumming up donations. She also met personally with President Lincoln, who discussed his plans for victory over the slave power. He gave her a renewed sense of energy and purpose. This was the Lincoln in whom she had guardedly placed her faith after the Republican convention, and the one she encouraged Illinoisans to rally behind. His Emancipation Proclamation, which took effect at the beginning of 1863, inspired her even more. Now the war to reunite the nation had also become a war against slavery. She would do everything she could to advance the cause.

After her visits to Union military hospitals, Mary gave an honest accounting to the Commission of all their misery and mismanagement. With a few exceptions, like the well-run General Hospital in Cairo, the facilities were riddled with filth and disrepair, and convalescent soldiers often acted as nurses, to the benefit of no one, least of all themselves. The hospitals needed improved sanitation, more and better medicine, fresh linens, and decent food. Everything would have to improve if the Union stood a chance of beating the Confederacy.

She also bitterly complained about the rivalries between different religious sects to offer aid to the soldiers. Many surgeons and officers only wanted nuns to provide relief to the troops, seeing that they rarely challenged authority and didn't go looking for a reporter to criticize conditions at their hospitals—unlike Protestant nurses. Mary fought against this sort of discrimination, but even among the Protestants she was suspect. Many churchmen didn't consider Universalism to be a valid denomination, because to them a religion without the threat of eternal punishment wasn't a real religion at all. Other nonorthodox sects like Unitarianism, whose ministers were heavily involved in running and promoting Sanitary Commission branches on the East Coast, came in for even more criticism from mainstream Christians, who depicted the Commission as an urban, secular organization whose members practiced a foreign religion or lacked faith altogether.

In response, a branch of the YMCA called the U.S. Christian Commission, which had formed in 1861 to provide relief to the troops, saw increasing success drawing donations from those uncomfortable with the worldliness of the Sanitary Commission. It also handed out religious literature and spread the gospel of evangelical Christianity in army camps. Mary saw it as a rival to her own organization, and feared that such missionaries would bring the wrong message. In her view, "dying soldiers needed to be told of God's love and forgiveness, not God's wrath."

Mary worried about a tide of new relief societies competing with each other and draining the enthusiasm of donors. She was determined to make the Chicago Sanitary Commission the focus of giving throughout the western states. To that end she vowed to start a new aid society for the Commission in every county in Illinois—and to find managers who would start new societies in every town in that county. By horse and by rail, she visited countless places in the state and persuaded, implored, and cajoled the locals to ally with her. All they had to do was send one box of supplies to Chicago per month. Ultimately this led to the creation of four thousand aid societies throughout Illinois and seventy thousand boxes arriving at her offices per month. She found that women on the home front contributed most of the goods:

> They rifled their houses of whatever bed-linen could be spared; denied their families canned and dried fruit; retrenched in the use of butter and eggs, that they might have more to take to market, and so more money to bestow on the soldiers; held festivals and dime parties; gave concerts; got up fairs,—in short, their ingenuity was as limitless as their patriotism.

As word of her successful operation spread beyond the state, she helped the women of neighboring states like Wisconsin and Iowa set up new societies and raise funds. She also traveled through the farm counties and saw images she could never have imagined before the war: women bringing in the harvest, driving reapers, binding and shocking wheat and loading grain, and performing other duties once reserved for men. In the small towns of the west, too, women had assumed jobs once strictly limited to their husbands and fathers—selling merchandise, operating heavy machinery, and keeping the family business running in tough economic times. At the same time they managed to stuff donation boxes full of shirts and bed linens, dried fruits and jams and jellies, and pickles in great abundance. It was hard, exhausting work, but the women of the west seemed to rise to it, and showed Mary she wasn't the only Northerner exhausting her energies for the cause. As she wrote, "My eyes were unsealed. The women in the harvest-field were invested with a new and heroic interest, and each hard-handed, brown, toiling woman was a heroine."

Mary's most momentous trip came in spring of 1863, when she and two other women from the Commission traveled down the Mississippi from Cairo nearly to Vicksburg, visiting the army hospitals along the way and disbursing food and supplies from 3,500 boxes. The largesse she brought was immense: everything from lemons and oranges (to relieve scurvy), to beef extract and codfish, from hospital sheets and bandages, to shirts, socks and shoes, and a small amount of good brandy.

At Memphis she vowed to visit every patient in all eleven hospitals— eight thousand men. She carefully went through the wards, no matter how dirty or cluttered, and found young men "disguised" with "mud, squalor, vermin, rags, and the wasting sickness of scurvy and swamp fever." She didn't flinch, though, and attended to their care and delivered the supplies as promised, making good on her vow to see every sick and wounded boy in the wards.

She found the cleanest and best-run facility to be Gayoso Hospital, where the troops were constantly overseen by some of the most skilled nurses and surgeons in the western theater. The nurse who ran the operation was said to be a stern figure who had a reputation as a bit of a hell-raiser. She also ran a hospital for smallpox patients down the river, and there she was notorious for her fury if she found hospital patients were mistreated or neglected. Few wanted to upset this woman and "arouse a moral earthquake, or let loose a small tornado of wrath." Mary met up with her at Gayoso Hospital, which also bore the nickname, "Mother Bickerdyke's Hospital."

Mary had known Mary Ann Bickerdyke since November 1862, when the former began her work with the Commission. She had heard of a strange middle-aged woman who had emerged from the wilds of Galesburg to become a commanding presence in army medicine. Mary wasn't sure how much of what she read in the newspapers was true—the reports described her rescuing people on the frozen battlefield of Fort Donelson, among other adventures. Plus, she herself knew to be skeptical of the way women were portrayed in the newspapers, based on her own treatment. So as a gesture of goodwill, even before meeting her formally, she invited this woman to use her home as a rest stop when on furlough from her duties at the front.

When Mary came home one evening, her cook told her of a tired, poor, sickly old lady who had come to stay, and who resembled her mother just before she died in Norway. She had come with a small carpetbag with her paltry possessions, had drawn herself a bath, and fallen asleep. She had ridden hundreds of miles to get to Chicago, and looked, and probably felt, half dead. Mother Bickerdyke had arrived.

After she awoke and they met formally, Mary was surprised by the woman's blunt, almost vulgar speech, which betrayed a certain crudeness and lack of education. She spoke with a thick country accent, dressed in tatty old garments, and offered no hint of a formal education. Mary wondered if she could even write. Soon, though, she won Mary over with her considerable vigor and charm, and with her tales of serving the troops on the great battlefields of the west. Mother Bickerdyke had cheerfully fought the surgeons and doctors who stood in her way, the male nurses who tried to strong-arm her out of power, and the occasional insults of soldiers. And still she persevered, and made the conditions of the hospitals she visited immeasurably better. But after more than a year without rest or recompense, she was also spent.

She would need time to recover at Mary's house and get her affairs in order. Mary helped her bring her sons from Galesburg and put them in a Chicago boarding school. She gave her a room to recover from her stresses, and enough decent food to nurse her back to a respectable condition. After that, Mother felt healthy enough to hit the road with Mary to drum up funds for the Commission, then to return to her duties in the army.

A few months later, on Mary's visit to Gayoso Hospital, she had a chance to see how Mother Bickerdyke operated in the field. She had recently approved her request for laundry equipment, which she used to set up a laundering facility. She employed a staff of fifty formerly enslaved black men and a white soldier nicknamed "Handy-Andy" to help her work.

The Commission allowed Mother to freely draw on its storehouses in Memphis, Cairo, and Chicago, and she had even finagled from General Grant himself an all-access pass behind Union lines—allowing her "into all camps and hospitals, past all pickets, with authority to draw on any quartermaster in his department for army wagons to transport sanitary or hospital stores." This included access to camps where other women were strictly forbidden.

So when Mary finally visited "Mother Bickerdyke's Hospital" in Memphis, she expected to see Mother hard at work with her new equipment and staff and improved health, and that she would offer her deep gratitude for Mary's help. She did not expect Mother to deliver a blunt insult to her face.

"You're a cowardly calf!" she said.

Mary was shocked and embarrassed by the charge. She had allowed this woman into her own home—had helped her accommodate her sons—and had brought her back to health. What had she possibly done to deserve such abuse?

It turns out she had said "no" to one of her schemes. It involved a doctor on the hospital staff with whom Mother was involved in a sort of running battle. In his latest salvo, the doctor had shut down a laundry facility that used several industrial washers the Commission had sent her. He didn't approve of her employment of black men and said he would not allow a "swarm of niggers" to defile his hospital. Instead he ordered them to report to the filthy "contraband camp" in the woods outside town, and never to return. When she found out, Mother was livid.

Rather than taking her aggression out on the doctor directly, she planned to go out into a driving rainstorm, track down a certain General Hurlbut who was in charge of the army post, rouse him from his sleep, and demand he countermand the doctor's orders and punish him to the greatest degree possible. And she wanted Mary Livermore to come along with her.

Mary refused. She would not sanction such an intrigue! It defied military order, proper manners, and common sense. But Mother Bickerdyke would not be denied. She left to wake the general, and branded Mary a craven bovine as she went. Her pride wounded, Mary had no choice but to follow.

Needless to say, the scheme worked. They splashed out into the rain, woke General Hurlbut from his bed, and presented their case with vigor. In turn the general overruled the doctor, criticized him for challenging the matron, and gave her license to operate all the laundries on the base as she saw fit.

At that point Mary realized this nurse had an even greater hold over the soldiers and officers than she expected, and an unmatched record in taking on her foes. As Mother said, "I guess you hadn't better get into a row with me, for whenever anybody does, one of us always goes to the wall. And it ain't never me!"

Mary was not used to such blatant cheek. This woman operated with the skill of a politician and the nerve of a prize-fighter. Mary would not typically have approved of such antics, yet she had to admit she felt strangely liberated. She had never before met anyone like this peculiar fireball of a woman. Unlike herself, Mother Bickerdyke never worried over consequences, never faltered in the pursuit of her goals, never aimed before she fired. She was a constant threat to the military bureaucracy and a sometime agent of chaos, and the troops adored her. And now she had her own hospital, too.

Seeing Mother Bickerdyke in action emboldened Mary to take actions she might never have contemplated before the war. First, she encountered a party of Southern women at the Gayoso House hotel where she was staying. Like herself, they were brought up to uphold proper decorum and to follow genteel middle-class customs. Unlike Mary, they supported the doctrine of secession and the enslavement of black people. And this she would not abide.

The women operated openly against the Union as spies and cast derision upon the Yankees staying there—referring to them as "Northern white trash," among other things. Mary tried to engage one of the women in a debate, but when the woman called Union soldiers "the dregs of your cities—gutter-snipes, drunken, ignorant," Mary angrily confronted her. The two nearly came to blows before the woman told her that federal troops had recently burned her family villa, destroying the dinner plates, carpets, and furniture. Mary informed her that, considering her rotten manners, she was lucky not to be burned up, too. She left while the woman was still screaming at her, her voice raised to a howling pitch.

Coming home from Memphis, Mary took her newfound vigor a step further. Angry words exchanged with a rebel woman were fine, but only actions would have a real effect on the war. So she resolved to do something that would go beyond even Mother Bickerdyke's own bold exploits. She would risk imprisonment by breaking the Black Law of Illinois.

Thanks to the 1853 statute that John Logan had championed, it was illegal for black Americans to migrate to Illinois, and for anyone to facilitate that migration. The wartime penalty for breaking this act was assignment to a contraband camp for blacks, and a thousand-dollar fine and a year's jail sentence for any whites who helped them. Nonetheless, when the former slave and abolitionist Ford Douglas asked Mary if she could help transport a young, formerly enslaved boy to Chicago to reunite with his mother, who had already fled north via the Underground Railroad, she agreed to break the law.

The child's name was Ben Morris, and he was not more than eight years of age. After Mary traveled upriver by boat, an associate of Douglas met her at the Illinois Central Railroad station in Cairo and transferred the boy to her care. She was already traveling with four orphaned girls she had picked up at Fort Pickering near Memphis—hoping to find adoptive parents for them back home—so she would have to make sure all the children would make it safely to Chicago. In Cairo, it would be especially dangerous to transport Ben, for here the railroad began its journey through Egypt, passing near Marion and Carbondale and all the other little towns where anger and hatred of black people burned hot and secession still had a lingering appeal. It would be 400 miles to Chicago, but the first 150 of them would be the hardest.

The provost marshal in Egypt was the greatest threat, inspecting each passenger's berth to make sure no prohibited items or people had been stowed aboard the train. At midnight, while many of the other passengers were asleep, Mary and Ben made their way to her sleeping car, and found the assistance of a black porter. He alerted them to a space underneath her bed that was just big enough for a large suitcase—or a small boy.

Within minutes, Ben was hidden away and sleeping. She could exhale for a moment.

Mary's comfort didn't last long. Below her bed, Ben began snoring loudly and waking some of the other passengers. This was a problem: Her only recourse was either to reveal his presence or pretend she was making the nasal racket herself—an unseemly image for a respectable woman. She pretended to be asleep.

The provost marshal later appeared in the sleeping car, checking berths for any stowaways. He came up to Mary and stopped for a moment, noticing the loudly snoring middle-class woman. Then he moved on to the next car.

Ben snored for hours under Mary's berth. In the morning it got to the point where some passengers asked the porter what was wrong with her—Was she going to lie in bed all day?—and the porter had to explain she was gravely ill from her travels and hadn't slept in six weeks. It wasn't far from the truth: Mary had indeed barely slept, and had a fever and many aches from her travels in the Deep South.

By the time they reached Centralia the danger was over. A new conductor took over the operation of the train, one who was also known to be a "conductor" for the Underground Railroad. Mary spent the last few hours of her journey home marveling she had summoned the courage for such an exploit, and thanking the Lord for shepherding them to safety—along with the porter and the conductor. In Chicago, she returned Ben to the care of his mother, and led the orphaned girls to her own Home for the Friendless, in hopes of finding them adoptive parents.

Helping a "contraband" find safety in defiance of the laws of her state was not a monumental gesture, but it was an important one. From now on Mary would act according to the dictates of her conscience, with less concern for propriety, even if it led to shouting matches and illicit actions and confrontations with officials. Still, one person she would not defy was the formidable Mother Bickerdyke. As Mary wrote, "I never knew anyone who deliberately disregarded her orders." This time, Mother needed another favor from Mary, even bigger than usual.

Thundering against the low quality of the "secesh" milk and eggs in Memphis, Mother had searched for months for an alternative that wouldn't make her Union boys sick with foul stomachs. Since she found the farmers in Tennessee impudent and condescending, and refused to negotiate with them, she decided instead to relocate the loyal "egg and milk producers" from the North to the South.

She traveled back to Illinois and asked the Commission to "stir up the aid societies as with a big spoon." Mary and her staff sent out a call for farm animals, and in a blaze of effort Mother secured the donation of a bevy of cows and chickens to be delivered to Memphis posthaste. But before that, she made sure the hens would be sent in batches to a central site for receiving and distribution—the Commission's own offices. Within days the site was a filthy mess, with cages stacked willy-nilly, feedstock littering the floor, and ghastly sounds and smells producing a rich and noxious atmosphere. As Mary remembered, "The din of crowing, cackling, and quarreling was unbearable; and, as the weather was warm, the odor was yet more insupportable."

Mary squirmed and turned up her nose, but Mother Bickerdyke seemed to delight in it—after all, she had witnessed much worse in army hospitals, and in any case, her absurd plan worked. She returned to her Gayoso Hospital in triumph, "forming a part of a bizarre procession of over one hundred cows and one thousand hens, strung all along the road from Chicago to Memphis." She had triumphed again despite the odds, and had given the Commission a celebrated victory, one whose smell Mary Livermore could never forget.

Yet the most remarkable aspect of Mother Bickerdyke's caper wasn't her own audacity. It was the energy and enthusiasm of hundreds of farmers—including many women—to donate their prized farm animals and drive them onto Illinois Central railcars in support of the Union effort. At the beginning of the war it would have been difficult to get farmers to part with their livestock, but now it was commonplace. Mary's unceasing work with the Commission had led to the creation of first dozens, then hundreds, and ultimately four thousand aid societies across Illinois and in neighboring states. So when Mother Bickerdyke made her call to the hinterlands for farm animals, she was sure to succeed. Mary Livermore had paved the way for her parade of "loyalist" creatures across the state.

When Mary's own parade and fair for soldiers in Chicago wrapped up in early November, it proved to validate her work. The creation of the aid societies led to the wagon train of produce; the contacts with industry and business led to the donated farm equipment; the power of her appeal led to singers, actors, and art patrons offering their services and holdings for free; and her relationship with the army led to the support of the troops and an array of complimentary flags and weapons. But despite the success of the North-Western Soldiers' Fair, and its estimated total of 100,000 visitors, one person was conspicuously absent.

During the autumn of 1863 Mother Bickerdyke was busy marching with the troops of the 15th Corps. General Sherman commanded that corps, and he would soon command the rest of the Army of the Tennessee. Although Sherman usually had little use for Commission agents, Mother was rumored to have a strange hold over him, and in Mary's words, she "became a special *attachée*" of his army.

Although Mother had been comfortable in her Memphis hospital, she did not hesitate to join Sherman's troops as they moved toward Chattanooga, joining up with his forces near Huntsville, Alabama. It was a long, difficult slog. She wore a pair of moccasins she fashioned from tree bark and army blankets, and her feet became blistered and bloody. The army faced an array of hardships, from freezing temperatures, to rebel snipers and guerrillas, to brutal mountain passes and ridges over broken and cobbled roads. But eventually she and her team—including Handy-Andy and fellow Commission agent Eliza Porter—made it to Chattanooga.

Mother arrived there four days before the battles that decided the city's fate. She witnessed the battle on Lookout Mountain as it happened, and barely had time to set up a field hospital near the base of Missionary Ridge before the final battle was over. She immediately faced a wave of 1,700 casualties from the 15th Corps' failed assault on Tunnel Hill. She did what she could to help them, but had few staff or resources this close to the front lines. The Commission called Eliza Porter away to another duty, so for nearly a month Mother was the only female nurse in camp.

Her duties were limitless: She made soup and toast for the boys, broiled mutton without a gridiron, baked bread, and served coffee and tea—all while attending to the wounded housed in makeshift shelters amid the trees. Few medical supplies and drugs were available, and army rations were low. By chance they did have plenty of whiskey available, which they took from an abandoned rebel still. Mother used it to make "panado," her own creation, a concoction of booze, hot water, and brown sugar mixed with hardtack crackers, which formed a sort of nutritious mush that convalescent soldiers ate with a spoon.

The nights were cold and unpleasant, and she and the soldiers burned wood in great "log-heaps." When they needed more firewood, she had them dismantle the breastworks the Confederates had used to repel Sherman's forces. Using mules and chains, the soldiers of the Pioneer Corps took apart the works and set them burning.

A major at the site, however, didn't approve of this. Destroying fortifications without permission was grounds for arrest, which he duly informed her. Mother nodded and kept about her labors: "All right, major, I'm arrested. Now don't bother me. I got work to do." Weeks later, she admitted her guilt at an official inquiry—and earned praise from the judges, who advised her to keep up the good work.

Despite the terrible conditions and oppressive chill, Mother labored at the field hospital through the new year. She nursed the dying through their final hours, ministered to the boys who feared death, and helped the wounded recover. Some of them had severed limbs from battlefield amputations, and they asked Mother to bury their lost arms and legs. She did so, dutifully covering them with dirt under a simple grave marker before offering a final prayer. And after her work was finally complete, she packed up and headed to the next Union camp down the line.

Mary somehow acquired a dress Mother wore during this trying time. It was a garment she had kept on for numberless days while cooking over a camp stove, and tending to the log fires, and constantly fighting off the embers. As Mary wrote, "It was burned so full of holes that it would hardly hang together when held up. It looked as if grape and canister had played hide-and-seek through it." She displayed the dress at the Commission's offices—a testament to Mother's labors at the front, a relic of her wartime service, an inspiration to anyone who saw it.

SIX

DAMN YOUR OFFICERS

T he train from Chattanooga had to fight its way into Georgia. Mile after mile, it battled over the ravines, attacked the mountain gaps, and cut through the oaks and pines. Its passengers nearly became casualties of the trip, clutching the handrails and bracing themselves against the seat backs to keep from being thrown to the floor. The Commission's agent, Eliza Porter, found herself airborne more than once, her ninety-pound frame jostled violently with each hard bump and dip.

The locomotive followed the path of the Northern invasion of the South in May 1864, moving past battlefields and skirmish lines that only days or weeks before had seen clashes between William Sherman's western armies of the United States of America and the combined troops of the Georgia militia and the Confederate States of America. The violence had driven the locals deep into the mountains, and the towns that passed by were mostly bleak and abandoned silhouettes, lit only by the lanterns of military guards and sentries.

After several hours the train pulled in at Ringgold, the end of the line. At the platform stood a sturdy, middle-aged woman in an old calico dress and weather-beaten sun bonnet. The woman's hair was unkempt, her posture was stooped, and the gray cloak she wore over her dress made her look suspiciously like a rebel. Eliza recognized her at once as her bosom friend and indispensable ally, Mary Ann Bickerdyke.

She led her toward a line of forty wagons, which contained rations and medical supplies from the Sanitary Commission, from tea, coffee, and milk, to rags, soap, and bandages, to crutches for amputees. The immense stores of the quartermaster and commissary were here, too, making for a huge mule-drawn parade of food and medicine that would help serve the needs of the 17,000 men of the 15th Corps of the U.S. Army. Mary Ann and Eliza were the only two women in sight.

A few days before, the soldiers of the 15th Corps had threaded their way through the hills and valleys of upstate Georgia with an array of cannons, mortars, rifles, and other weapons, most of it drawn by horses and mules too exhausted from several months of hard labor to complain. Among these troops was Eliza's own son, in a Chicago battery unit, whom she hadn't seen in several months but knew would be fighting somewhere near the front lines. His regiment and the rest of the corps had followed the path of Snake Creek, a thin artery that flowed deep into the woods past mountain crags and defiles and other narrow spaces perfect for ambushing an invading force, if any rebels in the area had a mind to.

Riding in an ambulance at the end of the mule train, Eliza looked out at the forbidding wilds. This forest was just the latest stop in her journey, which had taken her from little towns like Cairo and Corinth, to the rolling river country of Memphis, to the ridges and valleys of Chattanooga, and anywhere else sick and wounded soldiers of the war needed her aid and comfort. Some of the men called her the Angel of the Hospitals, but she didn't have the pride to accept such a moniker. She preferred Mary Ann's own term for her, "my little brown bird."

At fifty-seven, she was a decade older than Mary Ann and didn't have a fraction of her stamina. Slight of build, pale-skinned, suffering from chronic pain, and missing most of her teeth from an earlier illness, she struggled with the physical demands of being an army nurse and witnessing the gore and carnage that went with the job. Yet while Mary Ann may have bested her for strength and vigor, the petite Eliza had an outsize influence on her larger-than-life colleague.

When they first met, Mary Ann didn't think much of Eliza, seeing her puny frame as a hindrance to her labors and her health struggles as more befitting a hospital patient than a nurse. Moreover, her strange, mystical spirituality and her blatant displays of piety—such as praying on her knees with Commission donors—were more than "a little embarrassing." But Eliza had been doing the Lord's work for much longer than Mary Ann, and in places more remote and challenging than Galesburg, Illinois.

She had taught schoolchildren on the western frontier, educated freed slaves in Texas, helped run the Underground Railroad in Wisconsin, and taken an early and perilous stand for abolition. She had gone from being an office administrator at the Chicago Sanitary Commission to one of its field agents on the front lines of the invasion of the South. And while she expected no praise or honor for her labors, at the same time she would not accept being diminished or patronized by anyone who didn't appreciate her good works and keen intelligence—and that included Mary Ann Bickerdyke. Not surprisingly, Mary Ann came to respect her fire and feistiness, and the two became fast friends.

Eliza had gotten the Commission to enlist Mary Ann as a field agent, and even to pay her a salary, which she used for the care of her sons in Illinois. In return Mary Ann brought Eliza to most of the field hospitals where she worked, entrusted her with the care of even the sickest soldiers, and made sure she came along on the Georgia expedition. Mary Ann knew Eliza would have the stomach for it, and would not falter even in the face of the blackest horror of war.

After they passed through Snake Creek Gap, that is exactly what they saw. The horror began at daybreak, when they left their ambulance, walked across a meadow near the town of Resaca, and came to a pile of knapsacks. The pyramid of belongings spilled over with shirts and blankets and overcoats and letters home and other amenities that the soldiers of the 15th Corps had left behind, after they had finished their march and gone off to kill the enemy. And beyond the knapsacks lay the other discards, the results of their attack on the rebels: the arms and legs and fingers and jaws left in heaps around groves and culverts or wherever the orderlies could find space to dump them. Nearby, under the open sky, stood the operating tables—rough boards cut from trees, where the surgeons sawed away the injured and diseased parts of men they no longer had use for . . . since no one could walk on feet punctured with canister shot or fire a weapon with hands destroyed by gangrene. It was the purest sort of horror, but horror rendered familiar by its presence at the perimeter of every battlefield. Mary Ann and Eliza knew this was the right place, and began their work here.

While they were unloading supplies, an old friend greeted Mary Ann. Though it had been years since they had last spoken, she recognized him immediately—after all, he was the very reason she had gotten involved in the war in the first place. Dr. Benjamin Woodward put out his hand: "I am glad you are here. God knows women were never more welcome." They had both come a long way since Galesburg.

Word had spread over the years of Mary Ann's brash endeavors, and not only Dr. Woodward but many other officers saw her as a kind of talisman. Someone who could cure the sick and ease the pain of the dying with her ardent will and boundless energy. One of them was James McPherson, the general who currently commanded the Army of the Tennessee, now that William Sherman had been elevated to higher rank.

General McPherson had helped her secure the rations and medical supplies she needed, and was always willing to answer her requests and demands. And now, as he hurried from the battlefield, he had one for her: "My orderly is mortally wounded. Care for him, Mother, as best you can." Though the orderly was in grievous condition, Mary Ann made certain he had the best care she could muster.

While Mary Ann assisted the doctors and bandaged the wounds of the injured troops, Eliza spent the day washing blood from the faces of the wounded and dying. They lay on beds made from tree branches, with their own bloody shirts as their only pillows. Using buckets of fresh water and her handkerchief, she swabbed their cuts and gashes, spoke kind and comforting words to them, prayed with them, and hoped her own son would not be among them.

As day gave way to night, the warfare at Resaca increased in firepower and ferocity, and countless more injured men arrived at their makeshift field hospital in wagons and ambulances. Eliza looked over them with her lantern, trying to see distinct faces among the casualties, but saw no sign and heard no word from her son.

The thunder of shell fire grew louder. The blood, the carnage, the terror, it was all so close now. Her hands shook as she washed out her handkerchief with fresh water, and looked at the fearful eyes of the soldiers with a new sort of empathy for what they faced every moment of this war.

Suddenly she looked up as a young soldier ran toward her. As Mary Ann saw it:

> I can never forget the terrible scene, when the smoke was black as night and the earth vibrated beneath us as if an earthquake was actually shaking the land, when her son darted in like a deer exclaiming 'Mother, I'm all right!'—and as quickly and unceremoniously disappeared amid those midnight clouds of battle.

Eliza was relieved, able to hold back the fear for another moment, another hour, another day. Her hands stopped shaking and the cramp in her stomach abated. Her son's appearance had been a favorable omen. Soon after, the carnage lessened, the flow of casualties eased, and she and Mary Ann had time for a brief rest.

The two women spent the next several days visiting one field hospital after another, creating beds for the wounded made from blankets spread over pine boughs, and feeding the soldiers hardtack concocted into soups and panado. At first, they had only the medical supplies and rations they had brought down on the mule train, but they managed to stretch the provisions to feed and care for as many troops as they could. For the wounded in the 20th Army Corps, which included many Germans, they doled out sauerkraut and pickles, which in Eliza's words, "are never eaten but by famished men." For 260 soldiers on their way home by train, they brewed countless barrels of coffee to quench their thirst. And for the wounded who remained bedridden days after the battle had ended, Mary Ann and Eliza were able to set up regulation tents and cots, when the military finally sent relief supplies.

At Sugar Creek, four miles from the Resaca battlefield, Major General John Logan invited Mary Ann and Eliza to his headquarters, where they could arrange to have proper kitchens and nursing facilities set up. The general himself was engaged in combat with the enemy, and wouldn't be able to cross paths with the woman he had first met on the frozen landscape of Fort Donelson, but he gave his staff orders to provide Mary Ann and Eliza with whatever help they needed. Indeed, they had many fans among the generals, who appreciated their unwavering focus on their mission and perseverance in the face of obstacles—skills not unlike those it took to win a battle.

Generals Grant and Sherman especially liked Mary Ann, seeing her as a critical tool for making Union hospitals cleaner and more efficient. In return she leaned on them for favors and pushed their indulgence as far as it would go. She had received a general pass from General Grant into all camps and hospitals, and also persuaded, badgered, or browbeat General Sherman into doing her bidding, depending on her mood and the urgency of her need. Not only did she get him to make an exception to his prohibition on civilians and women following the army to Chattanooga, and then into Georgia, she also cajoled him into allowing two railcars per day of Commission supplies on military rolling stock. And she acquired his protection when she inevitably stirred up trouble.

In one well-known story, when a colonel's wife at Vicksburg had asked for medical care for her son afflicted with measles, and Mary Ann railed at the woman for wasting her time with a common childhood illness, the colonel took up the case with General Sherman directly. He demanded she punish the "nasty old woman" who had acted so impudently toward his spouse. Sherman just shrugged.

"Oh, well," he said. "You've picked on the one person around here who outranks me. If you want to lodge a complaint against her, you'll have to take it to President Lincoln."

She couldn't have chosen a more valuable ally than Sherman. When Lincoln elevated Grant to lieutenant general and commander of all federal armies in March 1864, Sherman gained in stature, too. He took over as head of the Military Division of the Mississippi, and commanded not just the Army of the Tennessee, but the armies of the Cumberland and Ohio, too, which were also engaged in the invasion. And where Sherman went, so went Mary Ann.

To Mary Livermore, Sherman was Mary Ann's "beau idéal," a perfect warrior who was "the special object of her idolatry. . . . She would count it a small thing to die for him." To Mary Ann, he was just "Billy Sherman," an honest old soldier with a grizzled charm and plainspoken demeanor, who just happened to be in charge of one of the largest armies in the western world. Curiously, she expressed her admiration for him not with obvious affection, but with impassioned demands and furious harangues—it almost seemed as if she were giving him marching orders. This behavior Sherman would never have countenanced in a lower-ranking officer, let alone a civilian. But because of his grudging respect for her and all that she offered his soldiers, he was willing to do her bidding.

A month and a half after Resaca, John Logan looked up at Kennesaw Mountain and knew he was in for a fight. General Sherman had been firm in his orders: Logan would prepare his troops to advance up the mountain and assault its defenders. At first Logan couldn't believe he was serious. The mountain wasn't just one peak—it was four, broken up by hills and ridges and topped with a formidable line of earthworks ringed with lines of artillery and soldiers in gray. To advance upon it "would only result in useless slaughter." He protested the action and implored Sherman to reconsider the attack, but his commander would not budge. Good military man that he was, Logan had no choice but to prepare for the assault. He wrote to his wife, Mary, "Our men are in good heart, though they have a bloody road before them."

This kind of attack had succeeded once before at Chattanooga, but that had been a command mistake that resulted in an unexpected victory for the Army of the Cumberland. This time, the Army of the Tennessee, Sherman's old command, would make the move, and the 15th Corps, Sherman's even older command, would be at the center of it—led by Logan as major general. And the Confederates would be ready for them.

Logan had been preparing for moments like this for months, ever since planning began for the spring campaign. In early March, Generals Grant and Sherman had agreed to attack their foes in tandem. While Grant battled Robert E. Lee's Army of Northern Virginia in that state, Sherman would attack Joe Johnston's rebel army in Georgia—confusingly called the Army of Tennessee—after Braxton Bragg had been sacked from command. Sherman's objective was to break up Johnston's army, cripple the war-fighting resources of the region, and move against Atlanta.

However, Grant had become bogged down in Virginia, and since early May Sherman's invasion had turned into an elaborate game of martial chess: Sherman and his three armies comprising 100,000 men would try to outflank Johnston's 60,000-strong corps. The brash Yankee general would make a bold opening move, only to find his way blocked by the rebel general's careful defensive tactics. Their forces would fight a few significant battles, but mostly bruise each other with skirmishing and artillery duels, and constantly build entrenchments across every hard-won mile. It was a tedious advance from pine forest to dry, barren scrubland, and the soldiers hated it—referring to this part of Georgia as "The Hell Hole." Yet slowly it began to work, and with each movement forward, Sherman would drive Johnston farther toward central Georgia. If Sherman could breach Johnston's works at Kennesaw Mountain, the federal armies would stand only twenty miles from Atlanta.

While Logan had his concerns about the plan, he had fought and suffered and triumphed enough times in the Union army that even a frontal assault could not daunt him. And though he expressed misgivings in private, in front of his troops he could do nothing but support it. His boys would expect nothing less.

In a war filled with brutality and ignoble behavior, an aura of old-fashioned glory clung to John Logan. As former colonel of the 31st Illinois Volunteer Infantry Regiment, previous leader of the Third Division of the 17th Corps, and now commanding general of the 15th Corps, he had risen far above what anyone could have expected from a congressman from southern Illinois. Most of President Lincoln's "political generals" had flamed out, from Nathaniel Banks to John McClernand, but Logan had emerged as a model commander in the field.

Thanks to the reporters following the Army of the Tennessee, Logan also had a national reputation as a daring and colorful leader of men, his brash feats and galvanizing rhetoric enhancing his stature with the troops and with the Northern public. Who could forget his sacrifice on the battlefield of Fort Donelson, where he had been shot full of holes, left for dead, and miraculously survived? Or how he rallied the troops at Raymond, Mississippi, charging against a fearsome wall of musket fire and grape shot? Or how he galloped along a ridgeline and inspired his men at Vicksburg, defying the rebel snipers who fired a hundred shots at him but couldn't bring him down? For these actions and more, General Grant had recommended Logan twice for promotion, and President Lincoln had agreed, elevating Logan first to brigadier general after Fort Donelson, and then to major general a year later. And as of last autumn he had taken command of the 15th Corps and added more laurels to his record, including:

- Standing boldly at Resaca on a hillock the rebels used for target practice, directing his artillery while remaining impervious to the exploding bombs around him.
- Plunging into Camp Creek and exhorting his men to swim to the other side to assault the rebels, under a deadly cannonade.
- Galloping along his lines at Dallas, Georgia, waving his hat and shouting "Fall in! Forward!" and driving his troops to beat back a surprise Confederate assault, "looking like the very god of war," as one soldier said.
- Taking a wound to the forearm, having it stitched up, then riding back to the front lines with his arm in a sling to lead his corpsmen to victory—and the next day getting shot again in the sleeve.

This was the "Black Jack" his troops knew and that he had become—a warrior on his black steed Slasher who knew no fear, gave no quarter, and always rebounded no matter how many times he had taken musket fire or been thrown from his horse. Logan even designed the badge for the 15th Corps—a cartridge box with "40 Rounds" written on it—and, rare for a commanding general, his men applauded him at the front and cheered his reckless, sometimes shocking bravado. As one soldier wrote, "the biggest coward in the world would stand on his head on top of the breastworks if Logan was present and told him to do so."

And he did it all with little respect for convention and order when in the midst of a fight. The troops loved it when he yelled at them to "Damn your regiments! Damn your officers! Forward and yell like hell!" He encouraged a scrum when it was needed, and even a bit of chaos if it helped to win the day. Such an approach came perilously close to fighting without orders, but in a Northern army that encouraged brash action and daring initiatives, it was welcome.

At least in some quarters. For anyone who angered him, his behavior could be frightening. His unchecked tirades, his wild gestures, his sharp profanity were all legendary, as was his willingness to pistol-whip (at Dallas) or threaten to kill (at Belmont) any soldier who behaved cowardly in the face of danger. But after the battle ended, he might take off his warrior mask and play the clown, telling ribald tales and silly jokes, giving impressions and speaking in colorful accents, including his famous Irish brogue. You never knew what you were going to get with Black Jack.

Away from the field of combat, Logan could be anxious, even morose at times. He worried about his health from all the abuse his body had taken. He ached with rheumatism and mysterious pains, and sometimes found it difficult to mount his horse. Throughout the western campaigns, he had been operated on several times, cracked his ribs, nearly died of exposure and fever, and been thrown from the saddle at least twice. And he began to think about his mortality. He had written to his wife just a few weeks before, informing her of $10,000 he had deposited with a trusted army colonel, which would be hers in the event of his death. And increasingly, his letters included the phrase, "If I do not survive."

He also tangled with the military hierarchy and his fellow generals, some of whom did not hold a "fighting general" like himself in the highest regard. They were especially wary of Logan if they had been trained at

West Point or were sticklers for maintaining rules and proper decorum. Some of them laced their feelings with contempt.

One such general was George Thomas, in charge of the Army of the Cumberland. Before the Atlanta campaign, Thomas had required passes for officers of the Army of the Tennessee to use the railroad his army controlled from Nashville to Chattanooga. Discovering this, Logan exploded. His men were not second-class citizens, subject to the whims of another army, and Thomas had no right to run the railway like his own private holding—it was an outrage! Logan raised hell, and Sherman had to intercede and overturn the railway policy. But Thomas would not forget the slight. As Sherman later said, "If there was a man on earth whom Thomas hated, it was Logan."

Even Logan's assumption of command over the 15th Corps had been a matter of dispute. Major General Frank Blair wanted to command that corps and Sherman agreed that he should, leaving Logan with the less-legendary 17th Corps. Logan responded with indignation, calling it unjust and telegraphing the president himself to express his displeasure. Lincoln and General Grant settled the argument in Logan's favor, but this conflict, like so many of the others, ensured him a reputation as an uncontrollable hothead, whose short fuse could be lit at the slightest provocation.

More than anyone else, James McPherson lit that fuse at Resaca, which had been the first major battle of the advance into Georgia. As the new commander of the Army of the Tennessee after Sherman became head of the western armies, McPherson and his nearly 25,000-man army had reached the outskirts of the town in May and were unable to determine the number of its defenders. McPherson preferred caution, and did not want to engage his army in combat with such uncertainties. Logan disagreed.

As he saw it, the 15th Corps alone could rush in and take the town, destroy a critical Confederate railway, and cut off the line of retreat for the rest of Joseph Johnston's army farther north—ensuring its doom. Didn't McPherson see he had a terrific opportunity to surprise the rebels, overwhelm their defenses, and possibly surround them? This would hasten the invasion of the Southern heartland and leave Atlanta helpless in the face of the attack. They had been battling the enemy for nearly three years, and rarely did they have a chance like this! Hadn't General Sherman called the Army of the Tennessee the Union's "whip snapper" for its rapid movements and quick maneuverability? Wasn't this the perfect time to snap the whip for a decisive victory over these implacable, these impudent, these godforsaken—these *goddamn*—secessionists? What were they waiting for?!

General McPherson carefully considered Logan's request, and just as carefully rejected it. Attacking now would be too big a risk and endanger the lives of many more troops. Logan couldn't believe it—he yelled, he swore, he almost denounced McPherson to his face, but nothing he said or did could force him to change his mind. Logan was shocked by the general's lack of nerve, his deficit of courage, and he stormed off, too furious to say or do anything else. Besides, his voice was hoarse.

A short time later, General Johnston discovered his army's vulnerability and brought in the bulk of his troops to defend Resaca. It turned out Logan was right: The town's initial defenders were no more than 4,000 troops, and the Army of the Tennessee outnumbered them six to one. The battle would have been a rout, had they fought it then. Sherman realized this when he reached the front, and said to McPherson, "Well, Mac, you have missed the opportunity of your life."

Since then, seven weeks had passed and thousands of soldiers had fallen. Johnston's army was never again so vulnerable, and the federals and rebels had managed to turn the western campaign into a slow, deadly slog. And now the 15th Corps prepared to attack Kennesaw Mountain at the foot of one of its peaks, Pigeon Hill.

Unlike Resaca, this was a much more dangerous mission, with a much lower chance of success. The "hill" was hardly a scrubby knoll; it was a rounded peak with craggy rocks and high cliffs—a "Gibraltar" protected by a thicket of cannons and a forest of muskets. The rebels had also dug trenches topped with forbidding parapets, to force any attacker to clamber over them in the face of what would surely be relentless rifle fire and an artillery barrage. Logan's corps had its own strengths—battle-hardened troops, sufficient weapons and ammunition, and plenty of courage—but he wondered: *Would it be enough this time?*

The drama of war and its mortal consequences appealed to Logan. The stakes were so great, the glory and tragedy so pronounced, it made his previous life as a politician pale in comparison. What oratorical battle in Congress could compare with real combat on a mountain range in Georgia? These days he preferred to think of himself as more a soldier than a politician. But his old life continued to call on him, in unexpected ways.

Friends and allies had been suggesting for more than a year that Logan return to the political fray, to run for Illinois governor in November 1864. In an about-face from their previous denunciation of his politics, many newspapers now openly supported him, especially the pro-war and anti-slavery papers that had once condemned him. He could run as a Republican, a Democrat, or on a new national unity ticket Lincoln had proposed for all supporters of the war, regardless of party stripe. None of this stirred him to action, though. Not when there was a war still to be won.

Politics, however, intruded into his life even in the army. And the country's greatest political question—just as it was its greatest moral and social and economic question—was what to do about slavery.

Racial matters continued to vex him. While still wary of radical Republicans and abolitionists, he was no longer the champion of white supremacy and race-baiter he once was. In Illinois, due to the Black Law he wrote that kept black people out of the state, there was little mixing of the races and Logan could freely spout whatever racial invective came to mind in Congress without having to defend himself to black neighbors or associates. In the South it was different. Here, the races commingled, and he was able to see the effect of slavery on black people, in all its horror.

Like other soldiers from the North, he had seen firsthand the elaborate plantations of the South and the owners and overseers who ran them, who kept slaves locked in leg and neck irons, bloodied them with whips, and otherwise abused and tortured them—all to force them to work in cotton and sugarcane fields in crushing subtropical weather. This made him question whether his earlier pro-Southern rhetoric hadn't done more harm than good, and whether his political career had been built on his own willful ignorance. Other sights and experiences marked Logan as well:

After the fall of Vicksburg, Grant gave Logan control of the city guard, and permitted each Confederate prisoner to leave the city with one "servant." The rebels abused the rule and tried to enslave blacks and force them to serve time in jail. Logan demanded an end to the practice, and Grant agreed to reverse the policy.

In Huntsville, Alabama, Logan led an inspection tour of houses he believed to harbor guerrillas. At one residence a woman noticed his dark complexion and asked him, "Whose boy are you?" Informed he was a Yankee general, the woman replied, "I tell you he's nothing of the kind. He's black."

Once Logan had been elevated in rank, Colonel "Doff" Ozburn took over the 31st Illinois Infantry. But Ozburn was a hostile foe of the Emancipation Proclamation, and vowed never "to fight to free the niggers." Logan sacked him in a profane tirade, "hot and thick from an outraged heart." Ozburn quit the army shortly thereafter.

In Jackson, Tennessee, a young girl escaped from a planter who had held her as a rape slave. Horrified by the situation, Logan quickly granted her protection from him. But feigning a mortal illness, the planter tricked her into visiting him, then kidnapped her and sold her off to a Georgia plantation. Logan never forgot the outrage.

His experiences culminated in a speaking tour of Egypt in the summer of 1863, in which he tried to rally his former constituents behind the policies of the Lincoln administration and address lingering sympathies toward secession in the region. It put him in a strange position: He would be speaking as an officer fighting a war he once fiercely opposed, under the command of a president he once firmly despised. But his time in the army had changed him, and he let it be known without any doubt, with the blunt force of rhetoric honed by years of practice.

Surprising some in the audience, he demanded their unconditional support of the Emancipation Proclamation and the arming of black soldiers. Promising this "wicked rebellion shall be utterly crushed," he defended both measures as a military necessity to whip the South. The proclamation would undercut the use of slaves to support the Confederate war effort, and black soldiery would give the North extra manpower to win the fight. Yes, as a congressman he had once argued for the preservation of human bondage where it existed, but no more! Instead, he would "sacrifice slavery and everything else to preserve the Union, and put down the rebellion."

Those who did not already know of Logan's changed beliefs listened in shock. To many of them he was still "Dirty Work" Logan, the author of the Black Law, the enemy of blacks and the scourge of Republicans. They appreciated his war record, but couldn't imagine he would support Lincoln's anti-slavery policies—and his emancipation policy no less! But Logan didn't stop there: He roundly condemned peace supporters and Southern sympathizers, among them many of his fellow Democrats, and praised the demolition of slavery without equivocation or regret. He spoke his most bracing, even stunning, words in Du Quoin, Illinois:

> [I]f they call me an Abolitionist, I can't help it. If fighting rebels and traitors be an Abolitionist, I suppose I must be counted in, and if that makes the soldiers Abolitionists, there are a good many of us. We don't care. God knows we are true to our country, and that is what is wanted.

Making this speech in his home region took nearly as much courage for John Logan as charging against artillery fire on a battlefield. For Egypt was its own kind of battlefield, and if some residents were happy to be persuaded by their former congressman, many others weren't. Foremost among the holdouts were his own family members.

While a few relatives like his brother-in-law, Hybert Cunningham, had turned away from the rebellion—deserting his Confederate unit and taking up arms with the North—others reacted venomously to his political awakening. His mother had practically disowned him, and still barred him from entering her house. His sister Annie had attacked his wife and received a beating from her in return, and still pledged her loyalty to the secessionists. And his brother Tom, whom Logan had helped make an officer with the 31st Illinois, used his time in the regiment to assault and attempt to rape several Southern women. He also got drunk on duty, and was known to shout "Hurrah for Jeff Davis!" in public, with glee.

Considering their wretched behavior, Logan had to concede most of his family might never accept his changed views, and would forever defend the Confederacy and make excuses for slavery. The same was true of other Egyptians who regarded his change of heart as ideological treason—including the various hecklers and catcallers during his speeches who decried his name and called him a turncoat for endorsing the policies of the Republicans. They despised him as they despised all Unionists. Some were even ready to back their sentiments with violence.

As many as 400 armed deserters were said to lurk in southern Illinois, threatening bloodshed against loyalists, and Mary told him insurrectionist groups like the Knights of the Golden Circle had unleashed terror against their enemies. His two former partners at a law firm he once worked at had both been arrested, and numerous other friends and associates now faced jail time for their subversive activities. In his speeches, Logan had called anti-Unionists a threat to the republic and had received death threats in return. How much further could he go without threatening the safety of his family? Could he continue to castigate pro-slavery "hellhounds and traitors" and demand they be hanged?

He couldn't forget how the previous November he had wandered into an Egyptian hotel with several of his officers and found himself face to face with a notorious secessionist. The hulking brute was supported by a rangy group of thugs and felt emboldened to insult Logan, calling him a traitor and a disgrace to his friends and family. Logan took the measure of the man and held his temper in check, but the ruffian only increased the severity of his insults and the loudness of his voice. Logan's honor was now at stake.

He quickly found a glass water pitcher and smashed it against the miscreant's head. The brute toppled to the ground and his motley associates charged toward the general with an eye to killing him. They were greeted with a line of army service revolvers aimed at their heads. Logan's officers had come to his defense. They beat a hasty retreat, but he knew they were lucky. The next time his enemies would come better armed.

Ironically, in some ways he was safer in the army, there among soldiers and officers who had seen many of the same things he had, at some distance from his home region and the guerrillas and subversives who threatened loyal citizens. But even in the army, there were many holdouts against the Emancipation Proclamation and especially the arming of black soldiers. One of them was his boss, William Sherman.

As Sherman had repeatedly vowed, black soldiers would not be part of his invasion force. Even though blacks counted among the most loyal of Unionists, constructed roads, bridges, trenches, and earthworks for the Army of the Tennessee, worked on railways, in hospitals and laundries, as spies in rebel territory, and as teamsters, wagon masters, carpenters, and blacksmiths, Sherman refused to allow them to carry weapons. He had his excuses—logistical, empirical, racial—but even in the face of great pressure from Washington, he would not budge. There would be no regiments made up of former slaves or freedmen in his armies.

Logan didn't understand this view. For if black Americans could do everything else to support the war, they could certainly be trusted to shoot Confederates. But he had his suspicions about Sherman's real motives— namely, that Sherman had failed to adapt to current military reality, and rejected any new idea if it wasn't taught at West Point.

A few black infantry regiments might have been very useful at Kennesaw Mountain. For Logan had 5,500 troops with which to assault Pigeon Hill, and any increase in infantry numbers would have helped improve the odds against such a formidable defensive line. Nonetheless, at 8 A.M. on June 27, 1864, Sherman ordered the attack to begin, and in tandem with units of the Army of the Cumberland farther south, Logan and his men advanced up the mountain.

They met with immediate and brutal resistance. The Confederates fired ceaseless rounds from their parapets and their batteries unleashed sheets of flame from their field guns. Unlike at Chattanooga, these shells found their mark and hundreds of men were cut to pieces by shrapnel or perforated by canister fire.

This didn't stop Logan. He bellowed at his men to follow him up the hillside, charging headlong into a blizzard of gunfire and minié balls. His brigades seized a first line of rifle pits and scattered the rebels, and then seized another, driving the defenders up the slope. The 15th Corps forced its way higher and higher and stopped just below the crest of the hill where the Confederates lodged behind their earthworks. A merciless cannonade provided the soundtrack, as Logan discovered his men had advanced farther than any other corps in the Army of the Tennessee.

He ordered another charge. His men rose up, went forward, and the Confederate guns drove them back. Again they charged, and again they were driven back. Logan then realized no matter how many times he exposed his troops to enemy fire or risked their lives, his corps was not going to go any farther up the mountain. Already six hundred men—a tenth of his force—had fallen, and the odds didn't improve as the sun went down.

For four days the lines remained frozen in place. Musket fire and artillery rounds peppered the air, some rebels threw rocks to taunt their Yankee foes, and the Union could gain no further ground. Finally, Sherman gave up. He turned to his old playbook and outflanked the rebel positions around the mountain. As before, Johnston beat a hasty retreat and moved his army back toward Atlanta. Logan's original prediction had been accurate: The assault on Kennesaw Mountain achieved nothing but the death and injury of 3,000 men—one of the worst battlefield losses in the Atlanta campaign.

This only made him question the tactics of William Sherman even more. For no amount of personal bravery could force a winning hand on a losing position. It was a foolish error to assault the mountain as he did, and as Logan wrote to his wife, "Sherman is a strange man and only seems to fight a portion of his army at a time"—meaning that in the face of uncertainty, he resorted to caution and only sent out battle units piecemeal to fight the enemy, instead of attacking in full force on all fronts. This ran contrary of the general's fearsome reputation, but he had done the same thing at Tunnel Hill in Chattanooga, with equally unsuccessful results. Logan now began to question Sherman's wisdom, and also wondered what motivated him, and the real purpose behind his failed mountain attack. As Logan later told an eastern colonel, he suspected Sherman did it because he was jealous of Grant gaining press attention for his battlefield exploits in Virginia, and he wanted to create his own headlines, positive or negative.

Yet, Sherman was more adept than Logan gave him credit for. The western commander soon learned from his mistake and drove the rebels south again. They abandoned their mountain redoubt and withdrew to the banks of the Chattahoochee River. And Sherman continued to advance, slowly and inexorably, into the heart of the Confederacy. As one rebel prisoner said, no matter how much Sherman was hated, he will "never go to hell, for he'll flank the devil and make heaven in spite of all the guards."

The sworn enemy of the South now stood less than twenty miles from Atlanta.

SEVEN

THE WHEEL

John McCline lay in his tent in the woods of north Georgia, listening to the autumn rain spatter the canvas with a steady rhythm. Other troops were huddled in their tents, playing cards or writing letters home or finding other ways to while away the time. Above them the canopy of pine trees absorbed most of the water, but there was enough of it left over to dampen their belongings and spirits, putting them in a gloomy mood ever since the drizzle began many days ago.

They camped at the foot of the Blue Ridge Mountains, amid the hollers and ravines of the Georgia hinterlands, in a landscape that had been occupied, fought over, bled upon, raided, and recaptured multiple times since the war began. The woods were said to be alive with guerrillas, who made war against the federals, against the rebels, against themselves, in constant bouts of bloodletting that refused to be stanched. Rumor had it, if a fellow wandered too far from his unit, he might find himself swinging from a tree or bleeding on the ground. Despite the danger, it made for a dark, strangely alluring world for a young man like John, who was not yet a teenager. He was still on a great journey, begun two years before when he escaped from the Hoggatt plantation. He was now at a new army camp, in a state nearly as exotic to him as Michigan, whose 13th Volunteer Infantry troops he counted among his closest friends and allies.

John and the 13th Michigan camped three miles from the Dalton depot. They were there to protect the lifeline of General Sherman's troops, the Western & Atlantic Railroad, from attacks by guerrillas. The thin iron artery brought the food, weapons, and provisions from the army's advance depot in Chattanooga to camps in the Atlanta area, and severing that artery became a priority to just about every secessionist in the state. Despite all the Union's armed guards on the trains, the garrisons protecting the depots and bridges and trestles, the blockhouses and the forts, the rebels still damaged the rails and roadbed with near impunity—constantly endangering the survival of the troops farther south. As Sherman said, "I am now 105 miles from Chattanooga and all our provisions have come over that single road, which is almost daily broken somewhere."

The troops weren't only in Dalton to guard the railroad. They were also there to vote their absentee ballots in the November election, still several weeks away. The newspapers said the race would be close, and President Lincoln needed every soldier's ballot he could get. So the Michiganders had a double duty: to vote for the candidate of their choice, Lincoln, against the deposed commander of the Army of the Potomac and current Democratic nominee, George McClellan, while they kept a close watch on the raiders who might attack at any time, jeopardizing the invasion as well as the president's reelection.

It was no idle threat. Just a few weeks before, General Joseph Wheeler's cavalry had attacked the Dalton garrison and battled federal troops from the Department of the Cumberland. The conflict took place before John and the 13th Michigan arrived, but the stories about the battle were still fresh. What was especially unusual was one group of soldiers who fought there. Although Sherman had tried to keep them out of his invading armies, the black troops of the 14th U.S. Colored Infantry played an important role in beating back the Confederate assault—the freedmen and former slaves driving the rebels from the field at a key point in the battle, as white Union soldiers waved their hats and cheered.

Were these the same black men who had so impressed John earlier in the war? He had never gotten the name of their regiment, but it was possible these horsemen had been among the same troops he had met in their barracks, with their spit polish and matchless style. By order of William Sherman, they would not be a part of his force. But in reality they had already helped protect that force, many miles away in another part of Georgia, whether "Uncle Billy" approved of it or not.

At nearly thirteen, John was not a soldier yet, but he was becoming a man. No longer a teamster, he had since traded in the reins to become an orderly to a captain, and received the first salary of his life—eight dollars per month. The work varied by the hour and the day, and often left him wet and muddy or sweaty and disheveled, but he embraced it. As he toiled with the rest of his unit, he learned new skills and discovered the practice of war meant more than just firing a musket.

After the battles of Chattanooga, he helped the regiment construct forts and warehouses and hospitals, as it did engineering duty throughout the winter of 1864. A few months later, when the regiment returned to its fighting form, he traveled with it, too, pursuing rebel general Nathan Bedford Forrest as he threatened Union-held towns and rail lines from northern Alabama to central Tennessee.

At Fort Pillow, Forrest was said to have massacred scores of troops trying to surrender, many of them black soldiers. The incident caused outrage in the North, and only made the Union army that much more determined to stop his attacks. John remembered early in the war when Forrest and his men stopped in at the plantation for a respite, devouring ham and cornbread before making their exit. He knew the danger of Forrest—and the death that awaited him if he were captured—but that didn't stop him from helping his regiment in any way he could. The 13th Michigan never caught the rebel general, but the pursuit brought John closer to the front lines than he had ever been, and he would get closer than that in the coming months. He would even fight if he had the chance.

Beyond anything else he had done in the army, one of John's greatest accomplishments was to educate himself, learning to read with the aid of a treasured spelling book. He never had the opportunity to learn when he was enslaved, but now that he had escaped, he became hungry for knowledge and experience. He picked up skills from wagoning to carpentry, learned about exotic new plants and wildlife he couldn't have imagined on the plantation, and heard stories of far-off places like Paw Paw, Michigan, where many of the troops were from, and which he one day hoped to visit. As he began to learn more about the war and life, and to grow up in the company of soldiers, he looked upon the new world he found with the eyes of an adult instead of a child, and saw it in all its tantalizing and terrifying power, its invigorating and intoxicating appeal.

John and his regiment finished their service in Dalton in mid-November and received orders to march south toward Atlanta. It was a place John had never seen but only heard tell of in his young life, first on the plantation from various white visitors who lived there, and then in camp from officers who had once passed through. Everyone knew how important it was, and how the entire recent campaign had been designed around its capture.

Atlanta was also known as the Gate City. The Georgians had given it the nickname as a testament to the many trains that entered the town and the tracks that passed through it, stitching the entire state together in an iron web of railroads. So when John left on his next journey, he fully expected to find a great city of industry, wealth, and commerce, a place central to Southern life and culture, where the massive roundhouse and depots and foundries and factories had powered the rebel armies for most of the war.

But when his regiment arrived in town, they found not a single one of those buildings standing, and much of the rest of the town also lay in ruin. The horizon was a jagged outline of broken walls and lonely chimneys, colored in brown and black char, in utter desolation and abandonment. No one lived there anymore, and many of the palatial and common homes, the grand and humble buildings, had been looted, or smashed to bits, or melted by flames. Even the trains that once gave the place its purpose stood demolished in heaps, and the railways surrounding the town had been twisted into corkscrews. The once-vital center of industry and commerce was now an infernal black hole—a great nowhere. Sherman had obliterated Atlanta from the map.

Four Months Earlier—

Captain Charles Wills stood on the banks of the Chattahoochee River north of Atlanta enjoying a mouthful of blackberries. They were plump and tart, and of a thoroughly pleasing variety. He and his colleagues in the 103rd Illinois had made a meal of them, along with grapes and green apples and Union beef. A few scurvy victims in the regiment—with black mouths and loose teeth—even devoured pickles. It was early July in the aftermath of Kennesaw Mountain, the weather was hot, and many of the boys had at last gotten a break from combat. Not that combat was ever far away—the Confederates had lined the other side of the river with massive arrowhead forts called "Shoupades" and some twenty Parrott field guns. But the cannons were quiet at the moment, and the regiment finally had a chance to exhale.

Last year in Chattanooga, Captain Wills had wanted a taste of battle. In the Atlanta campaign, he had gotten it. The 103rd Illinois had been under fire for fifty of the last sixty-two days. They had fought at Resaca, where many of the troops succumbed to death and disease, and witnessed a ferocious cannonade above their heads—"the most exciting show I ever saw," Wills wrote. They had met the enemy at Dallas, taking cover from a flurry of shells and case shot, and heard the rebels attack "with a yell the devil ought to copyright." They had skirmished at Adairsville as part of a division that lost 400 men, and camped in a stately house where the corpse of a rebel colonel lay uncovered in a garden amid hundreds of varieties of roses. And they saw action at Kennesaw Mountain, where a corporal Wills knew had been killed six feet from him and a spent minié ball glanced off his ankle. The regiment took fifty-seven casualties—a high number for one of the smaller units in the brigade—but Wills remained optimistic, and enjoyed an evening watching another captivating artillery show. General Sherman was even more sanguine about the battle, writing, "I begin to regard the death and mangling of a couple of thousand men as but a small affair."

Wills was hardly as cavalier about death as his commanding general, but he had become inured to it. The various horrors on view—the shocking mutilations, the cruel amputations, the thousands of dead horses and mules, the random and senseless killing, all of it—had become an inevitable part of his life in the army, and no longer surprised him.

It had been different early on, in his first year in uniform, when Wills could still be shaken by gore and brutality. He recalled his first encounter with the true nature of the war, after many months of ease with the Eighth Illinois "featherbed regiment." He was on patrol in Missouri when a regimental guard captured some twenty rebels, and with them a gunnysack stuffed with the bones of federal soldiers. The bodies were headless, the men's skulls having been put to use as soup bowls, and this heinous, inexplicable sight stunned him. As he wrote to his sister, he had never experienced anything like this, and "I thank God from my heart that dear old Illinois knows nothing of the horrors of this war."

Since then he had gotten used to them, learned to live with them, and tried to remain unfazed by them. He divided his attention between the pandemonium of the battlefield and the interesting new sights and creatures he saw in camp. When he wasn't marking time in a rifle pit, he enjoyed foraging in the countryside, chasing down a local chicken or pig, and catching fish and taking a dip in a cool stream. He took care to examine the quality of the Georgia soil—"only fit for turnips"—and the live oak trees and the curious moss growing on them. He took offense at the ants and chiggers that bit him without remorse, and the ground worms that clung to him without apology, but did enjoy catching the occasional scorpion, along with "a reddish brown bug not quite as large as a thrush, and as savage as a mad rat."

Within a few weeks, though, he had to leave the company of his six-legged friends and return to marching. General Sherman had planned a bold stroke against the rebels, and ordered the Army of the Tennessee to execute a "general right wheel." They would swing wide to the east, through the towns of Marietta and Roswell, and arc southward toward Decatur, where the troops would break up the Georgia Railroad and stage a surprise assault against Atlanta. Within a few days, the army turned the wheel splendidly, outmaneuvering Joe Johnston's forces on the Chattahoochee and forcing him to abandon his Shoupades just as he had abandoned his other defensive works in north Georgia.

By mid-July the army was lodged in Decatur. Here they used picks, hammers, and crowbars to disassemble the tracks, place the ties around trees, and build a fire under them. They would throw the rails over the blaze, heat them to red-hot, and wrap them around the trunks with the aid of mules—turning them into corkscrews the rebels called "Sherman's neckties." They also destroyed depots and water tanks and anything else the rebel army might use to feed and resupply itself by rail.

The regiment then received word Jefferson Davis had replaced Joe Johnston as rebel commander with a fiery Texas general named John Bell Hood, who had lost the use of his arm at Gettysburg and his entire leg at Chickamauga. Hood despised the concept of retreat, at which Johnston had become quite adept in recent months, and vowed to take the fight to the Yankees and attack them on all fronts. Hood had already done so in the first of his sorties, at Peachtree Creek north of Atlanta on July 20. The Army of the Cumberland fought off his rebels in a brisk, bloody battle that claimed almost 2,000 Union casualties in only a few hours. Next it would be the turn of the Army of the Tennessee and Wills's 103rd Illinois regiment to face Hood's army—before anyone realized it or could have even expected it.

James McPherson's Army of the Tennessee wasn't supposed to halt in Decatur. William Sherman had explicitly told him his objective was Atlanta. But whether out of an abundance of caution or a failure of nerve, McPherson came up two miles short. A minimal force of 2,500 Confederate cavalrymen had somehow deterred a rapidly advancing Union army seven times that size, as McPherson opted for the safe choice once more, playing defense just as he did at Resaca.

Nonetheless, even though the army didn't quite make it to Atlanta, its aerial bombs did. Twenty-pounder Parrott guns fired their shells into town, announcing the arrival of the army's 15th Corps. And at the head of that corps, giving the order to fire, was Major General John Logan.

He ordered his 15th Corps to dig entrenchments on their defensive line to match those of the rebels, who had sealed the town in a great ring of fortifications, breastworks, and abatis—three to four rows of pointed stakes and lengthy cordon of chevaux-de-frise. These fearsome defenses presented as steep a challenge to the Army of the Tennessee as they did to the Army of the Cumberland several miles to the west. Of course, Logan would happily crush their defenders if given the opportunity. But the opportunity was fleeting, and vanished when—

Two divisions of Confederate infantry smashed against the far left of the Union line.

It was a surprise assault: John Bell Hood's opening gift to the Army of the Tennessee.

The rebels seemed to attack in several places at once. Confusion broke out at Union headquarters. Which of the corps—the 15th, 16th, or 17th—were engaged? Where was the line of Confederate advance? How close were the rebels to breaking the Union line? How the hell had they gotten there in the first place?

From a bird's-eye view, it looked like this:

- Logan's 15th Corps, on the Union right, faced a frontal attack from the west, mostly skirmishers at first.
- Frank Blair's 17th Corps, in the middle, saw some rebel activity between his troops and those and the 16th Corps.
- Grenville Dodge's 16th Corps, on the Union left, bore the brunt of the initial assault.

The rebels had been marching all night, in a great southeastern arc, to strike against Dodge's soldiers. The rebels should have easily flanked the federal troops and rolled up their line; instead, Dodge's soldiers were waiting for them.

By happy accident, Dodge had realigned his corps earlier that day to face the Confederate assault, and beat it back over the course of an hour.

By unhappy accident, Frank Blair had not done the same with his corps, and now a rift opened between the 16th and 17th Corps. The rebels surged through the half-mile gap in the federal line—a gap equal in size to the one the rebels had exploited at Chickamauga to crush the federals.

Disorder followed. As the insurgents poured into the hole, troops became separated from their regiments, orders became muddled and contradictory, and corps leader Blair was nowhere to be seen on the field of combat. Instead he issued commands from his headquarters through signal officers. But if ever there was a time for a Union general to make his presence felt, it was now.

The general who did emerge to find out where the rebels were, and the exact location of the gap, was James McPherson. The leader of the Army of the Tennessee left his headquarters and rode south with his signal officers, trying to pinpoint the location of Confederate attackers. He found them soon enough.

In a patch of woods that just minutes before had been held by the Union, McPherson galloped into a pocket of Confederate troops. They pointed their muskets at him and demanded he surrender.

He wheeled his horse. As it turned sharply, he bowed and tipped his hat like a gentlemen, then rode away.

A rebel corporal with deadly aim shot him in the back. McPherson took the bullet near his heart and fell from his horse. After several minutes of hemorrhaging on the ground, he offered his last words, and breath. The rebels picked his pockets clean and returned to their lines.

Word soon got out the Army of the Tennessee was headless.

Confederate General Pat Cleburne—Sherman's nemesis from Tunnel Hill—took quick advantage of McPherson's death and the half-mile gap in the Union center. He drove his brigades behind the 17th Corps to attack it from the rear.

Suddenly the 17th Corps had to fight in three directions at once—front, flank, and rear—an almost impossible task. The battle turned nasty and chaotic.

Near Flat Shoals Road, Union troops realized their breastworks would do them no good when their enemy was shooting them in the back. They clambered over the works and, with their backs to Atlanta, took aim at the rebels charging from the east. As the rebels surged into their trenches, the federals pounced. They opened up on their attackers from close range, trying to drive them back. If that didn't work, they grabbed on to their uniforms, hauled them over their works, and savaged them into submission.

Other federal units weren't so lucky. Rebels surrounded several Union squads and companies and forced them to collapse or retreat. They also enveloped hundreds of troops in the Iowa 16th infantry and made prisoners out of the entire regiment.

The Union line became scattered and jagged, with some troops fighting on the east side of their works and some on the west, and trading sides several times during the afternoon as the fighting ebbed and flowed. Soldiers surrendered to troops who had surrendered to them just minutes before, and the opposing lines became as vague and diffuse as an inkblot—red instead of black.

The number of killed and wounded increased by one every two seconds for three hours.

Amid the tumult, General Charles Walcutt's brigade from the 15th Corps turned south to assist the 17th Corps. Captain Wills was in the brigade. He watched as the unit's massive twenty-four-pounder howitzers unleashed a blinding sheet of flame at the insurgents every time they advanced. They held back four rebel charges and took more than a hundred prisoners—all while shifting positions, east, west, and south. The Confederates came from almost every angle, and Walcutt's brigade repulsed them every time.

Among the fallen rebels, they found General McPherson's field glasses, hat, and dispatches, which had briefly been stolen from him by corpse robbers. Another brigade found McPherson's body later that day.

Wills was pleased by the success of his unit, but this was hard and brutal work—the kind he hadn't seen any time in the war, even at Kennesaw Mountain. Their foes fought with such intensity, such desperation, that only the perseverance and resolve of battle-hardened veterans like those in his regiment could force the attackers back.

Beyond the battle itself, there were sights he would never forget. One occurred when the troops found a Union boy in a ditch, with a bullet in his leg and several slashes to his face. Amazingly, the boy wasn't dead. Instead, he leaned up and smiled at his colleagues. He claimed he had shot a rebel officer, and received a gun blast and three spade blows for his trouble. But he had gotten his man, and he was delighted, despite all the blood.

Just west, a different group of federal troops set its defensive line at the apex of Bald Hill, a critical position where field guns like howitzers could rake their enemies with deadly fire. The knoll was the key to the fight, for if it were captured, the entire battle might be lost—or much more. Both sides knew how important the hill was, and it was here that 2,000 troops unleashed their most aggressive and wanton violence.

In some places the opposing forces stood twenty feet apart, or even less. They fixed bayonets, and fought hand to hand with "clubbed muskets, fisticuffs and wrestling." It wasn't a battle, it was a gunfight, a knife show, a boxing match. Boys pummeled each other with rifle butts, smashed each other with boot leather—wrestled, crushed, and choked.

The hellscape darkened when a fog of gunpowder clouded the field. Now the boys were almost indistinguishable in places. Attackers emerged from the smoke bearing steel blades, others were shot in the face. Rebel cannonballs from Atlanta hit rebels in the field. Officers cut throats with dress swords. Privates emptied chambers into corpses. A general hoisted an American flag—and got shot in the eye.

It became a close-range bloodbath, a hand-to-hand hecatomb. Troops fought without orders and swarmed and charged and collapsed in a grand surging vicious organism.

Amid the pandemonium, the Union boys learned who was now in charge of their army. Word spread through the ranks: Sherman had picked John Logan.

Logan had no time to celebrate. He took the reins of his horse Slasher and galloped south to confer with Dodge and Blair. They forged a plan to seal the gap in the Union center, just as—

The rebels tore a hole in the Union right—Logan's corps—when he wasn't there.

A fighting pastor named Lightburn, who temporarily ran the Second Division, was partly to blame. When the rebels charged into the railroad cut that ran through the center of the 15th Corps' line, he panicked and sprinted to the rear. His men followed in disorderly retreat—and a new Union gap opened up.

The attackers seized sixteen field guns and wheeled them around to set flame to the federals. Artillery blasts led to more panic, as the rebels took the Union's breastworks, kept coming, and seized prisoners. A boy in blue asked one in gray, "Are you going to kill all of us?" The answer was yes.

More Union troops retreated and saw "a great stream of grey pouring through the railroad cut." They were on the run, the fighting 15th, Logan's old boys, Sherman's older boys, in headlong retreat.

Sherman watched from his headquarters, just north. He still had tens of thousands of men on hand, held in reserve: the entire Army of the Ohio, and a few fresh brigades from the Army of the Cumberland. He did nothing, stood and watched. "Let the Army of the Tennessee fight it out," he said.

Then the Confederates captured more terrain, more prisoners, more Yankee courage. Sherman still refused to call the Ohio's infantry to rescue them. Instead he called on their batteries.

Sherman took personal command of the reserve artillery. He lined them up, gave them their targets, and sent shot and shell into rebel lines. Sherman fired his cannonade from beyond the Union far right, an unexpected angle, and tore the Johnny Rebs to pieces.

Then, the moment came. Logan arrived on horseback—

"on a coal-black charger streaked with foam, hatless, his long black hair flying, his eyes flashing with wrath—a human hurricane on horseback"

The boys screamed "Black Jack! Black Jack!"

He did not disappoint. He screamed, he exhorted, he drove, he propelled. He galloped up and down the line demanding his boys charge—for "McPherson and revenge!"

The troops whooped and cried, followed him as he went. Those who didn't attack got a smack from the flat side of his sword and a few sharp oaths. Then Logan offered more oaths for the Confederates—the damned rebels, the *goddamned* enemy—and he set his divisions into hard, unstoppable motion.

Logan rode and screamed till his voice nearly gave way, and held sway over the field. His troops counterattacked the Confederates and forced them to retreat and give up all but eight of the guns they had captured. They returned to their original lines shoddy, broken, and exhausted.

The line between triumph and tragedy was a thin one. Rebel victory over the 15th Corps had nearly been at hand. But Logan and his horse, and the inexhaustible work of his boys, prevented it.

By the end of the evening, July 22, the Battle of Atlanta was over. Three-thousand seven-hundred Union troops lay dead and wounded, and an uncertain number of Confederates—perhaps 6,000—had fallen as well. John Bell Hood's second sortie against the Yankees ended in failure. And John Logan became the new commander of the Army of the Tennessee.

But not for long. A few days later, when the time came to choose a permanent commander for that army, Sherman ignored the pleas of many of the Tennessean troops and chose—

Oliver O. Howard.

This was a surprise. Howard had no experience in the Army of the Tennessee. He was last seen in charge of the 20th Corps, and before that the 11th Corps and its many German troops, and before that, he had contributed to the debacle at Chancellorsville. He was a good man, losing an arm to combat and known as a kindly "Christian general," but his record was, at best, mixed. And he was no John Logan.

Logan did not take the news well. He beseeched Sherman to let him keep control of his beloved army at least through the end of the Atlanta campaign, but Sherman refused. His mind was set. Howard would take over command, and Logan would go back to running the 15th Corps.

Grenville Dodge found Logan soon after at his headquarters, grim and dejected. Logan fumed that despite all his success as a general, despite all the praise and adulation of the press and public—and most important, his boys!—Sherman had once again undermined him. And publicly this time.

Of course, Sherman had sent him a note that praised his soldierly qualities—and offered *no hard feelings*, in a matter of speaking—but

Logan did not find succor in such words. His grudge only deepened when he found out the real reason he had been forced from power: George Thomas.

Thomas had never forgotten how disdainful and contemptuous Logan had been to him about the Tennessee railroad matter. Over the course of months, he had nursed his grudge and fed it with new and imagined slights, until Logan became an insufferable foe. He acknowledged the former congressman's martial skills, but still didn't like him one bit. Thomas told Sherman that Oliver Howard was a good choice to command the Army of the Tennessee—"he is tractable and we can get along with him." But if Sherman were to give permanent command of that army to Logan, Thomas would quit. Sherman respected Thomas's threat and demoted Logan back to his old job. The Rock of Chickamauga had crushed him.

Later, Sherman salted the wound to his pride. He privately described men like Logan and Frank Blair as "civilians" and "ambitious men" and, even worse, "active politicians." He later wrote that while Logan had excellent skills as a battlefield warrior, he had less talent for logistics and strategy—and all three were critical to military command. He had summed up his philosophy in a letter to his brother several months earlier, writing that the value of a proper military education far exceeded that of gaining a field commission: "The army is a good school, but West Point is better."

Oliver Howard took command of the Army of the Tennessee but stayed in the background, letting field generals like Logan get the attention and many of the laurels. The enlisted men, of course, still adored Logan and many didn't understand why he hadn't been able to keep his job. They all had vivid and unforgettable experiences with their leader on the battlefield.

Charles Wills was a particular loyalist, and remembered how at Dallas, in the hottest part of the fight, "Logan came dashing up along our line, waved his hat, and told the boys to 'give them hell, boys.' You should have heard them cheer him." He stopped near Wills and asked, "It's all right, damn it, isn't it?" The captain told him it was. And a few days later, Wills saw Logan again and saluted. The general smiled and bowed in return.

Wills may have preferred Logan, but he was willing to give Howard a chance: "I think we'll like Howard first rate. If he is as good as McPherson, he'll do." Howard had a chance to prove his worth shortly after gaining command of the army, when Sherman ordered him to lead his troops on another great turn of the wheel—this time from the east side of Atlanta to the west, in a grand half-circle, counterclockwise around the town. The goal, as ever, was to seize control of more Confederate rail lines and destroy them.

When the federals reached Lick Skillet Road, they came upon an almshouse and a little house of worship called Ezra Church. Howard decided to entrench the army there, despite Sherman telling him the rebels would never attack so soon after such a devastating loss as the one a few days before. But Howard's instinct was right: A new Confederate corps commander named Stephen D. Lee chose that place to assault the federal line.

Commander Lee was no relation to Robert E. in genes or talent, and his leadership proved it. He sent wave after wave, division after division, of Southern troops to face the dug-in federal soldiers. Volleys of Union rifle fire greeted them, along with brutal rounds of shot, shell, and canister fire. As successive waves attacked, hundreds of Southerners fell in a great onslaught. It wasn't even a battle, it was a "turkey shoot." Or as one rebel soldier put it, "the Yankees had us like sittin' ducks on a pond, out in the open, and we could only see the smoke from their guns and muskets." Another called it "a perfect slaughter."

During the battle, Logan whipped up the enthusiasm of his boys in the 15th Corps, and the Army of the Tennessee held its position until the Confederates finally retreated in a bloody, broken mass. Charles Wills was in the thick of it, but to him the fight was far from glorious. As he wrote, "I am tired of seeing such butchery but if they will charge us that way once a day for a week, this corps will end the war in this section."

John Bell Hood's third sortie failed, in dreadful and dispiriting fashion. He caused more casualties in ten days of command than Joe Johnston had in ten weeks. No one knew exactly how many troops Bell sent to their deaths or to hospital beds. It was at least 10,000 and possibly many more.

The Union army took advantage of another rebel loss and extended its noose further around Atlanta, moving ever closer to cutting off its railroad supply lines. Now only two such routes entered the town from the south. Sherman just had to turn the wheel once more.

For the moment he could not. Both sides, injured and weary from the recent battles, settled in behind their field works. Sherman found no success with a further advance at Utoy Creek or with four cavalry attacks. So he decided to besiege Atlanta instead.

Union generals moved twenty-pounder Parrott field guns and other heavy-duty artillery to high positions overlooking the town and fired mercilessly at it. Often the shells and shot hit indiscriminately with unclear results—small explosions or smoke wafts in the distance. Reports indicated the rebels had well concealed their munitions stores and supply houses, and that most of the artillery rounds hit wide of the mark. But Sherman kept the guns in action for an entire month.

Logan oversaw the batteries of the 15th Corps as they did their demolition work, but his mind was elsewhere. His mind continued to harbor dark feelings for Sherman, and his grievances only seemed to mount. In the recent battle, his troops had praised him, his efforts had achieved great success, and even Oliver Howard said the victory at Ezra Church was "as much attributable to him as to any one man." Still, Sherman ruled supreme, and Logan found his dominion insufferable. He wrote to his wife, Mary, that the commander of the western armies was "an infernal brute" who lionized army bureaucrats from West Point above all others. Logan also began making plans for life after the army, which might come sooner rather than later.

Captain Wills, however, was again enjoying his adventures in the army during the siege. He had escaped his two battles of the 15th Corps with no major wounds, and felt once again relaxed and confident in their success. And he ate well, too—dining on potatoes and mixed vegetables, and even had his "extraordinary dreams" fulfilled with green corn and blackberries and sundry other edibles. The troops' stomachs were full, their clothes were clean and new, and there were plenty of rations to go around.

His men had a surplus of ammunition, too, and plenty of targets for it. He estimated the rebels fired one bullet for every forty of the Union's, as the Southern troops spent their time hunkered down in their trenches, "studying devilment." His regiment's artillery now bombarded Atlanta day and night.

By the end of August, the field guns of the 103rd Illinois and those of many other regiments had worn down the Confederates enough that Sherman gave up the siege. He would now make his final move against the town and its remaining railroad lines.

On August 25 Sherman's field and siege guns went silent. The rebels, who had grown used to their murderous, indiscriminate volleys and random explosions, could scarcely believe it. The next morning they found the federal lines deserted, the works cleared of Union troops, and the smell of gunpowder dissipated. Some of the more naive soldiers believed Sherman had simply given up, retreated, gone back to Ohio in shame. Others knew better, including the rebel commanders. The Union army was on the move somewhere, they just didn't know where.

Charles Wills and his regiment joined the rest of the Army of the Tennessee in leaving their field works in utter quietude. They muffled the wheels of their artillery, stripped their provisions down to the absolute essentials, and tried not to make a sound as they headed south, in another great arc that would nearly lead to a full revolution around Atlanta. The Army of the Tennessee was joined by the armies of the Cumberland and the Ohio—all pulling up stakes within a few hours of each other, under cover of darkness, and heading counterclockwise in a great curving motion, which Sherman called the "circle of desolation." Only one corps, the 20th, would remain behind to guard a rail bridge over the Chattahoochee River.

At some places in this advance southward, Wills and his Company C were only twenty-five yards from the rebels in their works, and could hear them chattering and rustling about. They camped near the Atlanta and West Point Railroad, one of the two lines still functioning around Atlanta. At noon the next day Sherman ordered them to destroy it. They did so with their bare hands, rending off the ties, stacking the wood, prying away the iron rails, and alighting the pile—then twisting the rails to create a tangle of Sherman's neckties where there had once been a railroad.

Closer to Atlanta, the Army of the Ohio was doing the same thing to the other railway still supplying the town, the Macon and Western Railroad. At a junction called Rough and Ready, the Ohio boys severed the line and cut off Atlanta from the rest of the South. Sherman had just achieved one of his major strategic objectives, and he wasn't finished yet.

Throughout the campaign, Sherman's former unit, the Army of the Tennessee, had ranged the widest around Atlanta, and now in the circle of desolation it occupied the outer ring of the federal attack. It lodged just outside the hamlet of Jonesboro, near the Macon rail line sixteen miles from town—and waited.

On the last day of August, John Bell Hood ordered William Hardee's rebel corps to assault the 20,000-strong federal line. Again, as at Ezra Church, the Confederates sent wave after wave of troops to attack the entrenched federal forces of the Army of the Tennessee, and wave after wave of them fell in a bloodbath. The Union batteries unloaded case shot, shell, and canister fire on the rebels' columns and devastated them. A Confederate soldier called it a "perfect hurricane of shot." A Union troop said it was "more like a butchery than a battle." By the end of the day, the Confederate forces were exhausted, almost spent. Wills said they had "lost a large mea[s]ure of vim, which counts a good deal in soldiering. Our loss in this fight is comparatively nothing."

When the sun rose again on Jonesboro, Sherman moved two corps from the Army of the Cumberland to finish the job. The first, led by an irascible general ironically named Jefferson Davis, smashed into the rebel lines from the north flank, rolling up their lines with merciless efficiency. Like the pandemonium at Bald Hill, the battle became a bloody scrum, as the opposing sides and troops resolved to crush each other with their fists and knives as well as their muskets. In the melee, Union troops fixed bayonets and stabbed and slashed at their enemy with mad fury, while officers on horseback gutted soldiers with their swords or fired revolvers at point blank range. As one observer saw it, "men acted like infuriated devils."

The Union surged deep into the rebel ranks, and the Confederates could not stop them. They smothered their foes from the north and west, nearly enveloping them in a murderous embrace that came close to annihilating the entire Southern force. A backup Union corps was due to deliver the final blow from the east, but it arrived too late in the day to take part. As Wills saw it, "Three hours more of daylight and Hardee would have had no corps left." The sun set on the Confederates after their monumental loss.

The next morning they were gone. John Bell Hood's army had escaped the noose by retreating to Lovejoy's Station farther south on the Macon line. But Atlanta had not escaped. Sherman now had the town under his control, and subject to his whim.

John Logan and his troops celebrated the victory with great joy. The 15th Corps had played a critical role in the battle on the first day of Jonesboro, fending off repeated attacks while Logan charged down the line in his signature fashion, exhorting his boys to fight while they responded with whoops of "Logan! Logan! Hurrah for Black Jack Logan!" His corps sustained only 200 losses—one-tenth the number of the rebels assaulting them.

Ten days later Logan gave a speech to his corpsmen in which he exalted them and their accomplishments, saying "The marches and labors performed by you during this campaign will hardly find a parallel in the history of war." He lauded their strength, courage, and fortitude to meet any test, and the character they had shown to defend the nation and crush the forces of treason and secession. The Atlanta campaign had concluded, and another was soon to follow. He told his boys they were assured of success in their next endeavor, and reuniting the country would doubtless be the highlight of their young lives.

He did not mention he would not be joining them. A few days later, he took leave from the army and went home to Illinois.

EIGHT

THE ANVIL

I n the early morning hours of September 2, the sky above Atlanta caught fire. From Decatur to Jonesboro all the way to Macon, Georgians in the region heard the sounds of warfare—artillery rounds igniting, bombs shaking the ground for miles around. Pillars of flame soared over the horizon, plumes of cinders rose to great heights, and the fog of gunpowder cast an eerie pall over the shadows of chimneys and the skeletons of buildings.

The next morning the smoke clung low to the ground, and in the dim cadaverous light Atlanta's citizens could see what had happened to their town when the Confederate army withdrew. Five train engines and more than eighty boxcars lay in ruin. Millions of cartridges had ignited, thousands of shells had exploded, and even more rounds of ammunition sat ominously on the ground waiting for someone to trigger them. Food, cotton, and medical supplies were melted, burned and wasted, and acres of homes and businesses around the rail yard were incinerated.

The inferno had started when John Bell Hood ordered his supply train to be destroyed just before his army left town, to keep the Yankees from taking the weapons and provisions. Now they sat in ruin, along with a fair portion of eastern Atlanta.

Into this dystopia marched the troops of the 20th Corps of the U.S. Army. Far from being stunned by the town's landscape, they were delighted. They marched in with smiles on their faces and patriotic tunes on their lips, giving praise to Old Glory and threatening to hang Jeff Davis from a sour apple tree. As the lone holdout of the various corps that had marched south to conquer Hood at sites like Rough and Ready and Jonesboro, they had spent the last week with their backs to the Chattahoochee River, guarding against a rebel attack. By this fluke they were the first army unit to enter the town, to accept the mayor's formal surrender, and to report the good news, as William Sherman would soon announce to the rest of the nation: "Atlanta is ours, and fairly won."

The soldiers of the 82nd Illinois Volunteer Infantry marched in among the dozens of regiments in the 20th Corps. They spared no ceremony, hoisting their flags and playing their songs, relieved and overwhelmed to be finished at last with the long hard slog of the Atlanta campaign—four months after it began. And no one was more proud than their commander, Lieutenant Colonel Edward Salomon.

Salomon led a regiment that had a cosmopolitan cast: There were, of course, plenty of Germans including Hessians, Bavarians, and Württembergers, from different parts of Illinois—Peoria, Bloomington, Belleville, as well as Chicago—and a sizable group from St. Louis, Missouri. Scandinavians had their own company, thick with Swedes and Norwegians, while Swiss sharpshooters formed a small and effective unit, and German Jews from Chicago organized their own company. It made for a diverse group of soldiers, missing only the colonel who had first commanded the regiment. He was nowhere near the front lines.

These days Friedrich Hecker resided on his farm in Belleville, Illinois, having left the U.S. Army six months before. He had nursed such expansive dreams of wartime glory—of rising in rank to general, commanding a division or even a corps, and showing the mettle of an intellectual-revolutionary-warrior in combat—that his goals proved impossible to meet. Not only had he failed to achieve them, his regiment and brigade attracted the enmity of the much-despised nativists, who claimed all German troops were cowards. This infuriated Hecker, and only made him more determined to prove his critics wrong. But the battles at Chattanooga had proven nothing. His brigade missed out on the triumph at Lookout Mountain, sat in helpless reserve at Tunnel Hill, and arrived late to Wauhatchie. And it was the result of the latter battle in particular that finally drove him to quit the army in a fit of pique.

His nemesis had once again been his commanding general, Joseph Hooker, who submitted an official report well after the battles of Chattanooga. In it he criticized the late arrival of the brigades in Carl Schurz's division to relieve John Geary's corps under attack at Wauhatchie. When Hecker found out about the charges after they appeared in a newspaper some weeks later, his temper boiled over and he demanded an official court of inquiry to investigate the matter.

The court met in February 1864, but did nothing to give Hecker satisfaction. Instead it reasoned Hooker's charges "were not intended to apply to [Hecker] or his command." At around the same time, a new round of army promotions had gone through at Washington, and Hecker's name was not among them. Even his old ally President Lincoln didn't see fit to give him the much-coveted single star of a brigadier general. With his pride thus wounded, Hecker had no choice but to give up his command and go home to nurse his grievances.

However, despite his absence from the battlefield, Hecker maintained a keen interest in his former regiment, and kept up with its progress any way he could. He cheered the news that Joseph Hooker had quit the army, after Sherman had passed him over (along with John Logan) for command of the Army of the Tennessee. He also learned of the regiment's movements, conduct, and gossip by corresponding with Rudolf Mueller, the former dry-goods clerk who had recently been promoted from lieutenant to captain. Though still in his twenties and too young to be a 48er, Mueller was an expat and just as committed as Hecker to republican principles and ideals. Mueller was also a Turner, or part of the

Turnverein organization, which reflected many of the political ideals of the 48ers, and encouraged its members to partake in military-style drills, riflery competitions, and a strict physical fitness regimen that included gymnastics.

Though Mueller lionized Hecker, he had much less respect for his current commander, Edward Salomon. Mueller saw him as an upstart, a relentless self-promoter who would do anything to ingratiate himself with the army brass and tout his achievements on the battlefield. In his letters, Mueller stirred Hecker's resentments, casting doubt upon the leadership of the regiment, and yearning for the old days when his friend ran things with crisp martial efficiency. He made Salomon a target of his derision, and soothed Hecker's injured pride by assuring him that no such usurper could ever equal his gallant record.

When Salomon also wrote to Hecker and offered praise for his old commander, Mueller assured him that such "sycophantic loyalty" derived from Salomon's "colossal impudence." He only flattered him to curry favor—it was all a naked, fraudulent ploy!

There was, however, one uncomfortable fact that Mueller had to acknowledge about his nemesis. Namely, Salomon had displayed great moral courage and performed well on the battlefield—especially at Gettysburg, where in Hecker's absence due to injury, Salomon led a bayonet charge that drove the much-feared Louisiana Tigers from their rifle pits, and received official commendation for showing "the highest order of coolness and determination under very trying circumstances." Still, no matter how brave Salomon may have been in combat, Mueller refused to see his commander as anything but a social climber who had risen beyond his station.

When Hecker left the regiment in March 1864, Mueller vowed he would not serve under Salomon, and would take a firm and uncompromising stand against the usurper. Yet when Salomon selected him to be captain of Company E, Mueller accepted, reasoning the lieutenant colonel had no choice but to elevate those men who had shown superior leadership on the field of combat, such as himself.

Even with the promotion, Mueller kept his jaundiced view of Salomon. Somehow, the more success his commander had in combat, the more he despised him. Which meant he loathed him quite a bit indeed, for

Salomon had driven the rebels from the field at Resaca; fought until his last rounds of ammunition were exhausted at New Hope Church; hung on bravely in a losing cause at Kennesaw Mountain; and defended against repeated attacks at Peachtree Creek, to the ultimate victory of the Army of the Cumberland.

Through Salomon's leadership, the success of the 82nd Illinois became so apparent in the campaign that its soldiers were nicknamed "Hooker's ironclads" (though Hooker had quit). But even for this, Mueller gave little credit to the lieutenant colonel. Rather, he assigned the regiment's recent glory to the skills Friedrich Hecker had drilled into it, with his phantom presence still guiding the troops from his farm in Belleville.

Of course, not everyone in the regiment saw things the same way. Outside of the epistolary universe of Rudolf Mueller and Friedrich Hecker, Salomon attracted much ardor and loyalty. The now-captain of Company F, Eugene Weigel, summed it up for many of the men, seeing Salomon as "well liked. He always keeps his cool, is calm and collected, and that's what makes him different from [Hecker]." General Carl Schurz saw it the same way. To him, Salomon "was the only soldier at Gettysburg who did not dodge when Lee's guns thundered; he stood up, smoked his cigar, and faced the cannon balls with the sangfroid of a Saladin."

In much the same manner, Salomon showed his valor in the campaign for Atlanta, and after the rebels retreated, he entered the town with the confident demeanor of a successful leader. He had proven his value in the field and now could expect weeks of recuperation while Sherman's forces readied for their next campaign. The 82nd Illinois first took the role of guarding rebel prisoners who had been captured in the recent conflicts, and after that shored up the army's fieldworks to prevent a surprise insurgent attack. These should have been halcyon days, in which the regiment could rebuild from its losses, treat its wounded, and prepare for the next great endeavor. Instead, Lieutenant Colonel Salomon had to deal with a revolt from his officer ranks.

The mutineers, not surprisingly, included Rudolf Mueller, who saw his leader as nothing more than a "popularity-seeking blister." He and some of his fellow officers had signed their names to a petition demanding his resignation. They no longer wished to be led by a man who disregarded their requests for reassignment or sick leave, who sought popularity in such a vulgar fashion, and who seemed entirely dispensable to the regiment. They even proposed the unit be made into a smaller force, with Salomon's position eliminated!

Salomon responded by taking the petition, ripping it up into tiny pieces, and throwing them out the window of his headquarters. This only enflamed the officers even more, and they responded with a flurry of rumors and innuendo—that the lieutenant colonel had experienced bouts of sickness, had taken up with an unsavory local woman named Madam Löventhal, had received a beating in return from Mr. Löventhal, and so on. They even threw a party and sang cheerful songs of praise for their beloved Friedrich Hecker, drinking so many toasts to him that several officers collapsed under the table, as Salomon watched with chagrin.

Since these tactics did not seem to bend Salomon to the will of the renegade officers, Mueller sought a furlough from the regiment to return to Peoria. But no such leave would be granted him for some time. Indeed, he would remain unhappy in the army and continue to stir with discontent, to plot open and futile rebellion against his commander, and to make increasingly snide and cynical comments about the state of affairs in the army. He even derided the people of his adopted country, seeing them as "a miserable nation of shopkeepers, these citizens of the Republic, who lack almost completely all characteristics of genuine republicans."

It made for an awkward set of beliefs. Mueller had vowed to defend the revolutionary ideology, the rights of man, the equality of all people, yet when given the opportunity, he reverted back to the worst aspects of the Old World—the hierarchy of class and rank, favoring those with an elite background over middling "shopkeepers"; the privilege of title and status, favoring the man with the noble pedigree over the ambitious civil servant; and underlying it all, the primacy of religion, favoring the Christian over the Jew.

While Hecker had publicly decried anti-Semitism, Mueller openly espoused it, comparing the 82nd to a "synagogue" since its commander was Jewish and an entire company consisted of Jews. He did all he could to convert his hero to the foul tenets of anti-Semitism, from mocking the religion Salomon practiced to giving him insulting nicknames to suggesting a great man like Hecker had no business associating with *these people*. As he wrote to Hecker while in the trenches around Atlanta in August:

> My dear colonel, I believe it is finally time that you disassociate yourself from anything with a trace of the *Creole* from Jerusalem. These people, as clever, smart, and sly as they are, rejoice so little about the beauties of nature; one sees or hears little of them laughing heartily, just as little do they understand you, or recognize the traits of your character, and don't know to appreciate it.

Such tactics met with failure. For no matter how much men like Rudolf Mueller tried to insult or deride him, Edward Salomon remained steadfast in his leadership of the regiment. He had come this far and would not yield.

Like Hecker, Salomon was an immigrant from the German states, but by choice, not by exile. He arrived in America as a merchant from Hamburg in 1855, worked his way up to clerk, bookkeeper, and lawyer in Chicago, and became an alderman for the Sixth Ward—one of the youngest in the city's history. He had met innumerable kinds of people from different backgrounds, and felt comfortable in their presence. He committed to the protection of his constituents, regardless of their skin color, and had shown his heroism even before the war began, rescuing a black passenger from an angry white mob on a trolley, at some risk to his own life and safety.

As a politician, he reveled in the mishmash of peoples and languages and accents he heard, and resolved to bring this sense of the New World into his own regiment. When he took command of the 82nd Illinois, he promoted men based on their ability, not which language they spoke. Soon the regiment became integrated in its cultures, and speakers of one language captained men of a different language, until the 82nd Illinois was no longer strictly a German unit, but a polyglot, mixed-up hybrid of peoples and tongues where the only criterion that mattered was success on the field of combat, which the regiment had shown with stunning results.

It didn't surprise Salomon that for all these reasons—for violating the boundaries of class and religion, of rank and privilege, of the very hierarchies that protected the elite—the German old guard continued to try to quash his rise and stifle him. And Mueller was no different, no matter how young he may have been.

But in this new America, three years of unremitting warfare had changed everything. The old pillars of caste began to crumble, new divisions began to form, and people like Edward Salomon began to rise to the levels of their own ability. As the commander of the 82nd Illinois Volunteer Infantry, he had already shown his talent. And he would continue to run the regiment his way, and rip his foes' objections into little pieces whenever he was given the opportunity.

A few days after the 20th Corps entered Atlanta, John Hight arrived in the siege-blasted town for the first time. He came by train from Chattanooga on the Western & Atlantic Railroad, not knowing exactly where to find his 58th Indiana regiment, what its role was in occupying the town, or how it had performed in the recent battles. He had spent the month of August recovering from a long illness in his hometown of Bloomington, but only when he returned to the camp of his regiment did he truly feel like he was "getting back home again."

Hight's chapel, which the camp mechanics had designed for him, had a roof composed of forest brush and walls thick with pine branches. The pews were little more than wooden planks, but Hight saw them as a good place to hear the gospel he preached. Nearby, a boatyard held supplies for pontoon bridges, with the accompanying canvas and ropes stored in adjoining houses. These were critical supplies, for since the beginning of the Atlanta campaign, the 58th Indiana had been assigned the duty of pontoniers, building bridges over the rivers of Georgia to help Sherman's armies invade the Southern heartland.

Once Reverend Hight got his bearings, he undertook a tour of Atlanta, looking to explore the town that had been his army's objective in the recent campaign. He found it hard to believe it was ever a place of any importance. Although many of its foundries, machine shops, and factories survived, it looked particularly desolate now that its rail yard had been blasted to pieces, its major buildings stood broken and battered from the cannonade, and Union soldiers had dismantled many of its houses for building materials to construct their camps. Even the cemetery was a wreck, with grave markers overturned and vaults pillaged. Hight thought it was "a sickening, loathsome sight" and it put him in a contemplative mood: "When I die, I want to be buried in the ground. I want no vandals to gaze on my dead face, nor do I wish to have my mummy hawked in the markets of future generations. I prefer to return to mother dust."

There was no way to escape the aura of death in the town. The array of shell damage alone was monumental. The walls and ceilings of many homes and storefronts had collapsed. Preheated cannonballs known as "hot shots" had caused wooden structures to ignite, while shrapnel from overhead blasts had riddled hundreds of other buildings. Shells that had failed to detonate dug furrows and craters in the streets.

The residents themselves had dug shelters under their homes and gardens to keep safe from the blasts. They lived in these "gopher holes" for weeks at a time, subsisting on whatever food they were able to scrounge in the area or were given by the rebel army. The most unlucky Atlantans were those who stepped too close to the munitions shops or supply warehouses or the railway roundhouse—regular targets for Sherman's massive siege guns—or found themselves outside on the wrong day at the wrong hour. Anywhere from 100 to 500 civilians had died in the shelling, though no one could be sure since many bodies were vaporized or severed into countless pieces by the blasts.

The Union army had no interest in the citizens who remained. Many depended on seeking charity or scavenging for their survival, which was difficult since the federal soldiers had priority to forage in the region. The troops eventually stripped the larders and corrals of just about every private home and farmstead they could find, leaving few provisions and livestock for anyone else to glean.

In camp Reverend Hight witnessed a parade of women and children visiting—"lean, lank, cadaverous people" on the edge of starvation. They tried bartering with soldiers for meat and necessities like medicine, offering what supplies of butter, green beans, tomatoes, and grapes they possessed, but most came away empty-handed. The minister felt pity for them, but understood why the Yankee troops did so little to help them—many of their male relatives still threatened the Union just outside town as soldiers and guerrillas, and they had no desire to support the families of their enemies. Other Union troops became even more dismissive of local suffering when their own comrades arrived in camp after having escaped from the rebels' infamous Andersonville prison, 120 miles away. These men had been captured at the Battle of Atlanta and, after only a few months in captivity, now resembled living skeletons. In their destitute condition they hardened the hearts of the federal soldiers against the Georgians even more.

The doctor for the 58th Indiana, James Patten, remained wary of the town folk, but kept his heart open to them. He gave out as many free supplies of medicine as he could, and took note of the terrible conditions of the battered citizenry. Some of the local women sold themselves for food, others begged in the streets, and even children were reduced to penury. One particular memory etched his mind deeply—"a little girl some six or seven years old had a piece of the raw bloody meat in both hands devouring it with the eagerness of a starving dog."

The impoverished in Atlanta did not include the local elite. As Hight saw it, "The rich and great have fled and left these poor women to the tender mercies of the detested Yankees." Those who helped fund the war, who profited from human bondage, who had staffs and servants and slaves—they had escaped town before the armies arrived. Those who remained were often poor, and included both white and black people. Formerly enslaved men and women were happy to welcome the Union army, now that the chains of bondage had been lifted, but the federal army could not feed or house them any more than it could the homeless whites in town. Moreover, Atlanta still had a population of refugees from north Georgia who had fled the upstate carnage, as well as refugees from downstate who feared the carnage to come. General Sherman wanted nothing to do with any of them.

On September 7, Sherman issued an order of expulsion for the remaining citizens in Atlanta—3,000 people—who were to evacuate their town within three weeks. The order excluded pro-Union families and Northern sympathizers, but otherwise almost all the residents had to leave.

Sherman claimed military necessity for the order, that it would be too difficult to offer 1,500 rations a day to the locals as Hood's army had, that countless subversives and guerrillas could if they lingered disrupt the work of the Union army, and that Atlanta's current breastworks required 30,000 soldiers to occupy. By tightening the fortifications just to surround the railroad facilities and the military-industrial plant, he could hold the town with one-sixth as many men. The logic of his order was clear, the strategy sound, the morality dubious. While Atlanta held some 20,000 people in the early summer, many had fled during the siege, and only about one percent of them would remain after the evacuation.

On September 26, the Union army effected the order, and all but fifty families left by train, by mule-drawn wagons, on horseback, and on foot, scrambling out of town to avoid being arrested. In many cases the destruction or dismantling of their houses had already left them homeless, and many had to abandon their remaining possessions because they would not all fit in a train car or wagonload. So by the time they got to outlying stops like Rough and Ready, many were in dire condition—the picture of poverty on the move.

Hood called Sherman's order an act of "studied and ingenious cruelty" unparalleled in "the dark history of war." Southern politicians and newspapers widely denounced the move, and even a few Northern soldiers and reporters condemned it. The Ohio newspaper that just three years before had pronounced Sherman insane now claimed he hadn't just invaded Atlanta, he had walked all over it. In the Union armies, the reaction was mostly positive, with the officers delighted to have dibs on the better, intact houses in town for their headquarters and the enlisted men free from caring for, or being troubled by, the desperate citizens in their midst.

Reverend Hight was not surprised by the brutality of the occupation and evacuation. He understood the depths of depravity the war had caused. He had seen it close-up in the field, and had borne witness to sights so horrifying he would have found them hard to fathom just a few years before. Atlanta was only the latest chapter in the dark volume of this war, with each turn of the page bringing a new and unexpected surprise or atrocity. Yet he persisted as minister. Nothing he saw would dissuade him from serving the troops.

Someone, after all, had to steer them away from the temptations of liquor, vice, sacrilege, and other sins that seemed to multiply daily. As he reflected, "sometimes it seems that His Satanic Majesty is in full control of our Regiment, and that his emissaries are especially engaged in creating trouble in camp." Yet he was more than a moral policeman, and had a higher calling in the war. For he was part of the ground crew smashing the machinery of slavery, in body and spirit.

He harbored no doubts about his purpose. It was one thing to preach the gospel and decry slavery from the comforts of a church in Indiana. It was quite another to come upon it where it lived and thrived and prospered—to attack in its homeland, and to help annihilate it. And he didn't need a gun, either.

A year before, still early in his ministry to the troops, he had been teaching former slaves to read, in a school he had set up in camp in Tennessee. They had been deprived of education by their masters, but learned quickly, using a *Bible Reader* to understand words and sentence structure. For Hight, this was his own contribution to the battle against human bondage, and he knew that "by this process the institution of slavery is surely being overthrown."

Since then, he had come to the aid of newly freed men and women on several occasions, encouraged the soldiers to help them as they could, and denounced anyone who profited from the trade in human flesh. And that made it easier to justify the wrongs done to Atlanta and other Southern towns. As he said regarding the miseries of the war and their effect on the Confederate homeland, "Why does God permit these things? It is because they are the champions of slavery, and we of freedom. The story of the war is long, but the moral is short."

Increasingly, he found himself among many ministers and soldiers and even generals who felt the same way. They had seen slavery in practice and it repulsed them. It caused them to endorse actions that, whether by military necessity or simple revenge, they might never have contemplated in earlier years: burning homes and plantations, stealing livestock from corrals, treating the enemy as something less than human. Sherman was their agent, their proxy, the man on horseback who lit the flame.

However, unlike Sherman, Hight wanted to see black soldiers in the field by the thousands. He cheered the recruitment of U.S. Colored Infantry regiments, demanded fair treatment for freedmen, and encouraged black men in or out of uniform who fought back against unfair treatment by the Union army. And he would do anything necessary to wipe out the scourge of human bondage, making abolition central to his gospel, standing in alliance with an angry Lord above:

> Slavery is a sin against man—against God. It is one of the most vile of all crimes. It is not only a sin itself, but hinders all virtue and breeds all vice. It opposes religion, education and virtue. It is the great crime of America. We can not be successful until it is utterly overthrown. Many wrongs have been, and still are, heaped upon the negro race. We must change our course and repent before God, and make restitution, before we can hope for complete success.

To help him forge this ideology of war and liberation in its molten state, Reverend Hight became involved with the U.S. Christian Commission, which distributed Bibles and religious literature to the troops, and sometimes dispensed food and other provisions. Like Hight himself, many of its field agents were ministers on leave from their congregations who spread an evangelical version of Christianity, praying with the troops and promoting a gospel of personal salvation.

Like so many other things that were not under his control, General Sherman had no patience for the group. Before the outset of the Atlanta campaign, when representatives from the organization had tried to book train travel to Chattanooga to reach the troops, he had forbidden it, writing, "There is more need of gunpowder and oats than any moral or religious instruction." After leaders of the Commission appealed to him personally, asking if they could at least send religious texts to camp, his reply was curt: "rations and ammunition are much better." But even though Sherman tried to forbid their proselytizing, they persisted in it. With the aid of nurses and surgeons in the field, the U.S. Christian Commission eventually got a foothold in Sherman's army and began to spread its version of The Word.

Reverend Hight gave the group whatever support he could muster. He also formed a regimental Christian organization that functioned as a sort of private brotherhood, distributed hundreds of the Commission's Bibles to the troops of the 58th Indiana, and spoke at the group's gatherings, preached at its rallies, and advanced its cause publicly, writing "Long may the Christian Commission flourish."

Abolition and Christianity now allied in a way they had never done before the war—fulfilling their vision through martial action. Since many of the missionaries from the North were also abolitionists, they developed close ties with ministers like Hight who were ardent foes of slavery, and together promoted the idea that the Lord desired above all else the destruction of slavery. Lighting a plantation on fire, therefore, was no longer an act of arson; it was an offering to God against the sin of slavery. And liberating a slave, or aiding him when he liberated himself, was no longer a distraction from the military's core duties; it was the job of any God-fearing Christian soldier. The Christian Commission created a muscular role for religion on the front lines, and ministers like John Hight were proud to use it to spread the gospel and aid the cause of human equality—seeing the demise of human bondage as a moral imperative, no matter the bloodshed, destruction, or violence it unleashed.

The principal unleasher of such carnage was, of course, General Sherman—though he made for an odd sort of liberator. Before the war, and often during it, he derided abolitionists, insulted and disparaged black people, and had no particular affection for ministers. His wife, Ellen, was a practicing Catholic and raised their children in the faith, but Sherman himself cared little about whatever deity there may have been, and, in any case, he didn't expect any god to rank him very highly after what he had done in the war. His enemies openly rooted for him to go to hell, and he just shrugged in response. As he told John Logan, "if we can't subdue these Rebels and the rebellion, the next best thing we can do is all go to hell together."

Far from being blind to the impression he made on his enemies, however, Sherman remained sharply aware of it, honed it, and crafted it with precision. They called him a tyrant—he laid waste to entire towns and cities. They called his actions infamous—he bombed civilians and turned them into refugees. They accused him of lunacy—he dressed like a rogue and behaved erratically. But no matter how severe their insults became, Sherman wore them as an ironic badge, with a touch of bemusement. Their contempt only fueled him.

Unlike Reverend Hight, Sherman despised the rebels not for their defense of slavery, but *because* they were rebels. As he wrote to the Confederate general Hood, he would never relent in his fight against them because they "in the midst of Peace and prosperity have plunged a nation into War, dark and cruel War, . . . dared and badgered us to battle, insulted our Flag, seized our arsenals and forts" and committed other transgressions that made them unworthy of mercy or leniency. He made it even more plain to General Henry Halleck: "If the people raise a howl against my barbarity & cruelty, I will answer that War is War & not popularity seeking. If they want Peace, they & their relations must stop War"—which meant unconditionally surrendering to him, which he knew would never happen. Not without a great deal of bloodshed and devastation first.

He had gotten quite skilled at ravaging the Southern heartland in recent years. It began on a large scale in Jackson, Mississippi, where by his own admission he ordered the ruin of crops and farmland for 30 miles around. Then in February 1864, it was the turn of Meridian, Mississippi, where he staged a massive raid that destroyed more than a hundred miles of railroad track, sixty-one bridges, three sawmills, and countless other private and military structures; his troops foraged liberally through the countryside; and he ensured the town would be unusable as a base for any future rebel operations. As Sherman relayed in his official report, "Meridian, with its depots, store-houses, arsenal, hospitals, offices, hotels, and cantonments, no longer exists."

Meridian was a warm-up for what was to come. Foraging had been an essential part of his armies' ability to live off the land, and arson too had a role in punishing the families of insurgents by annihilating their homes and property. Now Sherman would employ both tools as part of a new plan that would devastate the industrial and agricultural heart of Georgia. But before he could fully develop his idea, he had to put it on hold. He had to do something about John Bell Hood first.

After his armies lost more than 10,000 men in four battles spread over six weeks in the summer of 1864, John Bell Hood could well have been fired by Jefferson Davis. His aggressive strategy of attacking an enemy with superior numbers had been a disaster, and some of his troops called him incompetent at best, a butcher at worst. Yet even with his men in retreat, he held on to command. And by the end of September, he devised a new strategy to ensnare Sherman's forces. Instead of launching another insane sortie against them, he would lead them on a chase.

Hood knew Sherman's forces depended on a long, tenuous supply line, the Western & Atlantic Railroad, for their food, weapons, and provisions. By taking his remaining Confederate troops upstate and waging war against the rail line itself, along with the Union garrisons that protected it, Hood might possibly lure Sherman into a pursuit that would exhaust his army, or at least hamper it. It was hardly the sort of strategy that would lead to monumental victories, but it would distract Sherman and put his railroad under threat, and ultimately threaten his occupation of Georgia and, perhaps, Tennessee. On September 29, Hood marched north and began to execute his plan, and a few days later, Sherman had no choice but to follow him.

The rebel commander marched north and ruined depots at Big Shanty and Acworth and tried to capture a storehouse at Allatoona. Sherman had to divide his armies in response, sending George Thomas and part of the Army of the Cumberland to Nashville to protect Tennessee, while he led the rest of his troops to go after Hood. Only a single Union corps remained to protect Atlanta.

Sherman soon discovered he was chasing after a phantom, since Hood would not accept battle and his army proved too elusive to slow down, much less destroy. They advanced into north Georgia and ruined the tracks between Kingston and Resaca, waylaid any Yankees they could find, and put the garrison at Dalton under threat. They soon forced it to surrender, in one of the more shameful moments of the war.

Three-quarters of the Dalton garrison comprised black soldiers of the 44th U.S. Colored Infantry, part of a unit that had fought off the rebels in the August attempt to raid the town. Now in October, the rebels returned and their attacks met with success. While the white Union officers who surrendered received leniency, Hood promised no such treatment for the 600 black troops who laid down their arms. To rebel cries of "Kill every damn one of them!" the Confederates stripped their clothes, took their shoes as their own, and sent them on a perilous march back into captivity. Many went to Mississippi, still more to parts unknown, and the great majority died along the way—victims of sudden executions, or being worked to death, or other gross brutality and mistreatment. As a Charleston newspaper later reported, "the men of the army were in favor of hanging the last one of them on the nearest [tree] limbs."

These actions shocked and horrified many Northern soldiers and the public, but didn't surprise Sherman. In fact, he would have preferred there were no black soldiers at all in the western theater. He could tolerate some U.S. Colored Infantry troops manning garrisons, but would not go any further. President Lincoln and General Grant tried to argue for their expanded role on the front lines or anywhere else the army needed troops, but Sherman remained inflexible. The black man to him was "not the equal of the white man," and he would brook no dissent from the policy he had set. He would stick with the views he had laid out in July, in a controversial letter that found its way into the newspapers, regarding his prohibition on black men on the battlefield.

No one shall infer from this that I am not the friend of the negro as well as the white race. I contend that the treason and rebellion of the master freed the slave; and I and the armies I have commanded have conducted to safe points more negroes than those of any other general officer in the army, but I prefer some negroes as pioneers, teamsters, cooks, and servants,

others gradually to experiment in the art of the soldier, beginning with the duties of local garrison . . .

He had opened the door just a crack, but no more. If Lincoln didn't
like his approach, he would have to publicly fire him, and Sherman
knew that would never happen—not after the rousing success of capturing Atlanta, in the critical weeks before the presidential election.
Sure enough, Lincoln treated his disobedience gently, trying to mildly
persuade his subordinate to accept the arming of black men, and ending
one message to Sherman with the feeble request, "May I ask, therefore,
that you will give your hearty co-operation?"

But he would neither agree nor cooperate. He had become an icon
to the North, and his fame gave him free rein to maintain his policy
on black troops. If anything, that was the easy part. The hard part was
in changing the course of the war altogether. For in the early days of
October, he finally had the opportunity to develop his bold new plan—a
blueprint for destruction that would concern Ulysses S. Grant and deeply
trouble President Lincoln.

Sherman's own disgust at the current state of the war sped the creation of
the plan. He despised following Hood around the countryside, scurrying
after that "whole batch of devils" who tormented Union garrisons, damaged infrastructure, and terrorized anyone in or out of uniform associated
with the federal government. One day Hood and his cavalry might lay
waste to a depot or storehouse, the next day his infantry might pillage a
Union-held town, and Sherman would have to send his men trotting after
the rebels—trying to force them into a battle that never came, or at least
trying not to make the Union occupation of Georgia look like a bad joke.
But this was not the soul of proper warfare! He wanted desperately to take
the initiative, not to respond to his enemy's erratic travels. He would no
sooner accept being on the defensive than he would losing a battle, and this
entire campaign in October—which had no name other than the "pursuit
of Hood in Georgia"—felt like one long, depressing waste of time.

Almost since Hood's upstate journey began, Sherman had been trying
to convince Grant, Lincoln, and Henry Halleck of a different approach.

He argued for a war against the Southerners' resources and infrastructure, against their crops and cattle, to demoralize their home front, and cripple their production of foodstuffs and armaments. But as Grant had ordered in March, with Lincoln's strong assent, the destruction of Confederate *armies* remained paramount. The rebel infantry, batteries, and cavalry had started the war, and winning it meant defeating them.

Increasingly, though, Sherman failed to see the logic in this. Armies depended on logistics and on their supply lines, and by cutting out the heart of their infrastructure and resources, they could bring the Confederates to their knees. Hadn't he done so in Atlanta? Hadn't he brutalized that town with a siege and occupation and destroyed its war-fighting capability, even though Hood's army escaped? Yes, while his original goal had been, in the words of writer Shelby Foote, to hammer the rebels against the anvil of Atlanta, didn't they have just as much success in pounding the anvil itself? Why not do the same thing elsewhere in Georgia? Why not bring Atlanta to the rest of the South?

This didn't sit well with the commander-in-chief. Sherman was proposing a campaign of destruction across Georgia—smashing bridges, railroads, factories, and anything else that might have a military purpose—which could end in disaster if his armies ran out of food or weapons, or got hopelessly lost in the swamps. And to what end? Wouldn't Hood still be free to march into Tennessee, and subject Union troops to whatever innumerable horrors his mind could dream up as revenge for Sherman's walk upon Atlanta? Wouldn't that dampen the martial spirit of the North, and possibly get a Democrat elected president?

It took weeks for Sherman to deal with these objections. But as the time passed, and as he continued chasing the rebel army for nearly 300 miles with little result, he grew only more passionate that his plan was the only way to break the will of the South—Hood be damned. He could transfer two more army corps to help George Thomas protect Tennessee, and then take the rest of his 60,000 men into the heart of Georgia. With his regular messages to General Grant, he slowly convinced him the plan was a logical and effective way to speed the end of the war. Lincoln took more time to sway, conveying through Secretary of War Stanton that a "misstep by General Sherman might be fatal to his army," and perhaps his own election campaign.

Still, Sherman continued to push hard for the adoption of his strategy. It would help the North triumph—what else mattered? The popular appeal of generals and presidents was ephemeral, and the public was fickle—why kowtow to them? In a letter to his brother, he disparaged politicians and even the notion of democracy itself during wartime: "It is a ridiculous farce to be voting at all. No man should now vote unless he has a musket at his shoulder." And to his wife, "Grant Sheridan & I are now the popular favorites but neither of us will survive this war." He would sacrifice his good name and his reputation to the conflict—why not his life, too? In the early part of the war, he had embraced self-destruction with no purpose, but now his potential self-destruction had a noble end: the obliteration of the Confederacy.

In mid-October, he received the official okay from Washington. He quickly began marshaling his forces for what would become known as the March to the Sea, and on October 29, he sent his troops south, away from John Bell Hood's raiders. And so the two great antagonist armies of the west took off in separate directions—the rebels to invade Tennessee, the Yankees to invade southern Georgia. The army that had the most success in devastating its enemy's terrain would triumph not only in the contest, but possibly win the war itself.

Sherman had no doubt his army would be the victor. As he said in a message to Grant, "I can make the march, and make Georgia howl."

NINE

SHADOWY TERRITORY

n late September 1864, a passenger car on a train from Nashville to Louisville erupted with lively discussion. The subject was, of course, politics. With the presidential election a bit more than a month away, tempers were hot and partisan. This had been prime Democratic country before the war, and still retained a fair measure of sympathy for the party. Nonetheless, the loudest voice in the train car didn't care a whit for giving that party its proper respect—much less for its platform, which favored peace with the rebels and declared the war a failure. The man with the booming voice expressed his outrage at the results of the convention and especially the nomination of the "Copperhead" George Pendleton for vice president. He would no more cast a vote for him than he would for Jeff Davis himself! With his bold views and military bearing, the speaker commanded his listeners' attention, even if they didn't all agree with him. John Logan was in fine form on his way home.

When he disembarked at Carbondale, Illinois, Logan met his wife, Mary, for a poignant reunion. They hadn't seen each other or corresponded in months, and his broken body and battle-worn features showed just what an impact the Atlanta campaign had had on him. As she wrote, "The scenes through which he had passed had furrowed his brow, but the flashing light of his eyes was still there, and the return to home and his family made him happy." There wasn't much time for catching up, however. He had to hit the stump in just a few days.

Black Jack's military prowess was not lost on the people of Egypt, and throughout the year his heroic performance at battlefields like Resaca, Dallas, Atlanta, and Ezra Church had gripped the region, just as it had the state and much of the west. Now he would have to take the military capital he had earned and spend it on his old pursuit of politics. But much had changed in three years—namely, was he still a Democrat? And which party did he support?

Mary's brother-in-law felt sure Logan would never abandon his tribal loyalties to the Democratic Party. Though the platform and the party's vice presidential nominee were contemptible, to be sure, its presidential nominee was a fellow general, George McClellan, the commander of the Army of the Potomac in the early years of the war. Why would Logan desert such a man who shared a party and a uniform with him, especially now that McClellan had disavowed the platform just as he did?

Mary disagreed with her relative, and felt sure her husband would cast his lot with Honest Abe. She wagered 500 dollars—which her friends raised for her—in exchange for her brother-in-law's prized team of mules. The winner of the bet would be decided based on what Logan said at his first campaign rally, in Carbondale on October 1.

More than 10,000 people, and perhaps many more, waited to hear General Logan in the town square. When he stepped onto the platform, the crowd of Republicans and Democrats roared with excitement at their local hero's return. They knew he would give the war effort a hearty endorsement, but beyond that they weren't certain where his political loyalties lay. He quickly let them know.

He denounced the peace faction with vigor and venom. Declaring rhetorical war against those who "sympathize with the infamous and damnable treason," he demanded action against anyone who undermined the federal government, who smiled upon secession, who gave consideration to peace at any cost. Instead of weak-kneed pacifism, he urged "preserving the Union at all hazards" and gave his full-throated support to President Lincoln and denounced those associated with the platform of the Democratic Party. His stance was uncompromising and unequivocal, dispelled any doubt about his views, and won his wife a sturdy team of mules.

His speech met with cheers and fervent enthusiasm, as well as some vicious catcalls and protests. For he was in Egypt, after all, and the region was the home of many of the so-called traitors he had denounced, and not everyone cottoned to his idea of what a patriot was or should be. Still, many of the rally-goers got what they came for—their hero praising the war and denouncing his enemies, in colorful and dramatic language delivered at top volume. They didn't even mind if he was a bit more circumspect about his party affiliation, since he didn't claim to have changed parties, only to support the one in favor of the war.

With the leaders of the Republican Party, Logan worked out a schedule of sixteen speeches he would deliver around Illinois, mostly in the southern section, over the next few weeks. From Carbondale to Springfield to Belleville, Centralia, Du Quoin, and Clinton, Logan traveled the state and delivered his oratory near railroad depots, with his words at each stopover becoming more impassioned and zealous. In Carbondale he had vowed to "kill the last rebel—Jeff Davis himself" and stand over his corpse waving Old Glory. By the time he got to Alton, his words took on an even more sanguine hue, as he promised "I am willing to subjugate, burn, and I had almost said exterminate rather than not put down this rebellion." Even his old law partner, Josh Allen—running to represent Logan's old district in Congress—became a target of his attacks, as he claimed "a greater traitor and humbug walks not unhung" and that Allen had tried to persuade him into supporting treason at the outset of the war.

His angry, at times fanatical, rhetoric drew massive crowds, as his stump events took on a carnivalesque atmosphere. As Mary remembered, at one stop several pseudo-soldiers "in grotesque uniforms of red, white, and blue" presented him with a live eagle to carry around the state with him. At other stops, the crowds became jubilant, buoyant, or downright enraged, until "we were constantly vibrating between tears and laughter over the grave and comic scenes we witnessed." His passion fed off the crowd's energy, until by the climax of his orations he was declaiming furiously against treason and secession, castigating the cowards who shrank from a fight, calling out his enemies for their malign influence, and taking off the gloves against anyone who had the gall to disagree! Often, he stepped off the platform with a hoarse voice or an inflamed throat.

His unmatched rhetorical skills earned him much attention in the press, and encouraged Republicans in Washington to allow him to extend his army leave until the end of the political season. But as his campaigning continued, he began to attract a level of hostility that matched his own. Some Democratic papers alleged Logan had deserted the army, or at least had taken a sabbatical when he should have been fighting. Another paper called him a buffoon and a blackguard. Soon enough, his speeches began to draw as many boos and heckles as they did cheers.

At Benton, the opposition was downright embarrassing. As he tried to deliver one of his signature speeches, an unruly voice in the crowd kept disrupting him, screaming out support for secession and against the war. It belonged to none other than his sister Annie, who humiliated him in the most public way possible.

While his other family members were more private in their antagonism, they were just as truculent. His mother, Elizabeth, continued to refuse him entry to the family home in Murphysboro, and his brother Tom stood firmly against many of his positions on the war and slavery. Tom also had a difficult time keeping ahead of the law, having narrowly avoided prosecution for his latest rape attempt.

But if Logan's family remained a source of trouble, he faced more immediate and violent threats on the stump. No longer content to whistle and jeer at their former champion, many of Logan's foes began to threaten him with violence. At Mount Vernon, after a vigorous argument, a hostile Democrat pointed a pistol at him. He responded by wielding a glass pitcher as a weapon—just as he had the year before, when he smashed a notorious secessionist over the head with one. This time members of the crowd separated the combatants, but Logan knew the presence of armed and dangerous enemies lurked around him everywhere as he traveled through Egypt. The region remained home to a sizable group of secessionists and the terror group The Knights of the Golden Circle, who were only too happy to make threats on his life when they weren't burning the homes and stealing the livestock of loyalist Illinoisans. In response, Logan took to carrying a revolver with him on stage.

Despite the attendant danger, Logan continued his campaign of fiery oratory throughout the state until Election Day. And even in the face of angry resistance, his impassioned pleas and rousing words paid off. Not only did Abraham Lincoln win his reelection and carry his home state over George McClellan, but even the 13th District—the heart of Egypt—went for the president in a surprise upset. Logan's commanding presence had made all the difference to the victory of the Union party and, in the words of Illinois Representative Elihu Washburne, the "glorious triumph over Copperheadism."

It was a great victory, indeed, but Logan hadn't returned home only to ensure the triumph of the Republican Party. He also returned because he had grown frustrated with his commander, the "infernal brute," William Sherman, and needed a respite from his questionable policies and unjust decisions. After the campaign ended, Logan told Sherman he had throat inflammation from the campaign, but would be ready to return to the army whenever he was needed. Sherman informed him, "It is not possible to overtake your command. Remain at home until you recover."

Logan didn't mind keeping a distance from Sherman's armies. But he still itched to return to duty, any duty, whether military or political. After the Republicans gained control of the state legislature in the election, and would therefore pick the next U.S. senator from Illinois, some of Logan's allies tried to convince him to stand for the office. Logan was intrigued by the possibility, but he had no desire to publicly usurp the party favorite, outgoing Governor Richard Yates. He never publicly campaigned for the position and relied on party operatives like incoming Governor Richard Oglesby to advance his cause, assuming he would in the coming days.

Around the same time, Logan put his name forward for consideration as commander of the Department of Missouri. Word had spread that the current head, William Rosecrans—still tainted by the defeat at Chickamauga—was due to be replaced, and Logan thought himself to be a good candidate, especially since the job would keep him out of Sherman's grasp. In early December he met with President Lincoln to talk politics, the war, and presumably the position.

He was surprised by how much he enjoyed the president's company. The commander-in-chief told homespun stories, showed an absolute confidence in the victory of the Union over the Confederacy, and complimented Logan on his political and martial skills in his respective campaigns in Illinois and Atlanta. Logan took the measure of his former nemesis and found him perfectly reasonable, charming, and lucid. How wrong he had been in assuming the rail-splitter to be a radical and a danger to the Constitution. And even if Lincoln were an abolitionist, Logan applied the same term to himself occasionally—perhaps with a sense of irony—and no longer held the same animosity toward those who would destroy the system of human bondage. Logan had changed markedly in three years, and could now count Lincoln as a man worthy of his support both in and out of uniform. He left the White House feeling confident in the outcome of the war and the fate of the nation.

Three days later the command of the Department of Missouri went to Grenville Dodge, Logan's subordinate at the Battle of Atlanta. He had been passed over for promotion yet again—this time not by a general like Sherman he distrusted, but by a president he admired. As the cold set in at Washington, Logan now faced the prospect of an unclear future. Though he had found unmatched success on the battlefield, in the political arena, and among the nation's leaders, he had been left with nothing to show for it. Despite all his struggles and valiant efforts, the champion orator and would-be hero of the west remained unemployed.

John Logan wasn't the only speaker on the stump in the western states. Mary Livermore was also making the rounds. From small towns in Wisconsin, to social clubs in Chicago, to churches across the region, Mary hit the fund-raising circuit and delivered speeches to drum up donations for the Sanitary Commission and support for the troops. At first mortified at having to speak in front of large audiences, she honed her style until her oratory became electric. At one address in Iowa, she began to understand the power her voice commanded:

> I concentrated my mind upon what I had to say. For the first ten minutes I talked into utter darkness. It was as if the house was unlighted. I did not even hear the sound of my own voice—only a roaring, as if ten thousand mill-wheels were thundering about me. . . . [After the speech] I was interrupted by long and loud applause. I was so absorbed that I did not understand it for a moment, and looked around to see what had fallen. I thought some of the seats had given way.

The effect was bracing, and a bit surprising. Her listeners had come to see *her*, to listen to *her* declaim on the war, and to take in *her* ideas on how to crush the twin evils of slavery and secession. It was as if her reputation had grown to a size where even she didn't recognize it.

She had already raised her profile with the Sanitary Fair, which had become a sensation in charitable circles and spawned dozens of new fairs across the country, from Iowa to Brooklyn, that raised millions of dollars. And she was expanding the reach of her organization well beyond Illinois, to the point where she was known throughout the west. In fact, her branch of the Sanitary Commission had become so dominant in war relief—inspiring new chapters and bringing aid societies into a wide regional network—that its leaders dropped "Chicago" from the title and called it the Northwestern Sanitary Commission. As the face of that commission, she had to arouse the passion of her listeners to contribute their money and goods to the cause, to marshal their enthusiasm and quash their doubts, and to keep them from worrying about how their boys were faring in the war.

It was not easy. She had been to hospitals on the front lines, and she knew the damage a minié ball or grapeshot or shrapnel could do to a body. She had seen too many young men without arms or legs or jaws, and couldn't even begin to describe the pain they felt, or the isolation from their families, or their terror of dying. How could she convey in simple words the monumental importance of all this suffering? How could she tell her listeners everything would work out fine, when the troops faced cannonades and missiles as part of their job duty? And especially now, with Sherman's armies advancing deep into the no-man's-land of Georgia, how could she provide a rousing patriotic spin on things like mass violence and total war? While she supported the war to unite the country and destroy slavery, even she had a hard time stomaching the idea of sieges and starvation, women and children left homeless, collective punishment and scorched earth.

Though she couldn't help but remember all the "destitution, sickness, and suffering" she had seen in the war, her speeches steered clear of this shadowy territory. Better to keep the focus on family and the flag, on the material needs of the soldiers, on the nobility of the cause. To say anything else would lead to doubt and fear, and compromise her essential message. She had no time for any of that.

As the months passed in 1864, along with giving speeches around the region, Mary found herself with a huge and unwieldy number of tasks to accomplish at branch headquarters in Chicago. On a typical morning, she had to oversee the packaging and shipment of innumerable boxes of goods for army camps, including "Codfish and sauer-kraut, pickles and ale, onions and potatoes, smoked salmon and halibut, ginger and whiskey, salt mackerel and tobacco," and many other items with notoriously fragrant odors. Amid this frenzy of activity came a parade of visitors, all demanding her time and attention, "on every imaginable errand, in every known mental mood—grieved, angry, stupid, astonished, incredulous, delighted, agonized," and it was her job to answer their questions, placate their fears, investigate their claims, assuage their doubts, and buck up their spirits.

She also oversaw the new sewing rooms at Commission headquarters for seamstresses to create garments for soldiers' uniforms; helped fund the Chicago Soldiers' Home, dedicated to the care of injured and indigent veterans; and provided assistance to the young wives and widows of soldiers, many of them black and immigrant women—everything from buying food and medicine to paying for their rent and burial costs for their deceased husbands. To go along with all this, she continued to work with The Home of the Friendless to find adoptive homes for orphaned children and temporary housing for destitute Chicagoans. Plus, she had to raise her own children and see them off to school every morning, leaving almost no time for herself at any hour.

Mary wasn't alone. Her colleague Jane Hoge worked nearly as hard, as did women in other Sanitary Commission branches—and women in general—throughout the west. As Mary had first seen, farm wives had taken over the management of farmsteads, even laboring in the fields themselves. And now thousands more women in Illinois worked as teachers than before the war, and many more women earned paychecks in mills, arsenals, and factories, crafting the clothing and knapsacks and shoes and weapons their boys used on the front lines. It was no longer a question of Mary exhorting women to work beyond their traditional sphere—they were already doing so by the millions, without any need for endorsements or huzzahs or any other sort of encouragement. The work was simply there to do, and it had to be done.

It soon caused a backlash. Many critics seized on the question of whether women should be paid at all for their work. The image of the self-sacrificing lady of the home and hearth still held sway in many circles, and the very idea of a woman working for filthy lucre—especially an upper-middle-class woman like Mary Livermore—invited much derision. The *Chicago Times*, in particular, lionized the noble self-sacrifice of nuns in support of the war while spitting venom at Jane and Mary, who "draw a thousand dollars" in yearly salary but "scarcely raise a finger" to help the boys in blue. It was a scabrous charge, and frustrated Mary to no end.

Even more dangerous were the accusations she and other Sanitary Commission members had to answer about the misuse of relief supplies. Various donors claimed distribution agents made a habit of stealing goods meant for the soldiers—everything from jars of pickles to boxes of socks—and not only did these spurious charges decrease contributions to the organization, they had a toxic effect on staffers. Mary had to spend time during her speeches defending the Commission, and even claimed some donors wondered why a half-dozen cans of peaches weren't properly doled out to every boy in the Union army!

Other wags suggested the Commission was no better than a speculation firm, getting goods for free from rubes on the home front and selling them to buyers on the front lines at a considerable markup. Although there was no proof of this, the charges stuck in some parts of the west and potential donors—many of them women on farms and in small towns—turned away in alarm. Now frantic to prove the Commission's integrity, Mary and its other leaders assured the public no significant theft of donations had occurred, and the group had no interest in speculation. And if anyone ever did take such foul actions, they would be chucked out of the organization straightaway.

But no amount of assurance could comfort the lapsed donors, and the leaders of the Commission began to suspect the source of the rumors might be a rival organization. As William Patton, vice president of Mary's branch, said in the Commission's official bulletin, "I am sorry to say that lately these reports are represented to us as made by the agents of the Christian Commission, in order to divert supplies from us to themselves." He then wrote, "It would be easy for us to retaliate," and charged the Christian Commission with everything from purloining peaches to giving away shirts and socks to the wrong soldiers. He also accused the Christian society of distributing thousands of copies of a leaflet with false claims about the Sanitary Commission, asking "Was that *Christian*? The circular has now been suppressed in this vicinity from very shame."

Earlier in the war, Mary had expressed fears about the potential of other groups to steal the energy of her own organization, and now the Christian Commission seemed to be doing just that, emerging as its clearest and most threatening adversary. Occasional statements of support between the groups could scarcely hide the animosity they felt for each other, which only continued to grow throughout 1864—a year that saw explosive growth for the Christian Commission and struggles for the Sanitary Commission.

The Christian Commission had gained the upper hand by closely modeling its methods on its rival. No longer content to simply offer Bibles and words of spiritual support, it was now fully invested in raising cash and donations of homegrown vegetables, homemade food, hand-sewn socks and shirts, and other provisions to soldiers in its care. Along with that, the Christian group paid its agents to do their work in the field, almost as much as Mary herself earned as an associate manager, yet steered clear of being associated with the taint of money. Its field agents aided their cause by casting themselves as pious and self-sacrificing holy men interested only in advancing God's work through an organization He favored. The Sanitary Commission agents, by contrast, offered no such impression. And some critics hinted they weren't even Christian in the first place.

Henry Bellows, the president, was a Unitarian, as were many other officers in the national organization; and Mary Livermore was a closely related Universalist. She found herself again confronting that nagging prejudice against the open-minded, forgiving religion she practiced. In her youth, it had been the faith of her parents that had aggrieved her: the judgmental, deterministic creed of Baptism—with its emphasis on sin and punishment of wayward souls. And now her tormentors had returned in the form of the evangelical agents of the Christian Commission, who questioned how an organization so worldly, so secular, *perhaps* so irreligious, as the Sanitary Commission could ever truly devote itself to God's work.

Mary wrote to an ally that the group's agents publicly seemed amiable and uncompetitive, but in fact were "pretending friendliness while all the while seeking to undermine us." The Christian Commission's scope of endeavor expanded further as the year went on, until it outmuscled the Sanitary Commission for the loyalty of individual aid societies and their donors, and even began setting up its own donation fairs.

With the year drawing to a close, Mary was torn. She had never experienced such success in her personal endeavors—raising her national profile, commanding attention for her words and actions, doing all she could for charity and the war—yet she grew beleaguered. With each step forward she took, her critics spoke louder, and as they spoke louder, she herself had to raise her own voice, until the contest became caustic and nakedly political. No matter how distasteful the dialogue may have been, however, she knew she had to engage in it. With the march of the armies deep into Southern terrain, there was too much at stake—for her reputation, her faith, her family, and her country. Guided by the hand of Providence, no one could go back to the ways things used to be, before the first shots were fired, before the armed struggle began, when the supreme monstrosity of slavery held sway.

Deep in Georgia with General Sherman, Mary Ann Bickerdyke had her critics, too, but these days they were wise enough to keep silent around her, lest they do anything to provoke her wrath. For she could still tear the bark off an adversary without hesitation, and could deliver a tongue-lashing that would lacerate the pride of anyone who had the temerity to challenge her. She and her little brown bird, Eliza Porter, were working too hard to countenance any such foolishness, and would raise holy hell against those who interfered with their labors.

Mary Ann traveled with the troops from Resaca to Atlanta, following Sherman's armies as they crossed rivers, mountain ranges, and ravines, in all varieties of weather and hardship. She and Eliza prepared great kettles of soup, coffee, and panado for the boys; they baked 500 loaves of bread at a time in portable brick ovens; they created crude beds in the wilderness cut from pine and hemlock boughs and covered with blankets; they traveled with the troops in ambulances and cared for them in make-shift hospitals; they sang songs like "Shining Shore" to lessen the fears of the wounded; they did anything necessary to aid the comfort of the injured and comfort the souls of the dying. Mother even resorted to her time-honored botanical treatments when she had a chance, concocting a blackberry cordial for diarrhea, a wild cherry and bloodroot tonic for heart ailments, jimsonweed tea for pain, and brown soap for chigger bites.

She would use any tool she could to help her boys, and would employ any able-bodied soul she encountered to help out. And unlike the leaders of the Sanitary Commission, she was happy to work with the field agents of the Christian Commission. She secured them passes to get into army camps and even arranged for them to take over her nursing work in out-posts like Resaca after she had to leave with Sherman's army. She figured as long as these agents did good service for the troops, they were on the side of God and the Union, regardless of which organization got the credit. Many of the commissions' agents got along well with each other in the field—they took breakfast together, swapped stories, and helped each other out in a pinch. Some of them even worshipped side by side.

—⁓—

As the Atlanta campaign went on, and the needs of the soldiers multiplied, Mother and Eliza dug in, often without sleep, sometimes without food. Eliza sacrificed many of her rations and subsisted on a few morsels a day, while Mother refused any gifts of new or fancy clothing for herself, and insisted they be made into garments for the troops. Some of their actions in the field became legendary, almost beyond the limit of human endurance—in Kingston they distributed seventy-five tons of provisions, and in Allatoona they oversaw the care of 3,000 patients. At Marietta, they labored for four months during the long Atlanta campaign and occupation, caring for some 13,000 injured troops in great revival tents the soldiers called "Mother Bickerdyke's Circus." Here, a recovering soldier could enjoy a hearty meal, receive the medicine he needed, put on a new set of clothes, and sample Mother's famed pink lemonade, brewed from lemon extract and fresh raspberry juice.

She was at this hospital when she learned of General James McPherson's death. He had always been an ally of hers, and the demise of such a young and gallant warrior really shook her. Sherman was also crestfallen at his friend's untimely demise at the Battle of Atlanta, and had his body moved to his headquarters at the Howard House, on the northern edge of the fighting. He summoned Mother into the combat zone and had her make sure McPherson's body safely reached a field hospital. Once it arrived, she removed the general's bloodstained shirt and washed it with her own hands, then arranged it in a package she gave to Eliza. She said, "I want you to take that, and put it under lock and key, until you can send it to General McPherson's mother" in Clyde, Ohio. It was one of the few belongings that the rebels hadn't stripped or stolen from his corpse.

As Mother prepared the general for his last resting place, she completed a remarkable rise. From the middle-aged countrywoman who began as the object of ridicule, to the hospital infighter who had to stake her claim to serve the army, to the figure of increasing renown who overcame great obstacles, to the intimate of generals and the heroine of the troops, Mother had advanced further in the war than even her greatest champions could have expected. That made it all the more jarring when, at the pinnacle of her fame, she encountered a new obstacle that she couldn't overcome by force of will or evade with homespun craftiness: General Sherman ordered her to go home.

He shocked her with this demand. Hadn't she been a loyal servant of the troops, and given her boys all the sweat and blood and ferocity her role required? When had she ever failed, or given up, or withdrawn from exhaustion? She argued with the western commander as best she could, but no amount of protest could change his mind this time. He may have been her ally, and may have been won over by her courage and vigor, but it didn't matter—she had to go.

Sherman explained she had done nothing wrong. He simply wanted no wounded soldiers, no infirm troops, no hospitals or ambulances, no nurses, no women, no "pampering fripperies" of luxury or delicacy, and no hangers-on to hamper his March to the Sea. He only wanted the hardiest, strongest, most battle-tested veterans to come along with him. Under no circumstances would he abide a slow march through southern Georgia. He couldn't, because, with the army due to forage for much of its food, it had to travel quickly without a lengthy supply train or railroad to provision it. Otherwise it would bog down and starve.

Mother had no answer to his hard logic, and in the end couldn't resist it. But she did secure a promise from him that once he reached his destination of Savannah, he would summon her to aid the boys once more. After more than a month in the swamps and wilderness, they would need it.

Preparing to leave, over the next two months, she and Eliza transferred all the injured and wounded troops home to the North. They couldn't care for them in Atlanta, because there would soon be no Union presence in town, or even a town to speak of. They had to leave, and she and Eliza had to leave with them.

By early November, Eliza had already left for Chicago to go with her husband on new charitable endeavors. Mother took longer to depart, and when she did the final stages of Sherman's plans for northern Georgia were well underway. As she took one of the last "up" trains headed north, she looked out over the rugged and tortured landscape that had been her home for most of the year. She saw the rosy glow on the horizon, the crimson streaks ever brighter, and she knew the fires of William Sherman had already begun their march.

On the night of November 10, Rome was burning. The north Georgia town had seen some minor action in the war, but was mainly known for its ironworks and munitions shops. Because of this, General Sherman thought it had value for the Confederate military, so it had to go. He ordered all barracks, warehouses, foundries, bridges, factories, and related sites to be burned or otherwise destroyed. The troops who carried out the charge didn't stop there, however. They also torched private homes, and while that was against Sherman's orders, those orders were enforced loosely at best. As one soldier reported, "This Government is now Entering upon a new policy. We are ordered to burn Cities and Barns and Houses and Ever we go and lay waste the Entire Country." The new policy was synonymous with "hard war."

Rome was among the first towns to be destroyed, but there were more to come. In Kingston, the railroad, the water towers, even the telegraph poles went up in a massive conflagration, after which the town had "no houses, no fences, and the roadside strewn with dead mules and broken wagons." At Cartersville, Cassville, Big Shanty, and Acworth, the townscape became a wreckage of incinerated buildings and chimneys remaining as lone sentinels. Marietta too became a focus of destruction, the fires spreading to the business section, private homes, the courthouse, and almost anything that anyone could use to foster war, commerce, or civilization. Sherman's newest staff member, Henry Hitchcock, was so shocked by the immolation he assumed it had to be against official orders. Who would allow such barbarism to take place? He asked Sherman about it, and the response he received was curt and unapologetic: "I never ordered burning of any dwelling—didn't order this, but can't be helped. I say *Jeff Davis burnt them*."

The sudden change in strategy was jarring. Months or even weeks before, the armies of the west had given their blood and toil to conquer and then hold these towns. Their generals had fortified defensive lines to protect them, their troops had occupied trenches and breastworks to secure them, their wagon trains and rail lines had been designed to provision them. And now, with the stroke of Sherman's pen and a few military orders, everything those armies had done was going up in flames. He felt no regret about it, either. As he had written Grant weeks before, "Until we can repopulate Georgia, it is useless to occupy it, but the utter destruction of its roads, houses, and people will cripple their military resources."

Sherman remained strangely detached from the fires he had set, but he took a turn for the emotional and the sentimental when thinking of his family. He learned one of his sons, Charles, was ill, so he took a break from his town-wrecking and wrote a letter to his daughters, Minnie and Lizzie, hoping their brother would "live long and take poor Willy's place in our love." He still mourned Willy, now dead more than a year, and felt a sublime sadness in once more bearing the loss. He felt hollow, at some remove from normal human ambition or cares, and let his wife, Ellen, know his lingering feelings of pain and emptiness.

He also had time to write to his other son, Thomas, who had just turned eight a few weeks before. He had heard the boy enjoyed a frolic in the orchard, gathering apples and grapes, and warned him not to indulge in eating too much fruit. He recalled how Willy used to eat hickory nuts with vigor, delighted to have his own tasty bag to snack on. Perhaps Thomas would enjoy dining on hickory nuts and walnuts, too, and would step into the role of his departed sibling. Perhaps he would even become the man of the house someday. "Willy will never meet us again in this world and you and I must take care of the family as long as I live and then will be your turn. . . . Minnie & Lizzie will soon be young ladies, will marry and change their names, but you will always be a Sherman and must represent the family." He looked forward to ending the war and returning to his kin with a proud soul and a full heart. But for now he had a job to do—making Georgia howl.

In mid-November came the final act in Atlanta's four-month saga of tragedy and disaster. The town had been besieged, fought over, invaded, occupied, evacuated, starved, dismantled, hollowed out, and disfigured, and it hardly resembled whatever it may have once been or represented. When Captain Orlando Poe did the last work of destruction to the town on Sherman's orders, few citizens lingered to mourn for it, no rebels remained to fight for it, and no one bothered to save it.

To the great railroad depot, 80 by 200 feet long, Poe invented a battering ram and collapsed its piers, brick walls, and towering roof. To factory smokestacks, Poe used a battering ram and a rope to level the huge columns into tiny bits. To the massive granite roundhouse, the rolling mills, the factories, the foundries, and the munitions shops, Poe's men engineered quick and clever schemes to collapse walls, topple piers and beams, and create piles of rubble from the structures of once-imposing buildings. And then came the fires.

On November 15 much of the business district took flame, as officers with orders to burn and enlisted men with a taste for arson took matters in their own hands. The incendiary wave started downtown with a few hot spots, but it quickly grew and spread to other sections of town, consuming homes and barns and anything else in its path. The torrent of fire devoured storehouses, warehouses, hotels, churches, theaters, taverns, shops, and markets, until its flames shot hundreds of feet in the air and turned the black sky into red and the night into terrible day for many miles around. The men too were transformed, from individual soldiers into ominous silhouettes, their shadows running to escape the firestorm, the catastrophe they had unleashed.

The air was rich and dense with the smell of war as cinders cascaded high and fell as ash, and gunpowder ignited and burned until a fog of light smoke gave the horizon an eerie glow. Abandoned artillery shells exploded here and there, adding the sounds of phantom battle to the scene, until the flames, the bombs, the ash, the embers gave the nearest impression of the apocalypse anyone had ever seen.

His work nearly done in Atlanta, Sherman wrote a last message to General Thomas in Tennessee. He told him he expected the telegraph wires would soon be cut, and he would vanish into southern Georgia with limited means of communication. His armies of 60,000 men, well-armed and well-trained, would then advance into parts unknown, "expecting to live chiefly on the country"—their aim to crush the soul of the Confederacy with Godspeed.

He also composed a final, brief message to his wife, Ellen. He let her know he had received the new clothing she had sent, along with her letters. In return he offered her these closing words:

"Write no more till you hear of me. Good bye.—W.T. Sherman."

TEN

COMRADES IN DIRT

I t was Thursday, November 17, when the little town of Conyers, Georgia, awoke to news that the Yankees were coming. The residents knew all about the destruction they had wrought upon Atlanta and other north Georgia towns and could only guess what lay in store for theirs. Despite their anger, their fears, and their nagging sense they'd be better off anywhere else but in the path of a federal army, the residents turned out anyway to catch a glimpse of the invaders. They had no choice: With John Bell Hood's rebel army now a distant memory up in Tennessee, no one else could stand up for their village. No one else could talk the Yankees out of burning it to the ground.

Almost all the residents who showed up were women and children. Their men had either left to fight with Hood's army or the Georgia militia or chose to skedaddle away from trouble. Rumor had it the Yankees went easier on ladies, greeting their stubbornness or defiance with a laugh or a shrug, whereas their gentlemen might receive a bullet for their efforts.

The federals arrived in the afternoon to the sound of their regimental bands playing the likes of "Yankee Doodle Dandy" and "John Brown's Body." Leading the 14th Corps of the U.S. Army and its 14,000 men was none other than Jefferson C. Davis—not, of course, the Jeff Davis the people of Conyers claimed as their president, but a Yankee general of the same name. The 14th Corps marched in tandem with the similar-sized 20th Corps, and together they made up the left wing of Sherman's marchers, reconfigured as the Army of Georgia and led by General Henry Slocum. They were part a force of more than 60,000 men, spread across a width of sixty miles, marching almost 300 miles through Georgia.

Among the troops filing into town were Reverend John Hight and the 58th Indiana Volunteer Infantry. Like the rest of the corpsmen, Hight and his Indianans saw Conyers as a special place. Not only was it the first town they had seen in two days that wasn't blackened by fire, starved into submission, or outright abandoned, it was also the place where they could finally rustle up some food. For during the entire siege and occupation of Atlanta, the cribs and corrals and larders of that town had been so worked over by ravenous troops that the terrain for some twenty miles around lay barren. Now, hardly any soldiers could find decent "eatables" except for the provisions on their own wagon train, and Sherman had made sure those wagons would not carry enough comestibles to feed an entire army. The boys knew they would have to forage for their meals, and by the time they got to Conyers, that is just what they did.

It was after the peak of the harvest in the South, and the harvest had been a bountiful one. The state government of Georgia had many months before asked farmers to grow grain and vegetables instead of cotton, to feed hungry troops on the march. Few knew then those troops would be from the North, and that they would snatch their bounty without asking for it. And so, in fields, gardens, barns, bins, and cellars, almost everywhere they looked, Sherman's boys found the kind of sustenance that could fill their bellies and give them enough energy to march fifteen miles a day. There were chickens, hogs, sorghum syrup, sweet potatoes, molasses, and countless other delights, all of them delicious and all of them belonging to someone else. Naturally, Sherman had issued orders that detailed how commanding officers should organize foraging parties for their brigades, and how those parties should gather foodstuffs, and how those foodstuffs should be distributed within the brigade, but by the time the soldiers got to Conyers, it didn't matter. The rules seemed more like suggestions than commands. As Hight wrote, "Our men helped themselves to anything they desired to eat. No effort was made by the officers to restrain them."

They also destroyed things—the First Michigan Engineers and Mechanics had been dismantling the Macon & Western Railroad at Lithonia under Sherman's supervision, and torched a train depot and a few unfortunate nearby houses. But Conyers wasn't a town for burning. It was a stopover that could provide the boys a brief rest, a hearty meal, even a few new books or a set of clothes. And they gave thanks to Uncle Billy for all the largesse, even if it was their own initiative, and their talent for breaking through doors and windows, that got them just what they wanted.

Reverend Hight wasn't one for busting into people's barnyards and stealing their cows and pigs, nor would you find him swiping sweet potatoes from a farmer's garden, but he ate as well in Conyers as the rest of the boys. He had also watched—and cheered—as his regiment dismantled a railroad bridge near Atlanta, knocking out its braces and swinging it wide until part of its span collapsed. Then, with a biblical flourish, he described how "the timbers begin to tumble, like men in battle; they dash madly against each other, and amid flashing fire and splashing waters, the bridge comes thundering down, like Satan and his hosts, when hurled from Heaven to hell." The 58th Indiana's pontoniers were better known for erecting bridges than destroying them, but would happily lay waste to them if Sherman ordered it.

Hight reveled in the collapse of infrastructure that supported the rebel war effort, but he had much darker feelings about the Union army's firing of other structures. As he saw it, "there is no sense in making war on women and children . . . [or] in burning the houses of the poor. The order for the destruction of this property will demoralize our own men." It sickened him to see the abuse of the defenseless. He heard a rumor of an attempted rape in the area, and how a Georgia woman had killed her Yankee attacker. His reaction: "May all such villains die the same death."

He had not come this far with the 58th Indiana to see his boys degenerate into criminals and barbarians. Many of them had heard his sermons under pine boughs, had worshipped with him in their tents, had promised to open their hearts to the message of Jesus Christ. He had helped the Christian Commission deliver them Bibles, and provide them with other spiritual and material aid. He watched them grow into God-fearing men, and encouraged them to provide charity to the weak and justice to the sinful. He had even turned some of them into abolitionists. And if his words weren't persuasive enough, seeing the horror of slavery was.

But he knew there had to be a careful balance in redeeming the land from slavery and destroying things without mercy. God's revenge upon Sodom and Gomorrah was just and proper because its unrepentant sinners had defied Him. But what of the Union army's revenge upon Georgia? Was that the same thing, when dozens of homes of poor whites and blacks might be swept up in the same infernos that consumed the plantations? He wondered where to draw the line, especially with the troops becoming more adept in their vengeful labors by the hour.

Sherman and his corps commanders were not God's agents, but they did hold the power to control and discipline their troops, with orders forbidding the trespass, looting, or firing of private homes. Some commanders were lax in laying down the law; others threatened violators with the penalty of death.

Jefferson C. Davis was one of the hard-nosed commanders. The head of the 14th Corps became disgusted by the wave of unapproved thievery that had consumed the soldiers. At one point he stumbled upon a pair of scofflaws spiriting away some elegant dresses from a house. In short order he ordered them to be arrested and shamed into wearing the dresses— with the word "STOLEN" marked on them.

He also reserved the right to shoot arsonists in the ranks. Even though Reverend Hight had no affection for the fire-starters, he despised Davis for his new policy: "Just think of shooting American soldiers for the benefit of rebels. No man, who really loves our cause and our soldiers, could issue such an order. If an officer desires to shoot our men, let him join the rebel army at once." But in this case, Jefferson Davis commanded an army corps in blue.

After passing through Conyers, the 58th Indiana reached the Yellow River on the way to Covington. The river stood 100 feet wide, was bordered by steep banks, and presented a fair challenge to the regiment. Its troops had been assigned to pontoon duty since May 1, but this would be the first bridge they built on the March to the Sea. They floated out a series of wooden boats clad in canvas, anchored them to the banks, overlaid them with beams known as "balks," and crossed them with wooden planks known as "chess." It made for a narrow floating artery that allowed the troops, their horses, and their wagons of vital supplies and ammunition to cross unimpeded. The cattle the troops had stolen from local farms waded across downstream.

It was perilous and unheralded work for the 58th Indiana, but essential nonetheless. Because so many railroads and bridges had already been destroyed—including the ones over the Yellow River—pontoon bridges were the only way to ford the nine major rivers of the march. So while Sherman's foragers and arsonists attracted most of the attention, the entire army could march nowhere without the pontoniers.

Along with the soldiers, Hight began to notice people without guns crossing the pontoon bridges. Men, women, and children, strong and weak, old and young, healthy and infirm, made their first hesitant steps to follow the column as it wended past their farmsteads and villages. Many were hungry, most were impoverished, and all were black. They had left private homes and plantations where Georgians who claimed to own them kept them as property. They plowed fields, made beds, fed boilers, smithed metal, stitched garments, and raised cotton, all under the constant threat of violence at the whim of their "masters." Some had already escaped earlier in the war, gone north on the Underground Railroad, or found another way to leave their confinement. Others only had the opportunity when it passed by in the form of an invading army. Now they marched with Sherman—and, at least at first, his armies did little to stop them. John Hight worried over the safety of some of the people, especially women, when traveling with an army prone to devilment, but they came anyway because "liberty is sweet, and they seem to think it is now or never."

For many of them it was a fleeting opportunity, not to be had again for many more months. The planters, the owners, the self-appointed masters knew this as well, and did everything they could to keep their men and women in bondage from disappearing. They told them outlandish tales of Yankees drowning black women and children in the Chattahoochee River and locking slaves in buildings in Atlanta before burning them. They told them if they fled, they would march at the head of Sherman's column, to serve as cannon fodder for the rebels' guns. They would later tell women the Yankees would rape them and steal rings from their fingers and rip earrings from their earlobes. Despite hearing these lurid and creative fictions, many slaves escaped their bonds and followed the army anyway. As one man reasoned, his master hated the Yankees, and since his master was no friend to him, he figured the Yankees just might be.

John Hight and his pontoniers came to know the freedmen better as they followed the column winding through central Georgia. The 58th Indiana marched in the rear along with the wagon train and the cattle drovers, who managed an impressively large herd taken from livestock corrals along the route. The cows were insurance against the boys' hunger, providing a supply of meat in case the foragers couldn't find enough pork—which they, with their increasingly picky tastes, preferred.

They marched through fetching little hamlets like Covington and huge plantation centers like Shady Dale—home to 7,600 acres and 250 slaves. They traveled over rivers and creeks with names like Ulcofauhachee, Cedar, and Murder, and past woods and farmsteads where they could "forage liberally on the country," as Sherman had ordered. They tramped over the grounds of plantations large and small.

Some of the plantations they passed had hundreds or thousands of acres; others only a dozen. Some had dozens of buildings on-site, with a manor house, barns, cribs, smokehouses, and farmhouses; others just had a shack or two. Some were home to the most prominent figures in the state; others to hardscrabble farmers. But one thing almost all of them had in common—the presence of slaves.

In many cases word of Sherman's troops on the march inspired the planters to drag their slaves with them to southwest Georgia, well away from the invasion route. If they stayed, they might hide in a swamp or in the woods, and have their bondsmen answer the door of their houses when the Yankees arrived. But if they thought their "property" would happily lie for them or parrot back everything the planters told them to say to the Yankees, they were mistaken. Many black men and women quickly led the federals to the hiding places below the floorboards and in the cellars where the planters had stored their jewelry and other valuables. They directed them to the attics where they stashed their heirlooms. They helped them find horses and mules concealed in copses, bogs, and thickets. They opened the larders and cribs and gave the Yankees the provender inside. In return they asked the soldiers to destroy the task houses and cotton gins and other places where they had slaved, and to shoot the hounds and tracking dogs whose speed and fangs had once prevented their escape. Sherman's boys were only too happy to oblige.

As the march went on, the soldiers became more adept at ferreting out the plantation spoils, and spoiling the plantations in the process. As one observer saw it:

> A planter's house was overrun in a jiffy; boxes, drawers, and escritoires were ransacked with a laudable zeal, and emptied of their contents. If the spoils were ample, the depredators were satisfied, and went off in peace; if not, everything was torn and destroyed, and most likely the owner was tickled with sharp bayonets into a confession where he had his treasures hid. If he escaped, and was hiding in a thicket, this was prima facie evidence that he was a skulking rebel; and most likely some ruffian, in his zeal to get rid of such vipers, gave him a dose of lead, which cured him of his Secesh tendencies.

John Hight did not sanction murder, but he did approve of destroying these houses of slavery. Was that not the very reason he marched with the army, to see them in ruin? A few weeks before in Atlanta, he had come to a plantation that once belonged to "a rich southern planter—a rank rebel."

He marveled at the grandiosity of the manor now reduced to rubble and ashes, and how these elites could not have imagined, "in their haughty pride . . . that hated Yankees would dig up their fields, burn their fences, and tear down their houses." The greater the repute of the planters who owned these estates, the more Hight cheered their annihilation.

One such planter was Howell Cobb. He was a former Georgia governor, speaker of the U.S. House of Representatives, and American treasury secretary turned Confederate general, who now commanded the defenses of Macon, Georgia, which Sherman had tricked the rebels into believing he would attack. Cobb owned up to five plantations, each with about 100 slaves. He had absconded from this one in the days before the march, taking with him his horses, mules, cattle, and able-bodied male slaves. He left the women, the children, and the disabled bondsmen behind, without food and dressed in rags, having taken their provisions with him to Macon. Before he left, he demanded his enslaved people should stay on the plantation, despite informing them that, when Sherman arrived with his bloodthirsty Yankees, he would slash their throats and yoke them to his wagons. These scare stories, along with starvation and exposure to the elements in "miserable hovels," left them in a particularly dire condition—as one observer put it, trapped in a "state of terrorism."

The more Sherman saw, the more he was taken aback by the shameful condition of the slaves. He ordered his foragers to freely distribute the goods they found to the bondsmen, and let the troops ransack the premises. He became even angrier when a staff officer produced a copy of a speech Cobb had recently made in Macon—calling for the rebels "to burn and destroy everything in his front, and assail him on all sides." Sherman's judgment was swift. As Hight noted with approval, "Everything that can be, is being destroyed." They spared only the slave quarters.

Marching with the 13th Michigan, John McCline didn't pass by the Cobb slave cabins, but he had seen many others like them along the route. They reminded him of the ones he had grown up in on the Clover Bottoms plantation in Tennessee—simple, wood-framed structures with a bed and stove inside. They were little more than crude shacks, especially

J. D. DICKEY

compared to the elegant stylings of the Hoggatt family mansion, but he had no choice but to live in them. At least they kept out the rain.

He never regretted making his escape from that desperate existence, but he still missed his family deeply—his grandmother, his brothers, and his friends. The last encounter he had had with a family member was back in January, when by chance he saw his brother Jeff on horseback serving with the 6th Ohio Battery. They had a warm reunion, and Jeff assured him their relatives were in good health. He also told John of the changes on the old plantation, and how the manor house now sat abandoned, slowly being chewed up by rats.

The siblings vowed to meet up again soon during the war, but it never happened. In the months that followed, Sherman sent the 6th Ohio to Tennessee to help George Thomas fend off John Bell Hood, and the 13th Michigan marched in the opposite direction, to the sea. So John would again have to wait a long time until he saw Jeff, or anyone, from his family. It might not even happen until the end of the war, or the end of slavery, whichever came last.

While meeting up with blood relatives proved elusive, John had met people in his regiment who became like surrogate family members to him. Some pals like Aron had left his company, but others, like Bart Brown—another black boy on the cusp of becoming a man—had come along and kept his spirits high. That could be a challenge at times, especially during rain squalls and grinding hikes of up to twenty miles a day and unpleasant encounters with belligerent locals.

The regiment had been on this particular march longer than most of the other units in the 14th Corps. They had started in Dalton almost a month earlier, passed the burned-up shell of Atlanta, and had since made their way into central Georgia. In that time, John had seen his friends destroy a lot of railroads, set fire to a handful of factories and munitions shops, and gather stolen goods in massive raids. Now working at regimental headquarters, John found a comfortable position attending to Major Yerkes (recently breveted in rank from captain), and managed the setup and breakdown of army tents, the gathering of wood and water, and various odd jobs.

Yerkes treated John fairly and made sure he worked at headquarters instead of serving with his old company. And it was a good thing, too.

John despised its new Captain Flint, and had never forgotten his barbaric treatment at his hands just a few months before in Dalton, when Flint was still a lieutenant.

The trouble began when John took leave from camp. He went to play a card game with Bart called Old Dutch for 50 cents a hand. Over two hours, John showed an impressive skill for wagering, and by the end of their match, had won an entire month's wages from Bart—10 dollars! When he came back to camp, Flint was furious at him for being out later than he said he would be. In short order, he ordered John tied to a tree and left him there to be humiliated in front of his friends.

John had dealt with worse punishment on the plantation, and didn't allow Flint to intimidate him. With a pocket knife, he cut himself loose and chopped up the rope. He laid the broken pieces down before Flint and waited for him to do something about it. The lieutenant responded by ordering him to be arrested and sent to the guard house without food or water. John spent the day there playing cards with a few friends who had been locked up for minor infractions. Later, Bart came by with a plate of food, and a few hours later, Flint relented and let John go.

It may have been a minor episode in the history of his maltreatment, but John never forgot it. He had gained confidence from serving in the army, and strengthened his backbone to fight enemies like Flint, and that would serve him well in the months and years ahead. He also began to understand the regiment could hold enemies as well as friends, and people could still do him wrong just because he was young, or willful, or black. Escaping from the plantation had just been the first step in a long journey.

For now, he was enjoying the march. He had made so many memories it was sometimes hard to keep track of them all. But one undisputed highlight was meeting the head of the Military Division of the Mississippi under an oak tree. While the marchers paused for a rest, John headed to a creek to fill his canteen, and General Sherman called out to him and asked him his regiment and his age. John answered and Sherman replied, "Well, you are nearly big enough to carry a gun." John told him he did hold weapons now and then, if an exhausted soldier needed a hand. Sherman said, "That's right. Help all you can." Regardless of his commander's actual feelings about black troops, John couldn't help but admire him, and thought seeing this "grand old man" on horseback created "a real sensation" in the regiment. Sherman rode with John's unit for two days before moving on to the next brigade.

While John would never forget meeting the western commander in the field, his favorite moments were with his friends in the 13th Michigan. And nowhere on the March to the Sea did the boys have a better time than when they reached Milledgeville with the rest of the 14th Corps. The unimposing town served as the Georgia state capital, and it was here that state convention delegates had approved acts to secede from the Union and join the Confederacy. Since then, legislators continued to pass secessionist laws until Sherman arrived on their doorstep. They escaped in a panic.

John and the Michiganders had quite a time in the small burg, though their boyish antics were only possible thanks to the protection of a federal army. They broke into peanut sheds where the legumes dried for market, stuffing themselves while the farmers of the crop watched. They chased down a flock of chickens who had no interest in becoming that night's dinner, scampering through the yards of residents until they caught the headstrong hens. And they invaded the Confederate mint, stuffing their pockets with rebel currency just for fun, since the devalued dollars had almost no value at all.

The rest of the corps were enjoying themselves almost as much. Glad to be out of the rain after a recent downpour, the corpsmen had hauled 700 wagons and other vehicles, 30 artillery pieces, 5,000 cows, and 12,000 horses and mules into and around the town. It made for a huge display of military might—with the combined force of the 20th Corps, a total of 27,000 soldiers in a village home to only a tenth as many people.

Their numbers alone gave the troops license to do almost anything they wanted to. Although some brigade commanders clamped down on egregious thievery among their regiments, many more did not. And within a few days the town and the outlying region began to look a shambles, as soldiers swarmed over farms plundering their sheep, turkeys, hogs, mules, horses, and chickens; broke into private homes hunting for silverware and gold rings and other valuables; tore apart picket fences, outhouses, and, in a few cases, church pews to use as fuel for campfires; and hauled out all the corn, sweet potatoes, dried peaches, molasses, and honeycomb they could grab, even if it meant a swarm of bees chasing after them.

At the state arsenal the soldiers added to their arms, uncovering a cache of 10,000 butcher knives with twenty-inch blades; several thousand old-fashioned pikes and cutlasses; a collection of shotguns and muskets; and even a few antique pistols that looked like they dated to the revolutionary era. Shortly after, Sherman ordered the arsenal to be burned, along with various depots and factories and the state penitentiary. He also ruined the town's gristmills, gin houses, and 1,700 bales of cotton, and blew up the powder magazine with dynamite, in a colossal explosion. Fifteen hundred pounds of tobacco he kept, however, and gave out as gifts to the troops.

Few buildings without military value were burned or destroyed. But many were vandalized, including the governor's mansion and the state capitol. The somber stone building resembled nothing less than a medieval castle, and in it the boys of the 14th Corps held a mock legislative session, repealing the state's act of secession and parodying the panicked flight of the legislators. They also ransacked the capitol library, hauling off legal and archival books and throwing them out the windows. Major James Connolly, observing the spectacle, saw it as a "downright shame . . . Public libraries should be sacredly respected by all belligerents, and I am sure General Sherman will, someday, regret that he permitted this library to be destroyed and plundered."

Sherman didn't give orders for the capitol library, or any other structure propping up Georgia civilization, to be despoiled. But neither did he punish the troops responsible, who more often than not had free rein to unleash chaos upon the luckless inhabitants of this town and many others. While a sizable portion of Sherman's armies refrained from vandalism and kept their plundering limited to finding food for themselves, another fair portion threatened the locals at gunpoint and pillaged wherever they could. They acquired a colorful nickname, too—bummers.

Unlike the authorized foragers, the bummers advanced ahead of the army column, traveling in groups of a few men up to several dozen. They came armed with revolvers and carbines, often in shabby clothes or unusual attire stolen from private wardrobes, and had a keen nose for sniffing out food and treasure. Upon locating a farm or plantation that hadn't yet been worked over, they checked to make sure no rebel troops were on-site. If not, they immediately began their plunder. They hitched the farm's horses and mules to wagons, then loaded the wagons with barrels of flour, shovelfuls of corn, and meat from the smokehouses. They tied cattle to the rear of the wagons and butchered hogs and chickens on-site, and added their carcasses to the booty. They rummaged through the drawers and closets of a house looking for valuables and, if they found none to their liking, might ransack the dwelling instead. If the farm or plantation owner appeared and claimed not to have any hidden treasures, they might put a noose around his neck and threaten to hang him until he fessed up. If he wasn't around, they might do the same to one of his slaves.

The worst of the bummers slaughtered animals and only cut off the hindquarters, leaving the rest of the body to rot. And if they weren't hungry enough to eat the cows and pigs and chickens they caught, they bayoneted them instead and left them to bleed out. Better that, they reasoned, than to feed the Confederacy or its citizens. They swiped objects they could never use and things they didn't need, just on a lark, and abandoned those things by the side of the road—littering the waysides with everything from harps and rocking chairs to baby carriages, peacocks, and a pet monkey.

They attacked dwellings of all sizes, from great plantations to humble shacks, whether the owners were rich or poor, black or white. And after they had gathered their fill, they might dine on their spoils and take a few hours off before returning to the column. When they did return to the march, they distributed what they had stolen to their friends in the regiment. Meanwhile, many of their commanding officers looked the other way, preferring not to know exactly what they had been up to. Few of the bummers had regrets about their actions. They were, after all, "foraging liberally on the country," just as Sherman had ordered, or may have ordered. Most of the bummers weren't sure of the wording, since they hadn't bothered to consult his special field orders. Many hadn't even read them in the first place.

The indiscriminate raids of the bummers gave rise to fury among the locals, who saw their livestock stolen or gutted, their belongings rifled through, and their homes desecrated. They called these Yankee invaders "demons" or "wolves" or "vandals." And they took action. Within weeks some of the rogue foragers began to turn up missing or dead, with a bullet to the heart or a slash to the throat. Rebel cavalrymen took to ambushing them—slaying entire parties of bummers or, if they captured them first, executing them in cold blood. What had begun as a frolic for the young foragers had turned into a zealous pursuit and was now a deadly business. Living off the country meant fighting total war.

The Confederate cavalry—scourge of the bummers—was under the control of General Joseph Wheeler, who provided some of the limited resistance the rebels were able to muster against Sherman's armies. Wheeler and his horsemen spent most of the time engaged in skirmishes with the Northern cavalry leader, Hugh Judson Kilpatrick— whom Sherman described as "a hell of a damned fool," a gambler and womanizer who had been jailed earlier in the war for selling confiscated livestock for his own profit. He was a rogue and a criminal, but as Sherman said, "I want just that sort of man to command my cavalry on this expedition."

Despite their rivalry, Wheeler and Kilpatrick had one thing in common: They both ordered their men to forage liberally. The native Georgians expected this from the Yankees; but from the rebels, it was a shock. Wheeler's cavalry units had to live off the land just as Sherman's troops did, and at times even seemed to outmatch them for bumming. One Alabaman saw how his men "have become lawless to an alarming extent, steal and plunder indiscriminately regardless of age or sex." They ransacked homes and hunted for food, and preyed on country folk whose farms had already been worked over by Union troops. Soldiers in one rogue Texas regiment even held an entire town hostage until they received a ransom. And when the cavalrymen didn't receive their pay from the depleted coffers of the Confederate treasury, their foraging increased in severity, until "The citizens of Georgia have more animosity toward Wheeler's Cavalry than they have against the

Yankees." So for the residents of the state, the arrival of the cavalry—rebel or federal—became a source of great fear, and a reminder they had no allies on horseback.

While the 14th and 20th Corps of the U.S. Army were plundering Milledgeville, Kilpatrick was demonstrating against Macon to the west. This helped to distract Wheeler's forces and led the rebels to believe the federal infantry would follow with an attack there. However, the Confederates were too mobile to be pinned down in only one area, and ranged widely in their attacks.

John Hight had his worries about Wheeler. Since he and the 58th Indiana traveled at the back of the column with the wagon train and the cattle guards, he thought the Confederate cavalry might come along at any time to "swallow up" his pontoniers and the other luckless stragglers. A brigade from the 20th Corps had been protecting them in the first part of the march, but had since departed to tear up railroad tracks. Now they stood vulnerable to an ambush. The 58th Indiana's commander, George Buell, became incensed at their exposure to the rebel cavalry without protection, but there was little he could do about it. It frustrated Hight as well. Didn't General Jefferson C. Davis understand the peril of leaving his bridge builders in the lurch? If they were slaughtered in an ambush, then the whole fate of the army would be jeopardized. And no matter how many men or wagons or guns Sherman had brought, they would all be useless if they couldn't cross the next river.

Hight had growing doubts about generals Sherman and Davis. As for the former, even though Sherman had liberated dozens of plantations and occasionally gave the spoils to freed slaves, the general couldn't conceive of black men and women as anything other than field workers for his army. Hight grew angry at Sherman's pigheadedness, and insisted that any able-bodied individual regardless of color should be given a weapon and allowed to fight against oppression, to help win the war for the cause of union and abolition. He even outlined a detailed, four-point plan for doing so, including organizing an entire army of free black men for the benefit of the nation. Still, he knew that Sherman, while a strong unionist, had no real interest in destroying human bondage as a moral

FIGURE 1 (ABOVE): Republican
Convention, 1860.
FIGURE 2 (LEFT): Friedrich Hecker.
FIGURE 3 (BELOW): Mary Livermore.

FIGURE 4 (LEFT): Mary Ann Bickerdyke.
FIGURE 5 (CENTER): *Midnight on the Battle Field*, engraving of Bickerdyke at Fort Donelson.
FIGURE 6 (BOTTOM): Hospital Ship USS *Nashville*.

FIGURE 7 (ABOVE): Chickamauga Drawing by Alfred Waud.
FIGURE 8 (BELOW LEFT): John McCline in middle age.
FIGURE 9 (BELOW RIGHT): John Hight.

FIGURE 10 (ABOVE LEFT): Charles Wills. FIGURE 11 (ABOVE RIGHT): General Joseph Hooker.
FIGURE 12 (BELOW): Chattanooga.

FIGURE 13 (LEFT): General Ulysses Grant.
FIGURE 14 (BELOW): Illinois Monument at Missionary Ridge.

FIGURE 15 (ABOVE): Sanitary Commission Office in Richmond, 1865. FIGURE 16 (CENTER): Chicago Sanitary Commission Office in McVicker's Theatre. FIGURE 17 (RIGHT): General John Logan.

FIGURE 18 (ABOVE): Stereograph Card of Sanitary Commission Wagon Train.
FIGURE 19 (BELOW): Battle of Resaca by Alfred Waud.

FIGURE 20 (ABOVE): Railroad Track Destruction in Georgia.
FIGURE 21 (BELOW): "General Sherman's Rear Guard" of bummers and refugees, from *Harper's Weekly*.

FIGURE 22 (ABOVE): Destruction of Hood's Ordnance Train in Atlanta.
FIGURE 23 (LEFT): Rudolph Mueller.
FIGURE 24 (BELOW): Edward Salomon

FIGURE 25 (ABOVE): Pontoon Bridge at Decatur. FIGURE 26 (BELOW): Evacuation of Atlanta.

FIGURE 27 (RIGHT): Evacuation of Atlanta.

FIGURE 28 (CENTER): Christian Commission Field HQ in Maryland.

FIGURE 29 (BELOW): Disabled Petitioners at DC Office of Christian Commission.

FIGURE 30 (ABOVE): Atlanta After the Bombardment. FIGURE 31 (BELOW): Slave Dealers in Atlanta.

FIGURE 32 (TOP): Sherman by Mathew Brady.
FIGURE 32 (CENTER): *The Burning of Atlanta*, from *Harper's Weekly.*
FIGURE 34 (BOTTOM): The Bummer.

FIGURE 35 (ABOVE): Prospectors/Treasure Seekers.
FIGURE 36 (ELOW): Union Prisoners at Andersonville.

FIGURE 37 (ABOVE): Sherman's March to the Sea by FOC Darley.
FIGURE 38 (BELOW): Refugee Train.

FIGURE 39 (ABOVE): William Sherman and His Generals: Oliver Howard, John Logan, William Hazen, Sherman, Jefferson C. Davis, Henry Slocum, Joseph Mower.
FIGURE 40 (BELOW): Freedmen on the March.

FIGURE 41 (ABOVE): African Americans at St. Helena Island, SC.
FIGURE 42 (BELOW): Sherman's March at McPhersonville, SC.

FIGURE 43 (ABOVE): Officers of the 82nd Illinois Volunteer Infantry.
FIGURE 44 (BELOW): Burning of Columbia, SC.

FIGURE 45 (ABOVE): Ruins of Columbia.
FIGURE 46 (BELOW): Ruins of Columbia.

FIGURE 47 (ABOVE): Corduroying at Lynch's Creek.
FIGURE 48 (BELOW): Slave Quarters at St. Helena Island Plantation.

FIGURE 49 (ABOVE): Unionist Refugees.
FIGURE 50 (BELOW): Crossing the Long Bridge for the Grand Review.

FIGURE 51 (ABOVE): John Logan and Family. FIGURE 52 (BELOW LEFT): Mary Ann Bickerdyke.
FIGURE 53 (BELOW RIGHT): Edward Salomon.

FIGURE 54 (ABOVE): Grand Review of the Armies.
FIGURE 55 (LEFT): John McCline in postwar New Mexico.
FIGURE 56 (BELOW): Slave Prison in Alexandria, VA.

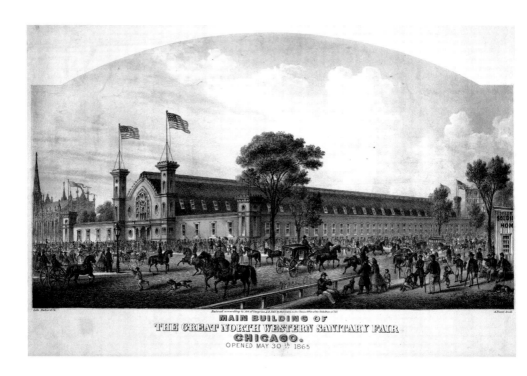

FIGURE 57 (ABOVE): Northwestern Sanitary Fair of 1865. FIGURE 58 (BELOW LEFT): Mary Livermore. FIGURE 59 (BELOW RIGHT): William Sherman in Retirement.

crusade. As he wrote, "He has been a pro-slavery man, and is unwilling to take high and manly ground on the slavery question."

As for General Davis, Hight had unmitigated contempt. Not only was he a martinet who threatened to shoot his own troops for their disobedience, he was nothing less than "a military tyrant, without one spark of humanity in his makeup. He was an ardent pro-slavery man before he entered the army, and has not changed his views since." Davis may have helped win the Battle of Jonesboro, and showed adept leadership in the field at times, but he also questioned Lincoln's racial policies and thought the Emancipation Proclamation would cause "mischief" in the army and society. Like Sherman, he would have happily preserved slavery if it preserved the union.

Even worse, Davis was an actual, bona fide murderer—a man who had shot and killed a superior officer, General William Nelson, in Louisville two years before. He had quarreled with Nelson in the minutes before the act, and took out his aggression on the much larger man with a bullet to the heart. Amazingly, Davis wasn't punished or even charged for the offense, since a major military campaign was then underway in Kentucky and the Union army couldn't afford to go without a handful of its commanding officers for a court martial. Davis remained not guilty in law, if not in reputation. Although he would never rise higher in rank than brigadier general of volunteers, he did find his way back to a prominent command. He had performed well enough in recent battles with the Army of the Cumberland that Sherman let him lead one of his four corps on the March to the Sea.

An *unapologetic* pro-slavery man . . . an *unrepentant* murderer. Hight didn't understand why men like Jefferson C. Davis were allowed to serve in the Northern armies—supposedly the armies of liberation against slavery and secession, but in reality littered with rogues and miscreants. If Hight had his way, Davis would already have been hanged for his crime, or at least imprisoned for life, but instead here he was, marching south from Milledgeville, one of the esteemed generals in one of the most famous armies on earth.

It disgusted the reverend, but he tried to rise above it. Sin was legion on earth, and the army was no different. Still, the unfairness of it all gnawed at him, vexed him, entangled his emotions and diminished his hopes. Army commanders should be wise, fatherly figures with large hearts and a humility before God, not clever scoundrels who could fire a gun. He hated to see wickedness take root in the ranks, hated the influence tyrants like Davis had over the soldiers.

Hight realized why he took it all so personally. This was no regular army—it was his home. He had made it so by turning away from Bloomington and embracing life among the troops, where death and salvation were such real and immediate concerns, and justice and righteousness such clear and tangible pursuits. He felt responsible for the uplift of these young men, guiding their path to transcendence.

He often wondered, though. Was he a fool for providing such guidance in a world where sin and tyranny held sway? He tried not to think about the consequences of all this destruction. How the gears of war crushed spirits and broke souls with irreparable finality. How churches had been burned and their pews used for kindling. How God's name had been profaned with blasphemy. How alcohol fueled widespread brutality and corruption. How the meekest upon the land—the poor, the children, even the bedraggled horses and mules—had been abused and degraded. How the leaders of what should have been a moral crusade delighted in their immorality. How a thousand other contradictions proved maddening and irreconcilable. He only knew that God had made him the shepherd of this flock. He had to fulfill his mission and help them follow a righteous path, wherever it led. But it was no easy task—these sheep were a rangy lot.

Reverend Hight had gained new members of his congregation over the summer when a few fresh souls transferred into the regiment. He was glad to see them, and not only because they might turn up for one of his sermons. They were soldiers who had developed a sterling reputation in the Atlanta campaign and were ready to test it on the road to Savannah. As Hight put it, "Many of our new men are Germans. These make the best of soldiers."

While there were a fair number of immigrant soldiers in the 58th Indiana and the 14th Corps, many more of them fought with the 20th Corps. Hight had grown familiar with one brigade from the 20th when they protected the pontoon train north of Milledgeville, acting as its rearguard. He was glad to have a shield from the rebel cavalry, especially with the threat of Wheeler's horsemen looming ever greater.

However, the feeling was not mutual among the corpsmen, who included the Germans of the 82nd Illinois Volunteer Infantry. Used to fighting and winning front-line battles as part of "Hooker's Ironclads," the regiment didn't enjoy marching at the back of the column. The troops grew frustrated at their tedious work, shadowing 300 wagons that regularly broke down and got stuck in the mud, and had to be shielded from snipers as they went. Even worse, the troops in the forward units got to forage over the country first, leaving hardly any decent eatables for the rear guard—just empty barns and plundered houses.

After they passed Milledgeville came the great day when the 82nd Illinois was transferred to the advance guard. They returned to the field with a flourish, skirmishing with the rebel cavalry, foraging for delicious provisions as well as a new supply of horses and mules, and tearing up railroad tracks as they went. They especially enjoyed ripping apart the roadbed and building fires that incinerated miles of rails and wooden stringers. As one soldier reported, after his unit finished its destructive work with a flourish, "[we] got so dirty, we looked like coal burners."

The sight of these troops covered in soot and coal tar would have greatly offended the regiment's original commander, Friedrich Hecker. The colonel once insisted his men should effect a crisp, clean, martial appearance, to go along with the rigid rules he had instituted. He could have no more imagined his soldiers coated in grime than he could their being reduced to guarding wagons or stealing food. But ever since Hecker had quit early in 1864, the men of the 82nd Illinois had done all those things, along with something else they didn't do while Hecker was their leader—win battles.

The success of the regiment increased the profile of its commander, Lieutenant Colonel Edward Salomon. He became highly regarded enough in the 20th Corps that he was assigned a new duty—messenger to George Thomas's forces in Tennessee, who were just about to face the remnants of John Bell Hood's army. Sherman had stopped following

Hood a month before, but the wily Texan remained dangerous, so transferring messages between Thomas's and Sherman's armies became a critical task. With Salomon taking a leave of absence from the 82nd Illinois, another German immigrant, Major Ferdinand Rolshausen, filled the role of commander. He was competent and well-liked by many of the soldiers—with the notable exception of Captain Rudolf Mueller, who thought of him as a "frightened hare" whose "back has grown quite bent from dodging the bullets so often." But Mueller tended to despise any superior officer not named Friedrich Hecker.

Although the 82nd Illinois still had a strong Teutonic element, its soldiers were no longer mainly German. Battlefield losses and furloughs had lowered its numbers, and new non-German recruits had diluted its old ethnic character even further. Increasingly the 82nd mixed Scandinavians, Jews, Swiss, and Germans with troops whose families had immigrated decades, or even centuries, before to America. It made for a colorful group rich with different languages and accents, and one that fit in well with the crazy quilt of cultures in the 20th Corps.

At the beginning of the march, the differences had been glaring between regiments raised for the western and eastern theaters in the 20th Corps. The eastern soldiers typically maintained a sharp dress code, adhered to proper rules and order, and drilled on parade grounds—giving them the look of a model army. If they didn't often win major battles in the east, at least they looked as if they could.

When Grant and Sherman moved twenty-six of these regiments west to compose half the units of what became the 20th Corps, the easterners were shocked by the slovenly appearance of their western counterparts. Their "raggedness and uncleanliness of apparel and looseness and negligence of appearance" alarmed them. Their slouch hats and frayed and weather-beaten garments showed a contempt for proper style, and their grizzled and unwashed faces, along with their crude behavior, made them "more like an armed rabble than an army." Many of the boys were dirty, profane, and rude, even to their commanders. They would holler for more food from officers if their rations weren't sufficient, mock their commanders as they rode by on horseback, and participate in all kinds of unapproved pranks and hijinks—everything from staging battles with pine cones to surprising each other with poisonous snakes. They indulged in lively, often violent, games as well. Cockfighting was a favorite sport for the boys, who set up nightly bouts of combat between their favorite chickens. The winning fowl received valorous names like "Bill Sherman" and "Johnny Logan." The losers got called "Bob Lee" and "Jeff Davis."

Unlike the easterners, who had a reputation for being fastidious prigs, the western boys were proud of their sloppy, unrefined ways and accepted or even reveled in the torments of the march. As one officer reported, "These two nights marching, groping through the woods, tumbling into ditches, and wading through mud, have been unable to dash the spirits of the men. Torn with brambles, burning their clothes and shoes, losing their hats, and mired from head to foot, and chilled to the marrow, they find fun in every accident."

Eventually the easterners in the 20th Corps began to appreciate the westerners' unusual ways. All the grime and disarray and violent hijinks and disorderly conduct and outright wildness kept the boys together, in a rousing, dirty camaraderie that no amount of rebel attacks or hard marching could diminish. As the campaign went on, the style of the east and west in the corps began to blend, just as the ethnic divisions within its regiments began to blur, until the soldiers became one rowdy mass of western fighters—united under the banner of William Sherman and his signature brand of warfare.

Southeast of Milledgeville the 14th and 20th Corps crossed paths, and each continued to march in parallel ten to thirty miles from each other. The pontoniers of the 58th Indiana still didn't have a rear guard, and continued to be exposed to the threat of Wheeler's cavalry. And the horsemen made their presence felt, even when they weren't firing muskets at their Yankee foes.

Wheeler had done his worst at Buffalo Creek, a 40-foot-wide channel bounded by seventy acres of swamps, which were crossed by nine bridges spanning 30 to 100 feet. Here the rebels had burned the 80-foot main bridge, damaged the trestles of the smaller ones, and even trashed the causeways that allowed access into the swamps. In order for the soldiers, wagons, and artillery pieces of both army corps to cross over the quagmire, the First Michigan Engineers and Mechanics had to first throw rails and logs over the swamp mud to build a corduroy road. Then the pontoniers would follow by bridging the main channel.

The work took no less than seven hours, ending just before midnight. As the nonengineering troops took a long break playing cards and other games, the First Michigan and 58th Indiana completed a massive engineering work in the middle of nowhere. Working from each side of the river, the pontoniers cut down trees, fashioned them into planks, and laid them down over rails, until they repaired all the bridges Wheeler and his troops had destroyed. Together with the First Michigan, they constructed a great wooden pathway that stretched a full quarter of a mile, over muddy swamps and marshes across Buffalo Creek and its channels to eventual dry ground. It was a true feat of engineering and a product of a heroic amount of effort—though one that few troops would see in the daylight, if they ever saw it again.

As November ended, the pontoniers built roads over the swamps of the Ogeechee River basin. The weather turned colder, and Reverend Hight noticed the character of the march changing. The sandy ground of central Georgia gave way to the swamps farther south, and the column moved slower over the sodden terrain. The regiment still scoured the country and collected a bevy of horses and mules, along with the likes of sweet potatoes, honey, peanuts, persimmons, and even a few gamecocks, but found many eatables were getting harder to locate. Sometimes foragers got lost and took the wrong roads; other times they came back empty-handed, and the regiment had to go without food for a meal or a day. And with the rebel horsemen capturing and executing any food gatherers they found, Hight saw "It is getting to be a dangerous business to forage."

The increased peril of finding food didn't only affect the troops. Upon the passage of Sherman's army, thousands of slaves had freed themselves from bondage and began following the column en masse. When Sherman paused the march at Louisville, Georgia, to regroup militarily, many more freedmen throughout the region congregated with the army. They arrived on foot, and in old buggies and wagons taken from farms. Women came holding their babies, teenage boys and girls followed with their siblings, and young and old men arrived alone or with their families. The majority escaped the plantation simply in hopes of a better, freer life; others did so to reunite their families that had been divided across town or county lines. Some sang hymns and praised God for delivering them from evil.

Although the Union generals worried how they would feed thousands of freed people, many of them had already been foraging on the country for years. As with the slaves on the Cobb plantation, their masters had kept them in a state of near-starvation, desperate for meat and reduced to penury. They had had no choice but to seek out food wherever they could find it, whether foraging in the woods or purloining hogs and chickens from farms in the region. They would continue to do so now, though with the protection of the Union army.

In return they provided Sherman with a huge source of free labor. Blacks now worked in large numbers in the Pioneer Corps, helping build corduroy roads through the swamps, as well as driving wagons, cooking meals, spying on Confederates, destroying railroads, navigating troops through the outback, and ferreting out buried treasures on plantations. They earned their keep on the march and did many thankless, arduous labors, and only received army rations after the troops had eaten. Still, they kept coming to march with Sherman.

The newly freed black marchers were still in the rear of the column when the 14th Corps found itself marching through yet another swamp. Wheeler's cavalry had earlier destroyed the bridge over Buckhead Creek and lurked nearby to attack the rear of the Yankee army if it had a chance. The pontoniers laid down a bridge to span the creek, and the troops crossed over quickly and without incident, delivering the soldiers, guns, and wagons to the opposite shore. Then General Jefferson C. Davis ordered the pontoons to be removed.

Before the black marchers could pass, Davis had his provost guard stop them at gunpoint, leaving them stranded on the far side of the creek—at clear risk of capture or murder by the horsemen. Panic soon broke out among the refugees, who let forth "a cry of agony that ought to have melted the stoniest heart." As the army leaders prepared to march on, the scene became more desperate for the freedmen:

> Some of them at once plunged into the water, and swam across. Others ran wildly up and down the bank, shrieking with terror and crying for help. It was too much for our humane officers and men. They threw pieces of plank and timber into the water, and rendered every assistance possible to the frantic refugees. Many of them succeeded in reaching our shore. They came up the bank and through the bushes, dripping wet, but happy in the thought that they had escaped. There was a shout of triumph among our men as they saw the refugees successfully stemming the current. But all did not get over. Some were drowned—how many is not known.

John Hight was horrified by the action, calling it "disgraceful to American history." The abandonment of refugees stood in defiance to everything Hight believed, to the ideals he preached about, to the very mercy of God. Brute villainy now ruled the 14th Corps in the form of Jefferson C. Davis, and it demanded condemnation regardless of consequence. But it wasn't the first time the general had tried to murder people, nor would it be the last.

ELEVEN

ALL AROUND THEM LIGHT AS DAY

C aptain Charles Wills was in high spirits and having a capital day. It was the morning of November 22, and his 103rd Illinois Volunteer Infantry, as part of a fighting brigade helmed by Charles Walcutt, had driven Joseph Wheeler's cavalry from the field ten miles outside of Macon. The brigade had performed splendidly, as Wills reported, and had "stampeded them. It was the richest thing I ever saw. We got highly complimented on the way we drove them." They had marched 114 miles from Atlanta in just a week, and this skirmish was their first major challenge. They had met it with aplomb, and were now ready for lunch.

They passed through nearby Griswoldville, whose capture had been their objective. The quaint little town had once been a minor manufacturing center, home to several dozen homes, a mansion, a gristmill, and a handful of factories producing everything from soap and bricks to Colt revolvers. Now it lay in ruins, after a Michigan cavalry unit had burned most of it to the ground. Nonetheless, Captain Wills looked forward to setting up camp there and settling in for a relaxing evening.

It looked to be another successful day on the march. In just over a week, he and his regiment had tramped over level, well-cultivated farm-land and were discovering new plants and animals—everything from Spanish moss and lemon trees to a coal-black squirrel. They feasted on the likes of pork and sweet potatoes, drank cow's milk for the first time in a year, and even experimented with exotic meats like opossum—which he found he liked very much! The highlight came when he visited a popular hot springs, where he uncovered a cache of peach brandy and "*destroyed*" it, meaning he guzzled it with delight. It all made for a wondrous journey, "the most gigantic pleasure excursion ever planned." He filled his belly with fresh food, breathed in the clean country air, and even met a few fine Southern ladies. One of them rewarded his company with a nice supper and an evening's rest. As he put it, "By the kindness of Mrs. Elizabeth Celia Pye, I occupy a feather bed to-night."

However, the day spoiled quickly. While he was luxuriating and for-getting his troubles, the sudden crack of musketry reminded him he was still fighting a war. Rebels were on the attack.

The acting commander of the 15th Corps, Peter Osterhaus, ordered Charles Walcutt to pull his brigade back to the edge of the woods, a little over a mile east of town. There, Wills and the 103rd Illinois and the other five regiments in the brigade constructed field works made of logs and rails stripped from a nearby railroad line. They set up a defen-sive perimeter flanked by swamps, and prepared to give the rebel cavalry another taste of defeat. General Wheeler didn't seem to know when he'd been whipped.

Except these attackers weren't the cavalry. Instead, Wills watched as "a fine line of Johnnies" in the Confederate infantry appeared, then another line emerged, and another. Roughly four brigades' worth of rebel soldiers now faced them, 2,400 men—900 more than Walcutt's brigade. In an instant they shattered the afternoon calm.

A quartet of rebel cannons wiped out the two federal guns opposing them, killing a handful of gunners and stripping the brigade of its artillery protection. The rebel cannoneers next turned their firepower against the Yankee field works, blasting the logs and rails, and exposing the brigade to a flurry of shot and shell.

After blowing holes in the federal defensive line, the rebels now had their moment. They charged across the open field.

With their flags flying, they moved fast, and got to within 250 yards of the federal line. It was the first major conflict of the March to the Sea, and Charles Wills was in the thick of it.

A Confederate shell struck the color guard for the Sixth Iowa, blowing a man's head off and covering the regiment's flag with his blood. The rebels advanced.

The Yankee regiments readied their first shots, aiming low with their single-shot Springfield rifles and Spencer repeating rifles. They hit many of the attackers in the first line, but more rebels followed.

The Yankees fired—reloaded—fired—reloaded—fired—reloaded, until the noise became deafening and the smoke blinding. The rebels kept coming.

They delivered a flurry of Union lead, round after round, until "our guns got so hot they burned our hands." But the rebel assault did not stop.

A shell burst near General Walcutt and pierced his leg with shrapnel, forcing him off the field. A new commander took over and realized the brigade was running out of ammunition. They'd have to make their remaining cartridges count.

The rebels got to within fifty yards of the Yankees, close enough to see their uniforms and their faces. They saw their enemy in plain view—but could not reach them. The fight became too hot to bear.

Dozens of men fell in heaps. The attackers took cover in a gully.

They paused in the trench and waited for their moment, then rose up and charged. The Union rifles beat them back with a hail of lead.

They fell into the gully once more. Then they rose up again, and faced the same sheet of flame. Three, four, perhaps seven times did the rebels attack their foes, trying desperately to cross those last fifty yards and overwhelm their defenses and gain a victory. But each time they met with a violent repulse, and their troops fell by the score. As Wills saw it, "one after another their lines crumbled to pieces."

Fewer men returned to the trench each time, with a general and two colonels among the casualties. With daylight leaching away, the attackers' spirits weakened and their effort collapsed. The last remaining troops quit the field and withdrew into the woods.

After the battle had concluded, Wills and the rest of the brigade advanced toward the gully to capture the remaining Confederates, or finish them off if they fought back. What they found shocked them: "Old grey-haired and weakly-looking men and little boys, not over 15 years old, lay dead or writhing in pain. I did pity those boys, they almost all who could talk, said the Rebel cavalry gathered them up and forced them in. . . . They knew nothing at all about fighting."

Walcutt's brigade had lost 100 men; the rebels, 600. But the Union troops soon discovered the battle hadn't involved Confederate regulars, but poorly trained Georgia militiamen, as green as the woods around them. Though they looked impressive from a distance, most of the militiamen's shots went twenty feet over the heads of Union troops. Most of the Union troops' shots found their mark.

In the trench, long after dark, the fallen men writhed in pain, cried for water, begged for mercy. One Iowan saw it as a "harvest of death." Fathers and uncles lay dead beside their sons and nephews, who lay dead beside friends and colleagues. As one wounded man said, "My entire neighborhood is ruined, these people are all my neighbors." Charles Wills felt sick to his stomach: "It was awful the way we slaughtered those men."

Federal troops spent a good portion of the night doing what they could to help those who could still breathe or walk, moving them to a field hospital and giving them water and medicine. The corpses they covered in blankets. It all made for a grim and disturbing scene, and a dark capstone to Captain Wills's capital day. He began to understand more fully what the war meant, and feared what it might become. As he wrote, "I hope we will never have to shoot at such men again."

Four days later and forty miles east, a group of much better-trained Confederate fighters decided to meet their foes at Sandersville. With its yellow-brick courthouse on the town square, a handful of stately homes, and a Greek Revival church, the small town itself had little military value. But Joseph Wheeler and his rebel cavalry had to make a stand there to try to delay the Yankee invaders before they could reach Augusta, or Savannah, or whatever major town they planned to strike next. He dismounted his horsemen and positioned them behind barricades, awaiting the inevitable approach of Union skirmishers. Some residents pleaded with Wheeler not to bring the fight to their town, not to draw the attention of the Northern vandals to their homes, but he ignored them. If Sandersville had to burn to save the Confederacy, so be it.

The skirmishers came in waves, first from the west, where the 20th Corps bore down on the rebels, and then from the north, where the 14th Corps attacked them in a pincers movement. A half-hour's worth of gunplay followed, until the Yankee skirmishers broke loose and assaulted Wheeler's cavalry in a frenzy. They severed their lines and chased them into the streets, across people's backyards, and anywhere they could find them. Pandemonium broke out as "women & children were frightened entirely out of their wits & increased the confusion by their screams." The chaos peaked as the Yankees forced the rebels out of town, galloping for their lives.

After the smoke cleared, a figure entered the town on horseback. With a calm expression on his face and an unlit cigar in his mouth, he surveyed the residents who watched him with quiet terror. William Sherman had arrived.

The commanding general of the Military Division of the Mississippi rode in and took the measure of the place. Wheeler's men had left a mess of broken barricades and a handful of wounded men behind. Riflemen had used the courthouse and private homes to cover the Confederates' retreat. And the church now had a dead rebel lying on its steps.

Union troops scouted the town and found a sizable brick house to use as their general's temporary headquarters. The owner was a doctor who had gone to Macon. His sister and her aunt had remained to face the invaders, and when one notable red-haired Yankee—with a grizzled face and unshaven whiskers—appeared in their parlor, they were in no mood to receive him. Still, they had no choice. Sherman would not brook dissent from a pair of lady rebels, even if it was in their own home.

He was especially peevish today. He told them their General Wheeler had no business using the town as a battle site, and the town folk had no right to shoot at his men to cover the cavalry's escape. It was contrary to the rules of war as he knew them, and an insult to martial honor. Also, he had seen burning piles of fodder west of town, and knew Wheeler had destroyed them to starve the Union cattle, mules, and horses, and by extension his men. He threatened to burn the entire town for these transgressions, or any town that allowed such treasonous behavior.

The general kept up the conversation and stayed for several hours. As he did with most civilians he encountered, he tried to explain to his hosts the folly of secession and the righteousness of his cause. He offered repeated justifications for his policies and vowed he didn't make war on women and children. The ladies listened decorously and allowed him to vent his emotions. Their strategy worked. By the time he left his anger had dissipated, and he promised only to burn the courthouse and the stocks of cotton and other goods that could support the Confederate war effort. It wasn't a complete victory for the women over Sherman's violent impulses, but it was as good as any town folk could expect to receive on the March to the Sea.

The residents of Sandersville were lucky. Just west at Buffalo Creek, Sherman had ordered a house to be torched because it sat near a bridge Wheeler's men had burned. He justified it to his aide Henry Hitchcock by remarking, "In war everything is right which prevents anything. If bridges are burned I have a right to burn all houses near it." His policy spread unchecked fear among the locals and gave rise to stories that the Yankee general not only burned houses, but freely massacred the people inside them.

Sherman grew frustrated at these rumors. Hadn't he repeated, over and over, that his men would only harm property in support of the rebel war effort? Had there been an outbreak of beatings or rapes or murders or other outrages upon the citizens of Georgia? Of course not! Their cotton may have been burned, their corn and hogs and sweet potatoes and molasses may have been gobbled, their slaves may have been freed, and their barns and storehouses occasionally burned, but never—never—had he ordered harm upon any civilian unless she fired a weapon at him. This in spite of all the loose talk from the locals about his men being vandals or demons or miscreants—expressed openly and in saucy, defiant tones! He had patiently endured such rude, uncivil behavior. Did that not make him a model commander in these desperate times?

Not all the Georgians he encountered were so impudent. At Covington they turned out to offer him provisions, and one woman even prepared a fine meal for him. (He chose to evade their kindnesses.) At other towns leading citizens turned out to meet him, offer him supplies, and implore him to protect their property with armed guards. He occasionally indulged them. And at Gum Creek, he calmed the concerns of an elderly woman and her middle-aged unmarried daughter, to such a degree that the mother even tried to arrange a pairing with Sherman's staff surgeon—saying her daughter was "a powerful fast knitter—could keep a bachelor's ankles mighty warm."

These were the exceptions, however. More often the locals hid from his advance or regarded him with cold disregard. Rather than seeing this as a product of his foraging policy and the abuses of the bummers, Sherman blamed their intransigence on Confederate leaders. He groused to Henry Hitchcock about the calumnies they had spread to their people, warning them of the bloodthirsty Yankees who reveled in the murder of innocents, who set angry slaves upon defenseless whites, who indulged in all manner of great and petty cruelties—crimes far worse than anything his troops had actually done. On more than one occasion, upon approaching a sizable house looking for a spot to eat or bed for the night, the woman meeting him showed a look of barely concealed terror, expecting to be bludgeoned at the conquering general's whim. At another home, he found the lady of the house and her children frozen in paralytic horror at his presence. They cried for mercy and expected to be killed by the great beast Sherman. He spoke to them in dulcet tones for many minutes and finally assuaged their fears, but such reactions maddened him and only made him more determined to crush the sham Confederacy that spread such lies.

Moreover, many of these same Georgians who cowered before him—with the notable exception of their slaves, who welcomed him—crafted their own lies they thought he would be gullible enough to believe. When he inquired as to why they supported the secessionists, they offered awkward and elaborate justifications for their men being impressed into the Confederate army, that they had been good and loyal citizens of the republic, that they only wished for peace, and on and on. Yet despite all their hems and haws, they never once volunteered to give up their slaves in support of national unity. Couldn't they just keep their human property and support the Union too? Sherman could only scoff. The time for that had long since passed; the war had come, and their way of life had to end, along with the rebellion.

In pursuit of this aim he had been quite artful. His great plans for the march had gone well over the last two weeks, resulting in what he called "the perfection of campaigning." As he saw it, not only had his armies managed to feed themselves with proper foraging, they had largely refrained from unapproved arson and pillaging—with the exception of certain "stragglers"—and had performed well in their skirmishes with Wheeler's cavalry and the rare fight at Griswoldville. Sherman had marched with the left wing, the Army of Georgia, for the last two weeks and now looked forward to traveling with his former command, the Army of the Tennessee, for the next two.

Now consisting of just the 15th and 17th Corps, the Army of the Tennessee was the right wing of the invasion force, and Sherman put the trusty Oliver Howard in charge of it. The army traveled on roads that were much harder going than those of the left wing, encountering far fewer people, much less productive farmland, and sandy soil that quickly gave way to swamps and quasi-quicksand in places. Still, Sherman respected the grit of the 15th Corps and expected it would be up for the challenge. It always had been.

Sherman had been in no hurry to call the political general John Logan back to command the 15th Corps. He respected his bravado, but thought his strategic skills were lacking, especially in a campaign where strategy meant everything, and fighting much less. In Logan's absence, he had chosen as corps commander the German immigrant Peter Osterhaus, who had already shown a keen mind in preparing for the rebel attack at Griswoldville, and would doubtless find more success in the campaign. Sherman himself planned to travel with the other part of the Army of the Tennessee, the 17th Corps, led by another political general, Frank Blair.

Thus far, all four corps had executed his plans brilliantly for the march, and had flummoxed star-crossed Confederate leaders like Howell Cobb, William Hardee, P.G.T. Beauregard, and even old Braxton Bragg, all of whom Jeff Davis had recycled to defend the Southern heartland. Sherman easily outfoxed them with pep and vigor.

At the outset near Atlanta, he had feinted in John Bell Hood's direction in Tennessee, making them think he would withdraw into north Georgia. Then once they knew he was headed south, he tricked them into thinking the industrial town of Macon was his target, and they reacted by fortifying the town and locking down a fair number of their troops. Once they knew he had no interest in Macon, they threw their weight into protecting Augusta, another manufacturing center. Accordingly, he sent General Kilpatrick's Union cavalry in that direction and forced them to tie down more troops in its defense. And now his recent moves had caused so much confusion and consternation among the rebel chieftains, they had no idea where his four corps were going—to Augusta, to Savannah, or to a destination much farther north. Perhaps his troops were even headed to the South Carolina coast, where they could cut off the railroad supply line and starve southern Georgia into submission! He enjoyed keeping them guessing.

Sherman's aide Henry Hitchcock greatly admired his boss for all of his tactics and stratagems, seeing him as "varied, quick, original, shrewd, full of anecdote, experience, and general information." He appreciated his nimble mind and brilliant, masterful plan to bring the South to its knees. But his ardor had its limits.

Hitchcock had served with Sherman since the scorched-earth campaign he had waged in north Georgia just before he burned Atlanta. He had challenged him then on the merits of his campaign of destruction, but now knew better than to question his commander's wisdom. Sherman had become a military icon; he was just a lawyer from Missouri. Still, Hitchcock didn't need a degree in military science to know that Sherman, despite being the owner of a great calculating mind, could also be plagued by anxiety and agitation. In camp, he had seen Sherman burst into rages, especially when the press reported his armies' movements or when plantation owners and Confederate leaders spread lies about him. He had seen him make decisions in nervy and restless fashion, especially when challenged. And he had seen him late at night, in his red flannel underwear and dressing gown, pacing, cogitating, delivering thoughts and theories to whomever would listen:

> He is proverbially the most restless man in the army at night,—never sleeps a night straight through, and frequently comes out and pokes round in this style, disregarding all remonstrance as to taking cold. His staff think that just such a freak at Rome [Georgia] brought on the neuralgia attack in his right arm and shoulder which has been troubling him for a month. Joined him and chatted a while about weather, climate, late hours, etc., etc.

His strong yet strangely erratic personality didn't diminish his popularity in the ranks, though. The troops gave him familiar nicknames like "old dad," "old Billy," or even "Crazy Billy." Some wags took it further, and when they passed by the general, called out "Forage liberally!" as they held armloads of stolen eatables—which Sherman responded to either with a quick lecture on proper foraging or outright indifference, depending on his mood. In one case he crossed paths with a soldier who had hung a cornucopia of vegetables from his uniform while clutching a dead chicken. Sherman cursed at him for violating official orders; the offender cursed back at him. Sherman demanded to know his name; the offender revealed himself to be an army chaplain. The plundering preacher then graciously invited him to dine with him that evening on the stolen bounty. Sherman declined.

As much as anyone, Henry Hitchcock grew disenchanted about these flagrant violations of Sherman's policies on foraging, and questioned whether the general had the ability, or even the interest, to control his own soldiers. As he wrote, "I am bound to say I think Sherman lacking in enforcing discipline. Brilliant and daring, fertile, rapid, and terrible, he does not seem to me to *carry things out* in this respect."

Many troops saw their commander's special orders as vague guidelines rather than firm edicts. Bummers continued to flourish in the ranks, and even common soldiers were not above busting open pantry doors to fill their pockets with eatables or rifling through cellars and attics in search of hidden treasure. At Louisville a scene of chaos ensued after a lively campaign of plunder, in which "foragers came in loaded down with hams and quarters of pigs and sheep, bags and teams full of vegetables, with mules girdled with turkeys and chickens, trundling in wheelbarrows barrels of sorghum syrup and wash-tubs full of honey." The looters ransacked mansions, drank the rare wine they found there, made off with the Brussels carpets and bed quilts, and even danced a "rough waltz" in a parlor while "some brother rascals were pounding music out of the five hundred dollar piano with musket butts, and dancing on the mahogany, smashed the piano and everything they could not lug off." After a rumor spread that a local girl had spat on a Yankee soldier, the troops responded by burning nearly the entire town. A few bummers even plundered graveyards in hopes of finding valuables where there should have been corpses. Sometimes they found both.

Not all regiments behaved so barbarically, and a good number executed Sherman's field orders to the letter. They foraged with discretion according to the proper protocols, left enough food at a farm so its owners wouldn't starve, and refrained from unnecessary theft and arson. Their officers enforced foraging orders with precision and threatened anyone who violated them, including other officers.

One such enforcer was Captain Orlando Poe, Sherman's chief engineer and, ironically, the man he had ordered to burn Atlanta. Poe grew especially disgusted at the officers who winked at their troops' brash thievery or even encouraged it. As he wrote to his wife describing his effort to stop it: "I lose my temper . . . and make pretty free use of my physical strength with which Providence has blessed me, as more than one 'bunged-up' face in the army can testify." But no amount of Poe's pummeling could stop the plundering. Eventually Sherman himself became worried about the epidemic of theft, too. He issued new field orders that reminded the troops of the proper methods of foraging, though it seemed to take little hold among the worst violators. As he told Hitchcock, "I have been three years fighting stragglers, and they are harder to conquer than the enemy."

The end result of all the plunder was nothing less than murder. The free-range foragers and bummers infuriated southern Georgians, and Joseph Wheeler's cavalry responded by treating them as hostile combatants, hanging them from trees or slashing their throats. Soon the rebel horsemen began treating captured Union cavalrymen the same way—by executing them. In his ongoing war with Wheeler, Union General Hugh Kilpatrick reported to Sherman his men had been found killed and mutilated by Southern savages. He asked for permission to fight back, to give the rebels a taste of their own bloody medicine. Sherman's response was succinct. Provided Kilpatrick had clear and incontrovertible evidence of such bestial crimes, he had his commander's approval to respond in kind. As Sherman told him, "you may hang and mutilate man for man without regard to rank."

One officer who did not believe in an eye for an eye, and resisted every urge to descend into animal savagery, was General Oliver Howard. The leader of the Army of the Tennessee and the well-known Christian general tried to remain a moral man on the march, yet he found it difficult. Swearing was widespread among some officers and enlisted men, arson and looting had become legion in certain units, and the sight of poor, beleaguered Georgians stripped of their possessions or forced from their homes sickened him. It called into question his purpose in the army and even the health of his soul. As he said, "For the past year there has seemed to be a cloud between me and my Savior." Unlike Sherman, though, he resolved to do something about it. In his Special Field Order No. 26, Howard gave license to his officers to shoot any pillagers they found; to enforce vigorously the rules against unauthorized foraging; and to punish anyone convicted of robbery or arson with death.

Charles Wills was very familiar with these new orders. Howard had issued them on the day of the victory at Griswoldville, and three days later, the troops of the 103rd Illinois heard them read aloud for about the twentieth time. They listened to them thoughtfully, paid them dutiful attention, and then ignored them. They were having too good a time at the town of Irwinton to bother with official army policy. Many of them were out "prospecting"—poking into the earth with sharpened sticks to discover any treasures the locals may have buried. They capped their visit to town by burning the courthouse and most of the public buildings.

Wills had always felt qualms about foraging and arson in the Army of the Tennessee. In the early days of the war, he had described the army as becoming "awfully depraved" in its thievery. Much later, in January 1864, he wrote that the 500 men in his mounted army unit "have committed more devilment than two divisions of regular cavalry could in five years." The men under his command were not responsible for the worst of it, and as captain, he had vigorously tried to control their behavior. He knew if he ever had to face an official board of inquiry, he would be responsible for their actions.

That was before the March to the Sea. Now, despite his edicts, many soldiers in the 103rd indulged in stealing and bumming at will. If anyone were to punish them, it would be a concerned commander on-site like Oliver Howard or Orlando Poe. But there weren't enough Christian generals or enraged engineers to put a stop to the abuses. Even Wills himself had feasted to excess on the rich harvest of the South, and if his conscience bothered him, he forgot to mention it in his diary.

What did bother him, though, were his recent experiences in battle. Griswoldville continued to haunt him, as it did most of the federal troops who had looked into that trench, into that abyss, and had seen the dead bodies of old men and children. In fact, Wills himself began to wonder whether it was worth it. He had left the headquarters of Richard Oglesby back in Lagrange, Tennessee, to become a real soldier with the 103rd in the summer of 1863. He had given up his material comforts—of free-flowing wine, delicious meals, lovely women, and lively dancing—for life on the march, all in hopes of "seeing the elephant" of battle and becoming a man. And in north Georgia, from Resaca to Kennesaw Mountain, he had done just that: experiencing the thrill and horror of war, and the sharp feeling of victory and defeat. At the Battle of Atlanta he had seen combat up close, as his brigade helped turn the tide against the rebels, and it had invigorated and shocked and terrified and emboldened him. But after that the valor of the campaign began to crumble.

At Ezra Church, wave after wave of Confederates had perished in a hail of lead—a gruesome spectacle that Wills called "butchery." Then at Jonesboro, more Confederates had fallen in a senseless slaughter, to Wills's disbelief. And now there was Griswoldville. Was this what it meant to be a Union soldier in Georgia? To annihilate lines of men whose commanders sacrificed them in vain hopes of an unlikely victory? Where was the glory in that kind of triumph?

He didn't know. He could only take comfort in the familiar, enjoying the food his unit foraged, seeing unusual wildlife in the woods, and finding pleasure when he could. At Irwinton, Wills met a lovely country lady named Miss Howell, "a charming girl, very accomplished," with whom he enjoyed "another romantic meeting" and spent the night at her house. Sadly, he had to depart with his regiment the next day. Soon after, the 15th Corps burned the town.

He could only wonder where she was now . . . where any of them had gone . . . and what had become of them.

In the second part of the march, after it crossed the Oconee River, the 15th Corps saw its opportunities for devilment diminish greatly. Its soldiers tramped through a landscape where stocks of grain and produce became smaller, the cows and horses looked thinner and hungrier, plantations gave way to humble farms, and people became fewer in number and much poorer. Feeding the army here meant taking food from a family that might have no way to replenish it.

The 15th had the most southerly route of the four corps, and by far the worst. General Howard had somehow ended up with incorrect, outdated maps, and his corps had to travel through the desolate countryside on what Wills described as "old Indian trails." The corps ended up strung out over twenty miles in places, and the four divisions within the corps ended up scattered—and would not reunite until the march was nearly over. It didn't take long for some units to get lost in a no-man's-land of pine barrens.

In some areas, the trees were so dense the troops had to slash their way through the underbrush. Day after day Wills's unit trudged through tracts of "awful pine forest, hardly broken by fence or clearing. I never saw such a lonesome place. Not a bird, not a sign of animal life, but the shrill notes of the tree frog. Not a twig of undergrowth, and no vegetable life but just grass and pitch pine." He began to despise the smell of pine, especially when it was burning. Worse, the troops had to cross remote swamps on pontoons and corduroy roads, and were repeatedly delayed at rivers like the Ogeechee. They also saw new, more menacing wildlife like scorpions and pine snakes.

Sometimes while they were lost in the thickets and swamps, the only way for soldiers to tell where they were would be to wait for a rise in elevation, a gentle hill, a clearing above the tree line. And there they would see them, just to the north. The great pillars of smoke—the burning railroads and cotton gins and barns and arsenals and warehouses that marked the path of each army corps. The routes of the 14th, the 20th, and the 17th were written in dark carbon plumes above the horizon. One officer saw it as "Columns of smoke by day, and 'pillars of fire' by night, for miles and miles . . ."

As the 15th Corps marched into parts unknown, the terrain became increasingly alien, the atmosphere more phantasmic. In the Third Division, the troops made a long trek into the wilderness on a narrow trail, illuminated on each side by burning fence rails made of pitch pine, which they had lit for warmth in the cold of the evening. One soldier recalled walking into a landscape that resembled a scene from the Old Testament, as his unit passed through "two walls of fire . . . extending as far as the eye could reach, with here and there burning cotton gins and out buildings, and the heavens above, and all before, around and behind them, light as day with the flames of the burning pitch."

In this bleak and remote landscape, Charles Wills found fewer eatables to his liking and fewer women for a dalliance. Yet he continued to meet and converse with the locals, as a relief from the drudgery of the journey. Most of those who remained to greet the army were black. They had escaped from hardscrabble farms and smallholder tracts of land—not the sort of plantations the left wing marched past. As Wills wrote, an "immense number of 'contrabands' now follow us, most of them able-bodied men, who intend going into the army." He did not dissuade them.

Three years of campaigning had changed Wills from an inveterate bigot to someone whose mind was beginning to open. Instead of mocking black people in his diary, he now reported the indignities he saw heaped upon them. Weeks before in north Georgia he watched the rebel army take 800 black men as captives, likely to be killed or sold into slavery, and it appalled him. Closer to Atlanta he watched planters run thousands of their slaves down a road, and saw some of them escape. And recently, in early December, he met a black girl who had no choice but to join the army column after she had led the 103rd Illinois to her farm's horses and mules. In return her owner beat her with a rail, broke her arm, and "bruised her shamefully." These incidents hardened Wills to pleas from the farmers and planters he met not to take their grain and livestock. What was worse—to lose property to an invading army, or to lose one's life or health to someone who claimed to own you?

Henry Hitchcock, traveling with Sherman, heard many of the same stories on farms and plantations they visited. Some slaves told them of masters who routinely tied them up and delivered 200 to 300 lashes with a strap. At one house, a black man had lost his leg when several white women shot him in an argument over the way he planted potatoes. And at another, the lovely young woman who greeted Sherman's troops had an entirely different character with her bondsmen. They reported she flogged them with a strap, beat them with hand saws and paddles with holes, and after savaging them, literally rubbed salt into their wounds. These masters were often the same people who demanded Sherman protect their property from theft—including their slaves.

Sherman would do no such thing. Destroying slavery meant crippling the labor base of the South, which in turn meant crippling the rebellion. On many occasions when he and his staff came to a plantation, they sought out the slaves first. "Don't want white man," the general would say, trusting almost nothing that came out of the mouths of planters and their families. Once Sherman summoned a bondsman, often an elderly man, he learned of the lies the plantation owners had spread of the Yankees' murdering ways, of their attempts to keep the people they "owned" from escaping while they hid from the army, and, of course, where the planters stashed their loot. He met slaves who were illiterate as well as those who had taught themselves to read and write despite the risks. He met slaves who were speechless at the sight of a liberator in their midst, as well as those who engaged him in lively discussions of history and politics. And he met slaves who asked him if it was wise to run away. One response he offered summed it up: "Go when you like,—we don't force any to be soldiers,—pay wages, and will pay you if you choose to come: but as *you* have family, better stay now and have general concert and leave hereafter. *But don't hurt your masters or their families*—we don't want that."

Remarkably, whether or not they heard Sherman's words, few freedmen did harm their former captors, despite the abuses they had endured—abuses that were etched on their bodies in countless places. Sherman and Hitchcock saw the whip marks that had lacerated their skin, the implements of pain and torture they suffered under, and the tracking dogs that made their lives miserable, snuffing out any chance of escape with the aid of a keen nose, lightning speed, and sharp teeth.

The troops of all four army corps saw these things, too, and it challenged their beliefs. Before the war, apologists for slavery had peddled romantic fables that many had believed—the benevolent master, the childlike slave, the patrician gentility, the graceful manners. Those myths crumbled when the troops saw what slavery looked like up close, as the soldier Theodore Upson did at one plantation: "stocks, iron collars with chains on them, several kinds of whips, and a paddle thing with a lot of holes on it."

Whether they were ardent abolitionists or committed bigots, the great majority of Sherman's men came to despise the planters who had started and funded the war—and knew slavery was the source of their livelihood. In response they destroyed the whipping posts where slaves had been abused and the workhouses where they had toiled, the pens where they had been confined and the auction blocks where they had been sold as chattel. They stole great quantities of food and livestock in places where the bondsmen told them to look. They saw the opulent manor houses of white secessionists next to the rude leaking shacks of black loyalists. And when the images of wealth and poverty, comfort and desperation, freedom and slavery became too much to reconcile, more than a few soldiers made the leap from enterprising foragers to angry avengers. As one observer saw, "If the negroes on the place told stories of great cruelty they had suffered, or of bitter hostility to the Union, or if there were bloodhounds about, which had been used to run down slaves, the injury was generally avenged by the torch." Many of the pillars of fire on the March to the Sea were houses of slavery on fire.

While most soldiers still harbored prejudice against blacks, the march forced some of them to confront it. And an increasing number of troops now wrote letters home talking about the "blasted and debased and damned" world they saw in "a system of wrong that no language can properly condemn," where the violence and terror visited upon slaves increased their conviction for emancipation and their enmity for rich planters—which only increased further as they witnessed more plantation violence. In turn, their words influenced the ideas of their parents and their neighbors, who had begun the war supporting only the preservation of the union, not abolition. Now they too understood fighting secession meant fighting slavery, and their own boys were doing it every day with muskets and matches.

All these thoughts of liberty and captivity, war and brutality, new friends and old enemies, finally coalesced when Union prisoners of war began to return to the ranks. As these men appeared in camp weary, starving, and emaciated, they told their colleagues of the few allies they had in prison pens like Andersonville. As one Ohio escapee said, "The slaves universally were the prisoners' friends," and did what they could to help them flee. The same bloodhounds that had tracked escaped slaves also tracked escaped prisoners, and that only made the Northern soldiers respect the freedmen, and hate the rebels and their attack dogs, that much more. The troops started shooting and killing the canines wherever they found them.

The rage of the soldiers grew after the 20th Corps passed through Camp Lawton, a short-lived camp where Yankee prisoners starved on meager rations and endured abuse at the hands of their captors. Here the corpsmen saw a 300-foot-square, pine-log stockade open to the elements, where guards would shoot men who wandered past a "dead line" boundary. They saw the "miserable hovels, hardly fit for swine to live in" that the prisoners were forced to build as their housing, and the graves they dug with their own hands. They saw unburied bodies that had been left behind when the guards relocated the living prisoners before Sherman's forces could get there. And they saw a cemetery with 650 burial plots.

The horror of the place left a deep impression on the soldiers who passed through it, and they vowed to avenge "this scene of suffering cruelty and murder." Sherman himself did not visit Camp Lawton, but he heard enough reports about it that he levied a quick judgment. He directed Frank Blair and the 17th Corps to take action against Millen, the town nearest to the camp.

As one soldier wrote, "We burned everything here that a match would ignite."

TWELVE

YELL LIKE THE DEVIL

John McCline woke up at dawn but couldn't see the sun. It was another December morning in the swamp, with the fog hanging low over the cypress trees and Spanish moss, and the thin road ahead seeming to vanish in the dense forest. The opaque clouds, the chilly air, the invisible sun—it all made for an unearthly world that none of the boys in the 13th Michigan had ever experienced. Only the roosters tied to some of the boys' knapsacks seemed to instinctively know the day was upon them. But by nightfall, most of them would end up on a roasting spit or in a stew pot.

Passing through the swamplands, the 14th Corps was running out of food. There was still enough beef from the droves of cattle that followed the army, and the troops slaughtered cows daily to provide sustenance for the marchers. But a side of beef quickly became loathsome when it was the only entrée on the plate, meal after meal. And the farm boys weren't used to these low-quality cuts. The army had run out of fodder, so the meat was tough and leathery, cut from the emaciated flesh of cows almost too weak to stand before they were killed. These "walking skeletons" were more bone than muscle, and to make their meat edible, troops had to boil it for hours. Still, despite their pitiable condition and foul smells, these poor creatures were all that stood between the marchers and starvation—the thin bovine line between the success and failure of Sherman's grand scheme.

Some foragers would not content themselves with the quality of their daily ration. They tried to find cattle and hogs on farms deep in swamp country. Since army orders had forbidden the wasting of ammunition on livestock, the boys had to wrestle the creatures to the ground while they were writhing and kicking. Sometimes they met with success, and grabbed the horns and pinned an animal down while an axeman did his worst. Other times the beasts got the best of them, and dragged their tormentors along the ground or trampled them. Hunting for food could be hard work in southern Georgia.

John McCline's unit was lucky. Some regiments like his in the 14th Corps still had sweet and white potatoes to consume. But many other units had to face the rugged labors of hulling rice by hand, or subsist on bad beef alone. The freedmen had taught the soldiers how to use a wooden pestle and mortar—foraged from houses in the area—to pound out enough edible rice for a meal or two. The process took up to eight hours per man. Otherwise, the troops had to dine on whatever foodstuffs they could scrounge, from oysters to acorns.

The glory days of foraging for the left wing of Sherman's forces had ended. Whereas just a week ago the boys had stuffed themselves with everything from pork and persimmons to corn on the cob, now their stomachs rumbled or even revolted when they had to eat the same meager fare day after day. Some of the troops recalled how they had once shot pigs and cattle without restraint—only removing the hindquarters for a takeaway meal, or leaving the entire carcass to rot so the rebels couldn't have any. How much good meat had they left rotting on the farms of central Georgia? No one could say. But they were certain it would taste mighty delicious if they had it now.

—◊—

Traveling near the border of South Carolina, the 13th Michigan was getting close to Savannah, though the journey had exhausted its troops in recent days. Everything was a challenge, from hunting for food, to keeping their clothes and gear dry, to keeping up the pace when mud bogged down their horses, mules, and wagons. When the trail became too congested, they walked alongside it, over the sodden ground. Here, the cypress trees had knobby knees that poked above the water line and tripped any hapless soldier who stumbled over them, sending him face first into the muck.

The strange terrain reminded John of how much things had changed. Less than two weeks before, he and his friends had enjoyed their idyll in Milledgeville, chasing chickens and swiping rebel money. Their bellies were full, their tempers were cheerful, and their hijinks were many. But John had seen too much in this war to expect the march to remain easy. Confederate cavalrymen began firing shots at their skirmishers. Guerrillas slashed the throats of their foragers. And the common folk looked at them with daggers as sharp as bayonets. And slowly his worries grew.

He had felt fear before, in bondage on the farm in Tennessee. He felt it again when he traveled through that state with a Union regiment. But this fear was different. It was the special kind of fear of a young man with dark skin in the deep Georgia woods. He did not know this country, and had no allies here. And if the kind of slavery he knew had been brutal, the kind practiced here was unimaginable. The iron collars, the shackles, the horror of it all. It knotted his stomach and troubled his mind. If he were captured, he would not be sent back to the Hoggatt farm, but sold for profit in the swamplands, and enslaved on a rice plantation. He knew rebel horsemen lurked in these woods with a mind to do just that.

Therefore, he resolved that if he faced danger, he would allow himself to be killed, but not captured. He would stick close to his friends with guns, and do what he could to help the Union army reach its destination. Anything to get out of the swamp and away from its unseen terrors.

To emerge from the hinterlands, John's regiment followed the path of a canal that led from the cypress swamp into a clearing and toward a simple, two-story, wood-frame house. It was empty and a perfect place to stay for the night. John and the rest of his friends in the regiment settled in, relaxing from another long day on the trail, telling stories and playing cards. They had come more than 250 miles from Atlanta, and couldn't wait to reach their destination of Savannah, rumored to be a pretty little town with a long history—the oldest in Georgia.

But no sooner had they started to imagine what might await them there, a Confederate barrage suddenly shattered the walls and windows. Shot and shell exploded and sent shrapnel and wood shards flying.

John sprinted out of the house, looking for a place to hide. On one side of him was a flooded rice paddy; on the other, huge stands of pine—and the treetops held snipers.

The sharpshooters took aim at the boys and struck down about two dozen.

No one could see the snipers, just the bursts of flame from the dark woods.

With the rebels attacking their regiment from above, the Yankees were easy targets. All they could do was build their field works higher and dig their trenches deeper.

In the face of the danger, officers ordered their men to stay low, not to reveal themselves. Even when they went for water from the canal, they had to travel in darkness.

The next morning, the invisible sun rose, the fog slowly brightened, and in late morning the sun burned through. The Confederate artillery batteries now had a much clearer view of their targets—and opened up on them for three hours.

John and Captain Flint were returning from the canal when the shelling began. One bomb burst over their heads and they dove for cover. The next round came in and hit the cattle pen. Panic overtook the cows. Though half-starved, they still had enough energy to charge out of their confines to escape the explosions. Soon the regiment had a stampede on its hands.

The drovers followed the cows into the woods, trying to corral as many as they could. Otherwise the corps would have no meat.

John and the captain made it back to the trenches, but they had been lucky. The shellfire had missed them. But they and the others in the regiment would have to return to the canal for more water. Each time they did, the rebel batteries and snipers would take aim at them, and some of their shots would find their mark.

The sudden violence marked a change. The Michiganders had thought they'd see no more battles before they reached Savannah. But as John and the rest of the regiment watched the bombs flying over their works, they knew the end of the campaign would be the toughest.

John was scared throughout the ordeal. He imagined the dangers that lurked in the woods, and how perilous his life had become. Somehow, though, he never lost his sense of wonder. As day passed to night, he looked up at the dark sky: "It was an amazing sight to me to lie on my back in my dugout and see the great shells bursting high up in the air."

The fireworks display would continue through the night, in all its fearsome and terrible beauty.

Farther back in the column of the 14th Corps, John Hight and the 58th Indiana faced a different kind of bombardment. They were waiting for their corpsmen to cross Ebenezer Creek on their pontoon bridge when a gunboat opened up on them from the nearby Savannah River. The rebel guns lobbed huge 64-pound shot at them—enough to shatter trees or bridges or bodies if the monstrous cannonballs came anywhere near them. The troops abandoned their cool reserve, "and we resolved, each for himself, to take our chances at dodging." One shot plowed into the creekside and others whizzed over their heads.

After a short time the firing ended. Then the pontoniers heard more batteries in action, closer to Savannah. General William Hardee was doing his best to resist Sherman's advance by pummeling his forces before they could assault the rebel defenses. On this day, the 14th Corps was in the line of fire.

The 58th Indiana troops also heard musket fire to the rear. It was from their old foe Joseph Wheeler, who had begun attacking the Yankee rear guard with his horsemen, taking aim at both cavalry and infantry units to try to slow down the marchers.

Less than a week before, Wheeler had lost the biggest cavalry skirmish of the march at Waynesboro—and 250 casualties—but remained undaunted. He now tried all manner of tactics against the invaders, fighting dismounted behind barricades, launching surprise attacks, capturing prisoners, and harassing any Union troops assigned to protect the corps' slow-moving wagons and their cargo.

There were also a good number of black refugees at the back of the column—anywhere from several hundred to a thousand. They had arrived in sizable numbers, though not as many as those who followed the other corps on the march. Ever since the incident at Buckhead Creek, word had spread about the hostility of the 14th Corps and its commander Jefferson C. Davis, and many former slaves had no interest in traveling in a corps led by a pro-slavery man.

The feeling was mutual. Two weeks before, Davis had written that "Useless negroes are being accumulated to an extent which would be suicide to a column which must be constantly stripped for battle and prepared for the utmost celerity of movement. . . . every additional mouth consumes food, which it requires risk to obtain." But Davis forgot or chose not to notice that the freedmen also foraged for food, and contributed essential labors to the corps—without which they would never be able to cross over the swamps.

By Sherman's own order, many black men worked in the Pioneer Corps, laboring at the front of the column while their wives or children marched at the back of it. Liberated from plantations just days before, the freedmen slashed timber, cut it up into manageable pieces, and assembled it plank by plank into improvised roadways that crossed streams, rivulets, marshes, creeks, and swamps. They could be quite creative in their work, even fashioning ad hoc roads from bundles of pine boughs and undergrowth, tying them with thick wires and laying them close together so wagons, troops, horses, and cows could pass over them. If timber wasn't available, they hunted for fence rails or railroad ties to lay across the murky waters. Any kind of wood would do, and they needed a lot of it. The ooze often swallowed up the first layer of planks, and another fresh collection of logs or rails or ties had to be placed on top of it, and sometimes another beyond that.

Mile after mile nearly 2,000 pioneers laid down these corduroy roads, and when they did the rest of Sherman's armies tramped over them and got ever closer to the Atlantic coast. It was hard, wet, and often thankless work, but the freedmen readily signed up for it. Not only were they helping the North invade the heart of the Confederacy, they were, for the first time in their lives, getting paid for their work.

But none of this mattered to Jefferson C. Davis. He saw blacks as a burden to his corps, and resolved to do something about it. His earlier gambit to strand them (to their likely deaths) at Buckhead Creek had not fully succeeded, so he had a second chance when his corps passed over Ebenezer and Lockner Creeks.

When Major James Connolly, a staff officer for General Absalom Baird, found out about Davis's plans for the freedmen, he was furious. In the middle of this grim landscape—which Connolly called "the most gloomy, dismal cypress swamp I ever saw"—Davis planned to lead his corpsmen over a repaired trestle bridge and then to prevent the freedmen from crossing with armed guards, exposing them to recapture by Wheeler's cavalry. As Connolly wrote in his journal:

> The idea of five or six hundred black women, children and old men being thus returned to slavery by such an infernal Copperhead as Jeff C. Davis was entirely too much for my Democracy; I suppose loss of sleep, and fatigue made me somewhat out of humor too, and I told his staff officers what I thought of such an inhuman, barbarous proceeding in language which may possibly result in a reprimand from his serene Highness, for I know his toadies will repeat it to him, but I don't care a fig. I am determined to expose this act of his publicly. . . . I expect this will cost me my Brevet as Lieut. Colonel, but let it go, I wouldn't barter my convictions of right, nor seal my mouth for any promotion.

Connolly's words had no immediate effect. Davis arranged for the freedmen to be told they could cross the trestle bridge once the rest of the army had done so, and they waited patiently for their chance. But once the column of the 14th Corps had passed over it, the rear guard of the corps suddenly intervened, to the surprise of the men, women, and children.

They pleaded with the guards to let them pass, but pleading could only do so much in the face of drawn rifles. Some tried to argue with the soldiers, or ran along the shoreline to find another crossing downstream. As the guards held them off, Davis ordered the entire trestle bridge to burn.

Their one chance for freedom was now on fire. Some freed slaves rushed into the water to brave the currents of the wide and swift stream. Other screamed out on the creek bank for help. Few of the women and children could make it across, so the hardier men swam first, aided by groups of sympathetic Union soldiers who threw them logs and branches to help.

Once these men crossed, some improvised makeshift rafts from scattered pieces of wood. Then they went back across the swollen creek to rescue their wives and sons and daughters, or anyone else who seemed incapable of making it across on their own.

The creekside resounded with cries and wails, as people who couldn't swim desperately lunged across the waters and drowned in the attempt. And despite the efforts of the men with rafts, there weren't enough saviors to rescue everyone who had been abandoned.

And then came Wheeler's cavalry. Terror followed panic, as the rebels fired with their carbines—first at the retreating Yankee soldiers on the far shore, then at the black people on the near shore. They shot and killed a number of them in cold blood. The rest they took into captivity, dragging them back into the murky darkness of swamp country and backwoods slavery.

One of Davis's greatest critics, John Hight, soon heard of the incident, and it almost broke his spirit. As he wrote, "I cannot find words to express my detestation of such cruelty and wickedness. May God Almighty save the Nation from the responsibility of General Davis' acts!" But Jefferson C. Davis wasn't finished yet.

At Lockner Creek, the general crossed his corps on pontoons provided by the 58th Indiana. Once they were across, he demanded the boats and planks be removed, and again ordered the rear guard to prevent the freedmen from crossing. There were fewer of them now, with so many having succumbed to drowning or capture at Ebenezer Creek. Still, the scene repeated itself, with plaintive cries and wails, attempts to cross defeated at gunpoint, desperate plunges into the water, and the inevitable drownings and recapture by Confederate horsemen.

His mission now accomplished, Jefferson C. Davis ordered his 14th Corps column to march on, deeper into the woods, on corduroy roads created by black pioneers. But while Ebenezer and Lockner Creeks soon disappeared into the mists of swamp country, the incidents that took place there did not. In a memoir written two decades later, one observer, Charles Kerr, could not forget the searing images he had witnessed on that day, December 9, 1864: "It was unjustifiable and perfidious, and across the stretch of twenty years my soul burns with indignation to-night as I recall it."

John Hight felt the same way, and had a difficult time containing his fury at the depraved actions of his corps commander. He would not go as far as the regimental doctor James Patten—who remarked, "If I had the power I would [hang] him as high as Haman"—or imagine him shot by his own troops, but he knew such wickedness had to be denounced and punished. The nefarious racist needed to face a court martial and be convicted and jailed for his crimes. But how could this be done, in a war in which moral outrages were common? And who would step forward to do such a deed, in an army under the command of William Sherman?

While Hight struggled with these questions, over the next few days, the 58th Indiana and the Pioneer Corps brought the corps closer and closer to Savannah, mile by mile, creek by creek, rice paddy by rice paddy. The coastal landscape became flatter and wetter, dotted with fields of sage grass and cedars, until finally, in the distance, appeared the town itself, surrounded by live oaks with hanging Spanish moss.

The regiment camped in fields, among the cypresses, and on the grounds of a deserted plantation. Occasionally Confederate gunboats emerged to lob a few shells in their direction, but they usually fell short. More dangerous was the lack of food. Though the regiment had dined on pork and potatoes just days before, their forage soon dwindled along with their fodder. Worse, many of their horses had taken ill, and "almost all the horses we had when we left the Chattahoochee [north of Atlanta], are either diseased or dead."

Passing by their camp was an earthen causeway. This road led into town and held the promise of drawing them into a place that had fresh food, comfortable lodgings, and relief from the miseries of the march. But it was a dead end. Like all roads around Savannah, it came to an abrupt halt at a Confederate line of defense.

General William Hardee had set up these lines to secure the town and the 18,000 rebels protecting it. The outer lines comprised little more than burned bridges, damaged roadways, and scattered field works holding infantry units. But the inner lines were more formidable, with flooded fields, sharpshooters, entrenched artillery, and fortified causeways surrounded by swamps.

Just west of the column of the 14th Corps, the 20th Corps faced some of the toughest obstacles along rebel lines. Some of its regiments had to brave the Monteith Swamp, sinking into mud up to their waists, to outflank the enemy. Others had to fight skirmishes in the pines and hack their way through acres of fallen timber and underbrush. Still others faced snipers and cannonades.

However, one of the regiments in the corps, the 82nd Illinois, actually enjoyed this part of the march. They were doing what they were good at—wrecking railroads.

The Charleston and Savannah Railroad, to be specific. The troops reveled in the destructive work of burning the ties and wrapping the rails around trees. They became skilled at damaging Confederate infrastructure, and preventing the rebel war machine from moving men and supplies over the iron road. It had been a welcome change from earlier in the march when they had to protect the wagon train in the rear. That kind of work they had put behind them, or so they thought.

On the evening of December 11, their luck turned. Brigade leader James Robinson transferred them back to the rear and kept them there for the next 10 days, watching over the wagons yet again. They had no choice but to do their duty and entrench four and a half miles from

Savannah, within sight of the town but still so far away. Around them were abandoned farmsteads overtaken by tracts of pine and cypress, humble shacks and tumbledown houses, and plantations that had already been ransacked by other units in the corps. The forage was poor, the eatables scarce.

They weren't reduced to scavenging for acorns yet, but knew they would have to do better than eating skin-and-bones cattle from their pens. The commander of the 82nd, Major Ferdinand Rolshausen, attempted to try to find new sources of food, and sent out foraging parties to prowl around the edges of the swamp looking for any victuals they could glean.

This was a less than gallant assignment. Having to scrape together an evening meal, after trudging through the mire, was beneath the dignity of some of the officers. One of them was Captain Rudolph Mueller, who already lacked respect for Major Rolshausen and had resorted to spreading gossip and bile about him and the other members of the regiment he didn't like. He even flirted with insubordination, and answered the major's command to forage by not showing up for duty.

In response, Rolshausen censured him. Mueller responded to that the only way he knew how: He exploded with rage.

How could he have possibly *known* he had been ordered to forage? No one had *told* him! It was an outrage—an *injustice*—that he had been admonished for an act *of which he was innocent!*

Lieutenant William Loeb had been assigned to tell Mueller of his foraging duty. He stated he had done so, and refuted Mueller's contention. He also called him a liar.

Mueller hit him across the face.

Loeb hurled a plate of food at him.

The brawl was on, as both men unleashed their furies.

After pummeling each other with sufficient violence and victuals, the men were finally separated. Major Rolshausen ordered both under arrest. Mueller resigned his commission, but thought better of it and demanded a court martial.

While in custody, he managed to write a letter to his old friend Friedrich Hecker, justifying his actions, spitting venom against his enemies, and plotting his vengeance. He had become, as he wrote, a "slumbering but revenge-seeking lion."

Thus, while his regiment prepared to invest Savannah with the rest of Sherman's forces and reach the climax of the March to the Sea, Mueller sat in military detention—held in "chains and bonds," his pride wounded, his grievances multiplying. Like the colonel he adored, Mueller would take his chances in front of a military tribunal, to decide whether he was a threat to "good order and discipline." If convicted, Mueller would be punished or thrown out of the army. If acquitted, he would serve once more under the command of officers whom he despised.

Little did he know that one of the officers he most despised was returning to the regiment in just a few weeks. Lieutenant Colonel Edward Salomon had served the Union army with distinction in Tennessee, and was coming back to command the 82nd Illinois once more.

By early December, news from that state had reached Sherman's headquarters of the victory John Schofield and his Army of the Ohio had won on November 30. John Bell Hood's Confederate forces had nearly trapped Schofield's army the night before, but after an artful escape, Schofield established a fortified defensive line at the town of Franklin. There, Hood assaulted his position with some 25,000 troops—and saw a quarter of them fall, along with a dozen generals. Despite the victory, Schofield withdrew his forces north and joined George Thomas's two corps from the Army of the Cumberland. Sherman now expected Hood would attack Thomas in his characteristic hell-bent style, though couldn't be certain of the outcome. As he wrote to General Grant a few days later: "I know full well that General Thomas is slow in mind and in action; but he is judicious and brave and the troops feel great confidence in him. I still hope he will out-manoeuvre and destroy Hood."

Sherman felt relieved not to have faced such great battles on the March to the Sea. He had seen enough mass killing around Atlanta, and remained certain that destroying the enemy's resources and its will to fight were paramount—not wiping out thousands of its soldiers. He felt the march had been a less savage alternative to traditional warfare, executed under proper rules and official control, with a measure of charity and benevolence when appropriate.

Indeed, he had made sure to leave Georgians' lives and bodies inviolate, and the honor of their women, and concentrated his destruction on their railroads, their cotton gins, their arsenals, and their magazines. He would never sanction wanton murder against them, would never embody the remorseless brute they imagined him to be. And for that reason the calumnies about him he read in their newspapers, and the lies they had spread about him to their slaves, continued to infuriate him—especially when *they* committed the kind of atrocities he had forbidden among his own infantry. His temper boiled over when he found one of his men with a missing foot.

Sherman and his aide Henry Hitchcock had been traveling with Frank Blair's 17th Corps, advancing to the interior defensive lines of Savannah, when they saw the poor fellow who now bore only a bloody stump where there had once been a lower leg. The weapon he had stepped on was a "torpedo"—a land mine set into the ground with a projecting trigger. The rebels had buried countless hundreds of these fearsome foot-long objects in the road bed, expecting the Yankee invaders to step on them and lose their lives or limbs. To Sherman, "This was not war, but murder, and it made me very angry." In response he forced his rebel prisoners to travel in front of the column, digging up the torpedoes as they found them.

Fortune favored William Sherman. Had he not been marching in a field away from his advance guard, he too might have been maimed or killed by such weapons. But he had walked away unscathed, initially oblivious to the threat of the mines. Henry Hitchcock wondered how long his luck could hold. How many times had he seen the general "quietly going ahead on foot without a word to anybody, and we not knowing it unless by watching him"? How many more times could he go his own way without risking death?

The perils became even more palpable once the general and his staff reached within five miles of Savannah on the Louisville Road. Here they found a modest house to use as a temporary base near the tracks of the Georgia Central Railroad. Union skirmishers had already made contact with rebel forces a quarter of a mile away, and Sherman wanted to find out more. He set off on foot, with Hitchcock close behind.

They soon heard the sharp burst of cannon fire—it sounded like a rocket. Hitchcock dove for the ground and landed in the sand, expecting a shell to explode at any moment and kill all of them.

He peeked up to see Sherman intact, deftly crossing the road. The general said, "This place is not safe, they are firing down the road—we had better go back." A 32-pound cannonball had narrowly missed them before ricocheting down the dirt avenue.

They stepped away from the road and reached the railroad cut, a four-foot-deep trench. Hitchcock was no more than ten paces from the tracks when another great *boom* echoed down the line.

A second cannonball seared the air—bounding over the rails—headed for the general. He took a quick step back as the shot nearly hit him. It killed a bystander instead, nearly decapitating him in a bloody and horrific scene.

Once again, the commander of the Military Division of the Mississippi had been lucky. With clear aim and an open path of fire, the Confederate cannoneers should have had him dead. If they had used explosive shells instead of solid shot, they would have.

But on this day, as on every day in the campaign, Sherman eluded injury and death just as he had eluded defeat. The March to the Sea had been a boon to his fortunes and a balm for his troubles. It clearly wasn't his time to be sacrificed to the war—not yet. Not before the final act he had planned for Savannah.

All that remained was to consolidate his forces and seal off the town from rebel reinforcement. He had crafted a plan whereby the 14th and the 20th Corps would march along the west side of the Savannah River, not far from South Carolina, while the 17th Corps would travel down the east bank of the Ogeechee River. All three corps would converge in an arc around the town's defensive perimeter. That left the lone corps of the 15th to do the dirty work.

Sherman had given his old command some gritty duties. Not only did they have to subsist in the pine barrens and endure some of the worst conditions in swamp country, they also had to march at a distance from the other three corps on the western edge of the advance, beyond the Ogeechee. Here in the Georgia tidewater, provisions were running out, as foragers repeatedly came up short and the troops began to get sick of hulling rice and scrounging for acorns. But the commanding general had faith in his boys. He planned for them to deliver the knockout blow to William Hardee's defense of Savannah.

The assault would come at Fort McAllister. Located four miles outside of the town's defensive line, the fort was the gateway to the Ogeechee River and to the resupply of Sherman's armies by sea. But with twenty-six heavy guns, it could also choke off reinforcements to those armies. If the fort could be captured, Sherman could ship in siege guns to pound Savannah into submission, along with new clothing and shoes, and rations like bacon and hardtack that the troops hadn't had in weeks. If it weren't captured, Sherman's forces could starve.

The Union had been trying to take the fort from the rebels for three years, and had failed each time. The seaward-facing guns made for a fearsome defense against naval attack, and the network of islands and estuaries, swamps and rice paddies, made a landward charge a heady undertaking. But one particular unit in the 15th Corps would have to manage it—the Second Division.

It was no accident Sherman chose the Second to make the assault. It had once been his own division, thick with Ohio regiments, some of which he had helped recruit. It was also the division he commanded at Shiloh when he and U.S. Grant fought off the Confederates on that now-legendary battlefield in April 1862, and where he had been twice wounded, in a bloody and relentless fight without quarter.

Now he expected the boys of the Second Division to repeat their success. General William Hazen would lead them in an afternoon attack, storming the fort while Sherman watched with his staff across the river, on the roof of a rice mill.

Midday arrived on December 13, the ideal moment to launch the attack. Sherman expected the Second Division to be ready—for Hazen to give the word—and for the march to meet its objective, or to reach its fate. But nothing happened.

The sun began to drop closer to the horizon. Sherman agitated. He learned Hazen didn't even have his forces in position. He grew nervous. What was taking him so long? Why weren't his men on the field?

The division's challenges came on the approaches to the fort, over the marshes and causeways. Hazen led nine regiments and eight more in reserve, and he had difficulty getting all 3,000 troops aligned. Some units had to cross swamps. Others had to negotiate fallen timber. Still others had to evade torpedoes. Hours went by before all the regiments could line up, and by that time, it was past 4 P.M. on one of the shortest days of the year. The shadows started to lengthen.

Just beyond the fort, a Union ship in the sound opened signal communication with Sherman. First, it asked who he was. Then it asked what he needed and who was in control of the fort. Sherman answered these questions and asked the ship to pound the fort with its heavy guns. But the ship had no such guns—it was a tugboat named Dandelion.

Sherman had finally had enough. He ordered his signal officer to tell Hazen to take the fort immediately. The flag had to wave over the compound by sunset.

A few moments later, Hazen's men emerged from the tree line and charged toward the fort. Puffs of artillery smoke and musket fire gave Sherman the clue he had been waiting for.

They moved at double-quick time across 700 yards of open field, exposed to rebel musket fire and cannon rounds. Most of the rounds went high—Hazen's men were lucky.

They had no such luck when they reached the abatis: cut timber, live oaks polished into spears, wooden-dagger defenses. The regiments converged near the spear points, ready to climb over them, when—

Torpedoes.

Small but deadly explosions, shearing off legs and feet. Land mines buried in the sand. Tearing through the men, bringing them down so marksmen could cut them up.

The carnage didn't stop them. Hazen's men kept coming, hurrying over the bomb field, grabbing sharpened wood.

A few brave souls worked their way through the abatis, then pushed them apart and opened up narrow slots. More men plunged into the wood pile, past the stakes.

The last layer was a ditch—twelve feet deep, with spikes at the bottom. Now the troops were too fired up to stop. They clambered into it, avoided the spears, and reached the walls of the fort. More troops followed, and more after them.

Now they were climbing the walls, clawing into the loose earth. Rebel gunfire peppered them at a steep angle. They gasped and surged and advanced, despite the danger. They didn't fire back—they had mounted bayonets.

They lunged over the parapets with their knives and began stabbing. The rebels held fast to their guns, got speared for their efforts. Hand-to-hand fighting in the tide of bluecoats. The defenders fell, bleeding from stab wounds, clubbed with musket butts, slashed with sabers, punched and choked.

The fort commander Major George Anderson dropped his sword and received a gun butt to his head. Groggy and confused, he watched a tide of Union soldiers surge over the fort, enveloping it, making it their own. A Union officer put him under arrest. It was General Hazen himself, an old acquaintance before the war.

"Get to the rear, George," he said, "and report to me later."

From the rice mill, Sherman and his staff watched the attack unfold to success. The haggard army commander's eyes filled with tears and he jumped up and down, filled with childlike delight. He saw the regimental flags wave, then saw Old Glory replace the rebel flag atop the fort. The other officers cheered, yelled, cried, embraced, and shook hands to celebrate the victory. Some men stamped and screamed so loudly, the communications chief worried the building would collapse.

Sherman dashed off a note to Henry Slocum, commanding the left wing farther east. He let him know the assault had been a great success, ending just before twilight and only lasting fifteen minutes. And he gave him one resolute order: "Take a good big drink, a long breath, and then yell like the devil."

The general was overcome with nervous excitement, wanting to celebrate in proper style but not from the roof of a rice mill. With some of his key staff members not present to counsel him, Sherman decided to paddle out to Fort McAllister himself—in an oyster boat.

No one could stop him—this was the commander's moment—so Army of the Tennessee leader Oliver Howard came along too, flush with excitement and delighted that one of his own divisions had conquered the fort. A quartet of their aides joined them, and the little team of Union officers paddled out to sea.

It was laborious work, rowing six nautical miles down the Ogeechee River against flood tide in the dark. Sherman steered the boat and pointed out obstacles along the way, mile by grueling mile. But he was not tired in the slightest.

His mind raced at thoughts of what capturing the fort meant. How his armies had reopened communication with the fleet, and seized a base to resupply their food and weapons and provisions. How it would only be a matter of days before Savannah fell by siege or assault or abandonment. How the war and his own reputation had turned a page. How the March to the Sea had finally reached it.

Finally, around 9 P.M., Sherman and his party of officers reached a landing point a mile and a half from the fort. A sentry met them and directed them to the plantation house General Hazen occupied as his new headquarters.

When Sherman and company arrived, they found the general just sitting down to eat. Hazen asked if they would like to partake in the meal; they readily accepted. Hazen then asked if an unexpected guest could join them—fort commander George Anderson, now being held in a corral of prisoners. Sherman agreed.

Anderson came in and was surprised to see the conquering general seated across from him. As Sherman wrote, "He looked at me hard to discover the horns and talons of the devil, for at that time my reputation was not good at the South; but, like myself, being hungry, he lay to on the ham, hard bread and coffee served out to us by our host."

After a moment, Anderson noticed one of the waiters was familiar to him. His name was Bob, and just a few hours before he had attended to him as his slave. Now he worked under his own free will for General Hazen.

Anderson looked at Sherman and thought about it, then said, "General, it looks to me as though the game is up."

Sherman nodded. "Yes, the game is up. Slavery is gone, and the Southern Confederacy is a thing of the past."

RECKONING

THIRTEEN

SENTINELS

The days before Christmas 1864 were a rich and festive time in the North. Not only had Abraham Lincoln been reelected president, but word spread that the Confederates had withdrawn from Savannah and the Union army had taken possession of the town. The news prompted joyful celebrations and jubilant rallies, and one could hardly pick up a newspaper without seeing thanks offered to Jesus Christ, Santa Claus, and William Sherman.

The press cheerfully offered hosannas in the name of the general—formerly their nemesis—calling him "gallant" as the "head of his heroic legions" who had triumphed over the South "in one grand continuous holiday excursion." They compared his feats to those of legendary commanders like Napoleon and the Duke of Wellington, and lauded him as a martial version of St. Nick, who gave the Union the gift of military conquest. Sherman in turn offered his largesse to President Lincoln, writing in a famous telegram, "I beg to present you as a Christmas-gift the city of Savannah, with one hundred and fifty heavy guns and plenty of ammunition, also about twenty-five thousand bales of cotton." The North delighted in his generosity.

A few days later, stories began to spread about just what kind of town Sherman's men had occupied. It was old and lovely, to be sure, but it was also in terrible shape—the victim of looting by town folk after the Confederates left, bad sanitation, shambling housing, and a lack of provisions. Relief organizations in Boston and New York City responded by organizing charity drives to help, raising money to purchase and ship to the town essentials like flour, cornmeal, meat, and vegetables. A much bigger flood of donations, though, went to Union soldiers through the U.S. Sanitary Commission. With Sherman's forces back on the map in Savannah, the relief society targeted its efforts to send the troops food, clothing, and medical supplies beyond what army quartermasters already provided. One of the forces behind this relief was Mary Livermore.

In the past few months, Mary's life had become busy beyond measure. Her Northwestern branch now presided over a huge array of fund-raising activities—"Fairs, large and small; festivals, comic and grotesque; conventions, processions, refreshment tables, concerts, and tableaux, were held in every nook and corner" of the western region. Many towns now held their own fairs, and women who before the war had known nothing but farm life came forward to found their own aid societies and coordinate charity relief from their friends and neighbors.

Mary and Jane Hoge even pioneered a new revenue system in which donors pledged a day's labor or income to the annual support of their commission branch. In addition, they oversaw the increasing number of duties of their branch—everything from inspecting army camps and hospitals; to providing food and supplies to the troops; to operating hospital ships and running convalescent homes; to providing nurses for ill and injured soldiers; to sending messages to families of the deceased and assisting their widows.

Mary also helped set up new societies, gave rousing public speeches, and became a lightning rod for praise and criticism—and none of it quashed her energies. She would cut back on her work for the *New Covenant*, curb her social activities in Chicago, and even hold sleep in abeyance before she would neglect any needs of the Sanitary Commission. As she said early in 1864, "*I can't be still, and I* WON'T *be still.*" The treasurer of the national commission, George Templeton Strong, was struck by her and Jane's many industrious endeavors, and could only admiringly describe their work ethic "in terms of droves of horses."

The competition with the Christian Commission only added to her fervor. Both competed for the same donated boxes of fruit and vegetables and socks and bandages, and both tried anything they could to become the sole focus of charity for soldiers in the war. For Mary the competition was invigorating, exhausting, and infuriating—sometimes all at once.

By the end of 1864, the Christian Commission nearly had as great a reputation as the Sanitary Commission, and had grown rapidly throughout the year, aided by the support of hundreds of ministers and field agents in army camps. These men not only distributed Bibles and relief supplies, they prayed and led church services with the troops. By contrast, the Northwestern Sanitary Commission struggled to fill its coffers, especially because the great size of its operation, and expanding number of duties, had depleted its treasury. Mary realized she would have to find some way of refilling it. The obvious solution was a second Sanitary Fair in Chicago.

She planned it to be the biggest and grandest of them all, with the goal of a half-million dollars in donations—two-thirds more than the previous record holder for Sanitary Fairs, in Brooklyn. It would take place around the time of Lincoln's second inauguration in 1865, and the president had promised to visit. Still, she encountered resistance from the Christian Commission, which insisted on a share of the fair's proceeds or its members would refuse to visit or in any way support it. Mary gave in and agreed to the Commission's demands, but wasn't happy about it. As she wrote while planning the event, "Our Fair progresses gloriously . . . despite the malignant efforts of the Chris. Com. to hinder it."

The diversion of part of the fair's proceeds to the Christian Commission didn't make it any easier for the event to turn a profit. Mary realized she needed to raise funds well beyond the western states. To do so she sent out agents to solicit donations from every businessman and social and political leader she could find, in every corner of the nation, from

New England to California, and in countries from Ireland to Italy to Russia to China. And once more she called upon her old ally in the fight to help the army boys, the one in whose loyalty she had implicit faith: Mary Ann Bickerdyke.

After her journey back from Atlanta, Mother Bickerdyke had been on the road for months. She would be returning to Chicago shortly, but had to stop off in Cairo, Illinois, the little town in Egypt where she had begun her career as an army nurse. She wanted to check the current conditions of the Soldiers' Home, one of thirty facilities and lodges the Sanitary Commission ran nationwide that catered to the needs of troops back from the war. It had twenty-five hospital beds, four guest chambers, a dining hall, and a slew of amenities to help the wounded make the transition back to civilian life.

When Mother arrived she was astonished by the progress of the Sanitary Commission's work there. Instead of the dismal, filthy, half-lit facilities she remembered in Cairo from early in the war—and which she had striven so diligently to clean up—the Soldiers' Home was a marvel. Its dining tables were spotless, its kitchen a model of efficiency, its laundry operations top-notch, and its hygiene unsurpassed. The woman who ran it was one Mrs. A.F. Grant, a preacher's widow whom she knew well. Mother had chosen her to take over her duties at the Gayoso Hospital in Memphis after she left with Sherman's army. Grant had since emerged as a dynamo to match the energy of Mother herself.

If anything Mrs. Grant had gone overboard in her zeal for order. Mother thought she was a pedant, someone whose obsession to free the world from minor stains and wrinkled bed sheets went well beyond normal bounds of cleanliness. Still, Mother was glad she now ran the Soldiers' Home and was proud of her advancement. Mrs. Grant was among dozens of women, perhaps hundreds, who had taken Mother's example and made it a model for their own charity work.

Mrs. Grant introduced Mother to one of the many Christian Commission agents she allowed to visit the home. It was Annie Wittenmyer, the founder of the Keokuk Ladies' Soldiers' Aid Society in Iowa. Mother didn't know her, but had heard about her notorious battles with Mary

Livermore, including one in which she challenged Mary publicly and demanded to see the itemized expenses of her Chicago branch—as if she were some kind of thief! As Mary wrote in a private letter, her encounter in Iowa was "the severest labor of my life. I would not do anything of the kind again, for even the Sanitary Commission."

Mother soon heard about Wittenmyer's latest project: special dietary kitchens for convalescent soldiers. Mother didn't think much of these facilities, calling them "kitchens-within-kitchens to turn out little dabs of soup and coddled eggs." Still, she was polite and listened graciously. Mother needed as many allies as she could get, and didn't want to make an enemy of someone like Wittenmyer. As she had vowed earlier in the war, Mother would work with anyone regardless of religion to help her boys, as long as they furnished her with the kind of supplies she needed. How else could she prevent the troops from getting scurvy, or keep them wrapped in clean bandages, or serve up her famous panado concoction?

Back in Chicago, Mother kept the Cairo visit to herself. Mary Livermore looked like she had more important things to worry about. Indeed, she asked Mother to help her on the speaking circuit, traveling around the country exhorting the wealthy to do more for the Commission and to push for donations of art, merchandise, and anything else that would make the next fair an appealing event. Mother didn't hesitate to answer: She readily agreed to it. She couldn't wait to get back in front of people and tell them all they should be doing to help out her boys.

She arrived in New York City and met with Dr. Henry Bellows, who ran the national office of the Sanitary Commission, to plan her speaking engagements and discuss what she would say to drum up donations for the fair. While she was in the city, she dropped in on Plymouth Church in Brooklyn to listen to the Sunday sermon of Henry Ward Beecher, brother of her hometown preacher in Galesburg and abolitionist of world renown. After he had finished his homily, she came forward to meet him. However, as she did, many members of the congregation recognized her—her celebrity had spread even to New York—and they wanted her to say a few words about her work. She agreed to speak to the parishioners in the Sunday school room. But only the women.

Once they all congregated there, Mother made sure the door was shut and began to tell stories. But these weren't designed to draw donations for the fair; they were tales of war. Of horrific injuries and brutal amputations. Of disease and illness. Of all the tortures of battle and the way they wracked pain and disfigurement on the bodies of innocent young men. Many in the crowd were shocked, even aghast, at hearing such explicit details of the effect of combat on human beings. Their newspapers didn't describe the horrors in such detail, and even their sons and husbands who had returned from the front kept quiet about what they had seen there. But Mother Bickerdyke had no fear of revealing it. She described how her boys suffered, and how they lay in misery in field hospitals for lack of supplies and proper hygiene.

With her listeners now stunned into silence, Mother switched to a lighter tone. She asked them about the fashions of the day—and how many petticoats they wore. It turned out the requisite number was five, to maintain a proper look and keep up with the proper upper-middle-class style. Mother listened politely and then told them of soldiers' wounds and amputated stumps having to be wrapped in gunnysack, instead of the nice clean muslin that they wore so discreetly. Then she made a request.

"Lift your dresses. There's no one but us women here. Ladies of Brooklyn, in the name of my boys, *drop that fifth petticoat!*"

With that she secured three trunk loads of women's petticoats to use as bandages and wound wrappings. Mother's oratory had been spellbinding, her presentation masterful. Few others, and certainly not Reverend Beecher, could have convinced these well-heeled women to give up their undergarments in support of the war. But Mother knew how to do it, and she did.

She brought the garments with her to Philadelphia, her next stop on the tour. However, it was there she learned she would have to cut her fund-raising short. William Sherman had summoned her to Savannah.

She figured the general had finally come to his senses and realized how much good she offered his troops. It was a little late—the March to the Sea had already reached it—but she would never turn down an offer from Billy Sherman. Of course she would leave on a steamboat and fill it full of donations to provide relief for his poor soldiers down in that humid and festering town. She had been waiting patiently for many weeks to return to the war, and this was her opportunity.

The only problem was there were no donations to give. The Philadelphia branch of the Sanitary Commission had already arranged for its relief supplies to go to Chicago for the fair, not to Georgia. Ironically, this became a hindrance rather than a benefit to Mother's new mission. She had few other options short of delivering speeches for several weeks to accrue enough donations to bring south. Then she remembered—this city was a bastion of the Christian Commission.

It took a good deal of humility, and a fair bit of audacity, but Mother Bickerdyke asked if the leaders of that commission would fill a ship full of supplies for her boys. They answered promptly, and said yes.

It didn't surprise her. Mother had long worked with agents from the Christian Commission. She prayed with them, secured them rail passes, trusted them with nursing duties, let them distribute Bibles, ate breakfast with them, and listened to their plans for special diet kitchens. She remained polite and thoughtful to her would-be rivals, and considered them allies instead of enemies. They liked and respected her in return, and now in Philadelphia, they came through for her.

They filled the military ship with an array of fruit, crackers, butter, cheese, tea, beef extract, condensed milk, cornstarch, and clothing, along with a team of mules and an ambulance, by her own request. With their fulsome aid, she was soon on her way to Savannah—and a long-awaited reunion with her old friend Billy.

By contrast, John Logan was none too happy to see the general again. It had been more than three months since he had seen Sherman, and when he returned to the 15th Corps, he found him in fine form, jocular and confident, ready for the next phase of his invasion. Logan, however, could not say the same of himself. His shadow campaign for U.S. Senate had been a bust, as Richard Oglesby and others failed to support him, and he now found himself back under the command of his adversary. He puzzled over his misfortune. If not for some bad luck and missed opportunities, he might have been the hero of the west, and not just another army general trying to win laurels for his boss.

Logan had come so close to redemption a few weeks before. At City Point, Virginia, in mid-December, he had met with Grant to assess the current state of the western forces. Sherman, of course, had vanished into the Georgia interior and left no clue as to the state or disposition of his troops. But Grant had a much better idea about George Thomas, who waited in middle Tennessee preparing to battle John Bell Hood's Confederates. And that was the problem.

On several occasions, Grant had ordered Thomas to attack Hood's outnumbered and exhausted rebels. They had been badly beaten by John Schofield's Army of the Ohio at the Battle of Franklin at the end of November, but Hood refused to withdraw and continued to threaten the Yankees. At first Grant was frustrated with Thomas's inaction, then became outright angry. What was he waiting for? At first Thomas's excuse was the lack of mounts for his cavalry; then it was the bad winter weather. Finally Grant had had enough, and told Logan to go to Nashville and relieve Thomas of his command *in person*, and take control of his corps from the Army of the Cumberland. Logan's mission—to destroy Hood's Confederates once and for all.

This was the opportunity Logan had long awaited. He left on a train for Tennessee immediately, with instructions not to inform anyone outside of his staff of his mission, and only to reveal his purpose when he met Thomas. The promise of taking command of some 50,000 men excited him, and he greatly appreciated Grant's faith in him. He transferred to Cincinnati and then Louisville confident that he could execute his orders to perfection and whip the rebels soundly.

But in Kentucky he learned George Thomas had already done just that. In an uncharacteristically bold move, Thomas launched a two-day assault against Hood's forces and crushed them. In the Battle of Nashville, Hood lost 6,000 men (twice the number of federals) and six commanding generals, and saw his army disintegrate in defeat. By smashing Hood's Confederates as a cohesive force, Thomas had achieved a greater victory in the field than any western commander since Grant at Vicksburg. By contrast, while Sherman's forces had allowed defeated rebel armies to escape on at least three occasions—at Resaca, Jonesboro, and Savannah—Thomas's men had completed the job. Hood was finished as a commander, and his army lay in disarray. This was the kind of complete victory that President Lincoln and General Grant had long demanded—to destroy a rebel army in the field—and the general known as "Slow Trot" had delivered it to them.

For Logan the triumph was bittersweet. He was delighted the Union had won such a major battle, and even happy for his old antagonist Thomas, but he saw the prospects were bleaker for himself. From Louisville he wrote to Grant of the jubilation in the west over Thomas's success, and his troops' newly restored confidence in him. Grant ordered Logan to return to Washington at once.

Logan took a cold and dreary overnight train to the District of Columbia, where he was due to meet President Lincoln once more and discuss his future plans. Lincoln still held him in great esteem, and for Logan the feeling was mutual. Logan expected Lincoln would offer him a proper role in the war, just as he had in October in the presidential election, when Lincoln had him barnstorm Illinois for the Republicans. Logan had achieved a signal success then, far beyond anyone's estimation. Instead of simply minimizing the party's losses in Egypt, he had delivered the region to Lincoln and helped him win the state. He had nearly single-handedly changed the political calculus in southern Illinois, from Republicans versus Democrats, to war supporters versus peace advocates, to patriots versus traitors. Illinois had become a bulwark for Lincoln's party, as had several other western states, and Logan had been instrumental in its conversion. Now he expected some sort of reward.

Logan considered running the Department of the South, which stretched from Florida to the Carolinas. It needed a new commander, and would give him the necessary distance from Sherman. It wouldn't be complete independence, but would at least provide him enough space that he could do the work as he saw fit. Grant recommended him for the job, and Logan began to imagine spending the winter in the subtropics. But just as soon as the opportunity opened, it closed. Ignoring Grant's endorsement, Secretary of War Edwin Stanton gave the command to someone else.

Thus, when Logan met Lincoln the day after Christmas, he saw his prospects diminishing along with his hope for advancement. Worse, he found that all the rail-splitter wanted to discuss were the glories of George Thomas and William Sherman.

Had Logan read the clever telegram Sherman just sent, offering him the holiday gift of Savannah? He thought it witty and succinct. And could he convey Lincoln's own response, in person, to the general? That would be a gracious and timely action, and would bring Logan back to the field to take part in Sherman's next campaign. And was he still interested in promotion to a higher command? If so, the president vowed to make an effort to help him. He promised he would.

As Logan suspected, this promise came to nothing. Within a few days he found himself in New York City, ready to board a ship to Savannah, to return to the command of his old nemesis—the man who thought him unfit for higher command since he hadn't attended West Point, and who derided him as a "political general." In a way Logan expected this from someone like Sherman, a professional army man whose loyalties were old and tribal. What he hadn't expected was how his new political allies in the Republican Party would treat him the same way. Just as Sherman had taken away his command of the Army of the Tennessee, so too did politicians like Richard Oglesby prevent his rise to the U.S. Senate, and the president failed to promote him to lead a military department. Even his longtime supporter U.S. Grant had dangled the possibility of his leading western armies to crush Hood, only to take it away when Thomas finally decided to become a warrior.

Logan wondered if he had fallen victim to some strange hex. He had done all he could on the field of battle—had bled and suffered, nearly died, led from the front, rallied again and again, and achieved a record in combat few could match. Yet here he was, carrying a congratulatory note from President Lincoln to General Sherman, a two-star errand boy in blue. The more he thought about it, the more his old temper began to rise. He fumed to Mary in his letters, disgusted at the lack of reward for all his sacrifices and the ingratitude of men he once considered allies. He wondered if "I do not deserve any better treatment as I was foolish enough to work for men who only had their own interest at heart. . . . I hope to help some of them again in the *same* way." Did he deserve this humiliation for an unknown transgression? Or was he simply a fool for placing so much faith in deceitful human nature?

Logan arrived in Savannah on January 6, promptly delivered the presidential message to General Sherman, and set off to explore the town. It didn't take him long to find the headquarters of the 15th Corps, where Peter Osterhaus led the unit in his absence. He expected to take command without ceremony and resume his work without notice. He was surprised by his reception.

The men broke out in cheers for their old commander, shook his hand vigorously, and overflowed with affection. At first their enthusiasm and ardor shocked Logan, but he quickly came to understand it. To veterans he was already a legend, and even the recent conscripts looked at him with awe. There before them was the man on the coal-black charger, the hero of Resaca and Dallas and Atlanta, their very own icon.

Their love humbled him, and he reveled in telling tales of his adventures up north and promised greater adventures still to come. With every one of their compliments and kind words, he felt his anger and vexation begin to fade, until he once again transformed into their bold and fearless leader. This was the general they knew, the one they would follow into any fight, and the one they would risk their lives for, with just a yell from his voice or a thrust from his saber. Black Jack had returned.

While John Logan reunited with his corpsmen, the rest of the officers and enlisted men were busy turning Savannah into a Union garrison. The provost guard established picket lines outside the town, allowing only those with an official pass to come and go. The army hired locals to retrofit buildings and man parapets to protect against rebel attack. The wharf became crowded with hundreds of ships, everything from steamboats and cargo ships to rowboats and rafts, most of them unloading supplies for the needs of the hungry and threadbare soldiers.

The residents of Savannah, along with the town itself, were in much worse shape than the soldiers. Most of them subsisted on rice and fish, supplemented by occasional deliveries of Union rations. And while the town still boasted parks with heritage trees, grand monuments, and spacious public squares, it also had a bleaker aspect. Hundreds of makeshift wooden huts, many of them "small, dilapidated, and forlorn," began to fill up those squares and plazas, their occupants often poor blacks and immigrants. Countless businesses had closed, and the roads and sidewalks lay in disrepair, with dozens of corpses of horses littering them. John Hight's 58th Indiana regiment was forced to camp at a "vile place" near piles of rice chaff and burning garbage, with wretched smells wafting from the open sewers, gales of sand blowing into people's eyes, and a nearby brothel catering to the more wayward men in the regiment. Surveying the terrible condition of the town, the outgoing head of the Department of the South, John G. Foster, described the residents as impoverished and in desperate need of relief supplies, until the town could once again begin to function normally.

One man who remained quite comfortable was William Sherman himself. After weeks sleeping in rough quarters, bivouacked in pine barrens and swamplands, occupying ramshackle hotels and abandoned dwellings, he had finally found accommodation suitable to his taste. An elderly gentleman, Charles Green—banker, cotton baron, and expatriate Liverpudlian—had graciously offered his two-story mansion to him, and he had accepted. And now Sherman and his staff lived in comfort, in an estate rich with European statuary and paintings, exquisite furniture, elegantly appointed rooms, and exotic species like banana plants. The owner didn't even seem angry that the general had seized his cotton holdings. He merely wanted him to be happy and satisfied, and to know that the good people of Savannah wished him no harm and would do nothing to merit the kind of wrath he had unleashed on other Georgia towns—like, say, Atlanta.

To this end Sherman entertained a parade of gracious and respectful local visitors. They included the mayor Richard Arnold, who had dropped by more than once, having freely surrendered his town just two weeks before, and the brother of General William Hardee and other local elites, who had an interest in keeping their property safe from confiscation and themselves free from military detention. Sherman found he enjoyed their company!

He had no particular enmity toward the town leaders. After all, they had not resisted his advance. Rather, they had thanked him for restoring order after looters briefly ran amok when the rebels withdrew. And with federal authority reestablished, some like Mayor Arnold had offered to discuss reconciliation with the rest of the Union, and praised the even-handed approach of General John Geary—whom Sherman had appointed to run the provost guard—for skillfully providing law and order.

No one seemed more pleased with Sherman's presence than black Savannahians. Ever since he had arrived in town, they surrounded him on the street wanting to shake hands and offer their support. Some quoted scripture to him; others asked for advice on obtaining work. Still others called on Sherman at his home, thanking him for freeing the town from slavery and comparing him favorably to Simeon and other biblical figures. Sherman, in turn, had the old auction blocks in town chopped up and made into firewood, and informed white Savannahians that while he would protect their material property from theft, he would not do the same for what they considered their human property. His armies had eradicated slavery in town, and they would have to accept it.

Privately, though, he found the idea of himself as a liberator to be curious, even a bit absurd. In a letter to his wife, Ellen, he wrote, "It would amuse you to See the Negroes, they flock to me old & young they pray and shout—and mix up my name with that of Moses, & Simon and other scriptural ones as well as Abram Linkum the Great Messiah of 'dis Jubilee.'" Still, despite his condescension, Sherman enjoyed the attention the freedmen gave him, seeing it as a welcome respite from the bile shown him by many of the white townspeople who weren't among the elite with property to lose. To them the Union army was worthy of contempt, to be greeted with defiance and insults like "sneaking Yankee" and "ruthless invader"—and gestures like wearing mourning black and refusing to walk under the banner of Old Glory as it hung over the streets. He figured they would persist in their hatred even to the day they faced annihilation—which, if not for Hardee's hasty withdrawal, they might well have.

Their behavior confounded Sherman. For all their impudence, he had treated them with mercy and kindness. He had allowed the town council to continue functioning, given to that council the provisions his troops had seized after taking control of the town, and offered to protect the property of the families of Confederate officers, and the honor of their wives and daughters. Still, many Savannahians expected him to reveal himself as the ignoble barbarian all their newspapers said he was. If anything they seemed disappointed that he wasn't. No matter what he did for them, they remained hateful and defiant and called him the "Vandal Chief." One woman even refused an invitation to meet him by wishing he be strapped onto a bed of pushpins!

Nonetheless, he knew the real source of their grievance wasn't his brusque manners or his style of occupation. It was the fact that he had triumphed in his March to the Sea, traveling nearly 300 miles in twenty-four days, and had crowned his victory by conquering their town. In an official report, Sherman bragged about his successes: 300 miles of railroads destroyed; 5,000 horses, 4,000 mules, and 13,000 cows confiscated; 9 to 11 million pounds of fodder seized; and innumerable cotton gins, mills, bridges, and telegraph lines rendered useless. It all made for some 100 million dollars' worth of damage to the economy of Georgia, at a cost of less than 600 casualties—out of 62,000 men. No one knew the exact number of Confederate casualties, although the number of stolen crops and livestock, emptied cribs and barns, and destroyed industrial equipment was immense. One part of Georgia near Sparta became known as the "Burnt Country" for the fires that had consumed it, while scattered throughout, "lone chimney-stacks, 'Sherman's Sentinels,' told of homes laid in ashes."

Sherman basked in the terrifying success of the campaign. And he received his greatest endorsement in the note John Logan handed him from President Lincoln. In it, the commander-in-chief praised him for having the courage to execute his campaign when Lincoln himself had his doubts—"the honor is all yours." The president would no longer get in the way of his strategic judgment and allowed him license to make war any way he chose: "I suppose it will be safe if I leave General Grant and yourself to decide."

Increasingly, reporters and a few politicians began to mention Sherman's name as a future candidate for senator or president, or more immediately as candidate for promotion to lieutenant general. This would give him the same rank as Grant, whose profile had taken a beating in recent months with the Army of the Potomac stymied in Virginia. But Sherman refused. He had no interest in threatening the position of Grant, or in being commander of all the U.S. armies, and he conveyed this refusal to anyone who cared to listen. He was more than happy in his current job, crushing the South in his own handcrafted invasion.

He marveled at how much had changed for him. No longer was he the beleaguered lunatic of popular disrepute, unable to command a military department. Now he was the conquering hero of the west, and it made all his previous struggles and assorted miseries diminish in memory. Where once he had been obsessed with potential failure, now he planned for inevitable victory.

Even the loss of another of his sons, Charles, a baby whom he had never seen, would not dampen his spirit. After Ellen informed him of the tragedy, he felt sorry for her own anguish, but remained impassive about Charles's passing. As he wrote to her, "I cannot say I grieve for him as I did Willy. . . . amid the Scenes of death and desolation through which I daily pass I cannot but become callous to death. It is so common, so familiar that it no longer impresses me as of old."

No longer would he allow a death in the family to detract from his mission. He had exhausted his emotional reserve in mourning for Willy the year before, and had let his passing plague his thoughts and weaken his faith. But something had changed in him since then. His spirit had hardened as his fortunes multiplied.

Lincoln's letter to Sherman marked the high point of his esteem in the North. But almost as soon as he read it, he was in trouble again.

Other letters followed Lincoln's from Washington, and these were far less complimentary. One from Chief of Staff Henry Halleck warned him that his policies toward freedmen and black troops had met with contempt in some quarters, namely among the Radical Republicans who were strong supporters of abolition and of punishing the South after the war. Halleck told him these factions accused him of bearing "an almost criminal dislike to the negro" and that he could have done far more to assist escaped slaves as they followed his army columns. Following Halleck's letter was one from Salmon Chase, the new chief justice of the Supreme Court. He charged Sherman had openly disobeyed the president's order to arm black troops and treated them "as a set of pariahs, almost without rights" and then reminded him that he had once classified black people with other stolen property of war like cattle.

Sherman was shocked by his sudden disrepute among the powers in Washington. Had the ground really shifted that much in the month he had been out of contact with them? Didn't they know black people praised him and shook his hand almost every day?

He quickly wrote back to Chase and outlined his views on the freedmen. He claimed 20,000 had followed his four corps (double the actual number who reached Savannah). While he had no animus toward escaped slaves, he did consider them "a dangerous impediment" to his army, "clogging my roads, and eating up our subsistence." He would consider employing blacks as soldiers at some point, but would not *force* them. After all, he had always felt that while black men and women should be made free, they should not have equality with whites.

With Halleck he was even more blunt. He realized he would be blamed for any transgressions on the march—"But the nigger? Why, in God's name, can't sensible men let him alone?" He rejected any accusations of his unfairness to freed slaves, and touted his fitness to be a fair protector of their interests, using one of his favorite terms for them: "I profess to be the best kind of friend to Sambo, and think that on such a question Sambo should be consulted."

Halleck and the rest of the military establishment decided to test his word. Secretary of War Stanton boarded a ship to Savannah immediately.

Sherman ranted to his wife about the army's treatment of him. In the midst of his spectacular success—which was "pure & unalloyed by the taint of parasitic flattery"—the military leaders had dared to question his judgment for the sake of that "Negro nonsense" involving the arming of black troops. He didn't care what they said—he wouldn't have it! And moreover, he knew his stance was proper and his feelings justified: "I am right & wont Change."

To that end he had already disarmed a regiment of black soldiers, the 110th U.S. Colored Infantry, who had arrived in Georgia with an eye toward manning the local garrison. This Sherman could not abide, especially since it might offend the sensibilities of the town folk who already despised him. As he wrote, "people have prejudices which must be regarded." He took the guns out of the hands of these black men and put them to work laboring for the army, driving wagons and serving white officers. And if they had to protect a military installation, Sherman preferred it be a coastal fort instead of a town full of white Southerners.

Many of the military brass, especially of an abolitionist bent, had no idea what Sherman was thinking. Throughout the U.S. there were already 140 black regiments totaling more than 100,000 troops—which would grow to 10 percent of the Union's entire fighting force. Didn't he understand that change was inevitable in the army? Hadn't he read the reports from Nashville? There, black soldiers had fought fiercely and bravely in their major battle in the western theater. At Overton Hill, for example, one regiment attacked a fortified Confederate position across a sodden bog, and despite losing 40 percent of its men, refused to retreat. Even commander George Thomas, a native Virginian, had to respect what he had seen with his own eyes, at that hill and other battle sites: "The question is settled: negro soldiers will fight." Sherman, however, had not seen it for he wasn't there; and what he didn't see, he refused to believe. For him, this was still a white man's war, and he would do everything in his power to keep it that way.

The troubles for blacks in Savannah went well beyond Sherman's prohibition on arming them as soldiers. While he protected the economic interests of Southern whites in town, blacks were fair game for any Union troops who still had a taste for plunder. Reports told of bummers stealing from freedmen and pillaging their property, stripping their homes of lumber to use as firewood, devouring their stocks of rice, and peppering them with the usual racial invective and other abuse. As on the March to the Sea, Sherman did little to stop any of this behavior.

Many of the former slaves who had escaped during the march now congregated in the town as refugees—without sufficient food, medicine, and clothing—and starved by the dozens, perhaps hundreds. Their condition became a cause of concern in the North, though relief supplies mostly went to white, well-heeled Savannahians. As one Union general wrote, "Charities from the North are given to rank secesh women in silks, while poor whites & destitute negroes are turned away, and told to go to work."

It was even worse for the black men and women just outside Savannah. While Sherman proclaimed how orderly the town had been under the control of his provost guard, in Liberty County conditions were very different under the sway of his cavalry. Without anyone to stop him, General Hugh Kilpatrick and his men stole from and ransacked any houses they could find. Often their targets were plantations, but they also included the homes of black residents. These former slaves had slowly, painstakingly scraped together enough money to buy small plots of land and tend gardens and maintain farms. Once Kilpatrick's boys arrived, they helped themselves to their belongings, pillaging everything they had. The cavalry snatched horses, hogs, and cows, swiped family heirlooms, and even stole the blankets from an elderly, bedridden black minister. At Midway Church, Kilpatrick corralled livestock in the graveyard, turned the sanctuary into a slaughterhouse, used the grave markers as kindling for cooking meat, and burned the church records. Again, Sherman did nothing to stop Kilpatrick from his depredations, and blacks whose property he had ruined had to wait ten to fifteen years after the war to file property claims against the U.S. government.

Secretary of War Stanton knew about many of these abuses when he arrived in Savannah on January 11. But he didn't come to talk only about the bummers, or black troops, or Sherman's racial attitudes. He wanted to know about Ebenezer Creek, and what Sherman knew and when he knew it.

Lieutenant Colonel James Connolly had never forgotten about the terrible events of December 9. Upon reaching Savannah, he wrote letters to his congressional representative and to his division commander Absalom Baird describing Jefferson C. Davis's willful abandonment of black refugees at that swollen creek and their subsequent drowning and recapture by Confederate horsemen. From there, General Baird publicized the letter by sending it to the *New York Tribune*, and also forwarded it to the secretary of war.

The story caused a national stir. Northern readers wondered if it could be true, and Radical Republicans condemned Sherman for employing a known racist and murderer to lead the 14th Corps. Worse, Davis was a Copperhead, a Southern sympathizer, an enemy of freedom, and if Sherman had given such a man his sanction, then surely Sherman must be aligned with his beliefs, too.

Sherman responded by denying the whole thing. He let Henry Halleck know "that cock-and-bull story of my turning back negroes that Wheeler might kill them is all humbug. I turned nobody back." When Stanton arrived in Savannah, Sherman was ready to repeat much the same defense to him in private.

However, the secretary of war was not a man for casual conversation. Instead he followed a formal procedure to uncover the truth about the accusations. At his headquarters, he asked Sherman a series of twelve detailed questions about his conduct of the war and actions toward escaped slaves.

Sherman made a cogent defense of his actions. He described the military necessity of a quick march, the overwhelming numbers of freedmen he had had to manage, and the danger of his own troops starving in order to feed thousands of refugees. He also defended General Davis, whom he called an excellent soldier, and sent for Davis himself to explain his actions. When Davis humbly appeared before the secretary, he vowed he never held any rancor toward blacks. He was simply doing his duty in withdrawing his pontoon bridge to protect his men. He claimed he meant no harm whatsoever.

Stanton wanted to know more. He summoned a group of twenty middle-aged and elderly black ministers—fifteen of them former slaves—and asked them a different series of questions about the war, the army, and freedom. Did they support the Emancipation Proclamation and the national government? Would black men fight for the Union? Were they capable of taking care of themselves once freed, and willing to follow the laws of the nation? And did they want to live among white people or away from them? The answer to all these questions was yes, except for the latter. To that, one of the respondents said, "I would prefer to live by ourselves, for there is a prejudice against us in the South that will take years to get over."

For his final question, Stanton asked Sherman to leave the room. Surprised by the request, Sherman felt insulted. He later complained about the absurdity of qualifying the testimony of a conquering general with the opinions of slaves whom he had freed. Nonetheless, he followed the order and went outside the room.

Now in private, the secretary bluntly asked the men what they thought of the commander and his conduct in recent weeks. They considered it for a moment, pondered the rare opportunity to address a leader of national stature like Stanton, and also realized Sherman was right outside the door.

They promptly expressed gratitude for Sherman performing his duty, and said his behavior was that "of a friend and a gentleman. We have confidence in General Sherman, and think that what concerns us could not be under better hands." And with that the meeting ended. Sherman returned to the room and discussed more particulars of the march, and the black ministers went home.

Stanton was satisfied with their answers, and issued no censure to Sherman or Davis for the events at Ebenezer Creek. The generals thus escaped punishment for allowing the tragedy and murder to occur, with Stanton believing their stories and approving of their leadership. But he had also heard something from the preachers that stuck with him:

"The way we can best take care of ourselves is to have land, and turn it and till it by our labor . . . and we can soon maintain ourselves and have something to spare."

The secretary of war considered it and thought this was a good idea. What could be more fitting than to offer these black men and women a form of recompense while also stripping the white Southerners of their lands to punish them for rebelling?

Before he left Savannah, he had Sherman draft an order that would address the topic of land distribution for freedmen. Surprisingly, Sherman was quick to comply and drew up the order posthaste. Stanton carefully reviewed his draft, making changes as necessary, until the two men agreed on a new policy that few could have predicted:

Newly freed slaves would take possession of the abandoned rice plantations of the Sea Islands and sections of the adjacent coastlines of Georgia and South Carolina. Each family would be entitled to a forty-acre plot of land, with the backing and protection of the U.S. government. The residents would exert control over their own affairs, cultivate their own farms and livestock, and no whites beyond military troops would be allowed to reside there.

When the order appeared, many in uniform were surprised and assumed Stanton had been its primary author. But Sherman not only wrote the new policy, he openly supported it, and had been advocating for such a plan for nearly a year. A full nine months before, as he had written to General Lorenzo Thomas, "I would prefer much to colonize the negroes on lands clearly forfeited to us by treason, and for the Government to buy or extinguish the claims of other and loyal people in the districts chosen." He suggested giving a huge swath of the Mississippi Delta region between Memphis and Vicksburg to freed slaves—including the plantation of rebel president Jefferson Davis. While the new policy wasn't as far-reaching, since it only included the Sea Islands and a nearby 30-mile-wide stretch of coastline, it still appealed to the Union commander. It would not only give the freedmen land on which to relocate after the March to the Sea, it would free Sherman from having to provide for them in Savannah, or in the army column during the next phase of the invasion. And that was his primary motivation.

And so, in the fallout from Ebenezer Creek and the creation of this new military edict, within weeks the U.S. government was helping 20,000 former slaves settle across 400,000 acres of land in the South. The figure behind this bold plan wasn't Lincoln or Stanton or another progressive leader, or even someone known for his sympathies for black people. Instead it was General William Sherman.

He spelled out the policy as part of his Special Field Order No. 15, but most people came to know it by another name: Forty Acres and a Mule.

FOURTEEN

FIRE AND SWORD

John Logan was in pain. It seemed like every winter he was in pain, but this time it was different. Rheumatism bedeviled his shoulder, and nagging aches crept down his torso. This gnawing aggressive discomfort had troubled him for years now, but it seemed worse in the South Carolina rains of late January 1865. The locals called this the most tempestuous weather they had seen in twenty years, an incessant frigid spray that turned the ground to muck and each movement into an ordeal. An inch of icy crust formed each night, only melting with the icy rain each morning. It was bad enough if you lived in a humble shack that leaked; it was unaccountably worse if your army was trying to invade the state.

He tried not to run through his mind the full catalog of injuries he had experienced—the times he had been thrown from his horse, peppered with minié balls, left for dead—but how could he forget them when raising his arm or craning his neck led to a sharp jolt of pain and a grimace? For all his boys knew, he wore this gritty expression not because of his own torment, but as a badge of scorn for the traitors whose homeland they were destroying.

Since leaving Savannah, Logan had led his 15th Corps from the army camp at Beaufort on Port Royal Island, across to the mainland, and on to the Salkehatchie River. It was wet and dismal country, but Logan pushed his boys through these soggy lowlands to play his part in William Sherman's latest campaign—crushing the state that instigated the rebellion or, as some of the troops called it, "the Hell hole of secession."

For the great raid into South Carolina, Sherman had again divided his army into two wings. The left would proceed north by northwest to threaten Augusta; the right would head north by northeast to threaten Charleston. Neither wing would actually attack those towns. Instead, their goal was to feint toward them, before converging around the state capital of Columbia, and from there move upstate and into North Carolina. The 14th and 20th Corps composed the left wing, still known as the Army of Georgia; the 17th and 15th composed the right wing, the Army of the Tennessee. Sherman traveled with the right wing.

On the way, Logan had a chance to talk strategy with his commanding general and sometimes nemesis. Because he had spent the March to the Sea up in Illinois stumping for the president, he was unaware of just how much theft of Georgians' property had taken place. Learning about these excesses, Logan resolved to forbid foraging in his own corps in the Carolinas campaign. Sherman quickly corrected him: His 15th Corps would forage just as it had in Georgia—if not more so.

While Logan did try to crack down on bumming in his orders to the troops, he could not contain the feelings of revenge many of them had for South Carolina, nor did he try. The politicians and many of the residents of the state had for years expressed contempt for the Union and threatened to leave it or "nullify" federal laws, going all the way back to Jacksonian times. To no one's surprise, they had launched the secession movement first: breaking up the nation before Lincoln could be inaugurated, joining a rump confederacy of aggrieved Southern states, and protecting their "peculiar institution" of slavery and defending it through violent action. The Union armies took four years to advance to the state's borders and deliver their own response, and now they had reached them—marching into the low country, stealing food anywhere they could, and burning anything of military or economic value. This was the vengeance they had long imagined, using "fire and sword" to crush the cradle of rebellion.

Hearing word of Sherman on the march again, most South Carolinians had fled, leaving thousands of vacant houses, farms, and barns behind. Many of these met with the Yankee torch, sometimes even before the troops could raid them for their foodstuffs and provisions. If residents were at home when the soldiers arrived, their houses would often be spared, but if not, they added to the column's growing trail of smoky plumes. Remote, little-known hamlets like Pocotaligo and McPhersonville fell to the flames, as did cotton gins, munitions shops, railroad depots, arsenals, magazines, warehouses, and factories. The southern part of South Carolina soon became even more desolate than it had been before the troops arrived—a wilderness of carbonized building skeletons and lone chimneys, devoid of inhabitants or anything resembling civilization.

The terrain was equally bleak. The boys thought they had seen the worst of it at the riverbed of the Big Salkehatchie: a great flooded watercourse with 15 tributaries that had to be crossed on pontoons or corduroy roads or even waded through in waist-deep water. Like their commander, the corpsmen faced the ice-cold streams with bravado and high spirits, until their legs began to go numb and their muscles stiffened up—and the torrential winter rain began to seem endless. Logan traveled side by side with his boys, encouraging them, exhorting them, helping them carry supplies, and leading the way, all while never betraying his own deep body pains in an environment that made them appreciably worse.

The Edisto River offered the greatest test. Here, the rebels had set their works and batteries on the far side of the river, and rather than surging ahead into range of their cannons, Logan ordered his troops to outflank them. This meant plunging into water that rose almost up to their armpits. They had to travel nearly three-quarters of a mile in the swamp, holding not only their cartridge boxes and their gear at the tips of their rifles above the waterline, but their pants, socks, and shoes, too. More than a few soldiers tripped over the cypress trees' submerged knees and went down into the frigid murk with all their belongings. The effect of wading half-naked in these waters led to bouts of fatigue and illness, even among some of the toughest veterans. Some literally froze up and could not move another foot; others refused to advance until the weather improved.

The boys had few opportunities for sleep amid their countless labors—everything from chopping wood for corduroy roads to dismantling railroad track—and some of them could barely keep their eyes open, running purely on willpower and whatever grub they could scrounge from the abandoned farmsteads in the area. Even the horses and mules had it better than they, and were led to the high ground while the soldiers themselves had to drag their artillery and wagons. Pulling and heaving with whatever reserves of strength they had left, they managed to bring their lumbering vehicles to the far side of the Edisto and force the rebels to evacuate their works. But they hardly had time to celebrate their successful maneuver. There were more rivers and swamps awaiting them in the miles ahead.

Logan tried to keep his mind focused on the march—on advancing, outflanking, surrounding, demolishing, advancing—but amid his repetitive labors, his thoughts couldn't help but drift. If not for politics and ill fortune, he might now be commanding a military department, or preparing for a term in the Senate, or running an army in Tennessee. Instead he was back under the sway of William Sherman, in the most dreadful sort of campaign. There was no glory in battling these swamps, or fighting the weather; and he could hardly cast a heroic image for his boys when their enemies were little more than cotton gins, train depots, old warehouses, and abandoned villages.

Resaca and Dallas and Atlanta now seemed like fond memories, classic battles against a powerful Confederate enemy, the noble gestures, the inspiring speeches, the supreme acts of courage that had made him a warrior. He would never again have an opportunity for that kind of valor, not in this murky benighted landscape. All he could do was keep his commitment to his boys, his great extended family who made for much better kin than his own relatives. It was for them that he fought and suffered, grew and transformed.

He spent his 39th birthday in the Edisto swamp. It was a milestone of how far he had come, how different in some ways he was from the politician who decried both traitors and warmongers when the conflict began. Now he prosecuted the rebellion with a spirit and a vigor that matched that of any abolitionist. In fact, since the war began he found himself more and more in sympathy with their arguments, now that he had witnessed slavery in practice. He had seen too much in Tennessee, in Mississippi, and now in South Carolina to forget, and these memories changed and possessed him. The latest example had been near the Salkehatchie River, where he came across a white slave.

This perplexed and troubled him. The Black Law Logan had written as a young legislator, his angry speeches in Congress, and his angrier words on the stump, had all been predicated on white supremacy—the racial doctrine that propped up the plantation system and justified the enslavement of millions of Africans. But here was a rangy white man with a scraggly beard and mangy hair, of French and Indian heritage, who could not be confused for a black man and yet was owned by a South Carolina planter, after being bought at auction for $91.

The man was, of course, an aberration—and unimportant compared to the massive numbers of black men and women who faced the lash and the strap daily. But Logan couldn't forget the man, because he undercut his assumptions and gave the lie to his justifications. He also gave Logan the last push he needed to change his mind about slavery. As he said to Sherman, meeting that slave alone would have "made an abolitionist of him."

John Hight needed no encouragement to become an abolitionist—he had been one since his early years and knew the basic moral calculus of human bondage. He greatly respected John Logan. As he said, "He impresses one as a man of talent," but if Logan and the other generals had fought mainly for the preservation of the Union, for Hight it was the cause of freedom that guided him. For slavery was evil incarnate, and needed to be purged from the earth, preferably through peaceful action, but if that proved impossible, then through bullets, cannonballs, and fire.

He still didn't carry a gun, but he did assist black men and women who joined the column of the 14th Corps, and he bore witness to the funeral pyres of slavery, in the form of the smoke and flames that billowed through the Carolina woods. In Barnwell, the corps incinerated the courthouse, the business district, and many houses, leading them to label the place "Burnwell." And as Hight saw, "The rebels are now reaping the just reward of their long oppression of the slaves."

The reverend was not the only man in the army who felt such anger at the slave masters. Others like Lieutenant Colonel George Nichols had many of the same feelings, seeing black people beaten and abused and debased like mules and oxen. As in Georgia, in South Carolina the whipping post, the collars and chains, the depravity of it all were again on display, and not to be forgotten. As Nichols wrote, "It makes one's blood boil to see the evidences of the heartlessness and cruelty of these white men. I firmly believe that we are God's instruments of justice, and that they are at last called to account for this shameless crime."

Hight felt the same way, but his quest for revenge was not limitless. Within a few days of the beginning of the campaign, he began to harbor doubts about its excesses. The houses became more shambling, the cropland looked more barren, and the landscape more forbidding. And the hungrier and more desperate the people looked, the more he realized how worthy they were of God's mercy. As Hight wrote:

> We saw but few people, in our march to-day, and they were poor enough to disarm all hatred, had we borne them any. One family was about moving to Savannah, where alms were more plentiful. At another house, a woman sat shivering by the mule pen, guarding the last mule. The old man trembled with the palsy. A young man, thinly clad, stood shivering, while an armless sleeve told a tale of rebel service, which I did not feel at liberty to draw from his lips by Yankee questions. No people reside in any of these parts, save the poor. As for slaves, there never were many, and still fewer now.

The vengeful delights of torching a rich plantation had grown scarce in this part of the South, and Hight felt his natural inclination toward compassion and charity return. It did the nation no good to punish the poor for their misfortune, or to strip indigent rural farmers of their last hopes. Where was the godliness in that? Only the devil could smile upon such endeavors, and, unfortunately, in this army corps there were more than a few.

Sherman assigned the 14th Corps to the left wing of the invasion force, and chose Jefferson C. Davis once more to lead it. It took Davis's corps many days to reach the crossing of the Savannah River at Sisters Ferry, since the rains had turned the dirt roads into deep muddy furrows. Hight and the pontoniers couldn't span the river until February 5—a full ten days behind the troops of the right wing to the east.

When they finally traversed the river, the corps began a monotonous plod through the Carolina outback, where the weather was uniformly cold, wet, and miserable. The terrain was a desolate landscape of pine trees and sandy soil, swamps and quicksand. The settlements were a mix of burned-out hamlets, hardscrabble plantations, and meager houses and farms. And the work was never easy.

To cross rivers like the Salkehatchie, the Edisto, the Saluda, the Congaree, and the Broad, the corpsmen had to first cross the tributaries and swamps that surrounded them, with the Pioneer Corps cutting hundreds of trees to construct corduroy roads. After that, the pontoniers worked for hours or days to bridge the torrents of water where rivers overflowed in the winter rains, using up to twenty-one boats, often spanning hundreds of feet.

Their reward for all this work was more work. The effect of these constant labors was deadening, and made worse when the men remained perpetually chilly and damp, and failed to get sufficient sleep after Sherman ordered regimental tents to be destroyed. He meant the order to lighten the wagons' loads, but all it did was make the troops angry and deprive them of rest and comfort. Hight especially derided the idea, for "At the very time orders are issued to destroy tents, there are hundreds of pounds of old and useless articles hauled by teamsters, guards, and others. Men in this train are hauling tobacco by the box, for purposes of speculation."

Still, despite all the hardship, Hight and the 58th Indiana persisted and carried out their role in the campaign. The reverend, after all, expected these kind of difficulties, especially in an invasion as fraught with peril and sacrifice as this one. What he could not abide, however, was Jefferson C. Davis.

Whatever respect Hight may have had for Davis had evaporated after Ebenezer Creek. His feelings of shame and disgust at that tragedy were well known, and only deepened after Davis's remorseless interview with Secretary of War Stanton in Savannah. The general had woven a tapestry of lies that had removed the moral stain from his name and ensured him another prominent command on the next march. And now here he was, issuing arbitrary edicts, ignoring good advice from his staff, and generally behaving like a strong-willed but weak-minded ogre.

Hight despised his "foolish and unreasonable" orders, such as making the pontoon train travel at the back of the corps column, exactly where it wasn't needed. When the troops came to a stream or river that needed bridging, the pontoniers had to trudge through the entire column to reach the front and begin their work. Did he not understand this was absurd? Other times, Davis forced the men to work two or three nights in a row without sleep, or demanded a river be bridged when he knew there weren't enough pontoons for the job—only to get angry when the last section of the span floated helplessly 200 feet from the other side. It made Hight wonder—*Is the man crazy?*

He simply didn't understand how this charlatan had been allowed to persist in his role, and came to envy the other corps on the march. The heroics of the 15th Corps, for example, were well known and unsurpassed on the battlefield. The "promptness, precision, and soldiery bearing" of the 20th Corps were admirable, too, and "In these respects they out-shine all the Corps of this army." But what did the 14th Corps have to offer? A leader known to be a murderer and a Copperhead? A reputation for abandoning freed slaves knowingly to their deaths?

He had to admit—it wasn't just Davis and his staff. Even before the corps had set foot in South Carolina, he had seen the boys begin to loosen their scruples, to drift from their ethical bearings, and indulge in all manner of vices. With whiskey rations offered to the men, drunkenness was rampant, "and many of them are going to the dogs." Profanity and gambling had become legion, and even on the night of the Sabbath, he could hear revelers fiddling and dancing without restraint. The new conscripts only added to the atmosphere, with rebel deserters, bounty jumpers, "shirks" and "butternuts" and other "scrapings of society" contributing to the camp's bestial revels.

Intemperance was the most grievous sin among the troops, and it sickened him to see men he had once thought to be upright souls indulging in foul oaths and fisticuffs after quaffing the devil's nectar. Yet the sight of all this debauchery exhausted him, and he found he couldn't even muster the energy to preach a sermon against the perils of strong drink or any of the other vices. And when he did find the energy, only a few random souls showed up to listen, shivering under a canopy of pines in the swamplands. Perhaps he shouldn't have been surprised. A message of humility before God couldn't stand a chance when there were bottles of whisky to swill, and houses to plunder, and a full catalog of sins to commit.

His old friends had long since left the 58th Indiana or been mustered out, and difficult questions now plagued him every day. What had become of him and his mission? Had it perished during the march? And what was missing in his ministry? The trials of war should have been the tools to guide his flock back to the grace of God. Instead, none of the boys seemed to care or notice what he said. And this hurt him more than anything the rebels could have done.

Hight felt himself alone and without direction or purpose: "I seem destined to outlive my usefulness in the Regiment." While he had made his home in the army and felt no desire to return to the comforts of Indiana, he wondered whether he should stay. He considered returning to civilian life once his term of service expired in March.

"At present, all my labor seems to be in vain. My way is hedged up; what am I to do? May God help me to do something. . . . The work of the Lord is under par, and His servant is neglected. When will a brighter day dawn? May God send it soon."

—⁂—

For Charles Wills, the brighter day had already dawned. On February 11, he received his commission as a major, after the 103rd Illinois's officers unanimously recommended him to fill an open position. He couldn't have been prouder, and saw it as a highlight of his two and a half years' service with the regiment. Unlike some of the men in the 15th Corps, he enjoyed the Carolinas campaign and saw it as an unusual and challenging enterprise.

While he had to battle through the swamps as everyone did, he also dined on the likes of ham, honey, and sweet potatoes; spent the night in a deserted resort "with mahogany furniture of the best quality . . . a fine piano, splendid plate mirror, and a fine library"; and saw new fauna such as "a school of porpoise which looked just like a drove of hogs in the water" while on a steamboat from Savannah to Beaufort. The only things missing were his impromptu encounters with local women, of which there had been very few since he had left Georgia.

He especially appreciated the kind of combat his regiment fought: skirmishes with cavalry and maneuvers to outflank rebel field works. There had been no repeats of Griswoldville or Ezra Church or Jonesboro, those bloody turkey shoots in Georgia that demoralized him and made him question what kind of war he was fighting. He even felt a bit of sympathy for the rebel soldiers he encountered, noticing their lack of proper clothing and gear, and all the losses they suffered trying to stop Sherman's advance. "Poor devils!"

Despite the sympathy Wills was able to muster for his enemy's forlorn condition, he knew the 15th Corps was doing all it could to worsen it. Wills wrote, "I never saw so much destruction of property before. Orders are strict as ever, but our men understand they are in South Carolina and are making good their old threats. Very few houses escape burning." The exceptions were those in which the family remained behind to guard their property. But even then, their cribs and larders were stripped and their livestock were stolen. At the same time, the corpsmen smashed the state's railroad lines, heating up the rails and giving them a double twist with a clamp and lever, to make sure no Confederate trains could pass over them, and helping deny the resupply of rebel troops upstate and farther north.

Once the troops got a taste for the destruction, it was hard to stop. When the 103rd set fire to a turpentine camp and set the massive pines ablaze, the conflagration burned out of control and nearly incinerated the regiment as well. Two nights before, a similar fire swept over the camp where Wills and his colleagues were sleeping. They awoke to the snap and crackle of the forest around them collapsing in the searing heat. The flames immolated his vest and jacket, and he and the other officers barely had time to escape their tents before they were scorched as well.

It took little effort for the pine forest to burn. Dead and dying pines that had been tapped for their pitch now became tinder—one spark was all it took for the branches to take flame and send the soldiers scurrying for cover. George Nichols reported how he passed through a forest "filled with flames and pitch-black smoke. . . . Wagons, horsemen, and foot soldiers, one by one disappeared in the gloom, to reappear here and there bathed in lurid light. Within, the fire singed our hair and clothes, while our maddened animals dashed hither and thither in an agony of fear."

Even in these hazardous conditions, nothing could slow down Wills and the rest of the 15th Corps. They bivouacked in the nastiest bottomlands. They outflanked Confederate positions by wading in swamp water up to their armpits. They corduroyed and pontooned through forests and wetlands and swamps no previous army would have dreamed of crossing. And they fought the rebels wherever they could find them. As Wills said when describing the force, "The men of this army surprise me every day with their endurance, spirit and recklessness."

For these reasons, the 15th Corps was Sherman's favorite in the western force, and he trusted it for everything from beating the rebels at Atlanta to storming Fort McAllister. And now that all four corps were pushing into central South Carolina, he gave the 15th the most prized opportunity—taking the state capital of Columbia.

To meet their objective, Wills and the 103rd Illinois fought as skirmishers, battling the Confederates along the Congaree River. They beat them back over the course of two days, driving them out of their works and crossing on pontoons in the face of artillery fire. Pushing on, mile by mile, their advance guard reached the junction of the Saluda and Broad rivers, with the capital well within their sights. They planned to attack it once the rest of the corps caught up. Instead, the rebels withdrew.

Columbia now lay before them, defenseless but for a few companies of rebel soldiers protecting the retreat. As part of a division commanded by Charles Woods, Wills and the 103rd Illinois became among the first troops to enter the town. General Logan chose Woods's division as the provost guard to protect the capital they had just conquered. But no one was in much of a mood to help the Columbians.

Almost as soon as the troops entered the capital on February 17, they were greeted by the sight of escaped prisoners joining their lines—filthy, emaciated, starving men who had been through hell to get out of the place they called Camp Sorghum, just outside town. There, the men had had to dig mud burrows for shelter, subsisted on scant rations, became targets for the guards if they crossed a "deadline" border, and ended up in ramshackle burial plots after their deaths. Not more than thirty escapees made it through the lines; the rest had been shipped to Charlotte, North Carolina. But the sight of these several dozen skeletal, abused men shocked the troops of Woods's division.

The stories the men told were worse than their appearances. Some POWs had not only been forced into subhuman living conditions, they had been paraded through the streets of Columbia itself. As one escapee remembered, "As we went along the streets a mob of people gathered around us, hooting and hissing their hatred at us. . . . A few wanted the guards to give them a chance to hang us. It was a sorry sight—this band of ragged, helpless, hungry loyalists being led like slaves and animals through the hooting, threatening crowd." It made many of the revenge-hungry men of Woods's division want to set fire to the town. They soon discovered the retreating rebels had nearly done the same thing.

General Wade Hampton had been detached from Robert E. Lee's forces in Virginia to manage the Confederate cavalry in South Carolina, and he had overseen the placement of large piles of cotton bales in the streets to destroy them. He had given no final order to burn them, but by the time the town was evacuated, some of the bales had taken flame.

No one knew the exact reason why. The night before, as the rebels retreated, mobs plundered stores and warehouses and some miscreants may have ignited the bales. Or it may have been rebel soldiers acting without orders, or Union artillery fire. Regardless of the cause, when Woods's division came marching in, a high wind scattered the tufts of cotton into trees and across the roads. Some of it fell like snow. Other pieces were smoldering.

Amid this strange atmosphere, the town residents came out to greet the arriving soldiers in Woods's division. Some of them were newly freed slaves; others were white loyalists who emerged from hiding. They were ecstatic to see the Union army in the capital, and rewarded them with their own sort of welcome gifts. In buckets and tin pans, they passed out free wine and liquor—some of which had been looted from local stores—and the troops drank it with delight. One regiment after another succumbed to the strong drink and forgot they were on duty to protect the town, or that they had any duty at all.

Charles Wills couldn't believe his eyes. His troops had been so driven and confident, so worthy of praise and admiration when they were campaigning in the wilderness. But the moment they encountered civilization in Columbia, they succumbed to their basest desires. The mass inebriation caused a breakdown of order, a disaster for an army unit trying to maintain law and order amid the near chaos of wartime. As Wills saw, "the boys loaded themselves with what they wanted. Whiskey and wine flowed like water, and the whole division is now drunk. This gobbling of things so, disgusts me much."

Woods ordered his men to protect private dwellings and public buildings, but turmoil broke out as the liquor continued to flow. Plunderers in the army broke into shops and scattered furniture and merchandise across the streets, rapacious residents joined them in the looting, and violent criminals added to the mayhem after escaping from a local penitentiary. A fierce wind began to blow the dry, combustible cotton everywhere, and soon, fire started to spread through the capital.

For once in the Carolinas campaign, this was nothing that Sherman or his generals wanted to happen. They had given assurances to the mayor and others the capital would be saved, that only the arsenals, foundries, machine shops, railroads, and such would be destroyed. Sherman had set a model for this kind of controlled destruction in Savannah, and he promised it would be followed here, too. But no matter what he or any of the officers said, the scenes of chaos expanded from one block to the next. Revenge seemed to have a mind of its own.

Charles Wills had witnessed arson and plunder many times before in the campaign, but this seemed especially baleful. No one was directing the violence—it just erupted from years of simmering anger, fueled by alcohol. He tried to stop the troops' reckless behavior, to curb their violence, but soon discovered he had no better ability to control anarchy as a major than he had as a captain. He couldn't manage chaos.

John Logan scarcely had time to rest when he entered the capital. Just a few hours after arriving, he learned of the fires threatening to destroy the town. One blaze even ignited six blocks away from his headquarters. Almost immediately, he marshaled his staff and whatever men he could find to battle the blazes that were consuming the business district along Richardson Street. The commander of the Army of the Tennessee, Oliver Howard, followed his lead and ordered up to 2,000 troops to extinguish the blazes, destroy sheds and out buildings that might allow the conflagration to spread, and get control over the wayward soldiers and convicts who were still running amok after midnight.

The citizens now faced more danger from rioters than from the fires themselves. Packs of self-styled bandits ran about in the streets breaking windows, busting open doors, and pillaging stores and homes of whatever loot they could grab. Some uncovered new stashes of liquor and guzzled it to add more fuel to the mayhem. Others ran rampant through private homes, assaulting anyone who tried to stop them. Responsible 15th Corps troops stationed themselves around these houses to protect them, and even guarded groups of town folk too terrified to walk home amid the pandemonium.

The scenes became more dangerous and phantasmagoric as the night wore on. Fierce, red-hot winds blew cascades of sparks and embers overhead, while the burning airborne cotton ignited homes and storefronts. Shadowy men pillaged in the darkness, then emerged glowing and demonic by the firelight. Soldiers arrested other soldiers, and luckless civilians ran for their lives. And all around them echoed the sound of buildings crackling and burning, as the Confederate capital stood on the verge of collapse.

At 1:30 A.M., Logan had had enough. He took a break from his firefighting to order General William Hazen to marshal a brigade for police duty—to quell the rioting that showed no sign of abating. The military police spread out across the business district and into the neighborhoods to arrest any hooligans they could find, and they found plenty. By dawn Hazen estimated some 2,500 rogue troops and escaped criminals had been arrested, with hundreds more still on the loose.

The violence and arson taxed whatever reserves of strength officers like Woods and Hazen and Logan had left. They had barely gotten any sleep for three nights, first having to battle the retreating rebels outside the capital, then their own soldiers inside of it. Despite their beleaguered condition, they did everything they could to keep the capital from being annihilated.

The wind died down overnight and kept any more structures from incineration. But as the morning of February 18 dawned, Columbia emerged as the picture of misery. Some 458 buildings—a third of the entire town—had been immolated and countless others damaged. Furniture, clothing, and blankets lay strewn across the streets, as the looters had plundered silverware, quilts, musical instruments, anything they could steal. Along the roads, little families of men, women, and children of all colors sat in destitute bunches, huddled with their trunks of clothes and keepsakes, having been burned out of their homes. The old state capitol with its library and extensive archives, the town's central avenues, its hotels and courthouses, countless businesses, eleven churches, a convent—all lay in ruin.

As in north Georgia and Atlanta, the greatest force of destruction in Columbia fell upon the poorest citizens. Hundreds of people roamed the streets, begging for food and looking for any assistance they could find, while their humble former houses stood in carbonized piles. These scenes of catastrophe went far beyond what anyone could have fathomed, and gave the lie to the idea that arson and pillaging could ever truly be managed, as Sherman had long claimed. The logic of hard war led to anarchy, and anarchy led to mass destruction, and the result of that immoral calculus was Columbia.

The ruin of the capital was a shocking sight, even for battle-hardened men. In response, many of the enlisted men opened their own haversacks and doled out what rations they had to the hungry people; others helped them gather food or supplies or protected them as they found shelter. The most engaged officer was Oliver Howard, who clamped down on the remaining lawbreakers with an aggressive police presence, and organized a force to protect the residents after the rest of his army left town. With Sherman's approval, he ordered 500 head of cattle to be given to the town folk for meat, and turned over any commissary stores and supplies to them as well, beyond what his own army required. He organized foraging parties to seek out food from the countryside for the residents, and even gave the mayor 100 rifles and many more rounds of ammunition to protect his town, should violence break out again in the coming weeks.

Many of the residents didn't want to test their luck, and set off with the army that had just wrecked their town. The column of the 15th Corps lengthened with black men and women just released from slavery, as well as white civilians who had lost everything in the fiery tempest and Union loyalists who feared for their lives. The corpsmen took them all in, until the march became a mix of soldiers and refugees, all headed to safer ground in North Carolina or wherever John Logan led them.

On its way out of town headed north, the 15th Corps did not neglect what it had come to Columbia to do in the first place. Under careful orders, the troops destroyed everything of military value, from the tracks and rolling stock of the railways, to the powder mill, armory, gasworks, foundry, printing plant, ammunition, gunpowder, rifles, bayonets, cannons, artillery shells, cartridge boxes, swords, and sabers. Among the final things they destroyed were 1,370 bales of cotton, which they burned carefully in the face of a gentle wind.

Though his corps had fulfilled their mission and left central South Carolina behind, John Logan could not forget the things he had seen in Columbia. He had never witnessed the March to the Sea, so had no sense of the arson, the pillaging, the bumming to which some generals had turned a blind eye. But he refused to do so. He would not be party to anarchy and mob rule—preventing these things was the very reason he had joined the war in the first place! Instead, he tightened his restrictions on mass plunder and arson, and threatened any rule-breakers with severe punishment. The malefactors in his corps would not be granted free rein to indulge their taste for bedlam, no matter how much enmity they had saved up for the birthplace of the rebellion.

Logan worried about the state of his troops. They had campaigned as Sherman's hard warriors for nearly a year now, and he feared the corruption of their spirit had set in. He knew most of his soldiers had remained in camp, or fought fires, or acted as provost guardsmen, but the sight of thousands of other marauders in blue uniforms—even if they were a minority—disgusted him beyond measure.

What had turned these valorous legions into rampaging rogues? He couldn't begin to explain or understand it. One thing he did know: The line between controlled vengeance and unchecked madness was a thin one, and Logan vowed his boys would not cross it again.

FIFTEEN

TO RALEIGH

William Sherman left South Carolina a smoldering wreck. His four corps had executed their revenge plans for the state by destroying much of its war-fighting ability and demoralizing the population by burning their towns, devouring their foodstuffs, and forcing them from their homes. If anything the devastation had been worse than in Georgia, and prompted mass denunciations of Sherman throughout the region, especially for the great pyre he had made of Columbia. The general cared little about the condemnation, though, and continued pushing his forces toward their next target: North Carolina.

By this time, the Confederate president Jefferson Davis began to appreciate the great failures of his war strategy, as none of his generals had managed to do anything to stop Sherman from laying waste to their heartland. Faced with what looked like inevitable defeat if he did not act, Davis appointed Robert E. Lee general-in-chief of all Confederate armies. Three weeks later, on February 23, Lee called up Joseph Johnston out of retirement to lead rebel forces once more, this time in the defense of the Tar Heel State.

Johnston was the last Southern general to have defeated Sherman in a major battle, nearly a year before at Kennesaw Mountain. For his defense of North Carolina, he had 21,000 troops, which were only a fraction of Union forces, and he was not optimistic about stopping the Yankees. Still, he had undeniable insight into Sherman's strategy. Unlike some Confederate generals, who assumed Sherman would attack Charlotte and its railway infrastructure, Johnston guessed Fayetteville was his next target. He guessed right. The Union general not only wanted to occupy that town to immolate its arsenal and factories, he chose it because it offered closer access to the port of Wilmington (100 miles to the southeast), which federal troops had recently captured to reestablish contact with Washington and allow for their resupply by sea of food, clothing, and weapons.

On March 12, Sherman's forces occupied Fayetteville. Although they disabled and destroyed its military infrastructure, the residents were surprised to discover most of their homes and livelihoods remained intact. General Baird even posted guards at public buildings and private homes. Unlike the neighboring state to the south, there would be no scorched earth in North Carolina.

This reflected a dramatic change in policy. From the moment they had crossed the border, Union soldiers refrained from mass pillaging and burning and reverted to their familiar, if still aggressive, approach to foraging. Few wanted to destroy the state, since it was one of the last to secede and was known to harbor a fair number of loyalists. However, two things didn't change across the border: the dismal weather and the hard slog through the swamps.

Few regiments had a harder road through this terrain than the 82nd Illinois. As part of the 20th Corps—on the left wing in the Army of Georgia—it had fought and waded and pontooned across some of the roughest country in the South. Its soldiers helped push wagons through the muck, build bridges, dismantle railroads, guard supply trains, and ward off surprise rebel attacks against their own regiment as well as others in the corps. Lieutenant Colonel Edward Salomon was back in command of the regiment, and drove his pan-European and American fighters with a spirit and energy that few other officers could match. They skirmished at waysides like Columbia Cross Roads and Chesterfield Court-House. They bridged rivers like the Cheraw and the Lumber, and built their tents on poles over flooded marshlands. They bivouacked in the swamps under relentless rains, and occasionally led the entire corps as the advance guard. Their campaign was arduous and often brutal, and by the time the men reached Fayetteville, they were exhausted and nearly played out.

They were, however, surprised and happy to receive letters from their friends and family for the first time in the Carolinas campaign, and to catch up on affairs with the outside world. It was also here that many refugees from the Carolinas—with estimates from 20,000 to 30,000—left the corps columns, with the former slaves headed to the Sea Islands, and the white refugees to settle in the North. The 82nd Illinois, however, would not be returning home just yet, but they would enjoy a respite from their grinding four-month campaign for the first time since their hiatus in Savannah.

Lieutenant Colonel Salomon, of course, had not spent his holidays in that Georgia seaport. Instead he had been with George Thomas's forces in Tennessee, which had devastated John Bell Hood's army and won the Battle of Nashville. The experience added to his lustrous record as a war fighter, and emboldened him on the current campaign despite its rigors.

Unlike some of the officers in the 20th Corps, Salomon maintained a firm sense of authority over his troops. He kept a clean and orderly camp and prevented drunkenness and horseplay in the ranks. The 82nd was one of the most well-drilled and disciplined units in the 20th Corps, and had a battle record to prove it. Thanks to his stalwart command of the regiment, most of Salomon's men respected him, with one notable exception.

Captain Rudolf Mueller had long disdained the lieutenant colonel, and liked him no better since he had returned to lead the regiment. If anything his meritorious conduct in Tennessee only added to Mueller's suspicions of him, as he continued to see him as an ambitious and prideful schemer. To Mueller, Salomon lacked the élan and martial bearing of the long-departed Friedrich Hecker. He ascribed any success the regiment enjoyed to his hero's enduring influence—not the theatrics of the interloper Salomon.

Mueller had had a checkered road in the 82nd in recent months. Not only had he openly warred against some of his fellow officers, he had been tried in a court martial two months before. Yet, while most onlookers had seen Mueller strike a lieutenant in a fit of rage, he had been acquitted of the charge, and his lower-ranking victim had been dismissed from the service (though later readmitted). This only heightened Mueller's sense of righteousness, and in his letters to Hecker, he continued to grouse about the quality of leadership of the regiment, as well as its moral conduct.

The captain had never experienced a campaign of destruction as he had during the March to the Sea, and in South Carolina it had only gotten worse. Still remembering his former commander's commitment to chivalry and high ideals, Mueller saw this new form of warfare as an odious affront to proper soldiery and civilized behavior. As he wrote, "Our army has taken on the character of bandits and murderous arsonist bands . . . and it is sad to have come so far that one must almost blush to say he belongs to Sherman's army and campaigned through S.C." Moreover, the troops' attire was tattered and many lacked socks and shoes, making them look like armed hooligans instead of proper warriors. The regiment's recent history and appearance so disgusted Mueller that he could only promise to provide his old friend Hecker with a full catalog of its "deeds and misdeeds" when he had more time.

For now, Mueller and the rest of the 82nd faced the next step in the campaign, heading northeast with the rest of Sherman's armies to the small town of Goldsboro. If necessary they would advance into Virginia and unite with General Grant's Army of the Potomac to smash Robert E. Lee's rebels and end the war with one great, decisive blow. But before that, they would have to beat Joseph Johnston's troops, who were waiting for them nearby, ready to strike against a foe that had long flummoxed them.

While Sherman's armies had faced little opposition in South Carolina other than rebel skirmishers, they met a stiffer test in North Carolina. A few days before, on March 9, the combined cavalry of Wade Hampton and Joseph Wheeler surprised Union general Hugh Kilpatrick, forcing him to run half-naked for his life into a swamp. The general later found his garments and rallied with his horsemen to fend off the rebels. This conflict, while officially known as the Battle of Monroe's Cross Roads, would be more popularly called the Battle of Kilpatrick's Pants.

The unexpected attack reflected General Johnston's new battle plan. Unlike the delay-and-withdraw approach he had taken to the invading Union armies in north Georgia, in North Carolina he chose a bolder gambit: He attacked them head on.

Outside the hamlet of Averasboro on March 16, Johnston ordered the corps of William Hardee to hit the 20th Corps when it was separated from the other units of Sherman's armies. The soldiers of the 82nd had spent the morning churning through a swamp in mud up to their waists, and were already exhausted from their labors. Still, they summoned whatever energy they had to hasten to the battlefield and relieve a brigade of the 20th under attack. Salomon's troops beat back several charges against them, but the battle didn't end until the 14th Corps arrived to threaten Hardee's position and force the rebel general to withdraw his corps.

The sudden aggression of Johnston's Confederates made a hard march that much harder. Within three days after Averasboro, the 82nd had to wade through the chilly waters of the Black River up to their belts, repair broken roads with corduroy, pull trapped wagons out of the muck with rope lines, and guard those wagons from attack. They got hardly any sleep, and by the time they did finally nod off, a booming cannonade awoke them. They were ordered to relieve another army unit under surprise Confederate assault, near a little-known hamlet called Bentonville.

This time it was the 14th Corps under attack. Two of its divisions had advanced into rebel territory thinking they faced only token opposition. They were gravely mistaken, as wave after wave of Southerners counterattacked and pushed them a half-mile in retreat. This opened up a huge gap in the Union center, and for a while it looked like Johnston would exploit it and rout the army completely.

On the Union left, the 20th Corps tried to hold its ground. The 82nd Illinois had been ordered to occupy a position facing a ravine, which marked the boundary of the disaster unfolding for the 14th Corps. But as soon as Salomon's men got to the front lines, they saw hundreds of men from the 14th fleeing the field in terror. Many stampeded into their ranks.

Chaos threatened to overwhelm the 82nd, but Salomon ordered his men to hold their ground. The discipline of his troops did not give way to panic, and the years of drilling, experience, and ingrained skill and intuition of these veteran fighters held with steady resolve.

Panic, however, did spread to the regiment alongside them, the 13th New Jersey. Their commander ordered his troops to withdraw, which would expose the 82nd to even greater rebel assault. Salomon knew what this meant: The Confederates would soon overrun them. He couldn't allow this to happen.

Despite holding no official power over the New Jerseyans, Salomon ordered them to hold their position—at gunpoint. Faced with the rifles of the 82nd Illinois, the New Jerseyans quit retreating and returned to their position. Their commander was the only one to run from the battlefield.

Edward Salomon now led two regiments to fend off the Confederate attack on the right flank of the 20th Corps. The Illinois and New Jersey soldiers, along with dozens of men from the 14th Corps who joined them piecemeal, held a critical piece of ground against the rebels. If they gave way, the collapse of the Union center would spread to the Union left, and provide a great, unexpected victory for Joseph Johnston.

Instead, Salomon's forces refused to buckle. They fought off four successive, bloody Confederate charges, and slowly pushed them back—aided by thundering rounds of shell and canister fire into the attackers' ranks. This action helped save the 14th Corps from destruction, and negated all the rebels' success earlier in the day.

That evening, March 19, Johnston's forces withdrew to their original positions. Two days later, the conflict ended with the arrival of Sherman's right wing forcing the rebels to retreat.

For the Chicago city alderman turned army lieutenant colonel, the Battle of Bentonville was a long-sought vindication. Just as he had taken a largely German expat force of Friedrich Hecker loyalists and turned it into a polyglot group of European and American warriors, so too had he pieced together two regiments from the 20th Corps and a hodgepodge of men from the 14th, and made one unified command that had held its ground and won the day. Even better for the veterans of the regiment, Bentonville was redemption for Chancellorsville—a well-deserved deliverance from the shame of that debacle, and a sign of what the 82nd could accomplish with the right leadership.

Even Rudolf Mueller had to acknowledge Salomon's success, however backhandedly. In yet another letter to Hecker, while criticizing the lieutenant colonel for his brashness and ambition, he couldn't help but allow a hint of admiration to seep through his thick irony. As he wrote, "the *great* man saved the rest of the army with his 172 men, in that we did not run . . . like a brig of the 14th Corps, but at most did our duty and remained there. . . . Was this not a heroic deed unlike any other?"

Edward Salomon didn't only rally his Illinoisans and the New Jerseyans. A fair number of Michiganders found his leadership compelling enough to abandon their retreat and take up arms with him. Among these troops were many of John McCline's friends.

During the Carolinas campaign, John and his fellow troops of the 13th Michigan had been stuck in the same swamps and quicksand and pine barrens as the rest of Sherman's forces. They had accommodated the great numbers of escaped slaves and white refugees that followed the corps en masse. And they had faced artillery rounds that lit up the skies like a fireworks display. But one thing they had not faced in a great while was the sort of major conflict that tried the faith of soldiers and cost the lives of many. The recruits of the 13th Michigan weren't used to the shock of close-quarters combat, and even the veterans hadn't tested their mettle since they had campaigned in Tennessee in the autumn of 1863. But at Bentonville, they were thrown into battle almost as soon as it started.

As combat began, their brigade commander, George Buell—until recently in charge of the 58th Indiana pontoniers—had ordered the 13th to assault a line of entrenched Confederates behind their works. They charged through forests and ravines to get within thirty yards of the rebels, only to be stunned by a cannonade and a torrent of rifle fire. The onslaught killed the regiment's commander, Major Willard Eaton, and sent the Michiganders into retreat. The newly energized rebels, with their battle cries and unexpected fury, inflicted further losses and drove back their entire division. By the late afternoon the regiment had become scattered and disorganized, and many soldiers stampeded through the lines of the 82nd Illinois. However, around fifty men of the 13th Michigan quit their retreat and helped the 82nd hold the line against the rebel attack. They did their part to keep the battle from becoming a rout, though their effort came at a price.

While John wasn't on the front lines, he could see the disarray of his colleagues when fragments of the regiment returned to camp. Some soldiers were still on the field with Edward Salomon; others had fallen on the field of combat. As it was for many other units in the 14th Corps, Bentonville had an unsparing effect on the 13th Michigan. John's friend Private David Shulters died in the failed ambush against the Confederates, and his occasional nemesis Lieutenant Flint was also a casualty. Flint still lived, but he had been shot through the skull, and would require extensive medical treatment before he was transferred home. John especially mourned Major Eaton, who had bravely led the regiment's attack, and whose body was later found stripped nearly naked and thrown into a mass grave.

With his pal Bart, John visited his friends in the field hospital, stunned at the wounds they had sustained. The 13th Michigan absorbed 110 casualties—a huge fraction of its soldiers in action. The regiment could not sustain losses like that and expect to continue as a cohesive fighting force. Luckily the battle ended before the regiment had to sacrifice any more of its troops.

John wondered how long had it been since he had lost so many good friends and allies in one place. Not since Chickamauga in 1863. There, he last felt the gut-wrenching sensation of pain and sadness. The crushing of spirit and hope. The fear that the rebels and slave masters might find a way to triumph. And the understanding he could do little about it. He was too young to fight, and could only watch as his friends and mentors came back to camp bloody and broken, or lost their limbs on operating tables, or expired in hospital beds. He felt these things again at Bentonville, exactly eighteen months to the day later.

Those battles had been brutal bookends of the Northern invasion. They troubled and saddened John, but they could not make him regret his choice to march with the army. His journey had been too rewarding, too enriching for him to abandon it in the face of death. He could scarcely have imagined this new life when he was trapped on the Hoggatt farm in Tennessee, and it remained strange and magical to him, despite all of its dangers.

He had met Aron and Larkin and Bart and countless other friends in the army, had led wagons over mountains and rivers, attended to colonels and other commanders, and learned things about life and human nature that he could not have found in any school book—though he had one of those, too, that he treasured. Going from plantation slavery into the great western army wasn't just a change of lifestyle; it was turning on the lights and discovering the world after being entombed in darkness.

And so it was on the first day of spring 1865 that John noticed the contrast between the beautiful weather dawning in this lovely Southern state and the lonely reality that so many of his friends would not enjoy it with him. They would not survive the war or ever see days like this again, but he would. He had escaped his bonds and had faced mortal danger as a child, which prepared him better than anything for the struggles of being an adult, and for his new role as a man.

Reverend John Hight and the pontoniers of the 58th Indiana did not see action at Bentonville. Instead they were a few miles away securing boats to cross 250 feet of the Neuse River. Although they weren't engaged in battle, nothing about their position was safe. All around them, Confederate operatives posed a threat. Guerrillas stole blue uniforms and lured soldiers into being captured or killed. Cavalrymen slayed food gatherers and decorated their corpses with signs reading "DEATH TO FORAGERS." And once again, the 58th Indiana didn't have a guard to protect it from danger. Despite all this, Hight was glad to see daylight after all their swamp travels, and to enjoy the first glimpse of spring: "We are coming out of the wilderness, thank God."

After the battle ended, the troops of the 14th and 20th Corps in the left wing marched over their pontoon bridges heading to

Goldsboro—destination of the campaign and only nine miles away. But before they could take up the pontoons and get out of danger, Hight and the 58th had to wait for one more army to cross: the 10th Corps of General Alfred Terry.

This was no typical army corps, and Terry was no typical general. Instead, this well-respected officer led a force of three divisions that had achieved greater things in North Carolina than any other federal unit— Sherman's armies included. Two months before they had captured Fort Fisher and conquered the last rebel stronghold on the Atlantic coast, which successive federal generals had failed to do throughout the war. Then they captured Wilmington, and thus secured an oceanic supply route that would keep the Union troops from relying solely on foraging to survive. But the most surprising thing about Terry's force was that it had an entire division of black soldiers.

The war record of these men undercut everything Sherman had ever argued about the inability of black men to fight for the Union. Across the nation, U.S.C.T. not only helped gain victories in North Carolina, they occupied Charleston, South Carolina, after Confederates abandoned it; they helped George Thomas win the Battle of Nashville; and they assisted U.S. Grant in the Army of the Potomac. But these troops were the first to operate in Sherman's midst and, for the moment, outside his control. Watching them dig entrenchments on one side of the Neuse, Hight was impressed. As he wrote:

> They are splendidly equipped, and march in good order, in marked contrast to Sherman's troops. Some of our people were a little disposed to twit the negroes, but, getting as good as they sent, they soon hush. You can say anything you please to an unarmed negro; but when you commence on a colored soldier, he will 'answer a fool according to his folly'—and the fool cannot help himself. Our men almost universally commend the soldierly appearance of the colored troops.

Still, there was only one division of black troops from Terry's corps camped here. And Hight knew they wouldn't be enough to hold off

Johnston's entire Confederate army if he chose to attack. There was talk John Schofield's 23rd Corps might be in the vicinity to provide relief, but Hight had no interest in waiting for it. He wanted to roll up the bridges and get to Sherman's encampment at Goldsboro as fast as possible. But danger found the 58th Indiana first.

At first the pontoniers only heard the occasional, distant blast of a cannon. As the minutes dragged on, though, the firing became louder and more insistent. The Battle of Bentonville didn't seem to have ended, only drawn closer.

A sudden volley of shellfire closed the distance in full.

One shell after another hit their lines, flew over their heads, blasted holes in their field works. The men entrenched behind their works, but the cannonade kept finding the weak spots.

Explosions of timber and river water crashed around them, as Hight and the 58th tried to hold their ground. Finally, they threw off their pontoon duties and became a combat unit once more.

How long had it been since they had readied their muskets and unfurled their banners? They had skirmished in Georgia and South Carolina occasionally, but the last time they had fought against a superior force was at Missionary Ridge in Chattanooga. Hight hoped the results would be the same.

Minié balls from Confederate rifles followed the report of the field guns. They were outnumbered, and "There is now nobody between us and the rebels, except the colored troops, and six guns, manned by white men." The rebels chose that moment to attack.

They came at Terry's lone division and the 58th Indiana with an excited spirit, fueled by adrenaline left over from Bentonville. They charged at the Union field works and the federals prepared for bloody combat at close quarters. But before they could be overrun, the Napoleons opened up in their defense.

These twelve-pounder brass cannons were only light artillery, but they did the job, blasting through the rebel lines and quashing their attack before it had a chance to succeed. Chastened by the noise and shattering effect of the guns, the Confederates disappeared back into the woods.

Hight drew a long, slow breath. He wondered if the attackers had been a reconnaissance force or a detachment. Certainly it wasn't all of Johnston's army. Still, he was glad to be alive for at least one more day, and knew the 58th wouldn't have stood a chance without Terry's black infantry and white cannoneers to protect them. A stroke of luck, and perhaps Providence, had saved them.

Over the next few days, the Army of the Tennessee and the Army of Georgia made camp in Goldsboro, which the 23rd Corps had seized. That corps, as part of the Army of the Ohio, had helped win two major battles in Tennessee just a few months before, and now brought Sherman's combined force to 88,000 troops. This was four times the size of Johnston's army, which was losing men quickly to desertion and an inability to properly feed and outfit them. But while they had the numbers, Sherman's troops didn't look much better than the Confederates.

By the time they reached Goldsboro, these soldiers had waded, marched, fought, corduroyed, and pontooned across 425 miles from Savannah in only fifty days, and their appearance showed it. Not more than one man in a dozen had proper military attire, and even then his coat was torn or frayed or full of holes. Some troops sported bare heads, others handkerchiefs, and others wore crushed and mutilated hats. A minority went without shirts under their jackets; a majority had trousers torn below the knee; and almost everyone lacked socks. Too many also lacked shoes, and sported feet caked with mud and dried blood.

As one observer saw, they "had worn their clothing pretty much to tatters and had not had time to wash even what they had left. They were dirty and ragged, as well as saucy, and were something else which was descriptive of tenants that had lodgings inside their flannels." Soap and river water would help take care of the vermin, but their hunger was harder to kill off. The railroad from Wilmington was not fully repaired, and upon reaching Goldsboro, the men found rations low and other provisions scarce—forcing them to resort to foraging once more. Some Union generals demanded the local quartermaster be punished for his inability to feed and refit the men, but Sherman chose to be patient. Once his engineers had rebuilt the rail line, the resupply could begin. No one's head had to roll just yet.

Eventually the Wilmington Railroad became operational again, and the troops received fresh food and gear, if a bit too slowly for some. Reverend Hight and his 58th Indiana soldiers were happy to get new rails and planks for their pontoons and twenty wagons full of bridging supplies. Like everyone else on the march, they were also relieved to take a few weeks off in town. Relief turned to joy on April 6, when word came that General Grant and the Army of the Potomac had captured Richmond and Petersburg, and Robert E. Lee's army was on the run.

The men cheered the great news, fired weapons into the air, sang patriotic songs their regimental bands played, and, of course, drank whiskey and toasted the inevitable demise of the Confederacy. Hight also got into the spirit of levity, and predicted the "slaveholders' rebellion" would be finished by the autumn. He allowed himself a measure of happiness, and was glad he had recently reenlisted, despite the ordeal of the recent campaign. He was now officially a veteran.

Although many of his old friends had left the regiment, Hight found that he despaired less over their departure than he had in previous months. New recruits filled their places and brought a fresh spirit with them. They and some of his old comrades even turned away from the bottle to give their renewed attention to the Lord. As Hight wrote, "There has been quite a moral reformation in the army during our stay at Goldsboro. Many soldiers have been converted. Could we have remained a while longer, I believe God would have given us a glorious revival in Sherman's army."

On April 10 the 58th Indiana joined the rest of the armies and moved out of Goldsboro on their way to Raleigh, the state capital. On the way he felt his old energy returning and the Holy Spirit rising up in him. The regiment came across a Methodist church, and as Hight prepared an evening sermon, he was surprised to see more and more soldiers enter the church, until it was full and they were ready to hear the word of God as Hight understood it. The war may have been winding down, but his passion had only increased and his faith strengthened.

It became a glorious night of praise and testimony. As he wrote, "I ascended the high pulpit, and, sweating, preached earnestly to the people.

The soldiers sang with a will. We had a good meeting, and hope for a revival."

John Hight felt imbued by the spirit, but the only reason it happened on the road to Raleigh was because of a sudden change in military strategy. Sherman had initially wanted to march north to Virginia and join with Grant's forces to smash Robert E. Lee's Confederate army. But when Grant met with Sherman at City Point, Virginia, he told him no. If the western armies helped defeat Lee, that would deprive the eastern armies of the glory, which would cause political problems. Grant did agree to allow Sherman to drive his armies into Virginia to play a supporting role in the fight against Lee, but only if the Army of the Potomac failed to capture his army first. Sherman went back to North Carolina to prepare for the march north, but on April 8, two days before he was to leave, Grant changed the plan. With Richmond and Petersburg captured, defeating Johnston's army would be Sherman's objective. He would stay in North Carolina until he completed the job.

Thus, when Sherman led his forces toward Raleigh, he wasn't just trying to capture the town, he was hoping to find Johnston and destroy his force. If he managed this feat, it would be the first time Sherman conquered a rebel army in full since he had risen to lead the Military Division of the Mississippi.

However, the loss of Richmond and Petersburg proved devastating to the Confederate cause. Most assumed General-in-Chief Lee would battle until the bitter end, and the rebel general tried to project as much confidence in the fight as he could. But the demise of the Confederate capital and one of its largest cities—which had been under siege for nine months—forced his hand. With his major Virginia bases lost, Lee had no choice but to break out and try to link up with Johnston's own forces in North Carolina, to have even the smallest hope of battling a much larger combined federal force. He never got the chance. On April 9, Grant outmaneuvered Lee's army and forced him to surrender at Appomattox Court House.

With the sudden collapse of the Army of Northern Virginia, the Confederacy had no real options left. Though some rebels advocated for continuing the fight with guerrilla warfare, more reasonable figures like Joseph Johnston thought otherwise. With difficulty and only a remote possibility of success, the general could try valiantly to make a show against Sherman's six corps in North Carolina; but to do the same against Grant's and Sherman's combined armies would be suicide. Surrender was the only logical—and, even in this brutal war, honorable—move left. On April 13, General Johnston sent word to Sherman that he was willing to negotiate to lay down arms.

The next day, in the Army of the Tennessee on the right wing, Major Charles Wills and the rest of his regiment entered Raleigh, a handsome town with lovely residences and gardens, expansive lawns and wide streets, a proud statehouse and other fine public buildings, almost all of which remained pristine despite the war. The capital had been left unguarded, and Sherman's men entered under a flag of truce. No Confederate state government remained in the capital—as at Milledgeville and Columbia, the legislators had departed in the days before—and Southern troops had also evacuated in advance of Sherman's arrival. Orders were strict on treating the residents with respect: no thieving, no looting, no burning. The capital would be kept safe and intact and not immolated, pillaged or otherwise molested.

Wills saw Confederate soldiers deserting from the ranks, coming through the lines of the 15th Corps to lay down their arms. Their fearsome war machine that had for years operated as a worthy foe on the battlefield was coming apart. The Southern forces were too small, too ill equipped, too underfed to mount an effective defense of the state. And in any case, Johnston was ready to give up.

Wills learned of the diplomacy between Sherman and Johnston and approved of it. He preferred the soldier's life to the civilian's, but even he had his limits. Fifty days of campaigning through swamps and wilderness had damaging effects on the high spirits of the men, and further rounds of combat would only be exhausting. Soon Wills's mind turned away from war to its unthinkable counterpart. As he wrote, "The whole four years seems to me more like a dream than reality. How anxious I am to shake hands with you all once more. 'How are you peace?'" But before he allowed such restful thoughts to fully pacify him, Wills learned the news that braced the nation:

President Lincoln had been assassinated.

Thoughts of peace immediately turned to rage. Honest Abe had been struck down by a gunman who had aimed at the back of his head, who had killed him in a public theater and escaped. No one knew what sort of villain could commit such an act, but theories spread and multiplied—it was surely the Confederate government behind the assassination, perhaps Jeff Davis himself! Others blamed the network of rebel conspirators known to operate across the country. Or perhaps it was the vice president, or traitors in Congress, or other traitors in hiding. Yet regardless of who had arranged for Lincoln's murder, the minds of the troops now set upon bloody revenge for the crime. As Wills wrote, "The army is crazy for vengeance. If we make another campaign it will be an awful one. . . . We hope Johnston will not surrender. God pity this country if he retreats or fights us." Another soldier reported, "The troops are in a blaze of excitement and bitterness of sad feeling," which they looked to express, possibly in violence.

General John Logan heard the news of Lincoln's assassination and it crushed him. Visitors at his headquarters saw him crying in reaction to Lincoln's death, which seemed so abrupt, so wicked, so shocking. When the war began, he thought of the chief executive as his adversary, a totem figure for the abolitionists to manipulate, someone who would cripple the nation. But not only had he been wrong about Lincoln, he had been wrong about himself. It was the chief executive's ideas that were the correct ones on slavery and emancipation, and only through campaigning in the South did Logan realize how right he had been. His views of Lincoln changed dramatically, until within the last few months he considered the president a loyal friend and ally, a kinsman from his state who had done it proud and elevated the nation. And now he was dead.

Generals Sherman and Howard received the news warily. They knew how raw the troops' feelings were over Lincoln's demise, and resolved to quell their anger before it could explode. They locked down all army camps and patrolled them with armed guards to keep any potential violence at bay.

However, a significant fraction of soldiers had no interest in being pacified by their peacemaking commanders. A group of 2,000 rogue troops from the Army of the Tennessee overran their guards and, bearing radiant torches and fury, began marching to the closest major target: the undefended capital of Raleigh.

Hearing of their advance, John Logan knew what he had to do. His body ached from rheumatism and the ceaseless labor of combat, his heart weakened at the death of his president, and his mind desperately needed more rest and sleep, but on the night of April 17, he put Slasher at a gallop to reach the rogue troops. When he caught up to them—sword held high, voice ringing—he issued a firm command.

They would put down their weapons and return to camp. If they dared injure any townspeople, the culprits would face severe punishment.

They ignored him and kept marching. For once his powerful words had no effect. These 2,000 troops would not stop until they had reduced Raleigh to cinders.

Some generals like Jacob Cox feared the worst, and thought little could be done to prevent the soldiers' destruction. But Logan had planned ahead.

As the men continued to march past him, they came upon a great row of artillery pieces—pointed not at Raleigh, but at them. The cannons held canister, designed to cut men to shreds.

Logan's message was simple: If they attacked the capital, he would kill them.

The men knew Black Jack all too well from his years of combat experience, and had seen him threaten cowardly troops and miscreants on the battlefield, but they had never seen this. They were openly disregarding his commands, and for that, they were the enemy.

Logan had vowed to himself after the burning of Columbia that such a wretched and shameful episode would not happen again under his watch. Even if he had to risk his life, he would stop anarchy from breaking out, and prevent pandemonium from holding sway.

The troops realized the danger they faced from the field guns, and knew Logan would not hesitate to fire them. Slowly they backed down and returned to camp. Their anger would not find its outlet, no matter how raw and bitter it was.

Because of his actions, Logan kept Raleigh free from the ravages of looters and arsonists in blue. He ensured the town would not end up like so many other Confederate state capitals in recent months—not pillaged like Milledgeville, ransacked like Jackson, or burned like Columbia. The war was nearly over, and Logan had secured peace for Raleigh at the end of a gun barrel.

Upon returning to his headquarters, Logan learned of the peace deal Sherman and Johnston had worked out. It allowed Confederate soldiers to march home and return their weapons to their state arsenals, then make a promise not to wage war against the United States again. The federal government would in turn recognize the Southern state governments as soon as their members took a loyalty oath, ignoring the fact that many of those members had voted to rebel in the first place. Upon hearing these wildly generous terms, Logan knew they would be rejected in Washington and Sherman would have to return to the negotiating table.

Logan was right: Secretary of War Stanton and other federal politicians were furious with Sherman's lack of negotiating skills, and forced him to negate the agreement and write a new document modeled on Lee's surrender to Grant. Johnston signed it a few days later just outside Durham, North Carolina, and with that, the war among the armies of the west ended.

Logan was relieved the conflict was finished, but had more important things to worry about than the details of the surrender agreement. He remained most concerned about the fate of the nation in the wake of the president's death, and mulled the political implications of the United States being led by Andrew Johnson, a Democratic loyalist from a rebel state. Even more, he fretted over the condition of his 15th Corps. Many of his troops were weather-beaten, poorly clothed, and lacked shoes. He harbored anger against Sherman's chief commissary officer for not delivering such items to the army in Goldsboro, and against Sherman for dismissing his own concerns.

Even worse, the march had not concluded even though the war had ended. The soldiers were due to tramp north hundreds of miles to reach Washington, D.C., to participate in a victory parade known as the Grand Review of the Armies. Logan knew their rations would not be sufficient to feed and support them all the way to the national capital.

Once again, he and his troops had been shortchanged. Conquering the South apparently didn't merit giving the men fresh rations, clean clothes, and new shoes. They would continue to suffer until they mustered out—until they left the service of their country and returned home where people would properly care for them. It galled him to no end, and he reacted by contacting the one person he knew who could help, without question or complaint.

He sent a telegram to Mary Ann Bickerdyke.

"On way to Washington. Short of rations. Meagre supply there. Go up. LOGAN"

Mother received the note in Beaufort, South Carolina. Although she was a long way from the front and from Logan, she vowed to help her second-favorite general any way she could.

She had spent much of the campaign in this coastal army post overseeing Union hospital facilities and assisting convalescent soldiers. Unlike Logan's 15th Corps, these injured troops were well fed and supplied. Her boys ate pork and healthy vegetables, and their hospital beds were well appointed with fresh pillows and blankets. Most of this, of course, had been stolen by foragers in the weeks before, but Mother made sure all these supplies ended up at the hospital, even confiscating them herself when she found them stashed in the troops' tents.

Like the other soldiers whom she helped, these convalescents praised the work she did, enjoyed her homespun stories and wisdom, and reveled in the songs and amusements she offered to brighten their grim recoveries. In thanks, they held a special parade in her honor since she would soon be leaving. On a fine spring day, they led a long line of dairy cows for her inspection, each with its horns and hooves polished, and bedecked them with small, colorful flags. A lively martial air accompanied the procession, which became known as the Cows Review and delighted her greatly. They were commemorating her legendary feat from years before—when she marshaled a great column of "loyalist" cows from Illinois to Memphis—and she couldn't have been more honored.

Days later, Mother Bickerdyke took a steamship to Washington, D.C., and left her boys in Beaufort in good hands with clean beds and decent food and medicine. Her trip north was another unexpected episode in what had been a war full of them. She figured it was all part of God's design, His plan for giving her a new life she never could have imagined before the war.

As the boat sailed past the North Carolina coast, she thought of all the boys still marching there. Their fight was over, but she knew how weary they must be. She hoped someone was there to succor their pain and comfort them through illness and death. She had spent time in the state earlier in the year, and had seen things she could not forget. Things that even a nursing veteran like her could still find shocking.

Mother had not meant to visit North Carolina on her late-winter voyage from New York. Thanks to the Christian Commission, she had a steamboat full of supplies—everything from crackers and cheese to beef extract, tapioca, and citrus fruit—meant for Sherman's troops in Savannah. Her ship had stopped in Wilmington only briefly, and she decided to explore the town after hearing tales of Union prisoners from Andersonville, Georgia, being lodged there after their release.

Looking into the many private homes and churches that acted as hospitals, Mother was repulsed by what she saw. Many former prisoners resembled skeletons, with running sores of the "prison pox" and rat bites on their skin, protruding ribs from starvation, and empty expressions of hopelessness. Some had succumbed to insanity from their torture while others seemed on the verge of death. Their gruesome and terrible injuries gave her no choice: She would abandon her journey to Savannah and give all her supplies to these men.

Over the next few weeks, she did all she could to nurse them back to health. Many were well beyond care, and she eased them through their final moments with kind words or a soothing song. Others she fed and cleaned and bandaged, making sure they had adequate food and linens and reproving any army doctors and nurses who failed to properly attend to them. She also wrote to the families of the deceased, telling them of their sons' deaths and offering her condolences.

Her work to fight the wounds and disease of these troops was beyond anything she had done in the war, and she had not finished it when she received orders to transfer to Beaufort. Now, two months later, as she sailed past North Carolina once more, she wondered what had happened to so many of her patients—whether they had regained their health and returned to their loved ones, or found a grave in this rebel state hundreds of miles from home. The war offered so many unanswered questions.

When Mother arrived in Washington, D.C., she returned her focus to the task at hand: finding provisions for Logan's corpsmen. She had little luck at first. The commissary stores had been given over to the Army of the Potomac and the inventories of the Sanitary Commission were empty, most of their supplies having been sent to Chicago for the upcoming fair. Mother didn't let this deter her.

She telegraphed the commission president, Henry Bellows, in New York and demanded supplies for "16,000 hungry men" since there was "not a cracker in the city." He promised to send them at once.

Within days a five-car train pulled into the Washington depot. It was loaded with everything from bread and butter to beefsteak and bacon, potatoes and onions, and coffee. An agent from the Sanitary Commission tried to send the largesse to a local warehouse, but Mother thwarted his plan. Instead she directed soldiers to send the supplies to Alexandria, Virginia, just across the Potomac, which would be the site for the 15th Corps to bivouac.

She secured enough provisions for Logan's boys that a surplus remained for other peckish soldiers who had already arrived in the capital. Among them was a cavalry unit led by General George Armstrong Custer, already a notable figure in the Army of the Potomac, who just a few weeks before had helped force Lee's surrender to Grant.

Watching this curious middle-aged woman in a bonnet arrive at his camp with several wagonloads of food, Custer didn't think much of her at first. He figured the government alone would provide enough supplies for his men. Soon, however, the general noticed the captivating effect she had on them, and how thankful they were that this unexpected figure had appeared from nowhere to nourish them. Then his staff informed him of who she was, and he finally understood. He was face to face with the famous Mother Bickerdyke.

Honored to meet this legendary nurse, Custer reached out his hand to greet her. "I don't wonder Sherman calls you one of his best generals," he said.

A few days later, the general herself would help lead the victory parade.

LEGACY

SIXTEEN

THE GRAND REVIEW

The war in the western theater ended when Generals Sherman and Johnston signed the final agreement of surrender at Bennett Place, North Carolina, on April 26, 1865. Confederate officers and enlisted men deposited their arms in Greensboro and returned to their homes. Union troops were ordered to stop foraging and burning and to treat any locals they encountered with respect and forbearance. For Joseph Johnston, the armistice was a peaceful if inglorious end to the campaign. For William Sherman, however, it was only the beginning of the trouble.

In the midst of what should have been his greatest triumph, Sherman learned he had been denounced throughout the country. *The New York Times* had reported his initial, generous terms of surrender and outrage ensued. Angry abolitionists and Radical Republicans demanded to know why he had tried to let the secessionists off so easily. Was he in league with the rebels, or had the stress of combat rendered him insane once more? Secretary of War Edwin Stanton fed the outrage, arguing that

Sherman knew he had no power to offer a liberal political settlement to the rebels, yet had gone ahead and done so anyway. As he saw it, Sherman's indulgence of Jeff Davis and the other traitors would have allowed the rebel president to slip away with the Confederate treasury and continue to wage war against the United States in absentia. Stanton spoke harsh public words against Sherman, fed leaks to the press condemning the general, and tried to channel the fury over the death of Abraham Lincoln in his direction. And it worked: By late April, many Republicans were convinced Sherman was a Copperhead at best, a traitor at worst.

Sherman had no choice but to acknowledge his errors in public. He wrote to Stanton to "admit my folly in embracing in a Military convention any Civil matters" and offered his regrets to U.S. Grant, who sympathized with his plight. But privately Sherman seethed. To him, Stanton was a "mean, scheming, vindictive politician" and a puppet for the radicals who wanted to punish the South even after the war was over, to ensure black equality with whites and to incite the fury of white reaction. He suspected this would only reignite the recent hostilities in the form of guerrilla warfare, and ensure a federal military presence in the South for generations, which he would adamantly refuse to support. Upon discovering that his onetime friend Henry Halleck was in league with Stanton's accusations, and had conspired to limit his military power, Sherman refused to allow his troops to pass for his review as they marched through Richmond. He would show Stanton the same disrespect when he had a chance.

Three weeks later, Sherman's anger had abated somewhat as he led his Army of the West—the renamed left and right wings of his forces— over 270 miles in less than three weeks to the District of Columbia. He looked forward to the Grand Review of the Armies and the opportunity to display his victorious troops before the public as the rough-hewn, battle-hardened veterans they were. Still, he simmered with frustration. His soldiers hadn't been paid in up to ten months, their provisions were low, their clothing was poor, and some Americans still saw the Army of the Potomac as the primary victor in the recent conflict. Worse, hostile newspapers continued their campaign of slander against him, and the weight of their slights vexed him. As he informed General John Rawlins before the review, the "Vandal Sherman" had bivouacked with his troops in Virginia, and "[t]hough in disgrace he is untamed and unconquered." If he could not clear his name, at least he could put on a good show.

The parade went brilliantly, even better than he had planned. Sherman dressed for the occasion—a rarity in this war—donning his uniform and looking every bit the noble general. He marched at the head of his troops alongside General Oliver Howard, who had already left the army to run the Freedmen's Bureau and oversee the advancement of newly freed slaves.

Sherman's sunburned, ragged warriors marched in a column that started fifteen miles from the avenue, with 60,000 troops—as many as the entire population of the capital—plus fourteen artillery batteries and a full complement of wagons, mules, and horsemen. Once the troops reached Pennsylvania Avenue, the onlookers couldn't contain their emotions. They wept and shouted for joy, waved handkerchiefs, cheered, prayed, and sang. Their enthusiasm stunned Sherman and choked him up. Amid all the raucous cries, the banners and battle flags, the honorary wreaths to the memory of Abe Lincoln, and the outpouring of affection, Sherman was most impressed by his men.

He looked back as the column of the Army of the West turned near the Treasury Building on its way to the White House, and saw "the sight was simply magnificent. The column was compact, and the glittering muskets looked like a solid mass of steel, moving with the regularity of a pendulum." The troops' attire may have been frayed, but their steps were precise and their martial bearing was without compare. He couldn't have been more enthralled as he watched, his breath momentarily stolen, his eyes now weeping.

As the head of the column approached the reviewing stand, Sherman saluted the dignitaries with his sword. They cheered, took off their hats, and gave him an ovation. He dismounted from his horse, walked to the reviewing stand, and began to shake hands with them. He warmly greeted his wife and family, President Andrew Johnson, Lieutenant General Grant, and the various cabinet members and notables sitting near them. After a moment he reached Secretary of War Stanton, who offered his hand in greeting, too.

With the Washington elite watching closely, Sherman looked at the secretary and paused, without a trace of emotion. Then he ignored his outstretched hand and took his seat among the generals.

Riding his black steed Slasher, John Logan followed just behind Sherman as the new commander of the Army of the Tennessee, leading 30,000 troops in the 15th and 17th Corps down Pennsylvania Avenue. He hadn't expected to be promoted just before the review, but he accepted the honor graciously. With a floral wreath around his neck, his favorite horse under him, and a crowd cheering and adulating him, Logan filled with pride.

Grant and Sherman had come to realize how essential he had been to the success of the western armies. On the night of the final Confederate surrender, they had offered Logan a position in the regular army as a brigadier general. Unlike other breveted generals, who would revert to colonels or lower ranks after the war, Logan would retain one star in the federal army. It was an unheard-of honor for a man Sherman once branded as a political general, and it convinced him that his superiors understood his talent and had no choice but to award him for it.

But he turned them down. He wanted to go back into politics instead.

After the war, Logan discarded his old alliances in the Democratic Party. Like other Union generals turned Republican politicians, he spoke out for abolition, black suffrage, and a rigid policy of Reconstruction for the South. He even turned against the infamous Black Law he himself had championed a dozen years before and saw it removed from the laws of Illinois. These stances put him in the camp of the Radical Republicans, the growing faction of the party devoted to the cause of civil rights and punishment for the South, and in firm opposition to the policies of President Andrew Johnson.

To him the change was inevitable. Who could have witnessed the abuses he had seen in places like Mississippi and Georgia and South Carolina and not be moved toward equal treatment for blacks? And once he had changed his position, he became zealous about it and exhorted his constituents to follow him. As he said at one campaign rally:

If you won't allow a man to vote because he has black skin, you have the same right to say I shall not vote because I have black hair. I don't care whether a man is black, red, blue, or white if he is a civilized man in a Christian community like ours . . . he has the right to say who the men shall be who control the Government.

During his two postwar terms in the House of Representatives and more than two terms in the Senate, Logan was fierce and uncompromising in his views. He helped lead the successful push for impeachment against President Johnson (who was saved from being removed from office by a single vote in the Senate). He fervently supported the presidency of Ulysses S. Grant and stumped for him with conviction, even if he didn't always agree with him. He promoted the patronage system to award his friends with public offices, and got caught up in a few financial scandals along the way. He waved the "bloody shirt" and charged treason against his former Democratic allies, and condemned them with force while campaigning for office. He won fame for his electrifying speeches—one of which Mark Twain compared to lightning flashing, making for "the most memorable night of my life"—and rode his celebrity to the Republican vice-presidential nomination in 1884 (though he and presidential candidate James Blaine lost). And he traveled the nation with enthusiasm from east to west, and so enthralled his listeners that they named schools and streets and counties and neighborhoods after him—including Logan Circle in Washington, D.C.

Even later in his life, amid a rising tide of racism and angry white reaction to equal rights for blacks, Logan maintained his beliefs and offered them to all who would listen. In Congress he stood behind bills to fight illiteracy and fund quality education for freedmen, to ensure fair treatment for former slaves, and to extend the franchise of civil equality wherever he could. Some thought it strange that the onetime nemesis of abolitionists could have made such a journey, but Logan did it, just as thousands of other former officers and enlisted men in the Union army did, irrevocably.

Logan could certainly never return to his old ways. He had fought too hard, burned too many bridges, and made too many new friends to ever go back. As Frederick Douglass, who occasionally shared a speaker's platform with Logan and fought on the same side of many political battles, said of him, "He has a backbone like the Brooklyn Bridge." Black civic groups gave Logan a new nickname for all his recent combat on the stump and in the halls of Congress: "the Black Eagle of Illinois."

If fighting for the cause of Radical Republicanism was a source of uplift for Logan, his family was an ongoing source of pain. His brother-in-law, Hybert Cunningham, had reformed, but died at a young age, as had Logan's adopted daughter, Kate. His brother Tom continued to be a shameless reprobate, freely attacking and humiliating women, while his sister Annie never dropped her secessionist views—even shouting down his public speeches when she had the chance. Only his relationship with his estranged mother, Elizabeth, improved. She finally reopened the door to her home to him, and the mother and son reunited, if only briefly. She died a year later.

Outside of the bonds with his wife, Mary, and his children, Logan never felt at home with his blood relatives. Instead, he found comfort in the soldiers he knew during wartime. And after the war ended, he maintained those bonds by helping build the Grand Army of the Republic into a national organization. With Logan as its second commander, the GAR enlisted former Union soldiers and established posts across the country, with a membership said to total nearly a half-million people by the end of the nineteenth century. The group pushed for veterans' pensions and public honors for their service, while also working as an ad hoc branch of the Republican Party. Logan made sure of that.

More than anything else, though, Logan's work with the GAR became timeless due to his General Order Number 11. In this action, he set the date of May 30 for adorning the graves of fallen soldiers. The holiday took place for the first time in 1868 under the name Decoration Day. One hundred and fifty years later, it continues to be celebrated on the last Monday in May, under the name Memorial Day.

—⁂—

Logan couldn't forget the memory of his fellow soldiers who had sacrificed themselves in combat for the 15th Corps. But on the morning of the Grand Review, he reserved one of the highest honors for a noncombatant: someone who had helped his boys from Mississippi to Georgia to Washington, D.C., and who had dressed his wounds, fed and clothed and bathed his troops, and provided the best nursing care any general could have ever hoped for. He demanded Mary Ann Bickerdyke take a position near him at the head of the Army of the Tennessee.

Mother didn't have a mind to accept his offer at first. She figured she had no business riding along with the general in a parade that was supposed to honor the troops. But he insisted: She would ride her horse Old Whitey down the avenue and accept the adulation that was long overdue. She reluctantly gave in.

Her boys created a garland of blue forget-me-nots for Old Whitey to wear like a blanket, while she would sport her trusty calico sundress and bonnet, which, like the uniforms of Sherman's soldiers, had been battered and frayed from years of service. Mother had never seen so many people in one place, jammed to the rafters, leaning out of windows, hooting and hollering in mad celebration. Not even Chicago was like this. She tried to keep from gawking like a country rube, or getting carried away with excitement. Instead she followed General Logan's lead—a steady trot, a respect for the crowd's enthusiasm, a smile and a nod of appreciation. The people loved her.

However, by the time she passed the reviewing stand, she had had enough. She got off Old Whitey and refused General Logan's attempts to have her meet the dignitaries. Before he could stop her, she scuttled away to a vacant lot just off the avenue. There she set up tents and offered lemonade, sandwiches, and first aid to the hungry and weary boys who had trudged seven hours from Virginia in the late-spring heat. Even on parade day, some of the convalescent troops had struggled to march, and working for a few extra hours to help them seemed only fair.

A few extra hours turned into ten extra months, as Mother traveled with Logan and his troops to Louisville and didn't quit her service until the last army volunteer from Illinois was mustered out—in March of 1866.

After that she tried to find her place in a world without war. First she went to Chicago and worked at Mary Livermore's charity The Home of the Friendless, though she chafed under the rule of its new superintendent, Mrs. Grant—the same woman who had been her subordinate in Memphis. Mother compared working with her to being stuck in a peck of produce.

Her son reminded her of a promise she had made allowing him to go to Kansas when he came of age. She granted it, and decided to follow him there. The Sunflower State offered great promise as a place where a settler could homestead 160 acres of public land and own them after living there for five years. The idea appealed to her, but rather than go it alone, she took out a bank loan for $10,000 to help fifty families settle there. She even appealed to William Sherman, who arranged for surplus army wagons to help convey their goods to the prairie. Soon she found herself operating a dining hall for the Kansas Pacific Railway in Salina, and it attracted a good number of hungry travelers. But the railway forced her out, and Mother once again had to find a new career.

General Logan came to her aid, and suggested she try to improve the lot of the poor in the slums of New York City. Surprisingly, the woman from the tiny town of Galesburg accepted the offer and moved to the nation's biggest city. She spent four years working with the Mission Board to improve the sanitation and care in the city's jails and asylums, and offered religious instruction as well to destitute children. This kind of work set the example for the rest of her life: physically demanding labor, often for little pay, to improve the life of anyone in a dire condition.

She moved back to Kansas just in time for a plague of grasshoppers to destroy the crops of thousands of farmers. In response she gave speeches and lectures in which she appealed for "grasshopper relief," persuaded her well-heeled friends like Mary Livermore to give generously to support the cause, and in the end helped bring 200 train carloads of food and clothing to the near-starving families of the state.

In later years she moved to San Francisco and served as a clerk at the U.S. Mint while working as a pension attorney—helping hundreds of disabled veterans receive recompense from the federal government for their years of service. She traveled widely gathering evidence, records, and testimony to support their claims, and summoned the aid of politicians like John Logan to help her mission. Introducing her before Congress, Senator Logan put it plainly: "Whatever she wants is right, and what she says will be the truth."

With Logan's aid, Mother also set up a branch of the Women's Relief Corps, tending to soldiers' graves and providing aid to their widows and orphans. In Kansas she oversaw the creation of the Mother Bickerdyke House for the care of former nurses and soldiers and their families; and The Grand Army of the Republic honored her with Mother Bickerdyke Day, held on her 80th birthday and commemorating all of her now-legendary endeavors.

There was much to celebrate. Mother Bickerdyke had made pioneering a way of life. Whether encouraging the wealthy to donate money for her causes, or helping the indigent in asylums and workhouses, she ventured into all corners of society. She did everything from cooking and cleaning to learning the law and testifying before Congress. She traveled south, then west, east, west, farther west, and east again in her life, not settling down long enough in a place to establish roots, but long enough so that few who lived there could forget what she had done.

In honor of her service, the U.S. government awarded her an army pension—one of the few ever given out to a woman in the era. The sum was $25 per month. It was an adequate stipend for a private, though far below what she should have received as a general.

Several blocks behind Mother Bickerdyke in the Grand Review, Major Charles Wills marched in the First Division of the 15th Corps. He was proud to march before the adoring crowd, but had no idea what he was going to do next. At Raleigh a few weeks before, the questions of postwar life left him without any answers. He even worried whether he would be unfit for the civilian world. As he wrote:

> I have almost a dread of being a citizen, of trying to be sharp, and trying to make money. I don't think I dread the work. I don't remember of shirking any work I ever attempted, but I am sure that civil life will go sorely against the grain for a

time. Citizens are not like soldiers, and I like soldier ways
much the best.

He became troubled by the uncertainty of his fate. What would he
do next, when there would be "No more finding the enemy driving in
his skirmishers, developing his line, getting into position, and retiring
every night"? The military provided no answers. After the review he was
recommended for promotion to lieutenant colonel, but was mustered out
before he could gain the breveted rank.

He returned to Canton adrift. His hometown seemed small and
isolated from the world-changing events he had experienced. He tried
to find a job, and ended up as a collector of soldiers' pension claims, but
the work didn't suit him. He felt a wanderlust, a restlessness, that didn't
seem to abate. He no longer found solace in the comforts of Illinois, and
began to consider leaving his home state.

Mary, his sister and correspondent during the war, wed a cavalry colonel
from Wills's first regiment named William Pitt Kellogg, and they moved
to New Orleans. For his service to the Republican Party, Kellogg got a
lucrative post as the port collector, and became one of the first "carpetbaggers" to relocate to the South from the North. Wills joined them, first as
a customs house agent then as a deputy collector of internal revenue. Like
other Yankees who settled in the South, Wills thought he could make a
new start in a place where all the old hierarchies and alliances had dissolved
in the devastation of the war. He and other former soldiers thought they
had much to offer the beleaguered region. Perhaps they could improve its
crop yield, or help it develop a proper sense of industry, or raise it from its
antiquated agricultural system, built on the ashes of slavery.

Wills had always enjoyed the good life, even in the army, and he tried
to find it in rural Louisiana. In the army, he had often pined for Southern
women, and he continued the practice in Iberia parish, marrying a local
woman named Katherine a few years after his arrival. Wills later took
possession of a sugar plantation, with his brother-in-law Kellogg as
co-owner, in the bayou country of southern Louisiana near Jeanerette.
Amazingly, after all his complaints about trekking through the swamps
of the South with Sherman, he decided to make his fortune living in one.

He worked for eight years at sugar planting, and succeeded at the task in which so many Northerners failed. He found a place for himself in the postwar world, in a state he once considered an enemy. But just as he brought his Northern sense of industry with him to Dixie, so too did he bring his Northern susceptibilities. A generation before, he had journeyed through the Confederacy with scarcely a cold or a scratch from combat. But now in middle age, the rigors of the subtropical climate began to take a toll. He suffered regularly from chills and other infirmities, and found himself in bed for months at a time. Malaria cut his life short, and he died at his plantation at age forty-two.

After the 15th Corps had passed in the Grand Review, the 17th Corps marched along the avenue. It took more than three hours to display all the guns, horses, and artillery in these two corps of the Army of the Tennessee, and the review was only half completed. The other major army still had to pass—the Army of Georgia, which contained part of the old Army of the Cumberland.

Many in the Washington crowd recognized the names of the regiments in the 20th Corps that followed. Some of these units had once been assigned to the east, and participated in battles from Antietam to Gettysburg. They had as stellar a record in combat as any other corpsmen, but mostly observers noticed how they appeared: sharply dressed, well drilled, finely polished. No other corps could match them for style. This was especially true of the 82nd Illinois. Lieutenant Colonel Edward Salomon led his men down the avenue with great finesse, in a sprightly display of gallantry.

Two weeks after the review, Salomon's men mustered out in Alexandria, Virginia. They returned to Springfield, Illinois, to receive their long-overdue pay, with a stopover in Chicago. Their reception there stunned them. The entire city seemed to erupt in joy when their train arrived. The locals greeted them with an artillery barrage over Lake Michigan, spirited music from marching bands, Roman candles firing into the air, and a fleet of carriages to convey them into the city, with torch bearers lighting the way. For a regiment that had experienced more glory and tragedy than almost any other in the corps, the welcome was a rousing and deeply appreciated endorsement of everything they had done. Even the press, which had been so hostile just two years before, lauded their achievements, as did local politicians and masses of well wishers.

More adulation followed when they visited the Northwestern Sanitary Fair, as word got out of just how much campaigning they had done in the South: 2,500 miles on foot, nearly as many by train, forty-three rivers crossed, and countless towns and prisoners captured from the Confederacy. The regiment had begun its service with 1,000 men, but only 300 remained to celebrate, "to receive the plaudits and praises of the entire Northwest."

The soldiers in the regiment reunited on Independence Day in 1869—the sixth anniversary of Gettysburg—and Edward Salomon became the first president of its veterans association and the regiment's most prominent success story. Before he retired from service, he received a breveted promotion to brigadier general, and was then elected clerk of Cook County. In his position he assisted veterans with their pension claims and helped certify their service and injuries in battle. But he didn't serve long: Newly elected President Ulysses S. Grant knew how valuable Salomon was politically, and appointed him governor of Washington Territory. Salomon served ably, but in one of the innumerable scandals of the Grant administration, he was forced to resign in 1872 after the press reported that he had directed money from the territorial treasury into his own speculative land deal.

He had no desire to stay in the thinly populated region after his resignation, but knew the Pacific coast suited him better than the east: There were more opportunities open to him, and fewer of the old tribal loyalties he had found so constricting. He relocated to California in 1875 and flourished. Over the next few decades, he ran for and won a seat in the state legislature, became assistant district attorney for San Francisco, and commanded the Bay Area post of the Grand Army of the Republic, along with other veterans groups. However, while Salomon was happy to spend the second half of his life in the Golden State, he never forgot the first state where he, as a young immigrant from Hamburg, had found a home.

He regularly returned to Illinois, took part in veterans ceremonies, and kept up with the old members of his regiment. In perhaps his most lasting effort, he lobbied for the creation of a monument to the 82nd Illinois Volunteer Infantry at Gettysburg, which wouldn't just represent their service at that battlefield, but all the places where they had fought, east and west. Salomon died in California, just two weeks after the 50th anniversary of the battle.

Salomon never forgot the man whose role he had taken as commander of the 82nd Illinois. He praised Friedrich Hecker publicly and was his regular correspondent during the war and occasionally after it. Hecker spent the last year of the war on his farm in Belleville, where he had retired after his abbreviated service in the 24th and 82nd Illinois. However, any thoughts he had about settling into the comfortable life of a farmer disappeared when his agricultural business struggled during an economic downturn. To make ends meet, he decided to elevate his public profile and hit the road once more.

Like the Hecker of old, he wrote articles and essays for the German-language press, and traveled the lecture circuit charging $100 per appearance, or 25 cents per listener, to declaim on the various topics that fueled his passions. He spoke out against temperance or any cause associated with nativists, criticized corporate monopolies as well as socialism and women's suffrage. His anti-clerical views caused the most controversy, and he was branded anti-Catholic for his verbal brickbats against the Pope and church dogma. He embraced the cause of civil service reform, and demanded an end to the patronage system that politicians of his own Republican Party used so skillfully—and, in his view, balefully. But he would only fight his adversaries in the party with words, not at the ballot box. He refused to run for public office despite many entreaties, preferring to stay unsullied by the grime of politics and the desperate pursuit of votes.

He made a triumphant return to a newly reunited Germany in 1873. Crowds from Ladenburg to Mannheim celebrated their expatriate favorite son, and lined the route of his return by coach. Some 10,000 people awaited his return, still remembering his fight for republican ideals twenty-five years before. When they saw him, they broke out in spirited hurrahs and "songs, hat swinging, scarf waving, wiping of tears." They weren't the only ones overcome in this "uninterrupted drone of jubilation." Hecker himself choked up, shaken by all the praise and affection from his fellow Germans.

Still, while he was delighted by his homecoming and happy the German states had unified, he was less impressed by the citizens' lack of civil liberties and political freedoms. When asked, he firmly rejected any suggestion he should return to his former homeland, calling himself an American and wondering about the very premise of the question: "What would I do there? Perhaps become a subject when I am already one of the two million sovereigns of Illinois? With sixty years soon on my back, one becomes too stiff to bend down to 'subjecthood' and regard it as fortunate." More than half of his adult life had been spent in the United States, and despite its infuriating politics, his lack of advancement in the military, and the public corruption he saw, he had no desire to leave his adopted homeland. He had become an American in mind and spirit.

Rudolph Mueller was much less enchanted with the nation. He never shared Hecker's enthusiasm for his adopted country, and wrote bitterly of it in his letters and compared its culture and traditions unfavorably to those of Germany. Still, he idolized his onetime commander, and looked to tighten his bond with him by becoming part of his family.

He succeeded shortly after mustering out of the 82nd Illinois, marrying Hecker's daughter, Malwina, in a grand ceremony on his Belleville farm. In the years following, he sired three grandchildren for his hero and maintained a close bond with him. This should have been the greatest achievement of his life, for remaining in his good graces was all that Mueller desired. But somehow, even after wedding Hecker's daughter and becoming part of the colonel's family, Mueller found himself restless and unsatisfied.

Unlike some of the German Americans he knew, he found assimilation into this country difficult. His old nemesis Salomon could go west and prosper even under the taint of scandal. His hero Hecker could reemerge after the war with his good name intact and his public esteem unmatched. Even the man he struck near Savannah, Lieutenant Loeb, could find a place for himself as a champion of veterans causes and co-builder of the

Gettysburg monument. But Mueller chafed at all of it. He continued to deride his adopted country's decadence, its people's poor sense of idealism, and its leaders' shameful avarice. He even besmirched the memory of President Lincoln, writing it was "good fortune for the country" for him to be assassinated.

Because of Mueller's pride, his family struggled financially and he bounced from one occupation to the next. In Peoria he sold dry goods, then moved to Chicago and made cigars, sold more dry goods, and booked travel; later he ended up in Minneapolis managing a beer-bottling plant, represented several brewhouses, and sold insurance. Nothing seemed to fit. He had more to offer than what he had been given, and saw himself a victim of all the corruption and venality of the era. He was also in constant pain from a debilitating fall, and this injury, as well as the injuries to his pride and character, proved too much for him to bear. By the last year of the century, few things stirred his passion anymore. Even family life held little appeal for him, or any kind of life as he knew it. He took his own in 1899, with a bullet to the head.

After the immigrants of the 82nd Illinois and the rest of the 20th Corps had proceeded in the Grand Review, the 14th Corps was the last corps to march. John McCline was there, too, with the 13th Michigan. He had enjoyed his time in the capital during the previous two days, visiting clothing shops and trying on new duds, eating ice cream, candy, and blackberries from street peddlers, and gambling at chuck-a-luck and other games of chance. But during the review the teenager was bored. He didn't carry a weapon or march in formation, so had to plod along with the wagons at the back of the column.

He walked with his friends from the regiment, and he noticed other former bondsmen in the review. In front of each division, General Sherman had placed the engineers and road builders of the Pioneer Corps. They carried spades and shovels and axes to remind the spectators of how their labors had opened the South to the invading troops—felling timber and corduroying roads in the bleakest swamps of the Georgia and Carolina low country. They were proud to march at the front of each division, but knew they had been set to this task because Sherman never allowed them to fight. Even the U.S. Colored Troops who came under his command he disarmed and outfitted with earth-moving tools.

Black troops made up a full 10 percent of Union forces, and fought at places like Nashville, Fort Fisher, and Petersburg, but none of their regiments were in the review. Sherman's hostility to them was well known, but even the Army of the Potomac didn't bother to summon them to D.C. for the parade—even though its leaders knew how valuable they were in combat. To the spectators and the dignitaries along Pennsylvania Avenue, the black men who had made such sacrifices were simply invisible.

In the South, though, U.S. Colored Troops were everywhere. They manned forts and garrisoned posts from Tennessee to Florida, flushed out the remaining rebel guerrillas in states like Texas, and had to deal with a hostile, often violent, white population who didn't know what to make of black men with guns—many of whom had been slaves only a few months before. Among these warriors were the 14th U.S. Colored Infantry, whom John had met back in Tennessee, and who now held a post in Chattanooga after fighting in the Battle of Nashville. John had never forgotten how they once asked if he wanted to join them. Now he could only wonder what that would have been like.

After the review, John followed the rest of his regiment back to Michigan. It was one of the Great Lakes states—yet another place he had only imagined from stories he heard from his friends. Rural and peaceful, it seemed a world away from the violence and horror he had seen on the battlefields and plantations in the South. First he went to Paw Paw, then Battle Creek, where he spent seven years doing odd jobs and working for a grocer. The town had been a stop on the Underground Railroad, and was the home of the great activist for abolition and racial equality, Sojourner Truth. He didn't mind the town, but by the time he reached adulthood, he was ready to see more of the world.

He came to Chicago in 1874 to find it looking just like Atlanta. The great fire of 1871 had wiped out many of its blocks, and the place was thick with ruins and charred buildings. But it was rebuilding, and John found work as a hotel waiter, spending two years slowly building up his income. Still, he yearned to see his family, and left the city to track down his brother Jeff in Indianapolis. The two siblings reunited after last seeing each other in January 1864, a dozen years before, and resolved to find the rest of the family back in Tennessee.

John had a warm reunion with two of his other brothers, who worked as sharecroppers near Nashville. John respected their honest labor, but had no desire to toil on a former plantation. So he decided to pay for classes at the Nashville Normal and Theological Institute, a school that had been set up late in the war to teach freedmen to become teachers and ministers. He had always wanted to educate himself, and the school gave him the opportunity, providing courses in math, grammar, and history over three years. After finishing his studies, he taught classes at the school, and seemed to be making a place for himself in Tennessee, the state that had treated him so shamefully as a child. However, when the school began to struggle financially and closed down, he had to leave and find a new path out west.

He had read stories of black cowboys on the range, of black homesteaders who farmed 160 acres after they served in the army, of opportunities on the railroads and in the growing towns of the prairie and the Rocky Mountains. He spent more than a decade trying to find his place there, first in St. Louis working as a waiter and hat checker, then in Colorado Springs funding a small business with an old colleague and losing a good deal of money. In the 1890s, he found his way to New Mexico.

He had the fortune to meet Herbert Hagerman in that U.S. territory, a stalwart of the Republican Party who had been ambassador to Russia and Secretary of the Interior, as well as an ally of Theodore Roosevelt. The Rough Rider appointed Hagerman governor in 1906, and he brought John with him to the governor's mansion. There, John acted as a combination butler, chief of staff, and informal policy advisor. John had taken an interest in politics over the years, and made newspaper clippings of important stories and events he thought relevant to the governor's interests. Hagerman looked to change the territorial government and its corrupt policies, but his approach to reform was too much for the power brokers out west. They protested his reforms and had Roosevelt sack him.

Hagerman spent the next few decades as a rancher, a commissioner for Indian affairs, and a lawyer in Santa Fe. John worked for him off and on, and ultimately established himself as a leader in the black community there. The social climate in the early twentieth century in America was almost uniformly hostile to the advancement of black people, and in the Southwest it was especially so, since African Americans were small in number and faced great prejudice. But John did what he could to help his friends and colleagues as he had always done, and managed a decent life for himself without ever getting married or having children. He lived through the Spanish-American War, World War I, and World War II, becoming one of the last people in the nation to have a memory of the mighty Civil War. He died in Santa Fe at the age of ninety-six.

Many former slaves like John had marched with the U.S. Army. Some had labored in the Pioneer Corps and marched in front of each division, but still more marched at the rear—mostly women and children, some with their mules and belongings, others with little more than ragged clothes and bare feet. They had come hundreds of miles with Sherman's forces, had resisted being sent to the Sea Islands or anywhere else, and had followed the troops to the national capital.

The onlookers didn't know what to make of the ranks of freedmen that passed before them. There was some jeering and mockery, and some applause, but mostly people watched with an uneasy familiarity. A decade before the war, Washington, D.C., had been a massive slave mart, with pens and prisoners for people in bondage and several major dealers in slaves who sold and treated them as animals or worse. The memory of these brutal years still etched the minds of Washingtonians. And now great crowds of black men and women had returned to the city, not as captives, but as free people by their own choice. They had foraged and marched through the South with the soldiers, and had earned their place in the review as much as anyone who used a weapon.

Among the freedmen at the back of the column, there were also ambulances that had transported the wounded and wagons still stuffed with forage—anything from turkeys and cows to chicken coops and other goods the bummers had pilfered. And following them was the unmistakable sight of the pontoon train. These wagons conveyed the floating

bridges for Sherman's invading armies, and with them came the pontoniers who built those bridges—John Hight and the 58th Indiana.

Hight and his troops enjoyed the review and were glad for the war to
be over. But once the parade had concluded, they did not return home
quickly as other units did. Instead they were ordered to provost duty in
Louisville, to guard whiskey dealers and brothels from robbery, and allow
them to carry out their trade. Hight found this work "demoralizing" and
simply wanted to return home, but he had reenlisted and now had to
follow orders, however infernal they may have been.

Many of the men in the regiment regularly allowed alcohol to whip
them senseless, or they became foolish and debauched under its influence. On one occasion, a soldier even followed a minister's sermon by
preaching his own message for temperance—while he was stone-cold
drunk. Such license and ill behavior always made Hight's temper rise. In
his last sermon in late July, about ten days before the regiment mustered
out, the reverend expressed his feelings about the effect of war in clear
and sharp words: "The hypocrite is unmasked; the really worthless is
shown to be such. He who can be spoiled by camp corruption is hardly
worth saving. He is but a poor weak thing at best. A holy war, such as
this, makes men better, physically, intellectually and morally."

While fewer troops attended his sermons in the closing months of their
service, there was little doubt they had a cumulative effect. His preaching
and that of hundreds of other chaplains, combined with the Christian
Commission's distribution of free Bibles and its use of field agents, led
to a widespread religious revival in the Union army. Estimates claimed
anywhere from 100,000 to 200,000 men turned toward Christianity
during the war, about 5 to 10 percent of the Union army. While Hight's
regimental Christian organization would disband at the close of the
conflict, more groups would take their place on the home front, as the
tide of evangelism surged throughout the North.

Hight did his part with spreading the word. He returned to Bloomington and became an agent for the Indiana Methodist Episcopal Conference, educating and converting new souls to the gospel and becoming
a presiding elder of his organization. He concentrated his energies for
temperance, as did activists who pushed for new prohibitions against

liquor throughout the U.S. and warned of its effect on men's souls. Hight hadn't forgotten his earlier beliefs, though, and became active in the Freedmen's Aid Society working for housing and education for freed blacks in the South, and for the passage of civil liberties laws that countered the rising tide of white supremacy. He also participated in the Grand Army of the Republic, like so many of his peers, though he had his doubts about the ethics of the Republican Party with which it was associated.

Amid all his work, Hight wanted to become a family man again. His first wife had died, and within two years after the end of the war he had remarried and soon fathered a daughter. By 1875 his family relocated to Cincinnati and he became the assistant editor of the *Western Christian Advocate*, a publication committed to temperance and other evangelical causes. He wrote and published and advocated for these causes for more than a decade and became an important part of the religious community there. But while his soul soared in his profession, his body refused to cooperate. Crippling paralysis gripped him as a middle-aged man, and he succumbed to it at the age of fifty-one.

After all the soldiers had made their review before the president and the crowds along Pennsylvania Avenue had gone home, most regiments began the final process of mustering out and heading back to their respective states. But across the country there were still a number of public events and showcases to be held to raise funds and supplies for the troops, of which the Northwestern Sanitary Fair of 1865 was the most prominent.

It was the grand final effort of Mary Livermore and Jane Hoge, and the commission's assistant managers had worked vigorously to make it happen. There was an opening-day parade complete with dignitaries, two corps of war veterans, various industrial and agricultural equipment, and a notable group of black Masons. Inside the exhibit halls, the spectacles included heroic oil paintings of recent battles, mock naval sea duels fought with miniature ships, various weapons and trophies and flags, Lincoln's reassembled childhood log cabin complete with a walk-in lecture from his relatives, and a replica wax figure of Jefferson Davis dressed as an old woman, his rumored disguise when captured. It all made for a lively and engaging event and raised $325,000 in support of the Sanitary

Commission—four times the profits from the 1863 fair, though well short of Mary Livermore's half-million-dollar goal.

By October it was time for Mary to resign from the commission, as the organization itself was ending its mission after the war. It had been phenomenally successful at not only its goal of providing aid and supplies to soldiers in the field, but in drawing mass numbers of volunteers to help win the war. Up to 12,000 aid societies came into existence during the conflict—of which Mary and Jane were responsible for organizing a sizable fraction—and they ultimately employed some 200,000 women across different races, classes, religions, and sections of the country. The commission raised $25 million for the needs of soldiers and their armies and, just as important, helped change women's role in the war and society. They had overseen farmsteads, run businesses, sold goods at market, and managed large organizations—all things largely forbidden to them before the war. As Mary wrote:

> Not only did these women broaden in their views; they grew practical and executive in work. They learned how to cooperate intelligently with men; became expert in conducting public business, in calling and presiding over public meetings, even when men made a large part of the audience; learned how to draft constitutions and bylaws, to act as secretaries and committees; how to keep accounts with precision and system; how to answer, indorse, and file letters; how to sort their stores and keep an accurate account of stock; they attended meetings with regularity and promptness, and became punctilious in observance of official etiquette; in short, they developed rapidly a remarkable aptitude for business, on which men looked and wondered. 'Where were these superior women before the war?'

One of the best examples of a woman who had changed thoroughly because of the war was Mary herself, having gone from a middle-class philanthropist in Chicago to a figure of national renown. She continued her efforts in the postwar era.

In politics she had fallen into the Radical Republican camp and argued for a "hard" Reconstruction for the South and greater attention to the civil rights of the freedmen, and criticized Andrew Johnson for his lack of attention to such matters. In religion she pushed her Universalist Church to support women's missionary activity and—in a radical step for the late 1860s—the ordination of female ministers. Mary's friend Olympia Brown duly became the denomination's first woman minister. And in social activism, she hadn't forgotten her great moral crusade of temperance, and regularly wrote columns inveighing against the evils of strong drink and the iniquities of the liquor trade. Yet, as fervently as she supported these causes, she made a new pursuit paramount to her efforts: suffrage.

With the passage of the 15th Amendment to the U.S. Constitution, which gave the right to vote to men of any race, many women's groups argued the franchise should be extended further to allow for the right to vote regardless of gender. Mary argued the case in her columns and organized Chicago's first women's rights convention. It drew a broad array of participants of both genders, everyone from Edward Beecher (Mother Bickerdyke's hometown preacher in Galesburg) to such luminaries at Elizabeth Cady Stanton and Susan B. Anthony. The convention proved to be a success, and gave Mary a platform to advance suffrage and her related goals: economic equality for women—to be paid the same as men for the same work—and greater educational opportunities for girls and women; fighting violence against women in the home and ill treatment on the job; elevating women to an equal role in society with men; and mass organizing for political and economic gain, which she later called "cooperative womanhood."

She moved to Boston before the great fire that consumed much of Chicago, and there she became the editor of the *Woman's Journal*, the most prominent platform yet for her views. She encouraged girls and women to integrate all-male universities by submitting applications and pushed publicly for fair treatment for all students; and she decried the unequal treatment of black students at major universities. She lobbied for the proper care and treatment of women prisoners, and for an end to the many abuses to which they were subjected. She highlighted the poor treatment of women working as seamstresses, nurses, chambermaids, waitresses, and clerks, and encouraged them to cooperate to advance their economic interests. And she railed against the "insane and vulgar greed for riches that actuates corporations, monopolies, trusts, and other like organizations, whose tendency is to deprive the wage-earner of a fair share of the wealth that he helps create." She even promoted "Christian Socialism" as a substitute for laissez-faire capitalism—as difficult a battle as any at the height of the Gilded Age. She summed up her objective for achieving success in the very first column she wrote for the *Woman's Journal*, and never deviated from that mission: "Push Things."

For all her groundbreaking, revolutionary, and sometimes iconoclastic views, Mary's words and opinions were wildly popular in some circles, especially on the East Coast and in major Northern cities. Whereas she might have been labeled a pariah before the war for these ideas, after it she became a beacon to the cause of reform. She hit the lecture circuit to publicize her goals, and visited places from the largest cities to the smallest wayside hamlets. Some little towns had never before seen a woman speak in public. In other places she debated men hostile to temperance or suffrage, and encouraged the women in the crowd to speak their opinions publicly, and take social and political action to advance their interests. The effect was electrifying, even to her foes. As one newspaper wrote, "If she can't convince, she at least commands respect."

Her increasingly lucrative and lengthy oratory tours made her the most successful woman speaker in the nation, in an era when public speaking was a principal source of education and entertainment. She spoke to thousands of men and women at a time, commanded substantial fees for major appearances, and laced her words with humor, passion, and a bit of self-deprecation.

Throughout her career, she never forgot to remind the audience of the great Civil War between the North and South, which later in her life receded in memory, more than a generation in the past. She remarked how much it had changed for women, and how the advances they had made in that era had made possible all their gains since then: greater integration of higher education, more legal rights, activism in the public square, and, eventually she assumed, the right to vote.

Abolition, black suffrage, temperance, women's rights, a revival of religious enthusiasm—all had risen in the tumult of war. Some causes had triumphed, others awaited their day. Mary was convinced the industrial energy and political fervor of the west had guided this progress. The pioneer states had driven the nation with their dynamic force, had changed and transformed that nation with their ideas, and saved that nation from collapse with leaders like Lincoln and armies like Sherman's. With their labor and sacrifice, westerners like Mary had created a new country—bold, dynamic, and still unvanquished—from the brilliant and terrible battles of the past.

EPILOGUE

THE FIRES TO COME

I t was a midwinter day in 1879 that the city of Atlanta awoke to the arrival of a visitor from the North. He was no typical Yankee, coming to consider buying a farmstead or investing in a local business. Instead, he was the general-in-chief of the U.S. Army, a legend around these parts who knew the town all too well. He had last come more than fourteen years before and knew the town's layout, its barracks and buildings, its railroads and industry, and the character of its people. And he was impressed by all these things, along with how much progress the town had made in recent years, considering he had once burned it to the ground.

William Sherman had decided to visit Atlanta as part of his return to the South. He hadn't come to gloat or to preside over a defeated enemy, but to take stock of what he saw there and to offer his encouragement to the growth of the region. And because of this, Atlanta's leaders didn't mind his presence at all. Perhaps with enough publicity from his visit, they thought, Sherman could encourage more Yankee investors to consider putting their money into the rebuilt town, which was now no longer just a burned-out railroad junction, but the dynamic and enterprising capital of Georgia.

He had already traveled through Chattanooga, and was similarly impressed by the progress these Southerners had made, and would later return to Savannah and tour major towns in Florida before heading on to Mobile and New Orleans. (He did not make it to Columbia, South Carolina.) Surprisingly, most of his hosts took a fancy to him. He spoke mainly of the old war in military terms, and lauded the locals for their commitment to economic growth and opportunity. He especially pleased them with his criticisms of Reconstruction. He thought it unfair that for a dozen years after the war, Northern radicals had maintained a military presence in the region and interfered with its affairs. The new president, Rutherford Hayes, had put an end to all that, and the new Democratic Congress had passed policies that allowed the white elites in the South to have their way—economically, socially, and racially.

The Southerners soon realized that their onetime nemesis sympathized with them, even if he had once leveled their towns and stolen their livestock and crops. Not only did Sherman admire the region—he had been a college president in Louisiana before the war and enjoyed the society there—but he firmly approved of its racial policies. He argued blacks were best kept in an inferior social position; that the national controversy over racist violence and the rise of the Ku Klux Klan had been overblown; that sending troops to monitor equal voting rights and the treatment of blacks, as his old friend Ulysses Grant had done as president, was "simply ridiculous"; and that trying to force the South to comply with a national civil rights agenda would lead to military dictatorship.

He had even, just after the war ended, explained to President Andrew Johnson that his Special Field Order No. 15—his most famous policy, known as Forty Acres and a Mule—was a measure of military necessity only. He claimed he hadn't intended to allow blacks to permanently occupy the land once held by white slave owners, and had no interest in seeing the policy continued. With Sherman's assent, the president happily revoked the order and gave the land back to its former white owners, and forced the freedmen off the land they had been promised. Sherman's interests, in short, seemed to align quite closely with those of the South. Indeed, sometimes it seemed the white former rebels were among his few allies in the post-Reconstruction world of the United States.

As the head of the army for nearly a decade, he became identified with many controversial policies, none more so than the removal of Native tribes from their land, the breaking of treaties with them, and the many brutal wars that resulted. He duly became a target for public denunciation in the press and in Congress, with critics calling his policies murderous and barbaric, especially when army troops burned entire villages and attacked women and children.

Despite his considerable public profile, his actual powers were quite limited. Repeated presidents had crippled his authority by forcing him to answer to domineering secretaries of war. His memoirs of the war had offended many of his old colleagues by diminishing their service or taking credit for their achievements as generals. And his relations with Congress were frequently frosty, if not openly hostile. His old subordinate John Logan—a Radical Republican and enemy of Southern sympathizers—had never forgotten being removed from power as head of the Army of the Tennessee after the Battle of Atlanta, and as a U.S. congressman and senator, he had tried to make Sherman's life unpleasant. He voted to reduce the size and troops of the federal army, cut the salaries of its leaders including Sherman's, and called into question many of his policies. At one congressional session, Logan even criticized the number of "West Pointers" in the service and their fat salaries, which came at the expense of "wooden-legged and one-armed men, and the widows and the orphans." Sherman became so enraged he stormed out of the chamber.

By the end of the 1870s, William Sherman retained his popularity with the public, but even that could not salve his wounded pride. He refused to run for office, despite many entreaties from both parties, and grew to despise politicians and the corrupt actions they took. He watched his son Thomas turn away from his education in the law, and a potentially profitable career, to become a Jesuit priest—a tragedy that cut the unreligious Sherman nearly as deep as the death of his son Willy in 1863. He separated from his wife, Ellen, and spent a Christmas in 1878 alone and ashamed, after she issued him an ultimatum to quit his imperious attitude over the family and treat her as an equal partner—otherwise she would be the sole "commander" of the future of their children. She had tolerated his callous behavior toward her before the war, but in this changed era, would no longer accept it. Reports of his philandering, which had leaked out in the press, didn't help matters.

More trouble came in 1881, when his old enemy, rebel president Jefferson Davis—whom Sherman had refused to meet on his victory lap in Dixie—came out with a memoir entitled *The Rise and Fall of the Confederate Government*. In it he compared Sherman to a barbarian and condemned his destruction of the Southern homeland, using startling examples—some real, some invented—of the general's base character and wanton cruelty. Sherman was furious and carried out a duel in words through the press, but Davis's criticisms found their mark. On the general's next trip to the South, he was given a cool reception, and as the last decade of his life passed, he found that Davis had helped to cast him as a crazed ruffian in uniform, a mad demon in human form.

It wasn't just Davis who did it. As future decades passed, Southern women whom he had never met, with names like Dolly Lunt Burge, Fanny Cohen, and Mary Chesnut, described the horrors of the March to the Sea and the Carolinas campaign. Sherman now became a figure worthy of contempt, a murderer and a charlatan who had stolen and annihilated everything he could. In many of these accountings of his campaigns, a new "Lost Cause" myth arose in which the innocent people of Georgia and the Carolinas only wanted respect for their states' rights, and slaves were innocent and childlike creatures unable to take care of themselves, and noble plantation owners wished only to protect their family members, black and white, from the depredations of Northern generals and, later, Yankee carpetbaggers and politicians. The cumulative weight of Lost Cause books and diaries sank Sherman's reputation as fully as anything Jefferson Davis could have written, and resembled the stories the planters told to keep their slaves from fleeing their bondage before the marchers arrived. And in the next century, the new media of cinema would ensure the long-term ruin of his name, with films like *The Birth of a Nation* and *Gone with the Wind* casting Southern slave holders as heroes and Northern generals as villains. Even many audiences in the North came to believe it.

However, William Sherman in the 1880s could not have predicted these things. He only knew that his allies had dwindled and the region he admired had turned against him. But it was at this time the general began to have his own doubts about what he had long believed. Aside from places like Atlanta, the industrial, productive South he saw on the rise never quite came into being. Instead, the region settled into a system of agricultural peonage and sharecropping, hostile to outside interests, especially if they happened to be Yankees. The racial caste system he saw as the most conducive to social harmony instead caused chaos and anarchy, with Southern states enshrining segregation in their constitutions and ensuring blacks would have no right to vote, no recourse to fair treatment under the law, and no freedom from brutality and violence—evident in the viral spread of lynching across the region.

As Sherman now saw, the rise of former Confederates to national power only crippled the size and funding of his army, and resulted in his onetime enemies occupying positions of power in the presidential cabinet, in Congress, and on the Supreme Court. He worried that all his efforts on the battlefield might have been for naught, as "what the Union armies conquered in war . . . the South conquered in politics." And in the guise of national reconciliation, the influence of that section had reached across the nation, as a new, bitter climate of racial hostility and oppression developed. Alarmed by this result, which he had willfully ignored for so long, Sherman urged action. To his brother John in Congress he wrote, "the Republican party which gave the negro the vote, must make that vote good" and argued for measures to control the power and influence of the South over electoral politics.

He also took a public stance. In an article for the *North American Review*, Sherman revealed some of his antiquated views of blacks and whites, but on the core question of civil rights he showed a marked change of perspective. He recalled the "despotic severity" of the slave masters and the countless abuses to which black men, women, and children had been subjected. He wrote of "the everlasting principles of human nature which tolerate all races and all colors, leaving each human being to seek in his own sphere 'the enjoyment of life, liberty and happiness'"—words that could have come from the pen of John Logan, with whom he had recently reconciled. And he issued a threat.

"I say to the South, Let the negro vote, and count his vote honestly." For if blacks continued to be denied their rights, "The Northern people will not long tolerate the negro vote to be suppressed." And as a consequence:

> Otherwise, so sure as there is a God in Heaven, you will have another war, more cruel than the last, when the torch and dagger will take the place of the muskets of well-ordered battalions. The negro is gaining in experience and intelligence every day, and he has read Byron: 'Hereditary bondsmen, know ye not, who would be free, them selves must strike the blow?' Should the negro strike that blow, in seeming justice, there will be millions to assist them.

And thus the "great vandal" of the Civil War finally came to understand the full measure of what had been at stake in the war. How equal justice and civil rights were more than just political slogans, and how the idea of land and freedom and opportunity to those who had been enslaved could never be forgotten. The policy could be revoked, but not its promise.

Though an old man, he offered to take up arms again, this time with a full appreciation for the gravity of the fight. While he would never again be a warrior, dying in New York City in 1891, Sherman did make for a chilling prophet, predicting the fires of a new rebellion in the years to come.

REFERENCES

GENERAL REFERENCES

There are several key primary sources that any history of the Civil War is bound to reference. The most important is the monumental Official Records of the War of the Rebellion (Washington, D.C.: Government Printing Office, 1880–1901), which comprises a comprehensive set of volumes of Union army orders, reports, and correspondence spread over 128 volumes. It can be a daunting prospect to research, but for the purposes of this book the key parts are almost all in Series I, including Volumes XXX and XXXI, Parts I and II in both volumes (Operations in Kentucky, Southwest Virginia, Tennessee, Mississippi, North Alabama, and North Georgia, August 11–December 31, 1863); Volume XXXVIII, Parts I, II, and III (The Atlanta Campaign, May 1–September 8, 1864); Volume XLIV (Operations in South Carolina, Georgia, and Florida, November 14–December 31, 1864); and Volume XLVII, Parts I, II, and III (Operations in North Carolina, South Carolina, Southern Georgia, and East Florida, January 1–June 30, 1865). Key statistics and quotations from the records are cited where appropriate in the chapter bibliographies and notes.

Also essential is Frederick Dyer's exhaustive *A Compendium of the War of the Rebellion* (Des Moines, Iowa: Dyer, 1908), nearly 1,800 pages describing the organization and records of Union military units, including their leaders, battle records, wartime engagements, and other data, as well as a lengthy description of individual regimental histories. Valuable supplemental sources include William F. Fox's *Regimental Losses in the Civil War* (Albany, N.Y.: Albany, 1889), detailing the wounded and killed throughout the war, as well as casualties from disease and other factors, and statistics and histories for 300 Union regiments; and, for most of the units mentioned in this book, General J.N. Reece's *Report of the Adjutant General of the State of Illinois* (Springfield, Ill.: Phillips Brothers, 1901), which breaks down the state's regiments by officers and enlisted men and describes their enlistment, date of muster, and fate in the war, whether discharged, injured, or killed in action. William B. Tubbs also offers a useful guide to the published sources related to individual units in his article "A Bibliography of Illinois Civil War Regimental Sources in the Illinois State Historical Library" (*Illinois Historical Journal* 87:3 (1994), 185–232). For a list of soldiers' self-told stories of the war, Albert E. Smith Jr. presents an array of sources in *Civil War Diaries and Personal Narratives* (Washington, D.C.: Library of Congress, 1998), arranged by name and cross-referenced by state regiment.

Nineteenth-century primary sources are critical for the data they preserve on the war, but more contemporary secondary sources provide a better analysis of how and why it happened. The best introduction to the restive politics of the prewar era that led, in part, to the conflict is David M. Potter's *The Impending Crisis: 1848–1861* (New York: Harper & Row, 1976), while the finest one-volume history of the war is still James McPherson's much-loved *Battle Cry of Freedom* (New York: Oxford Univ. Press, 1988). More comprehensive histories that include the Southern invasion are Bruce Catton's third volume of his war trilogy, *Never Call Retreat* (New York: Doubleday, 1965), and Shelby Foote's *The Civil War, A Narrative: Red River to Appomattox* (New York: Vintage, 1974). Somewhat drier, yet no less relevant, is the granular analysis of Herman Hattaway and Archer Jones's *How the North Won: A Military History of the Civil War* (Champaign: Univ. of Illinois Press, 1983), which argues for the importance of strategy and logistics in the Union victory. Another helpful reference is John C. Frederiksen's *Civil War Almanac* (New York: Checkmark, 2007), with its detailed descriptions of the daily happenings in the various theaters of the war.

For a closer look at the social, economic, and cultural worlds of the wartime North and South, Phillip Shaw Paludan's *A People's Contest: The Union and Civil War, 1861–1865* (New York: Harper & Row, 1988), and Emory Thomas's *The Confederate Nation: 1861–1865* (New York: Harper & Row, 1979) both provide worthy overviews. Bruce Levine further investigates the war's effect on the class structure of the South in his recent *The Fall of the House of Dixie: The Civil War and the Social Revolution That Transformed the South* (New York: Random House, 2013).

Although proponents of the Lost Cause claim "The War Between the States" was fought over the issue of states rights, the fundamental reason for the Civil War was slavery. The individual narratives of bondsmen are presented in *Slave Testimony*, John W. Blassingame, ed. (Baton Rouge, La.: Louisiana State Univ. Press, 1977), as well as the Library of Congress's sizable collection *Slave Narratives: A Folk History of Slavery in the United States from Interviews with Former Slaves* (Washington, D.C.: Federal Writers Project, 1941), though most of the latter's oral narratives were collected in the 1930s—more than 70 years after the end of the war. Useful academic studies include

James McPherson's *The Negro's Civil War: How American Blacks Felt and Acted During the War for the Union* (New York: Pantheon, 1965) and, for the immediate concerns of the present book, Clarence Mohr's *On the Threshold of Freedom: Masters and Slaves in Civil War Georgia* (Baton Rouge: Louisiana State Univ. Press, 2001). Benjamin Quarles outlines the wide range of roles blacks played in the conflict in *The Negro in the Civil War* (New York: Little, Brown, 1953).

Since William Sherman forbade black troops from serving in his forces, African American soldiers figure only tangentially in the current volume. However, there are numerous worthwhile sources, many of them contemporary, that provide an overview of their service: Noah Andre Trudeau, *Like Men of War: Black Troops in the Civil War, 1862–1865* (New York: Little, Brown, 1998); John David Smith, ed., *Black Soldiers in Blue: African American Troops in the Civil War Era* (Chapel Hill: Univ. of North Carolina Press, 2002); Edwin S. Redkey, *A Grand Army of Black Men* (New York: Cambridge Univ. Press, 1992); Joseph T. Glatthaar, *Forged in Battle: The Civil War Alliance of Black Soldiers and White Officers* (New York: Free Press, 1990); and Dudley Taylor Cornish, *The Sable Arm: Negro Troops in the Union Army, 1861–1865* (New York: Longmans, Green, 1956).

The Prairie State of Illinois figures prominently in the early part of this book, and sources relevant to its role in the war are detailed in the Chapter 1 citations below. For general information, Harry Hansen's *Illinois: A Descriptive and Historical Guide* (New York: Hastings House, 1974) is a classic text that describes the history and features of innumerable small towns, some of which are mentioned in this text. Worthwhile general histories of the state include Roger Biles's *Illinois: A History of the Land and Its People* (DeKalb, Ill.: Northern Illinois University Press, 2005) and James E. Davis's *Frontier Illinois* (Bloomington, Ind.: Indiana University Press, 1998). For a closer look at the military engagements of Illinois troops and some of the key leaders in the fight, both Mark Hubbard's *Illinois's War: The Civil War in Documents* (Athens: Ohio University Press, 2013) and Victor Hicken's *Illinois in the Civil War* (Chicago: Univ. of Illinois Press, 1991) feature useful references, analysis, and documentation.

A colorful memoir of life in prewar Egypt is Daniel Harmon Brush's *Growing Up in Southern Illinois* (Chicago: R.R. Donnelley & Sons, 1944), which details some of the social and cultural distinctions common to that region. *Tales and Songs of Southern Illinois*, by Charles Neely (Carbondale: Southern Illinois Univ. Press, 1938), adds a winsome element of regional folklore and country ballads. On the opposite end of the state, the second volume (1857–1871) of A.T. Andreas's *History of Chicago* (Chicago: Lakeside Press, 1885) is a bit antiquated, but covers key aspects of the city in such detail—from its railroads, hospitals, and schools to its literature, theater, and Masonic lodges—that its few modern rivals are nowhere near as comprehensive.

Finally, for a closer look at the kind of images shown in the insert, Alexander Gardner's *Photographic Sketch Book of the War* (Washington, D.C.: Philip & Solomons, 1866) and *Mathew Brady: Portraits of a Nation*, by Robert Wilson (New York: Bloomsbury, 2013), provide a masterful view of wartime photography and, in the case of the latter, a rich biographical story as well. For a good explanation of the drawings and etchings of the war published in national journals, William Fletcher Thompson Jr.'s article

"Illustrating the Civil War" (*The Wisconsin Magazine of History* 45:1 (1961), 10–20) is an excellent place to begin. Harry Katz and Vincent Virga's *Civil War Sketch Book: Drawings from the Battlefront* (New York: W.W. Norton, 2012) is a worthy long-form treatment of the same subject.

INTRODUCTION—TWO ARMIES IN WASHINGTON

Some of the better primary sources on Washington, D.C., in the months after the war and the procession of the march include the "General News" column of *The New York Times* on May 24 and May 25, 1865; George Ward Nichols, *The Story of the Great March from the Diary of a Staff Officer* (New York: Harper & Brothers, 1865); S.H.M. Byers, *With Fire and Sword* (New York: Neale, 1911); William B. Hazen, *A Narrative of Military Service* (Boston: Ticknor, 1885); and F.Y. Hedley, *Marching Through Georgia: Pen-Pictures of Every-Day Life in General Sherman's Army, from the Beginning of the Atlanta Campaign Until the Close of the War* (Chicago: Donohue, Henneberry, 1890).

Modern views of the same event include Ann McShea's article "Hazleton Soldiers in the Civil War Marched on After Lee's Surrender" (*The Standard-Speaker*, December 20, 2015), Reid D. Ross's "Civil War Grand Review" (*America's Civil War Magazine*, December 9, 2015; accessed at www.historynet.com/civil-war-grand-review.htm) and Steven E. Woodworth's book *Nothing but Victory: The Army of the Tennessee, 1861–1865* (New York: Knopf, 2005).

Several history blogs also offer a concise overview, including William Stroock's "The Grand Review of 1865" at Warfare History Network (accessed at http://warfarehistorynetwork.com/daily/civil-war/the-grand-review-of-1865/, March 27, 2017).

SELECTED REFERENCES:

p. vx   "my poor tatterdemalion corps": Burke Davis, *Sherman's March* (New York: Random House (1980), 288).

p. vx   "dingy, as if the smoke of numberless battlefields had dyed their garments": James Grant Wilson, "Two Modern Knights Errant" (*The Cosmopolitan* 11:1 (1891), 300).

p. xvi   "There had been no such army since the days of Julius Caesar": Bruce Catton, *This Hallowed Ground: The Story of the Union Side of the Civil War* (New York: Doubleday (1956), 373).

CHAPTER 1—THE WESTERN EDGE

The description of wartime Chicago is drawn in part from Theodore J. Karamanski's *Rally 'Round the Flag: Chicago and the Civil War* (Lanham, Md.: Rowman & Littlefield, 2006), while the story of the legendary Republican convention derives from P. Orman Ray, *The Convention That Nominated Lincoln* (Chicago: University of Chicago Press, 1906), as well as Gustave Koerner's *Memoirs: 1809–1896*, vol. 2 (Cedar Rapids, Iowa.: Torch Press, 1909), which also provide much insight about Koerner himself. An overview of the Wide Awakes and other political/paramilitary organizations can be found in

Koerner, as well as in Michael E. McGerr, *The Decline of Popular Politics: The American North, 1865–1928* (New York: Oxford University Press, 1988).

The victories and struggles of Mary Livermore are drawn from her *My Story of the War: A Woman's Narrative of Four Years Personal Experience* (Hartford, Conn.: A.D. Worthington, 1889), as well as *The Story of My Life, or The Sunshine and Shadow of Seventy Years* (Hartford, Conn.: A.D. Worthington, 1897). Generally, the former describes her wartime activities and the latter most of the other events in her life. Wendy Hamand Venet's *A Strong-Minded Woman: The Life of Mary A. Livermore* (Amherst: University of Massachusetts Press, 2005) is the best modern biographical source.

The description of Illinois's society, economy, and folkways derives from the general sources mentioned previously: Harry Hansen, ed., *Illinois: A Descriptive and Historical Guide*; Roger Biles, *Illinois: A History of the Land and Its People*; James E. Davis, *Frontier Illinois*; and Mark Hubbard, ed., *Illinois's War: The Civil War in Documents*. Another valuable reference was Richard Lyle Power's *Planting Corn Belt Culture: The Impress of the Upland Southerner and the Yankee in the Old Northwest* (Indianapolis: Indiana Historical Society, 1953).

Sabine Freitag's *Friedrich Hecker: Two Lives for Liberty* (St. Louis: St. Louis Mercantile Library: 2006) is the key source for the life of the revolutionary turned army colonel. Critical supplements include the collection of Friedrich Hecker Papers at the State Historical Society of Missouri (1825–1987; http://shsmo.org/manuscripts/stlouis /s0451.pdf), and, for a glimpse of the colonel's bucolic life near Belleville, Frederic Trautman's "Eight Weeks on a St. Clair County Farm in 1851: Letters by a Young German" (*Journal of the Illinois State Historical Society* 75:3 (1982)). Other essential texts about the role played by German immigrants before and during the Civil War include the following: Bruce Levine, *The Spirit of 1848: German Immigrants, Labor Conflict and the Coming of the Civil War* (Chicago: University of Illinois Press: 1992); the respective chapters by James M. Bergquist, "People and Politics in Transition: The Illinois Germans, 1850–1860," Jay Monaghan, "Did Abraham Lincoln Receive the Illinois German Vote?" and Donnal V. Smith, "The Influence of the Foreign-Born of the Northwest in the Election of 1860," all in *Ethnic Voters and the Election of Lincoln*, Frederick C. Luebke, ed. (Lincoln: University of Nebraska Press, 1971); Susanne Martha Schick, "'For God, Mac, and Country': The Political Worlds of Midwestern Germans During the Civil War Era" (Ph.D. dissertation, University of Illinois at Urbana-Champaign, 1994); Dean B. Mahin, *The Blessed Place of Freedom: Europeans in Civil War America* (Dulles, Va.: Brassey's Inc., 2002); and the Koerner *Memoirs* mentioned earlier.

Although the narrative of the 82nd Illinois Volunteer Infantry appears in later chapters, early discussions of German immigrant military activity are drawn from Joseph R. Reinhart, ed., *Yankee Dutchmen Under Fire: Civil War Letters from the 82nd Infantry* (Kent, Ohio: Kent State University Press, 2013); Eric Benjaminson, "A Regiment of Immigrants: The 82nd Illinois Volunteer Infantry and the Letters of Captain Rudolph Mueller" (*Journal of the Illinois State Historical Society* 94:2 (2001)); and Wilhelm Kaufmann, *The Germans in the American Civil War* (Munich: R. Oldenbourg, 1911).

SELECTED REFERENCES:

p. 3   "banner cry of Hell": Karamanski, *Rally 'Round the Flag*, 28.

p. 4   "gigantic pantomime" to "insanity of gladness": Livermore, *My Story of the War*, 550–552.

p. 7   "one of the most just, kind and indulgent of men": Koerner, *Memoirs*, 112.

p. 8   "a foreboding of the eventfulness of the moment," ibid., 94.

p. 8   "Is it certain Mr. Lincoln is an uncompromising slavery man?": Livermore, *My Story of the War*, 552.

p. 9   "hold sleep in abeyance": Livermore, *The Story of My Life*, 457.

p. 10   "the days of Orthodoxy are fast being numbered!": Venet, *A Strong-Willed Woman*, 68.

p. 10   "somewhat astonishing city" to "compulsory gymnastics": Livermore, *The Story of My Life*, 457–460.

p. 11   "endless punishment" and "utter ignorance": Venet, *A Strong-Willed Woman*, 68.

p. 11   "dragged the white ermine": Livermore, *The Story of My Life*, 436–437.

p. 12   "steeped to the lips," ibid., 365.

p. 13   "the most influential German in America": Freitag, *Two Lives for Liberty*, 169.

p. 13   "humiliation incumbent on chasing offices," ibid., 139.

p. 14   "like a pilgrim at Golgotha": Trautman, "Eight Weeks," 164.

p. 15   "a devilish rascal": Freitag, *Two Lives for Liberty*, 130.

p. 15   "he is considered the very Anti-Christ": Gustave Koerner letter to Abraham Lincoln, July 17, 1858, Lincoln Manuscripts, Library of Congress.

p. 16   "revolution—undisguised revolution": Karamanski, *Rally 'Round the Flag*, 44.

p. 17   "the low and the foreign born": Livermore, *The Story of My Life*, 435.

p. 19   "hostile act": Resolution to Call the Election of Abraham Lincoln as U.S. President a Hostile Act and to Communicate to Other Southern States South Carolina's Desire to Secede from the Union, South Carolina General Assembly, November 9, 1860.

p. 20   "the real contest [is] between slavery and freedom" to "deluge the land with blood": Livermore, *My Story of the War*, 88–89.

p. 21   "Southern aristocracy be broken": Freitag, *Two Lives for Liberty*, 220.

p. 21   "There was but one cry—'To arms! To arms!'": Koerner, *Memoirs*, 119–120.

CHAPTER 2—TIP OF THE SWORD

The John Alexander Logan family papers (Manuscript Division, Library of Congress, Washington, D.C., 1836–1925; http://hdl.loc.gov/loc.mss/eadmss.ms001029) are among the key sources for the Illinois politician and his wife, Mary, encompassing letters and reports, speeches, and various articles and memorabilia on his career and their life together. The *Congressional Globe* also records Logan's speeches in the U.S. House in their full, fiery detail (see quoted references for citations). Also useful as complementary sources are modern biographies including James Pickett Jones, *Black Jack: John A. Logan and Southern Illinois in the Civil War Era* (Tallahassee: Florida State University, 1967), and Gary Ecelbarger, *Black Jack Logan: An Extraordinary Life in Peace and War* (Guilford, Conn.: Lyons Press, 2005). Older biographies with less detailed information include

REFERENCES

George Francis Dawson, *Life and Services of Gen. John A. Logan, Soldier and Statesman* (New York: Belford, Clarke, 1887), and Byron Andrew, *A Biography of General John A. Logan, with an Account of His Public Services in Peace and in War* (New York: H.S. Goodspeed, 1884). Mary Logan's own *Reminiscences of a Soldier's Wife: An Autobiography* (New York: Charles Scribner's Sons, 1913) is also compelling, its author a notable public figure in her own right. For John Logan's early military career, the above sources provide useful information, as does W.S. Morris, L.D. Hartwell, and J.B. Kuykendall, *History 31st Regiment Illinois Volunteers* (Evansville, Ind.: Keller Print. and Pub., 1902; reprint Carbondale: Southern Illinois Univ. Press, 1998).

Descriptions of the political and social setting of the early war in Illinois are drawn from three key articles in the *Journal of the Illinois State Historical Society:* Robert I. Girardi, "Illinois' First Response to the Civil War" (105:2–3 (2012)); Wayne N. Duerkes, "I for One Am Ready to Do My Part: The Initial Motivations That Inspired Men from Northern Illinois to Enlist in the U.S. Army, 1861–1862" (105:4 (2012)); and Stanley L. Jones, "Agrarian Radicalism in Illinois' Constitutional Convention of 1862" (48:3 (1955)), as well as William L. Burton, *Melting Pot Soldiers: The Union's Ethnic Regiments* (Ames: Iowa State Univ. Press, 1988). Previously cited works such as Victor Hicken, *Illinois in the Civil War*; Mark Hubbard, *Illinois's War: The Civil War in Documents*; Richard Lyle Power, *Planting Corn Belt Culture*; and Theodore Karamanski, *Rally 'Round the Flag*, also illustrate the atmosphere at the time of initial enlistment and combat. Philip Shaw Paludan, *A People's Contest*, and Henry Hattaway and Archer Jones, *How the North Won*, provide a more national perspective on conditions in the early war era.

A collection of various primary sources for Mother Bickerdyke can be found in the Mary Ann Bickerdyke Papers (Manuscript Division, Library of Congress, Washington, D.C., 1847–1905; http://hdl.loc.gov/loc.mss/collmss.ms000057). However, even with its many letters and lists and biographical details, the collection provides incomplete information on the full scope of her duties in the war (many more of the items relate to her family life and postwar career). Her short, unfinished memoir, for example, includes handwritten accounts of her work during the battles of Belmont and Fort Donelson, but little about her duties in later campaigns.

As supplements, two critical modern sources for the rise of Mother Bickerdyke are Nina Brown Baker, *Cyclone in Calico* (Boston: Little, Brown, 1952); and Martin Litvin, *The Young Mary: Early Years of Mother Bickerdyke, America's Florence Nightingale, and Patron Saint of Kansas* (Galesburg, Ill.: Log City Books, 1976). Several biographies on Bickerdyke appeared near the end of her life, and employ a bit more hyperbole, though Julia A. Houghton Chase, *Mary A. Bickerdyke, "Mother"* (Lawrence, Kans.: Journal Publishing, 1896), is the best of these.

For a more general look at women's accomplishments in the era, including the substantial role of Mother Bickerdyke, Agatha Young, *The Women and the Crisis: Women of the North in the Civil War* (New York: McDowell, Obolensky, 1959), and William C. King and W.P. Derby, *Campfire Sketches and Battle-Field Echoes of 61–5* (Springfield, Mass.: King, Richardson, 1889), have considerable merit. Other background information was drawn from Judith E. Harper, *Women During the Civil War: An Encyclopedia*

(London: Routledge, 2003), and Robert E. Denney, *The Distaff Civil War* (Bloomington, Ind.: Trafford, 2002). Finally, while Mary Ann Bickerdyke is the subject of Chapter 2 instead of Mary Livermore, the latter's *My Story of the War* offers critical facts and anecdotes about Bickerdyke that are missing from some of the other sources.

SELECTED REFERENCES:

p. 23   "God knows that I have differed": Speech of John Logan to U.S. House of Representatives, *Congressional Globe*, 36th Congress, 1st Session, 86.

p. 25   "not suited to be placed upon a level with white men": Ecelbarger, *Black Jack Logan*, 28–29.

p. 25   "perform that dirty work": Speech of John Logan to U.S. House of Representatives, *Congressional Globe*, 36th Congress, 1st Session, 85.

p. 26   "Yes, I would. . . , I know Logan": Ecelbarger, *Black Jack Logan*, 64.

p. 26   "noble Spartans" to "never, never!": *Congressional Globe*, 36th Congress, 2nd Session, Appendix, 178–181, quoted in Jones, *Black Jack*, 71–72.

p. 27   "sold out the Democratic Party": *Chicago Times*, October 31, 1876, quoted in Jones, *Black Jack*, 80–81.

p. 27   "I'll be damned if I will": Ecelbarger, *Black Jack Logan*, 72.

p. 32   "From the Lord God almighty": Young, *The Women and the Crisis*, 93.

p. 33   "I worship with the Methodists" to "Sister Bickerdyke": Baker, *Cyclone in Calico*, 36.

p. 33   "He wanted me to do everything his way": Livermore, *My Story of the War*, 478–479.

p. 34   "strong as a man" to "pesky ossifiers": King and Derby, *Campfire Sketches*, 98–99.

p. 35   "the matter is easily disposed of" to "I talked sense to him": Baker, *Cyclone in Calico*, 54–55.

p. 35   "I felt sure I could at least scream": Mary Logan, *Reminiscences*, 97.

p. 36   "The time has come when a man": ibid., 98.

p. 37   "Go away from my house" to "smacking her sister-in-law over the head with it": Ecelbarger, *Black Jack Logan*, 88–89.

p. 37   "the 'hardest' swearers in the army": Hicken, *Illinois in the Civil War*, 158.

p. 43   "a braver or more gallant man is not to be found": Letter from Ulysses S. Grant to Elihu Washburne, February 22, 1862, quoted in John Y. Simon, ed., *The Papers of Ulysses S. Grant, January 8–March 31, 1862* (Carbondale, Ill.: Southern Illinois Univ. Press, 1972), 274.

p. 44   "I . . . have faith in you": Charles Bracelen Flood, *Grant and Sherman: The Friendship That Won the Civil War* (New York: Harper Perennial, 2006), 88.

CHAPTER 3—ECHOES OF CHICKAMAUGA

The Battle of Chickamauga has inspired several monographs, but the most detailed and far-reaching is by Peter Cozzens, *This Terrible Sound: The Battle of Chickamauga* (Chicago: Univ. of Illinois Press, 1992). Other sources providing useful descriptions of the battle include James Lee McDonough, *Chattanooga—A Death Grip on the Confederacy* (Knoxville: Univ. of Tennessee Press, 1984), and Steven E. Woodworth, *Six Armies in Tennessee: The Chickamauga and Chattanooga Campaigns* (Lincoln: Univ. of Nebraska

Press, 1998). The struggles of the Army of the Cumberland during and after the battle, from the ground level, are described in *Three Years with the 92d Illinois: The Civil War Diary of John M. King*, Claire E. Swedberg, ed. (Mechanicsburg, Penn.: Stackpole Books, 1999), and in James A. Connolly, *Three Years in the Army of the Cumberland: The Letters and Diary of James A. Connolly*, Paul M. Angle, ed. (Bloomington: Indiana Univ. Press, 1959). The principal source for the Chickamauga narrative of John J. Hight is the reverend's *History of the Fifty-Eighth Regiment of Indiana Volunteer Infantry* (Princeton, N.J.: Press of the Clarion, 1895).

John McCline describes his impression of the battle's aftermath—as well as his escape from slavery and role in the Union army and in the 13th Michigan—in *Slavery in the Clover Bottoms: John McCline's Narrative of His Life During Slavery and the Civil War*, Jan Furman, ed. (Knoxville: Univ. of Tennessee Press, 1998). Michael Culp offers additional information on the unit in "The Formation of Kalamazoo's Own 13th Michigan Infantry" (Michigan Live, October 16, 2011, accessed at mlive.com). The larger context of chattel slavery in Tennessee is drawn from Bobby L. Lovett, "The Negro in Tennessee, 1861–1866: A Socio-Military History of the Civil War Era" (Ph.D. dissertation, University of Arkansas, 1969), and John Cimprich, *Slavery's End in Tennessee, 1861–1865* (Tuscaloosa: Univ. of Alabama Press, 1985). The early days of the recruitment of blacks for the Union army is discussed in Dudley Taylor Cornish, *The Sable Arm: Black Troops in the Union Army, 1861–1865* (Lawrence: Univ. Press of Kansas, 1956), and Howard C. Westwood, "Grant's Role in Beginning Black Soldiery" (*Illinois Historical Journal* 79:3 (1986), 197–212).

The essential primary sources for the career of William T. Sherman are the general's own *The Memoirs of William T. Sherman*, vols. 1 and 2 (New York: D. Appleton, 1886), *Sherman's Civil War: Selected Correspondence of William T. Sherman, 1860–1865*, Brooks D. Simpson and Jean V. Berlin, eds. (Chapel Hill: Univ. of North Carolina Press, 1999), and *Home Letters of William Sherman*, M.A. DeWolfe Howe, ed. (New York: Charles Scribner's Sons, 1909). The William T. Sherman Papers in the Library of Congress (Manuscript Division, Library of Congress, Washington, D.C., 1810–1897; http://hdl.loc.gov/loc.mss/eadmss.ms009309) also offer a voluminous array of letters, reports, journals, articles, and memorabilia from the general's lengthy military service.

Sherman continues to inspire biographies by the dozen, but the best overviews are still a quarter-century old: Michael Fellman, *Citizen Sherman: A Life of William Tecumseh Sherman* (New York: Random House, 1994), and John F. Marszalek, *Sherman: A Soldier's Passion for Order* (New York: Free Press-Macmillan, 1993). Both offer contrasting judgments on the strengths and flaws of the general. More contemporary references are Robert L. O'Connell, *Fierce Patriot: The Tangled Lives of William Tecumseh Sherman* (New York: Random House, 2014), and James Lee McDonough, *William Tecumseh Sherman: In the Service of My Country, a Life* (New York: W.W. Norton, 2016). Supplementary sources include Stephen E. Bower, "The Theology of the Battlefield: William Tecumseh Sherman and the U.S. Civil War" (*The Journal of Military History* 64:4 (2000), 1005–1034), and Steven F. Woodworth, *Nothing but Victory: The Army of the Tennessee, 1861–1865* (New York: Knopf, 2005).

REFERENCES

Sherman's role in the development of "total war" and his assorted campaigns of destruction—and their moral and legal implications—are laid out in Debra Reddin Van Tuyll, "Scalawags and Scoundrels? The Moral and Legal Dimensions of Sherman's Last Campaigns" (*Studies in Popular Culture* 22:2 (1999), 33–45), John Bennett Walters, "General William T. Sherman and Total War" (*The Journal of Southern History* 14:4 (1948), 447–480), and Mark Grimsley, *The Hard Hand of War: Union Military Policy Toward Southern Civilians, 1861–1865* (New York: Cambridge University Press, 1995).

SELECTED REFERENCES:

p. 47   "the ugliest noise that any mortal ever heard": Ambrose Bierce, "A Little of Chickamauga," *San Francisco Examiner*, April 24, 1898.

p. 47   "our broken columns" to "infernal regions might well find delight": Hight, *History of the Fifty-Eighth Regiment*, 190.

p. 48   "in the wildest disorder" to "ran like turkeys": Cozzens, *This Terrible Sound*, 216–218.

p. 50   "some of the panic stricken": Hight, *History of the Fifty-Eighth Regiment*, 198.

p. 50   "the rebels utterly despise Yankee preachers": ibid., 186.

p. 51   "men suffering untold agony" to "I never expected to see either of them again": ibid., 185–187.

p. 51   "It was my first sight" to "the same distrust of myself": ibid., 44–46.

p. 52   block quotation: "I have become cosmopolitan": ibid., 267.

p. 54   "Come on, Johnny": McCline, *Slavery in the Clover Bottoms*, 51.

p. 56   "a world of tents" to "a real Yankee soldier": ibid., 53.

p. 57   "it gives you courage": ibid., 65.

p. 58   "I won't trust . . .": Letter from William Sherman to John Sherman, April 26, 1863, quoted in Simpson and Berlin, *Sherman's Civil War*, 461.

p. 58   "general equality and amalgamation": Letter from William Sherman to Ellen Sherman, July 10, 1860, quoted in Howe, *Home Letters*, 178.

p. 58   "old women and grannies of New England": Letter from William Sherman to Ellen Sherman, January 5, 1861, quoted in Howe, *Home Letters*, 189.

p. 58   "the political nonsense of Slave Rights": Letter from William Sherman to Roswell M. Sawyer, January 31, 1864, quoted in Simpson and Berlin, *Sherman's Civil War*, 600.

p. 58   "California to Maine, any man could do murder": Letter from William Sherman to Ellen Sherman, January 5, 1861, quoted in Howe, *Home Letters*, 189.

p. 58   "vindicating its just and rightful authority": Letter from William Sherman to Henry Halleck, October 10, 1863, quoted in Official Records of the War of the Rebellion, Series I, Volume XXX, Part IV, 235.

p. 59   "I look upon myself as a dead cock in the pit": Letter from William Sherman to Ellen Sherman, April 15, 1859, quoted in Marszalek, *Passion for Order*, 333.

p. 59   "My only hope for the salvation of the Constitution": Letter from William Sherman to George Mason Graham, January 5, 1861, quoted in Simpson and Berlin, *Sherman's Civil War*, 29.

p. 60   "this is the only death I have ever had": Letter from William Sherman to Ulysses S. Grant, October 4, 1863, quoted in Fellman, *Citizen Sherman*, 199.

p. 60   "The child who bore my name": Letter from William Sherman to Charles C. Smith, October 4, 1863, quoted in Simpson and Berlin, *Sherman's Civil War*, 551–552.

p. 60   "Why oh Why should that child": Letter from William Sherman to Ellen Sherman, October 6, 1863, quoted in Simpson and Berlin, *Sherman's Civil War*, 552–553.

p. 60   "moaning in death" to "grow up to care for you?": Letter from William Sherman to Ellen Sherman, October 10, 1863, quoted in Simpson and Berlin, *Sherman's Civil War*, 556.

p. 62   "I find myself riding a whirlwind": Letter from William Sherman to Ellen Sherman, November 1, 1861, quoted in Fellman, *Citizen Sherman*, 97.

p. 62   "GENERAL WM. T. SHERMAN INSANE": General News, *Cincinnati Commercial*, December 11, 1861.

p. 63   "I believe hundreds would have freely died": Letter from William Sherman to Ellen Sherman, October 14, 1863, quoted in Simpson and Berlin, *Sherman's Civil War*, 558.

p. 63   "brave and manly" to "alter ego": Fellman, *Citizen Sherman*, 204–205.

p. 64   "I must work on purely and exclusively": Letter from William Sherman to Admiral D.D. Porter, October 14, 1863, quoted in Official Records of the War of the Rebellion, Series I, Volume XXV, Part I, 469.

p. 64   "absolutely stripping the country of corn": Telegram from William Sherman to Ulysses S. Grant, July 14, 1863, in Official Records of the War of the Rebellion, Series I, Volume XXIV, Part II, 526.

p. 64   "The inhabitants are subjugated": Telegram from William Sherman to Ulysses S. Grant, July 18, 1863, in Official Records of the War of the Rebellion, Series I, Volume XXIV, Part II, 529.

p. 64   "Jackson is utterly destroyed": Telegram from William Sherman to Ulysses S. Grant, July 20, 1863, in Official Records of the War of the Rebellion, Series I, Volume XXIV, Part II, 530.

p. 64   "if any enemy of good government": Telegram from William Sherman to Stephen Hurlbut, October 24, 1863, quoted in Official Records of the War of the Rebellion, Series I, Volume XXXI, Part I, 719.

p. 65   "Show them no mercy": Telegram from William Sherman to G.M. Dodge, November 12, 1863, quoted in Official Records of the War of the Rebellion, Series I, Volume XXXI, Part III, 131.

p. 65   "To secure the safety of the navigation": Letter from William Sherman to John Logan, December 21, 1863, quoted in Official Records of the War of the Rebellion, Series I, Volume XXXI, Part III, 459.

CHAPTER 4—THREE VIEWS OF CHATTANOOGA

The notes and commentary of Charles Wills in *Army Life of an Illinois Soldier: The Letters and Diary of Charles W. Wills* (Toronto: Globe Printing, 1906) are invaluable material in understanding the role of a junior officer in the Army of the Tennessee. Other significant sources are H.H. Orendorff and G.M. Anderson, et al., *Reminiscences of the Civil War: From Diaries of Members of the 103rd Illinois Volunteer Infantry* (Chicago: J.F. Leaming,

1904), covering Wills's regiment, and Steven Woodworth's previously mentioned *Nothing but Victory: The Army of the Tennessee, 1861–1865.*

Friedrich Hecker's storied life and career are extensively documented in the Friedrich Hecker Papers at the State Historical Society of Missouri (1825–1987; http://shsmo .org/manuscripts/stlouis/s0451.pdf). The wartime collection offers numerous letters and reports mostly in English, while Hecker's prewar activities are written in an antique German script and difficult to translate even for German scholars. The best biography in English of the revolutionary turned U.S. Army colonel is by Sabine Freitag's *Friedrich Hecker: Two Lives for Liberty*, with Frederic Trautman's "Eight Weeks on a St. Clair County Farm in 1851: Letters by a Young German" and Oswald Garrison Villard's "The 'Latin Peasants' of Belleville, Illinois" (*Journal of the Illinois State Historical Society* 35:1 (1942)) as useful supplements.

The story of Hecker's ill-fated 24th Illinois regiment plays out in David Graham, "A Fight for a Principle: The 24th Illinois Volunteer Infantry Regiment" (*Journal of the Illinois State Historical Society* 104:1/2 (2011)) and in William Wagner, *History of the 24th Illinois Volunteer Infantry Regiment* (Chicago: Illinois Staats Zeitung, 1864), with an abbreviated description in William L. Burton, *Melting Pot Soldiers: The Union's Ethnic Regiments* (Ames: Iowa State Univ. Press, 1988). The narrative of Hecker's second regiment, the 82nd Illinois, is well described through the letters of its soldiers, in Eric Benjaminson, "A Regiment of Immigrants: The 82nd Illinois Volunteer Infantry and the Letters of Captain Rudolph Mueller," and Joseph R. Reinhart, ed., *Yankee Dutchmen Under Fire: Civil War Letters from the 82nd Infantry.* Mark A. Dluger provides an even broader look at the regiment's members and their postwar lives in "A Regimental Community: The Men of the 82nd Illinois Infantry Before, During, and After the American Civil War" (Ph.D. Dissertation, Loyola University Chicago, 2009).

A general perspective on Teutonic forces in the war is drawn from Wilhelm Kaufmann, *The Germans in the American Civil War* (Carlisle, Pa.: John Kallmann, 1999), and Christian B. Keller, *Chancellorsville and the Germans: Nativism, Ethnicity, and Civil War Memory* (New York: Fordham Univ. Press, 2007). Useful primary sources on the German regiments include Friedrich August Braeutigam, "Civil War Diary of Friedrich August Braeutigam" (*The Palatine Immigrant* 14:4 (1989–1990)), Gustave Koerner, *Memoirs: 1809–1896*, vol. 2, and Carl Schurz, *The Reminiscences of Carl Schurz: Volume 3, 1863–1869* (New York: McClure, 1908). For a discussion of German American immigrant units in the context of other ethnic regiments, William L. Burton's *Melting Pot Soldiers: The Union's Ethnic Regiments* and that author's "'Title Deed to America': Union Ethnic Regiments in the Civil War" (*Proceedings of the American Philosophical Society* 124:6 (1980)) are both vital interpretations, while Dean B. Mahin's *The Blessed Place of Freedom: Europeans in Civil War America* (Dulles, Va.: Brassey's, 2002) is a more general overview.

The battles at Tunnel Hill, Lookout Mountain, and Missionary Ridge are documented in Peter Cozzens, *The Shipwreck of Their Hopes: The Battles for Chattanooga*; James Lee McDonough, *Chattanooga—A Death Grip on the Confederacy*; and Steven E.

Woodworth, *Six Armies in Tennessee: The Chickamauga and Chattanooga Campaigns*. John Hight's *History of the Fifty-Eighth Regiment of Indiana Volunteer Infantry* also underscores this section, as well as Claire E. Swedberg, ed., *Three Years with the 92d Illinois: The Civil War Diary of John M. King*; James A. Connolly, *Three Years in the Army of the Cumberland*; and James Barnett, "Willich's Thirty-Second Indiana Volunteers" (*Cincinnati Historical Society Bulletin* 37 (1979)).

The violent world of Tennessee beyond the battlefield derives in part from B. Franklin Cooling, "A People's War: Partisan Conflict in Tennessee and Kentucky," from *Confederates, Unionists, and Violence on the Confederate Home Front*, ed. Daniel E. Sutherland (Fayetteville: Univ. of Arkansas Press, 1999); Jonathan D. Sarris, "Anatomy of an Atrocity: The Madden Branch Massacre and Guerrilla Warfare in North Georgia, 1861–1865" (*Georgia Historical Quarterly* 77:4 (1993), 679–710); and Paul A. Whelan, "Unconventional Warfare in East Tennessee, 1861–1865 (M.A. thesis, Univ. of Tennessee, 1963).

SELECTED REFERENCES:

p. 66   "a miserable hole": Wills, *Army Life*, 188.

p. 67   "the citizens were required": Orendorff and Anderson, *Reminiscences*, 21.

p. 67   "the army is becoming awfully depraved" to "pointless wickedness": Wills, *Army Life*, 136.

p. 68   "the marks of the 'Vandal Yankees'" to "entirely of bone and cuticle": ibid., 161–163.

p. 68   "it is pretty well understood in this army": ibid., 145.

p. 69   "the very ideal of a chivalric" to "fun and humor in his conversation": ibid., 183.

p. 69   "girls, fun, etc.": ibid., 187.

p. 69   "lots of pretty girls": ibid., 59–60.

p. 69   "you have no idea": ibid., 127.

p. 69   "forty-six of the ugliest": ibid., 17.

p. 70   "the size of my stone inkstand": ibid., 215.

p. 70   "go down the Mississippi": ibid., 176–177.

p. 70   "an honest confession": ibid., 183–184.

p. 72   "struck me on the calves": ibid., 201.

p. 77   "These men are no cowards!": Freitag, *Two Lives for Liberty*, 244.

p. 77   "No one says of me": ibid., 239.

p. 82   "destroy immense quantities" to "the mortification of turning my eyes": Wills, *Army Life*, 204.

p. 84   "exceedingly scarce": Hight, *History of the Fifty-Eighth Regiment*, 212.

p. 85   "every soldier felt the necessity": Report of Gen. August Willich, December 31, 1863, Official Records of the War of the Rebellion, Series I, Volume XXXI, Part II, 264.

p. 85   "an enfilading fire": Hight, *History of the Fifty-Eighth Regiment*, 221.

p. 86   "Chickamauga! Chickamauga!": Connolly, *Three Years*, 158.

p. 87   "To my left, long lines of men" to "most gloriously by courage": Hight, *History of the Fifty-Eighth Regiment*, 221–222.

p. 87   "anything from a siege gun" to "crowded into a day": ibid., 223–224.

CHAPTER 5—HEROES IN THE FIELD

The Research Center of the Chicago History Museum (www.chicagohistory.org) contains selected copies of the *New Covenant* newspaper, for which Mary Livermore wrote and which she and her husband, Daniel, published. Some of these writings form the basis for her biography, but more often her story is best conveyed in the well-written *My Story of the War: A Woman's Narrative of Four Years Personal Experience*, and *The Story of My Life, or The Sunshine and Shadow of Seventy Years*, with Wendy Hamand Venet's *A Strong-Minded Woman: The Life of Mary A. Livermore* as a useful supplement. For Jane Hoge's take on the same events Livermore describes, *The Boys in Blue; or, Heroes of the "Rank and File"* (New York: E.B. Treat, 1867) offers a more homespun approach and writing style, while Nina Brown Baker's *Cyclone in Calico* is a good reference for Livermore's interactions with Mary Ann Bickerdyke.

By far the best primary source for the workings of the Sanitary Commission, beyond those provided by Mary Livermore, is Sarah Edwards Henshaw's *Our Branch and Its Tributaries; Being a History of the Work of the Northwestern Sanitary Commission and Its Auxiliaries, During the War of the Rebellion* (Chicago: Alfred L. Sewell, 1868). J.S. Newberry's *U.S. Sanitary Commission in the Valley of the Mississippi, During the War of the Rebellion, 1861–1866* (Cleveland: Fairbanks, Benedict, 1871) provides additional details of the operation of the branch in its part two, second chapter, "North-Western Sanitary Commission: Chicago Branch." By contrast, the organization's official history—Charles J. Stillé, *History of the United States Sanitary Commission, Being the General Report of Its Work During the War of the Rebellion* (Philadelphia: J.B. Lippincott, 1866)—pointedly leaves out much of the work done by its women employees and managers.

More contemporary interpretations of the Sanitary Commission include Judith Ann Giesberg, *Civil War Sisterhood: The U.S. Sanitary Commission and Women's Politics in Transition* (Boston: Northeastern Univ. Press, 2000), and Pam Tise, "A Fragile Legacy: The Contributions of Women in the United States Sanitary Commission to the United States Administrative State" (M.P.A. thesis, Texas State University–San Marcos, 2013). As regards the commission's rivalry with the U.S. Christian Commission, see Jeanie Attie, *Patriotic Toil: Northern Women and the American Civil War* (Ithaca, N.Y.: Cornell Univ. Press, 1998), and (as Rejean Attie) "'A Swindling Concern': The United States Sanitary Commission and the Northern Female Public, 1861–1865" (Ph.D. dissertation, Columbia University, 1987).

The best overview of the first Sanitary Fair is by the Chicago Sanitary Commission, *History of the North-Western Soldiers' Fair* (Chicago: Dunlop, Sewell & Spalding, 1864), though William Y. Thompson, "Sanitary Fairs of the Civil War" (*Civil War History* 4:1 (1958)) adds helpful background information. The auctioning of the Emancipation Proclamation is a fascinating tale best told by Harold Holzer in "America's Second Declaration of Independence: Lincoln's Emancipation Proclamation" (HistoryNet, November 8, 2012, accessed at www.historynet.com/americas-second-declaration-of -independence.htm).

The discussion of the work of Mary Livermore only touches on the broad range of duties women undertook during the war. Some of the sources for this include L.P.

Brockett and Mary C. Vaughan, *Women's Work in the Civil War: A Record of Heroism, Patriotism and Patience* (Chicago: Zeigler, McCurdy, 1867), Agatha Young, *The Women and the Crisis: Women of the North in the Civil War* (New York: McDowell, Obolensky, 1959), Nina Silber, *Daughters of the Union: Northern Women Fight the Civil War* (Cambridge, Mass.: Harvard Univ. Press, 2005), Mary Gardner Holland, *Our Army Nurses: Stories from Women in the Civil War* (Roseville, Minn.: Edinborough Press, 1998), and Jane E. Schultz, *Women at the Front: Hospital Workers in Civil War America* (Chapel Hill: Univ. of North Carolina Press, 2004).

SELECTED REFERENCES:

p. 90   "barely tolerated it" and "doubtful of its success": Livermore, *My Story of the War*, 412–413.

p. 91   "overbearing and unladylike": Venet, *A Strong-Minded Woman*, 111.

p. 93   "dying soldiers needed to be told": ibid., 92.

p. 94   block quotation: "they rifled their houses": Livermore, *My Story of the War*, 144.

p. 94   "My eyes were unsealed": ibid., 149.

p. 95   "mud, squalor, vermin, rags" to "arouse a moral earthquake": ibid., 288–289.

p. 97   "into all camps and hospitals": ibid., 504.

p. 97   "You're a cowardly calf!" to "And it ain't never me!": Baker, *Cyclone in Calico*, 144–151.

p. 98   "Northern white trash" to "gutter-snipes, drunken, ignorant": Livermore, *My Story of the War*, 291–292.

p. 100–02 "I never knew anyone" to "became a special *attachée*": ibid., 510–516.

p. 103   "All right, major, I'm arrested.": Baker, *Cyclone in Calico*, 178.

p. 103   "It was burned so full of holes": Livermore, *My Story of the War*, 520.

CHAPTER 6—DAMN YOUR OFFICERS

As in Chapter 2, John Logan's narrative is based on his collection of papers in the Library of Congress, along with the biographies by Byron Andrews, *A Biography of General John A. Logan, with an Account of His Public Services in Peace and in War*; Gary Ecelbarger, *Black Jack Logan: An Extraordinary Life in Peace and War*; James Pickett Jones, *Black Jack: John A. Logan and Southern Illinois in the Civil War Era*; and Mary Logan, *Reminiscences of a Soldier's Wife: An Autobiography*. William F.G. Shanks's *Personal Recollections of Distinguished Generals* (New York: Harper & Brothers, 1866) also offers valuable information on Logan's role in some of the major Georgia battles, while Charles Wolcott Balestier, *James G. Blaine: A Sketch of His Life, with a Brief Record of the Life of John A. Logan* (New York: R. Worthington, 1884) features an interesting short sketch of the general.

Mother Bickerdyke's story is drawn from Nina Brown Baker, *Cyclone in Calico*, and Julia A. Chase, *Mary A. Bickerdyke, "Mother,"* with additional details from Margaret B. Davis, *Mother Bickerdyke: Her Life and Labors for the Relief of Our Soldiers; Sketches of Battle Scenes and Incidents of the Sanitary Service* (San Francisco: A.T. Dewey, 1886), and Mary H. Porter's *Eliza Chappell Porter: A Memoir* (Chicago: Fleming H. Revell, 1892). Previously cited sources focus on the larger role of women in the Union campaigns:

Nina Silber, *Daughters of the Union*; Jane E. Schultz, *Women at the Front*; Judith Ann Giesberg, *Civil War Sisterhood*; and Agatha Young, *The Women and the Crisis*.

The broad scope of the Georgia campaign derives in part from the U.S. Army's official analysis of it, in J. Britt McCarley, *The Atlanta and Savannah Campaigns, 1864* (Washington, D.C.: Center of Military History, U.S. Army, 2014). Additional sources of documentation for the invasion include Lee Kennett, *Marching Through Georgia: The Story of Soldiers and Civilians During Sherman's Campaign* (New York: HarperPerennial, 1996); John F. Marszalek, *Sherman: A Soldier's Passion for Order*; Mark Hubbard, ed. *Illinois's War: The Civil War in Documents*; and the soldier's diary of John Hill Ferguson, *On to Atlanta* (Lincoln: Univ. of Nebraska Press, 2001). The sources for the details of specific battles include the Official Records of the War of the Rebellion, along with Philip L. Secrist, *The Battle of Resaca: Atlanta Campaign, 1864* (Macon, Ga.: Mercer Univ. Press, 2010); Earl J. Hess, *Kennesaw Mountain: Sherman, Johnston, and the Atlanta Campaign* (Chapel Hill: Univ. of North Carolina Press, 2013); and Daniel J. Vermilya, *The Battle of Kennesaw Mountain* (Charleston, S.C.: The History Press, 2014).

SELECTED REFERENCES:

p. 107   "I am glad you are here.": Chase, *Mary A. Bickerdyke*, 69.

p. 107   "My orderly is mortally wounded.": ibid., 71.

p. 108   block quotation: "I can never forget the terrible scene": Porter, *Eliza Chappell Porter*, 185.

p. 108   "are never eaten but by famished men": ibid., 199.

p. 109   "You've picked on the one person": Baker, *Cyclone in Calico*, 160.

p. 110   "beau idéal" to "small thing to die for him": Livermore, *My Story of the War*, 515.

p. 110   "would only result in useless slaughter": Andrews, *Biography of Gen. John A. Logan*, 460.

p. 110   "Our men are in good heart": Letter from John A. Logan to Mary Logan, June 26, 1864, quoted in Jones, *Black Jack*, 208.

p. 112   "Fall in! Forward!": Andrews, *Biography of Gen. John A. Logan*, 453.

p. 112   "looking like the very god of war" to "the biggest coward in the world": Woodworth, *Nothing but Victory*, 515.

p. 113   "Damn your regiments!": Andrews, *Biography of Gen. John A. Logan*, 454.

p. 113   "if I do not survive": Letter from John A. Logan to Mary Logan, May 23, 1864, quoted in Jones, *Black Jack*, 201.

p. 114   "If there was a man on earth": Letter from William Sherman to John Sherman, July 21, 1884, quoted in Marszalek, *A Soldier's Passion for Order*, 279.

p. 115   "Well, Mac, you have missed the opportunity": Ecelbarger, *Black Jack Logan*, 169.

p. 117   "I tell you he's nothing of the kind!": Virginia Clay-Clopton, *A Belle of the Fifties: Memoirs of Mrs. Clay, of Alabama* (London: Wm. Heinemann, 1905), 185.

p. 117   "hot and thick from an outraged heart": Balestier, *James G. Blaine*, 257.

p. 118   "wicked rebellion" to "put down the rebellion": Ecelbarger, *Black Jack Logan*, 128.

p. 118   block quotation: "If they call me an Abolitionist": "General John A. Logan at DuQuoin," *Illinois State Journal*, August 5, 1863, quoted in Ecelbarger, *Black Jack Logan*, 155.

p. 121   "Sherman is a strange man": Letter from John Logan to Mary Logan, July 16, 1864, quoted in Jones, *Black Jack*, 210–211.

p. 122   "never go to hell": Wills, *Army Life*, 256.

CHAPTER 7—THE WHEEL

Although recorded in the 1930s, when he was in his mid-80s, John McCline's memoir *Slavery in the Clover Bottoms* remains the essential source for its author's story. Because the book contains a few factual errors, some of its details have been checked against Dudley Taylor Cornish, *The Sable Arm: Black Troops in the Union Army, 1861–1865*; Noah Andre Trudeau, *Like Men of War: Black Troops in the Civil War, 1862–1865*; and Robert S. Davis Jr., "White and Black in Blue: The Recruitment of Federal Units in Civil War North Georgia" (*Georgia Historical Quarterly* 85:3 (2001), 347–374).

Charles Wills's *Army Life of an Illinois Soldier: The Letters and Diary of Charles W. Wills* describes the rise of the army captain, with Steven W. Woodworth's *Nothing but Victory: The Army of the Tennessee, 1861–1865* adding details on the arduous movement of that army from Mississippi to Chattanooga. General John Logan's battlefield exploits also feature prominently in that volume, along with Byron Andrews, *A Biography of General John A. Logan, with an Account of His Public*; George Francis Dawson, *Life and Services of Gen. John A. Logan, Soldier and Statesman*; Gary Ecelbarger, *Black Jack Logan: An Extraordinary Life in Peace and War*; and James Pickett Jones, *Black Jack: John A. Logan and Southern Illinois in the Civil War Era*. Many of Logan's activities are also detailed in the reports and letters contained in Series I, Volume XXXVIII, Parts I–III of the Official Records of the War of the Rebellion.

Those records are critical to understanding the logic of Sherman's Atlanta campaign, as are primary sources such as General Jacob D. Cox's *Atlanta: Campaigns of the Civil War IX* (New York: Charles Scribner's Sons: 1882), told from his perspective as an officer in the Army of the Ohio; the collectively written *The Story of the Fifty-Fifth Regiment Illinois Volunteer Infantry in the Civil War, 1861–1865* (Clinton, Mass.: W.J. Coulter, 1887); and John Hill Ferguson's diary, *On to Atlanta*. Contemporary, secondary references include the formal military analysis of Marlin G. Kime, "Sherman's Gordian Knot: Logistical Problems in the Atlanta Campaign" (*The Georgia Historical Quarterly* 70:1 (1986)); J. Britt McCarley, *The Atlanta and Savannah Campaigns, 1864*; and Herman Hattaway and Archer Jones, *How the North Won: A Military History of the Civil War*.

Many fine monographs of the battles of and around Atlanta have been published in recent years, the best of which include Gary Ecelbarger, *The Day Dixie Died: The Battle of Atlanta* (New York: St. Martin's Press, 2010), and Russell S. Bonds, *War Like the Thunderbolt: The Battle and Burning of Atlanta* (Yardley, Penn.: Westholme, 2009). The best overall look at those battles in the context of the larger invasion remains Albert Castel, *Decision in the West: The Atlanta Campaign of 1864* (Lawrence.: Univ. Press of Kansas, 1992). Some accounts of the terror wrought by the bombing of the city are drawn from Marc Wortman, *The Bonfire: The Siege and Burning of Atlanta* (New York:

PublicAffairs, 2009), and Stephen Davis, "A Very Barbarous Mode of Carrying on War: Sherman's Artillery Bombardment of Atlanta, July 20–August 24, 1864" (*The Georgia Historical Quarterly* 79:1 (1995)).

SELECTED REFERENCES:

p. 124   "I am now 105 miles from Chattanooga": Letter from William Sherman to Ellen Sherman, June 26, 1864, quoted in Howe, *Home Letters*, 298.

p. 127   "the most exciting show I ever saw": Wills, *Army Life*, 241.

p. 127   "with a yell the devil ought to copyright": ibid., 250.

p. 128   "I begin to regard the death and mangling": Letter from William Sherman to Ellen Sherman, June 30, 1864, quoted in Simpson and Berlin, *Sherman's Civil War*, 660.

p. 128   "I thank God from my heart": Wills, *Army Life*, 61.

p. 128   "only fit for turnips" and "reddish brown bug": ibid., 281–282.

p. 128   "general right wheel": Sherman, *Memoirs*, vol. 2, 71.

p. 133   "clubbed muskets, fisticuffs and wrestling": Ecelbarger, *The Day Dixie Died*, 143.

p. 134   "Are you going to kill all of us?" and "a great stream of grey": Bonds, *Thunderbolt*, 166.

p. 134   "Let the Army of the Tennessee fight it out": Castel, *Decision in the West*, 414.

p. 134   "on a coal-black charger": *The Story of the Fifty-Fifth Regiment Illinois Volunteer Infantry in the Civil War, 1861–1865* (Clinton, Mass.: W.J. Coulter, 1887), 341.

p. 134   "Black Jack! Black Jack!": Bonds, *Thunderbolt*, 169.

p. 134   "McPherson and revenge!": Mary Logan, *Reminiscences*, 158.

p. 136   "he is tractable" to "active politicians": Dawson, *Life and Services*, 517.

p. 136   "The army is a good school": Letter from William Sherman to John Sherman, December 29, 1863, quoted in Simpson and Berlin, *Sherman's Civil War*, 577.

p. 136   "Logan came dashing up" to "It's all right, damn it, isn't it?": Wills, *Army Life*, 251–252.

p. 137   "I think we'll like Howard": ibid., 289.

p. 137   "the Yankees had us like sittin' ducks" and "a perfect slaughter": Bonds, *Thunderbolt*, 198–199.

p. 137   "I am tired of seeing such butchery": Wills, *Army Life*, 287.

p. 138   "as much attributable to him": Sherman, *Memoirs*, vol. 2, 91.

p. 138   "infernal brute": Letter from John Logan to Mary Logan, August 6, 1864, quoted in Jones, *Black Jack*, 224.

p. 138–39   "extraordinary dreams" and "studying devilment": Wills, *Army Life*, 288–290.

p. 139   "circle of desolation": Sherman, *Memoirs*, vol. 2, 102.

p. 140   "a perfect hurricane of shot" and "more like a butchery": Bonds, *Thunderbolt*, 262.

p. 140   "lost a large measure of *vim*": Wills, *Army Life*, 295.

p. 140   "men acted like infuriated devils": Bonds, *Thunderbolt*, 270.

p. 141   "three hours more of daylight": Wills, *Army Life*, 297.

p. 141   "Logan! Logan!": Dawson, *Life and Services*, 81.

p. 141   "The marches and labors performed by you": Logan address to 15th Corps, September 11, 1864, quoted in Balestier, *James G. Blaine*, 488.

CHAPTER 8—THE ANVIL

The story of the 82nd Illinois—from experiencing debacles on the Eastern theater to triumphs in the West—easily merits its own full-length study, but only selected parts of its lengthy narrative can be presented here. One of the most fascinating figures in the regiment, Lieutenant Colonel Edward Salomon, is profiled in David Gleicher, "From Jewish Immigrant to Union General in Under Ten Years" (*Chicago Jewish History* 15:2 (1992)), and in the collectively written *Biographical Sketches of the Leading Men of Chicago* (Chicago: Wilson & St. Clair, 1868). Salomon's nemesis emerges vividly in Eric Benjaminson, "A Regiment of Immigrants: The 82nd Illinois Volunteer Infantry and the Letters of Captain Rudolph Mueller," as well as Joseph R. Reinhart, ed. *Yankee Dutchmen Under Fire: Civil War Letters from the 82nd Infantry.* The story of the departed colonel who founded the regiment is drawn from Sabine Freitag, *Friedrich Hecker: Two Lives for Liberty*, while Mark A. Dluger offers a wider view of the regiment in "A Regimental Community: The Men of the 82nd Illinois Infantry Before, During, and After the American Civil War." Wilhelm Kaufmann, *The Germans in the American Civil War*, is a general guide to the German American soldiers of the conflict.

The shelling of Atlanta was, and continues to be, one of the most contentious aspects of Sherman's campaign. Some of these perspectives are laid out in Stephen Davis, "'A Very Barbarous Mode of Carrying on War': Sherman's Artillery Bombardment of Atlanta, July 20–August 24, 1864"; Mark Grimsley, *The Hard Hand of War: Union Military Policy Toward Southern Civilians, 1861–1865*; and Marc Wortman, *The Bonfire: The Siege and Burning of Atlanta*. John Hight, in his *History of the Fifty-Eighth Regiment of Indiana Volunteer Infantry*, is reluctantly supportive of the action, but the regimental doctor, James Patten, offers a more critical view in Robert G. Athearn, "An Indiana Doctor Marches with Sherman: The Diary of James Comfort Patten" (*Indiana Magazine of History* 49:4 (1953)).

Along with Hight's own writings, useful sources on the role and rise of the U.S. Christian Commission in the Union army include Lemuel Moss, *Annals of the United States Christian Commission* (Philadelphia: J.B. Lippincott, 1868), and Annie Wittenmyer, *Under the Guns: A Woman's Reminiscences of the Civil War* (Boston: E.B. Stillings, 1895). For more on the work of the Christian Commission in opposition to the Sanitary Commission, see Jeanie Attie, *Patriotic Toil: Northern Women and the American Civil War*.

Anne J. Bailey puts Sherman's invasion of Georgia into the context of John Bell Hood's own Confederate moves and countermoves in *The Chessboard of War: Sherman and Hood in the Autumn Campaigns of 1864* (Lincoln: Univ. of Nebraska Press, 2000). Earlier noted accounts of the campaign include Russell S. Bonds, *War Like the Thunderbolt: The Battle and Burning of Atlanta*; Albert Castel, *Decision in the West: The Atlanta Campaign of 1864*; and Steven E. Woodworth, *Nothing but Victory: The Army of the Tennessee, 1861–1865*. Shelby Foote's *The Civil War: A Narrative, Red River to Appomattox* offers additional perspective including the Southern reaction to the campaign. Several volumes also provide insight into the destruction of Atlanta as a precursor to the March to the Sea, among them Lee Kennett, *Marching Through Georgia: The Story of Soldiers and Civilians During Sherman's Campaign*; J. Britt

REFERENCES

McCarley, *The Atlanta and Savannah Campaigns, 1864*; and the comprehensive and definitive volume by Noah Andre Trudeau, *Southern Storm: Sherman's March to the Sea* (New York: HarperCollins, 2008).

Lastly, for Sherman's own strategy for and his personal design of the Atlanta campaign, see John F. Marszalek, *Sherman: A Soldier's Passion for Order*; Sherman himself in *The Memoirs of William T. Sherman*, vol. 2; Brooks D. Simpson and Jean V. Berlin, eds. *Sherman's Civil War: Selected Correspondence of William T. Sherman, 1860–1865.*; and the general's various notes and reports included in the Official Records, Series I, Volumes XXXI, XXXII, and XXXVIII.

SELECTED REFERENCES:

p. 143 — "Atlanta is ours, and fairly won": Telegram from William Sherman to Henry Halleck, September 3, 1864, in Official Records, Series I, Volume XXXVIII, Part V, 777.

p. 144 — "were not intended to apply to [Hecker]": Court of Inquiry Records, Department of the Cumberland, January 23, 1864, in Official Records, Series I, Volume XXXI, Part I, 210.

p. 145 — "sycophantic loyalty" and "colossal impudence": Letter from Rudolph Mueller to Friedrich Hecker, August 13, 1864, quoted in Reinhart, *Yankee Dutchmen*, 148.

p. 145 — "the highest order of coolness and determination": *Biographical Sketches*, 392.

p. 146 — "He always keeps his cool": Benjaminson, "A Regiment of Immigrants," 159.

p. 146 — "the only soldier at Gettysburg who did not dodge": Dluger, "Regimental Community," 284.

p. 146 — "popularity-seeking blister": Letter from Rudolph Mueller to Friedrich Hecker, October 25, 1864, quoted in Reinhart, *Yankee Dutchmen*, 163.

p. 147 — "a miserable nation of shopkeepers": Benjaminson, "A Regiment of Immigrants," 175.

p. 148 — block quotation: "My dear colonel, I believe it is finally time": Letter from Rudolph Mueller to Friedrich Hecker, August 13, 1864, quoted in Reinhart, *Yankee Dutchmen*, 148.

p. 149 — "getting back home again": Hight, *History of the Fifty-Eighth Regiment*, 361.

p. 150 — "a sickening, loathsome sight" to "return to mother dust": ibid., 370.

p. 150 — "lean, lank, cadaverous people": ibid., 373.

p. 151 — "a little girl some six or seven years old": Athearn, "An Indiana Doctor," 409.

p. 151 — "the rich and great have fled": Hight, *History of the Fifty-Eighth Regiment*, 373.

p. 152 — "studied and ingenious cruelty": Letter from John Bell Hood to William Sherman, September 9, 1864, quoted in Sherman, *Memoirs*, vol. 2, 119.

p. 153 — "sometimes it seems that His Satanic Majesty": Hight, *History of the Fifty-Eighth Regiment*, 382.

p. 153 — "by this process the institution of slavery": Hight, Report to the Indiana Conference, August 22, 1863, quoted in Hight, *History of the Fifty-Eighth Regiment*, 565.

p. 153 — "Why does God permit these things?": Hight, *History of the Fifty-Eighth Regiment*, 391.

p. 154 — block quotation: "Slavery is a sin against man": ibid., 273.

p. 154 — "There is more need of gunpowder and oats": Moss, *Annals of the Christian Commission*, 496.

p. 154   "Rations and ammunition are much better": David P. Conyngham, *Sherman's March Through the South: Sketches and Incidents of the Campaign* (New York: Sheldon, 1865), 76.

p. 155   "Long may the Christian Commission flourish": Hight, *History of the Fifty-Eighth Regiment*, 252.

p. 156   "if we can't subdue these rebels": Wills, *Army Life*, 292.

p. 156   "in the midst of peace and prosperity": Letter from William Sherman to John Bell Hood, September 10, 1864, quoted in Sherman, *Memoirs*, vol. 2, 120.

p. 156   "If the people raise a howl": Telegram from William Sherman to Henry Halleck, September 4, 1864, in Official Records, Series I, Volume XXXVIII, Part V, 794.

p. 156   "Meridian, with its depots, store-houses, arsenal": Report to J.A. Rawlins from William Sherman, March 7, 1864, in Official Records, Series I, Volume XXXII, Part I, 176.

p. 158   "Kill every damn one of them!": Bailey, *Chessboard of War*, 36.

p. 158   "the men of the army were in favor of hanging": *Charleston Mercury*, October 24, 1864, quoted in Bailey, *Chessboard of War*, 38.

p. 158   "not the equal of the white man": Letter from William Sherman to John A. Spooner, in Official Records, Series I, Volume XXXVIII, Part V, 306.

p. 158   block quotation: "No one shall infer from this": ibid.

p. 159   "May I ask, therefore, that you will give your hearty co-operation?": Telegram from Abraham Lincoln to William Sherman, July 18, 1864, in Official Records, Series I, Volume XXXVIII, Part V, 169.

p. 159   "whole batch of devils": Telegram from William Sherman to Ulysses S. Grant, October 9, 1864, quoted in Sherman, *Memoirs*, vol. 2, 152.

p. 161   "misstep by General Sherman might be fatal": Telegram from Edwin Stanton to Ulysses S. Grant, October 12, 1864, in Official Records, Series I, Volume XXXIX, Part III, 222.

p. 161   "It is a ridiculous farce to be voting at all": Letter from William Sherman to John Sherman, October 11, 1864, quoted in Simpson and Berlin, *Sherman's Civil War*, 733.

p. 161   "Grant Sheridan & I are now the popular favorites": Letter from William Sherman to Ellen Sherman, October 27, 1864, quoted in Simpson and Berlin, *Sherman's Civil War*, 743.

p. 161   "I can make the march and make Georgia howl": Telegram from William Sherman to Ulysses S. Grant, October 9, 1864, in Official Records, Series I, Volume XXXIX, Part III, 162.

CHAPTER 9—SHADOWY TERRITORY

John Logan's papers in the Library of Congress give some sense of his mission during the fall of 1864—militarily, as well as politically. Since he withdraws into the civilian world during this period, the Official Records of the War of the Rebellion are of little help tracing his actions. The standard biographies fill in the gaps: Byron Andrews, *A Biography of General John A. Logan, with an Account of His Public Services in Peace and in War*; George Francis Dawson, *Life and Services of Gen. John A. Logan, Soldier and Statesman*; Gary Ecelbarger, *Black Jack Logan: An Extraordinary Life in Peace and War*; and James Pickett Jones, *Black Jack: John A. Logan and Southern Illinois in the Civil War Era*. Mary Logan's *Reminiscences of a Soldier's Wife: An Autobiography* is also valuable for its depiction of Logan's electioneering and his life on the home front. John N. Dickinson's "The Civil War Years of John Alexander Logan" (*Journal of the Illinois State Historical Society* 56:2 (1963), 212–232) is a helpful summary of the general's wartime career.

Logan's politicking and speechmaking at this time were in proximity to Mary Livermore's own public speeches and appeals for donations to the Sanitary Commission. These episodes are vividly described in her *My Story of the War: A Woman's Narrative of Four Years*, with Wendy Hamand Venet's *A Strong-Minded Woman: The Life of Mary A. Livermore* as a useful adjunct. Also engaging, with a contemporaneous perspective, is Jane Hoge's *The Boys in Blue; or, Heroes of the "Rank and File,"* which details the considerable work Livermore and Hoge as assistant managers did for the commission.

For a broader look at the organization's role in the context of the invasion of the South, this chapter draws from William W. Patton, "The Sanitary Commission in the Army" (*The Sanitary Reporter* 2:17 (Jan. 15, 1865), 129–130), and Sarah Edwards Henshaw, *Our Branch and Its Tributaries*. Modern references include Judith Ann Giesberg, *Civil War Sisterhood: The U.S. Sanitary Commission and Women's Politics in Transition*; Nina Silber, *Daughters of the Union: Northern Women Fight the Civil War*; Jeanie Attie, "'A Swindling Concern': The United States Sanitary Commission and the Northern Female Public, 1861–1865"; and the latter author's *Patriotic Toil: Northern Women and the American Civil War*.

Nina Brown Baker's *Cyclone in Calico* is the most comprehensive source for the wartime actions of Mary Ann Bickerdyke—though the other aspects of her life are best explored through her family papers at the Library of Congress. Mary H. Porter follows the tumultuous narrative of Bickerdyke's associate in *Eliza Chappell Porter: A Memoir* (Chicago: Fleming H. Revell, 1892), while Julia A. Houghton Chase, in *Mary A. Bickerdyke, "Mother,"* and Margaret B. Davis, in *Mother Bickerdyke: Her Life and Labors for the Relief of Our Soldiers*, round out the stories of Bickerdyke's efforts during the war.

The Official Records are by far the best primary source for the actions and movements of Sherman's armies prior to the March to the Sea, along with the general's own writings in Brooks D. Simpson and Jean V. Berlin, eds., *Sherman's Civil War: Selected Correspondence of William T. Sherman, 1860–1865*, while the military analysis of J. Britt McCarley, *The Atlanta and Savannah Campaigns, 1864*, provides a clear view of the logistics and strategy involved. As supplementary sources, there are several volumes that offer contrasting views of the morality and efficacy of Sherman's campaigns. These include John F. Marszalek, *Sherman: A Soldier's Passion for Order*; Anne J. Bailey, *The Chessboard of War: Sherman and Hood in the Autumn Campaigns of 1864*; Noah Andre Trudeau, *Southern Storm: Sherman's March to the Sea*; and Steven E. Woodworth, *Nothing but Victory: The Army of the Tennessee, 1861–1865*.

The destruction of Atlanta is an oft-told story that has figured prominently in the narratives of postwar Southern writers wishing to depict Sherman as a demon. This volume draws on critical views of the conflagration—Marc Wortman, *The Bonfire: The Siege and Burning of Atlanta*; Russell S. Bonds, *War Like the Thunderbolt: The Battle and Burning of Atlanta*; Lee Kennett, *Marching Through Georgia: The Story of Soldiers and Civilians During Sherman's Campaign*—as well as the perspective of Union soldiers in the letters and journals mentioned in earlier chapters. One of the best views from the Union side is by Sherman's aide Henry Hitchcock, whose diary entries published as *Marching with Sherman* (New Haven, Conn.: Yale Univ. Press, 1927) cover not only the demise of Atlanta in mid-November 1864, but several north Georgia towns as well that were immolated in the days before.

SELECTED REFERENCES:

p. 163   "The scenes through which he had passed": Mary Logan, *Reminiscences*, 174.

p. 163   "sympathize with infamous and damnable treason" and "preserving the Union": Jones, *Black Jack*, 234–235.

p. 164   "kill the last rebel—Jeff Davis himself": Ecelbarger, *Black Jack Logan*, 191.

p. 164   "I am willing to subjugate, burn" and "a greater traitor and humbug": Jones, *Black Jack*, 236–237.

p. 164   "in grotesque uniforms" and "we were constantly vibrating": Mary Logan, *Reminiscences*, 180.

p. 166   "glorious triumph over Copperheadism": Jones, *Black Jack*, 239.

p. 166   "It is not possible to overtake your command": Telegram from R.M. Sawyer (on behalf of William Sherman) to John Logan, November 15, 1864, Official Records, Series I, Volume XLIV, 465.

p. 168   block quotation: "I concentrated my mind": Livermore, *My Story of the War*, 608.

p. 169   "destitution, sickness, and suffering": ibid.

p. 169   "codfish and sauer-kraut" to "every imaginable errand": ibid., 156.

p. 170   "draw a thousand dollars" and "scarcely raise a finger": Venet, *Strong-Minded Woman*, 111.

p. 171   "I am sorry to say" to "Was that *Christian*?": William Patton, "The Sanitary Commission," in *The Sanitary Reporter*, January 15, 1865, 2.

p. 172   "pretending friendliness while all the while": Venet, *Strong-Minded Woman*, 93.

p. 174   "Mother Bickerdyke's circus": Baker, *Cyclone in Calico*, 193.

p. 174   "I want you to take that, and put it under lock and key": Henshaw, *Our Branch*, 268.

p. 176   "This Government is now Entering upon a new policy": Kennett, *Marching Through Georgia*, 232.

p. 176   "no houses, no fences": ibid., 233.

p. 176   "I never ordered burning of any dwelling": Hitchcock, *Marching with Sherman*, 53.

p. 177   "Until we can repopulate Georgia": Telegram from William Sherman to Ulysses S. Grant, October 9, 1864, in Official Records, Series I, Volume XXXIX, Part III, 162.

p. 177   "live long and take poor Willy's place": Letter from William Sherman to Maria Boyle and Mary Elizabeth Sherman, November 9, 1864, quoted in Simpson and Berlin, *Sherman's Civil War*, 754.

p. 177   "Willy will never meet us again in this world": Letter from William Sherman to
          Thomas Sherman, November 10, 1864, quoted in Simpson and Berlin, *Sherman's
          Civil War*, 756.

p. 178   "expecting to live chiefly on the country": Telegram from William Sherman to
          George Thomas, November 11, 1864, in Official Records, Series I, Volume XXXIX,
          Part III, 747.

p. 178   "Write no more till you hear of me": Letter from William Sherman to Ellen Sherman,
          November 12, 1864, quoted in Simpson and Berlin, *Sherman's Civil War*, 758.

CHAPTER 10—COMRADES IN DIRT

The March to the Sea attracted considerable national attention once its significance became understood, during and after the war. Although numerous news accounts provided fragmentary views of the march, the best accounts were from the soldiers who participated in it, in the form of journal entries and letters home. Some of the most vivid narratives of the activity of the left wing of Sherman's forces include *Three Years in the Army of the Cumberland: The Letters and Diary of James A. Connolly*, Paul M. Angle, ed. (Bloomington: Indiana Univ. Press, 1959); "The John Van Duser Diary of Sherman's March from Atlanta to Hilton Head," Charles J. Brockman, ed. (*The Georgia Historical Quarterly* 53:2 (1969), 220–240); Manning Ferguson Force, "From Atlanta to Savannah: The Civil War Journal of Manning F. Force, November 15, 1864–January 3, 1865" (*The Georgia Historical Quarterly* 91:2 (2007), 185–205); and Charles D. Kerr, "From Atlanta to Raleigh," in *Glimpses of the Nation's Struggle* (St. Paul, Minn.: St. Paul Book and Stationery Company, 1887). The aides George Ward Nichols, in *The Story of the Great March, from the Diary of a Staff Officer* (New York: Harper & Brothers, 1865), and Henry Hitchcock, in *Marching with Sherman*, also offer a useful perspective on their commanders who led the sometimes wayward troops on the march. Other essential writings include David P. Conyngham, *Sherman's March Through the South: Sketches and Incidents of the Campaign* (New York: Sheldon, 1865), and "Sherman's March: Journal of an Eye-Witness" (*The New York Times*, December 23, 1864).

Modern descriptions of the March to the Sea provide more context on the trek, but do not resolve its controversies. Some of the more salient contemporary views include James C. Bonner, "Sherman at Milledgeville in 1864" (*The Journal of Southern History* 22:3 (1956), 273–291); D.J. De Laubenfels, "Where Sherman Passed By" (*Geographical Review* 47:3 (1957), 381–395); Bruce Levine, *The Fall of the House of Dixie: The Civil War and the Social Revolution That Transformed the South* (New York: Random House, 2013); and the thoroughly engaging volume by Joseph T. Glatthaar, *The March to the Sea and Beyond: Sherman's Troops in the Savannah and Carolinas Campaigns* (New York: New York Univ. Press, 1985). Previously cited works include Mark Grimsley, *The Hard Hand of War: Union Military Policy Toward Southern Civilians, 1861–1865*; Burke Davis, *Sherman's March*; Lee Kennett, *Marching Through Georgia: The Story of Soldiers and Civilians During Sherman's Campaign*; Noah Andre Trudeau, *Southern Storm: Sherman's March to the Sea*; and J. Britt McCarley, *The Atlanta and Savannah Campaigns, 1864*. Also illuminating is

John F. Marszalek, *Sherman: A Soldier's Passion for Order*, for the commanding general's strategy and design of the march.

Even more controversial than William Sherman is Union general Jefferson C. Davis, whose actions still inspire debate more than 150 years later. Some of these varying perspectives are laid out in Nathaniel Cheairs Hughes Jr. and Gordon D. Whitney, *Jefferson Davis in Blue: The Life of Sherman's Relentless Warrior* (Baton Rouge: Louisiana State Univ. Press, 2002), and James P. Jones, "General Jeff C. Davis, U.S.A. and Sherman's Georgia Campaign" (*The Georgia Historical Quarterly* 47:3 (1963), 231–248). The most critical view of Davis continues to be that of Reverend John Hight, in his *History of the Fifty-Eighth Regiment of Indiana Volunteer Infantry*, which provides a searing portrait of the general and a sober perspective on the march generally.

John McCline's escape from slavery provides a fitting background to his narrative of the March to the Sea, in *Slavery in the Clover Bottoms: John McCline's Narrative of His Life During Slavery and the Civil War*. A more localized view of slavery in Georgia is offered by several contemporary sources, largely drawn from individual wartime accounts and factual analyses: Edmund L. Drago, "How Sherman's March Through Georgia Affected the Slaves" (*The Georgia Historical Quarterly* 57:3 (1973), 361–375); Carole Emberton, "A Hungry Belly and Freedom" (accessed at We're History, November 25, 2014, werehistory.org/hungry-belly-and-freedom/); Clarence L. Mohr, "Before Sherman: Georgia Blacks and the Union War Effort" (*The Journal of Southern History* 45:3 (1979), 331–352); and Paul D. Escott, "The Context of Freedom: Georgia's Slaves During the Civil War" (*The Georgia Historical Quarterly* 58:1 (1974), 79–104). James M. Guthrie, *Camp-Fires of the Afro-American, or, The Colored Man as a Patriot* (Philadelphia: Afro-American Publishing, 1899) is also a useful historical resource on this aspect of the march.

The Official Records provide a helpful, if limited, view of the activity of immigrant regiments during the march, notably German American units. For additional detail, see Eric Benjaminson, "A Regiment of Immigrants: The 82nd Illinois Volunteer Infantry and the Letters of Captain Rudolph Mueller"; Mark A. Dluger, "A Regimental Community: The Men of the 82nd Illinois Infantry Before, During, and After the American Civil War"; and Joseph R. Reinhart, ed. *Yankee Dutchmen Under Fire: Civil War Letters from the 82nd Infantry*.

SELECTED REFERENCES:

p. 182   "Our men helped themselves to anything": Hight, *History of the Fifty-Eighth Regiment*, 416.

p. 182   "The timbers begin to tumble": ibid., 405.

p. 182   "there is no sense making war on women and children": ibid., 318.

p. 182   "May all such villains die the same death" to "liberty is sweet": ibid., 416–419.

p. 185   "forage liberally on the country": Special Field Order No. 120, L.M. Dayton (by order of William Sherman), November 9, 1864, in Official Records, Series I, Volume XXXIX, Part III, 713.

p. 186   "A planter's house was overrun in a jiffy": Conyngham, *Sherman's March Through the South*, 269.

p. 186   "a rich southern planter—a rank rebel" to "tear down their houses": Hight, *History of the Fifty-Eighth Regiment*, 391.

p. 187   "miserable hovels": ibid., 422.

p. 187   "state of terrorism": Conyngham, *Sherman's March Through the South*, 271.

p. 187   "to burn and destroy everything in his front": Nichols, *The Story of the Great March*, 30–31.

p. 187   "Everything that can be, is being destroyed": Hight, *History of the Fifty-Eighth Regiment*, 422.

p. 189   "Well, you are nearly big enough to carry a gun" to "a real sensation": McCline, *Slavery in the Clover Bottoms*, 93.

p. 191   "downright shame" to "destroyed and plundered": Connolly, *Three Years*, 318–319.

p. 193   "a hell of a damned fool" and "I want just that sort of man": Davis, *Sherman's March*, 70.

p. 193   "have become lawless to an alarming extent" to "The citizens of Georgia have more animosity": Glatthaar, *March to the Sea and Beyond*, 152.

p. 195   "He has been a pro-slavery man": Hight, *History of the Fifty-Eighth Regiment*, 415.

p. 195   "a military tyrant, without one spark of humanity": ibid., 426.

p. 196   "Many of our new men are Germans": ibid., 398

p. 197   "[we] got so dirty, we looked like coal burners": Dluger, "Regimental Community," 352.

p. 198   "frightened hare" and "back has grown quite bent": Benjaminson, "Regiment of Immigrants," 167.

p. 198   "raggedness and uncleanliness of apparel": Letter from Frederick Winkler to his wife, December 19, 1864, quoted in Glatthaar, *March to the Sea and Beyond*, 32.

p. 198   "more like an armed rabble than an army": Glatthaar, *March to the Sea and Beyond*, 32.

p. 199   "These two nights marching, groping through the woods": Manning Force, journal entry of November 20, 1864, quoted in Force, "From Atlanta to Savannah," 187.

p. 200   "It is getting to be a dangerous business to forage" to "a cry of agony": Hight, *History of the Fifty-Eighth Regiment*, 426–427.

p. 202   "Some of them at once plunged into the water" and "disgraceful to American history," ibid.

CHAPTER 11—ALL AROUND THEM LIGHT AS DAY

The progress of Sherman's right wing on the March to the Sea is a subject that has captured comparatively less attention than the movements of the left wing farther north. However, soldiers of the 15th and 17th Corps kept numerous diaries and journals and wrote countless letters home that together offer a vivid picture of this half of the invading force. The more engaging and useful of these sources are F.Y. Hedley, *Marching Through Georgia: Pen-Pictures of Every-Day Life in General Sherman's Army, from the Beginning of the Atlanta Campaign Until the Close of the War*; Theodore F. Upson, *With Sherman to the Sea* (Baton Rouge: Louisiana Univ. Press, 1943); Matthew H. Jamison, *Recollections of Pioneer and Army Life* (Kansas City, Mo.: Hudson Press, 1911); George Sharland, *Knapsack Notes of General Sherman's Grand Campaign Through the Empire State of the South* (Springfield, Ill.: Johnson & Bradford, 1865); D. Leib. Ambrose, *History of the Seventh*

Regiment Illinois Volunteer Infantry (Springfield: Illinois Journal Company, 1868); Samuel H. Hurst, *Journal-History of the 73rd Ohio Volunteer Infantry* (Chillicothe, Ohio, 1866); and Alexander G. Downing, *Downing's Civil War Diary, August 15, 1861–July 31, 1865*, ed. Olynthus B. Clark (Des Moines: The Historical Department of Iowa, 1916).

Charles W. Wills's own letters and diary entries in *Army Life of an Illinois Soldier: The Letters and Diary of Charles W. Wills*, are particularly compelling, since his unit was one of the few to participate in the only inland infantry battle of the March, Griswoldville. For additional context, Steven E. Woodworth's *Nothing but Victory: The Army of the Tennessee, 1861–1865*, is a useful supplemental source, as is the work of F. Edward Schwabe Jr. in *The March to the Sea: The Operational Role of Sherman's Right Wing* (Newport, R.I.: Naval War College, 1986), which is an obscure but invaluable analysis of the mission and purpose of this part of Sherman's force.

Although this chapter principally concerns the right wing, several previously cited works offer context on the comparable activities of the left wing: Charles J. Brockman Jr., ed., "The John Van Duser Diary of Sherman's March from Atlanta to Hilton Head"; James A. Connolly, *Three Years in the Army of the Cumberland: The Letters and Diary of James A. Connolly*; Charles D. Kerr, "From Atlanta to Raleigh," in *Glimpses of the Nation's Struggle*; and George Ward Nichols, *The Story of the Great March, from the Diary of a Staff Officer.* Adin Underwood's *The Three Years' Service of the Thirty-Third Mass. Infantry Regiment, 1862–1865* (Boston: A. Williams, 1881) also provides eye-opening anecdotes about the march, as does David P. Conyngham, *Sherman's March Through the South: Sketches and Incidents of the Campaign*, and the article "Sherman's March: Journal of an Eye-Witness" in *The New York Times*, December 23, 1864.

Other works that draw a broader picture of the march through the Georgia heartland include Joseph T. Glatthaar, *The March to the Sea and Beyond: Sherman's Troops in the Savannah and Carolinas Campaigns*; Anne J. Bailey, *The Chessboard of War: Sherman and Hood in the Autumn Campaigns of 1864*; Lee Kennett, *Marching Through Georgia: The Story of Soldiers and Civilians During Sherman's Campaign*; Noah Andre Trudeau, *Southern Storm: Sherman's March to the Sea*; and Debra Reddin Van Tuyll, "Scalawags and Scoundrels? The Moral and Legal Dimensions of Sherman's Last Campaigns."

The mass escape of enslaved peoples is another aspect of this part of the March that was among its most significant legacies. Some perspective on this movement is offered by Edmund L. Drago, "How Sherman's March Through Georgia Affected the Slaves" (*The Georgia Historical Quarterly* 57:3 (1973), 361v375); Paul D. Escott, "The Context of Freedom: Georgia's Slaves During the Civil War" (*The Georgia Historical Quarterly* 58:1 (1974), 79v104); and Clarence L. Mohr, "Before Sherman: Georgia Blacks and the Union War Effort" (*The Journal of Southern History* 45:3 (1979), 331–352). The activity of destitute whites in the invasion path is drawn in part from Stephen V. Ash, "Poor Whites in the Occupied South" (*The Journal of Southern History* 57:1 (1991), 39–62).

As regards the commander of the March, several volumes offer insight into the strategy and mind-set of William Sherman as he executed his campaign. Among these are Michael Fellman, *Citizen Sherman: A Life of William Tecumseh Sherman*; Henry Hitchcock, *Marching with Sherman*; John F. Marszalek, *Sherman: A Soldier's Passion for*

Order; and the general himself in *The Memoirs of William T. Sherman*, vol. 2, along with his assorted reports that appear in the Official Records (though nearly all of these were written well after the March concluded). For a look at Sherman's favored cavalry general, in all his unexpected success and depravity, Samuel J. Martin's *Kill-Cavalry: The Life of Union General Hugh Judson Kilpatrick* (Mechanicsburg, Pa.: Stackpole Books, 2000) is one of the few significant works on the commander, along with James Moore's less worthwhile *Kilpatrick and Our Cavalry* (New York: W.J. Widdleton, 1865).

SELECTED REFERENCES:

p. 203   "It was the richest thing I ever saw": Wills, *Army Life*, 322.

p. 204   "the most gigantic pleasure excursion ever planned" to "By the kindness of Mrs. Elizabeth Celia Pye": ibid., 320–321.

p. 204   "a fine line of Johnnies": ibid., 323.

p. 205   "our guns got so hot they burned our hands": Trudeau, *Southern Storm*, 209.

p. 205   "one after another their lines crumbled" to "old grey-haired and weakly-looking men": Wills, *Army Life*, 323–324.

p. 206   "harvest of death" and "My entire neighborhood is ruined": Trudeau, *Southern Storm*, 212–213.

p. 206   "It was awful the way we slaughtered those men" to "I hope we will never have to shoot": Wills, *Army Life*, 323–324.

p. 207   "women & children were frightened entirely": Trudeau, *Southern Storm*, 258.

p. 208   "In war everything is right which prevents anything": Hitchcock, *Marching with Sherman*, 92.

p. 209   "powerful fast knitter": ibid., 89.

p. 210   "the perfection of campaigning" to "varied, quick, original, shrewd": ibid., 110.

p. 212   "He is proverbially the most restless man in the army": ibid., 112–113.

p. 212   "I am bound to say I think Sherman lacking in discipline": ibid., 86–87.

p. 213   "foragers came in loaded down" to "some brother rascals were pounding music": Underwood, *Three Years' Service*, 249.

p. 213   "I lose my temper . . . and make pretty free use": Letter from Orlando M. Poe to Richard Delafield, October 8, 1865.

p. 214   "I have been three years fighting stragglers": Hitchcock, *Marching with Sherman*, 75.

p. 214   "you may hang and mutilate man for man": Telegram from L.M. Dayton (by order of William Sherman) to Hugh Kilpatrick, December 1, 1864, in Official Records, Series I, Volume XLIV, 271.

p. 214   "For the past year there has seemed to be a cloud": Kennett, *Marching Through Georgia*, 271.

p. 215   "awfully depraved": Wills, *Army Life*, 136.

p. 215   "have committed more devilment": ibid., 209.

p. 216   "a charming girl" and "another romantic meeting": ibid. 325.

p. 217   "awful pine forest, hardly broken by fence or clearing": ibid., 328.

p. 217   "Columns of smoke by day, and 'pillars of fire' by night": Connolly, *Three Years*, 314.

p. 217   "two walls of fire . . . extending as far as the eye could reach": Underwood, *Three Years' Service*, 248.

p. 217–18   "an immense number of 'contrabands'" to "bruised her shamefully": Wills, *Army Life*, 330–332.

p. 218   "Don't want white man" to "Go when you like": Hitchcock, *Marching with Sherman*, 66–67.

p. 219   "stocks, iron collars with chains on them": Upson, *With Sherman to the Sea*, 135.

p. 220   "If the negroes on the place told stories": Hedley, *Marching Through Georgia*, 270.

p. 220   "blasted and debased and damned": Hurst, *Journal-History of the 73rd Ohio*, 156.

p. 220   "The slaves universally were the prisoners' friends": S.H.M. Byers, *With Fire and Sword* (New York: Neale Publishing, 1911).

p. 221   "miserable hovels, hardly fit for swine to live in": Bailey, *Chessboard of War*, 114.

p. 221   "this scene of suffering cruelty and murder": Glatthaar, *The March to the Sea and Beyond*, 77.

p. 221   "We burned everything here": Downing, *Civil War Diary*, 234.

CHAPTER 12—YELL LIKE THE DEVIL

Some of the clearest and most vivid writing of the end stage of Sherman's March to the Sea comes from soldiers' letters and diaries. The critical sources for providing a firsthand view include the following: Charles J. Brockman Jr., ed., "The John Van Duser Diary of Sherman's March from Atlanta to Hilton Head"; Charles D. Kerr, "From Atlanta to Raleigh," in *Glimpses of the Nation's Struggle*; Henry Hitchcock, *Marching with Sherman*; George Ward Nichols, *The Story of the Great March, from the Diary of a Staff Officer*; George Sharland, *Knapsack Notes of General Sherman's Grand Campaign Through the Empire State of the South*; and Matthew H. Jamison, *Recollections of Pioneer and Army Life*. Further context is provided by reporters who traveled with the army, including David P. Conyngham, *Sherman's March Through the South: Sketches and Incidents of the Campaign*, and "Sherman's March: Journal of an Eye-Witness," *The New York Times*, December 23, 1864.

Some of the aforementioned references also offer a close view of the attack on Fort McAllister, which prompted all manner of news and magazine articles in the weeks after, though the perspective of the soldiers involved tends to remain the most accurate. General William B. Hazen, for one, who oversaw the attack, provides a ground-view look at this and other events in *A Narrative of Military Service* (Boston: Ticknor, 1885), while Sherman himself, in the article "Old Shady, with a Moral" (*North American Review* 147:383 (1888), 361–368), gives a brief glimpse of his own actions during the event. Other volumes such as the general's *Memoirs of William T. Sherman*, vol. 2, and John F. Marszalek, *Sherman: A Soldier's Passion for Order*, are also helpful in giving a sense of the strategy behind the attack. For a more current perspective, William E. Strong, "The Capture of Fort McAllister, December 13, 1864" (*The Georgia Historical Quarterly* 88:3 (2004), 406–421), offers a good analysis and summary.

The other significant event in the chapter, the tragedy at Ebenezer Creek, became more widely known after the March to the Sea had concluded. Some of the better firsthand accounts include James A. Connolly, *Three Years in the Army of the Cumberland: The Letters and Diary of James A. Connolly*; Charles D. Kerr, "From Atlanta to Raleigh"; Robert G. Athearn, "An Indiana Doctor Marches with Sherman: The Diary of James Comfort Patten" (*Indiana Magazine of History* 49:4 (1953)); and John Hight's *History of the Fifty-Eighth Regiment of Indiana Volunteer Infantry*. The actions of Jefferson C. Davis are further drawn from Nathaniel Cheairs Hughes Jr. and Gordon D. Whitney, *Jefferson Davis in Blue: The Life of Sherman's Relentless Warrior*, and James P. Jones, "General Jeff C. Davis, U.S.A. and Sherman's Georgia Campaign."

Other characters' stories in this chapter are derived from their own narratives: John McCline in *Slavery in the Clover Bottoms: John McCline's Narrative of His Life During Slavery and the Civil War*, and the Germans of the 82nd Illinois in Eric Benjaminson, "A Regiment of Immigrants: The 82nd Illinois Volunteer Infantry and the Letters of Captain Rudolph Mueller" and Joseph R. Reinhart, ed., *Yankee Dutchmen Under Fire: Civil War Letters from the 82nd Infantry*. Mark A. Dluger, in "A Regimental Community: The Men of the 82nd Illinois Infantry Before, During, and After the American Civil War," offers a definitive account of the unit.

Several contemporary works are also useful for illuminating the actions and controversies of the last phase of the March to the Sea. These include Joseph T. Glatthaar, *The March to the Sea and Beyond: Sherman's Troops in the Savannah and Carolinas Campaigns*; Lee Kennett, *Marching Through Georgia: The Story of Soldiers and Civilians During Sherman's Campaign*; Noah Andre Trudeau, *Southern Storm: Sherman's March to the Sea*; Steven E. Woodworth, *Nothing but Victory: The Army of the Tennessee, 1861–1865*; and J. Britt McCarley, *The Atlanta and Savannah Campaigns, 1864*. One of the rare volumes to describe the logistical importance of the right wing in the march, and the way it determined the success of the operation, is F. Edward Schwabe Jr., *The March to the Sea: The Operational Role of Sherman's Right Wing*, whose insights cannot be underestimated.

SELECTED REFERENCES:

p. 226   "It was an amazing sight": McCline, *Slavery in the Clover Bottoms*, 95.

p. 226   "and we resolved, each for himself": Hight, *History of the Fifty-Eighth Regiment*, 431.

p. 227   "Useless negroes are being accumulated": Telegram from A.C. McClurg (by order of Jefferson C. Davis), General Order No. 22, November 20, 1864, in Official Records, Series I, Volume XLIV, 502.

p. 228   "the most gloomy, dismal cypress swamp I ever saw": Connolly, *Three Years*, 353.

p. 228   "The idea of five or six hundred black women": ibid., 354–355.

p. 229   "I cannot find words to express my detestation": Hight, *History of the Fifty-Eighth Regiment*, 432.

p. 230   "It was unjustifiable and perfidious": Kerr, "From Atlanta to Raleigh," 216.

p. 230   "If I had the power I would [hang] him as high as Haman": Patten, "An Indiana Doctor Marches," 419.

p. 231   "almost all the horses we had when we left": Hight, *History of the Fifty-Eighth Regiment*, 434.

p. 232   "slumbering but revenge-seeking lion" to "good order and discipline": Letter from
          Rudolf Mueller to Friedrich Hecker, December 19, 1864, in Reinhart, *Yankee*
          Dutchmen, 168.

p. 233   "I know full well that General Thomas is slow in mind and in action": Telegram
          from William Sherman to Ulysses S. Grant, December 16, 1864, in Official
          Records, Series I, Volume XLIV, 728.

p. 234   "This was not war, but murder": Sherman, *Memoirs*, vol. 2, 194.

p. 234   "quietly going ahead on foot without a word to anybody": Hitchcock, *Marching with*
          Sherman, 163.

p. 235   "This place is not safe, they are firing down the road": ibid., 170.

p. 238   "Get to the rear, George": Trudeau, *Southern Storm*, 438.

p. 238   "Take a good big drink, a long breath, and then yell like the devil.": Telegram from
          L.M. Dayton (by order of William Sherman) to Henry Slocum, December 13, 1864,
          in Official Records, Series I, Volume XLIV, 704.

p. 239   "He looked at me hard to discover the horns" to "Yes, the game is up": Sherman,
          "Old Shady," 368.

CHAPTER 13—SENTINELS

William Sherman's March to the Sea and occupation of Savannah were the pinnacle of his military career. This period is colorfully detailed in Stanley Weintraub, *General Sherman's Christmas: Savannah, 1864* (New York: HarperCollins, 2009). The Northern reaction to the conditions its soldiers found in Savannah is drawn from John P. Dyer, "Northern Relief for Savannah During Sherman's Occupation" (*The Journal of Southern History* 19:4 (1953), 457–472), while the condition of black refugees is detailed in William A. Byrne, "'Uncle Billy' Sherman Comes to Town: The Free Winter of Black Savannah" (*The Georgia Historical Quarterly* 79:1 (1995), 91–116), and Edmund L. Drago, "How Sherman's March Through Georgia Affected the Slaves."

The depredations of cavalry general Hugh Kilpatrick were many, and affected white and black Southerners alike. Descriptions of his terrible adventures are drawn from Dylan Penningroth, "Slavery, Freedom, and Social Claims to Property Among African Americans in Liberty County, Georgia, 1850–1880" (*The Journal of American History* 84:2 (1997), 405–435); George A. Rogers and R.F. Saunders, "The Scourge of Sherman's Men in Liberty County, Georgia" (*The Georgia Historical Quarterly* 60:4 (1976), 356–369); and Samuel J. Martin, *Kill-Cavalry: The Life of Union General Hugh Judson Kilpatrick.*

The presence and status of black soldiers in occupied Savannah was a topic of controversy at the time, and is detailed in John David Smith, ed., *Black Soldiers in Blue: African American Troops in the Civil War Era*, and Noah Andre Trudeau, *Like Men of War: Black Troops in the Civil War, 1862–1865.* The tragedy of Ebenezer Creek is based on contemporaneous accounts, official records, and later discussions, including James A. Connolly, *Three Years in the Army of the Cumberland: The Letters and Diary of James A. Connolly*; John J. Hight, *History of the Fifty-Eighth Regiment of Indiana Volunteer Infantry*;

Nathaniel Cheairs Hughes Jr. and Gordon D. Whitney, *Jefferson Davis in Blue: The Life of Sherman's Relentless Warrior*; and James P. Jones, "General Jeff C. Davis, U.S.A. and Sherman's Georgia Campaign." The delayed fallout from the event, which led in part to the creation of Special Field Order No. 15, is described in the Official Records as noted, as well as Howard C. Westwood, "Sherman Marched: And Proclaimed 'Land for the Landless'" (*The South Carolina Historical Magazine* 79:1 (1984), 33–50).

General discussions of the plans and attitude of William Sherman in Savannah are offered in Henry Hitchcock, *Marching with Sherman*; George Ward Nichols, *The Story of the Great March, from the Diary of a Staff Officer*; Michael Fellman, *Citizen Sherman: A Life of William Tecumseh Sherman*; John F. Marszalek, *Sherman: A Soldier's Passion for Order*; and in the general's own words in Brooks D. Simpson and Jean V. Berlin, eds., *Sherman's Civil War: Selected Correspondence of William T. Sherman, 1860–1865*, and M.A. DeWolfe Howe, ed., *Home Letters of William Sherman*. For a wider perspective on the place of the Savannah campaign within the context of overall Union strategy, the following were also valuable: Anne J. Bailey, *The Chessboard of War: Sherman and Hood in the Autumn Campaigns of 1864;* Ulysses S. Grant, *Personal Memoirs of Ulysses S. Grant.*, vol. 2 (New York: Charles L. Webster, 1886); Lee Kennett, *Marching Through Georgia: The Story of Soldiers and Civilians During Sherman's Campaign*; and Noah Andre Trudeau, *Southern Storm: Sherman's March to the Sea*. The general's preparations and early strategy for his next campaign in the Carolinas are depicted in John G. Barrett, *Sherman's March Through the Carolinas* (Chapel Hill: Univ. of North Carolina Press, 1956), and Joseph T. Glatthaar, *The March to the Sea and Beyond: Sherman's Troops in the Savannah and Carolinas Campaigns*.

For controversies related to the policy of "hard war" as applied to the residents of the South, several sources were useful: Mark Grimsley, *The Hard Hand of War: Union Military Policy Toward Southern Civilians, 1861–1865*; Debra Reddin Van Tuyll, "Scalawags and Scoundrels? The Moral and Legal Dimensions of Sherman's Last Campaigns"; Anne Sarah Rubin, *Through the Heart of Dixie: Sherman's March and American Memory* (Chapel Hill: Univ. of North Carolina Press, 2014); and Bruce Levine, *The Fall of the House of Dixie: The Civil War and the Social Revolution That Transformed the South*.

Outside Savannah, Chapter 13 returns to the narrative of several characters at some remove from the invading armies. Mary Ann Bickerdyke's story is drawn from Nina Brown Baker, *Cyclone in Calico;* Julia A. Houghton Chase, *Mary A. Bickerdyke, "Mother"*; and Margaret B. Davis, *Mother Bickerdyke: Her Life and Labors for the Relief of Our Soldiers; Sketches of Battle Scenes and Incidents of the Sanitary Service*. John Logan's struggles in official Washington derive from George Francis Dawson, *Life and Services of Gen. John A. Logan, Soldier and Statesman*; Gary Ecelbarger, *Black Jack Logan: An Extraordinary Life in Peace and War*; James P. Jones, *Black Jack: John A. Logan and Southern Illinois in the Civil War Era*; and Mary A. Logan, *Reminiscences of a Soldier's Wife: An Autobiography*.

Mary Livermore's life was perhaps at its busiest and most hectic in late 1864, and several sources convey her myriad duties at this time: her own wartime biography *My Story of the War: A Woman's Narrative of Four Years Personal Experience;* Wendy Hamand Venet, *A Strong-Minded Woman: The Life of Mary A. Livermore*; and Jane Hoge, *The Boys in Blue; or, Heroes of the "Rank and File."* Her adversary Annie Wittenmyer's role with the Christian Commission is described in her own *Under the Guns: A Woman's Reminiscences of the Civil War.* For information on the activity of the Sanitary Commission generally, the following were key sources: Sarah Edwards Henshaw, *Our Branch and Its Tributaries; Being a History of the Work of the Northwestern Sanitary Commission and Its Auxiliaries, During the War of the Rebellion*; Judith Ann Giesberg, *Civil War Sisterhood: The U.S. Sanitary Commission and Women's Politics in Transition*; and Pam Tise, "A Fragile Legacy: The Contributions of Women in the United States Sanitary Commission to the United States Administrative State."

SELECTED REFERENCES:

p. 243   "head of his heroic legions": Trudeau, *Southern Storm*, 516.

p. 243   "in one grand continuous holiday excursion": Weintraub, *General Sherman's Christmas*, 170.

p. 243   "I beg to present you as a Christmas-gift": Telegram from William Sherman to Abraham Lincoln, December 22, 1864, in Official Records, Series I, Volume XLIV, 783.

p. 244   "Fairs, large and small; festivals, comic and grotesque": Henshaw, *Our Branch*, 273.

p. 245   *"I can't be still, and I* WON'T *be still"*: Venet, *A Strong-Minded Woman*, 121.

p. 245   "in terms of droves of horses": George Templeton Strong, *Diary of the Civil War, 1860–1865* (New York: Macmillan, 1962), 562.

p. 245   "Our Fair progresses gloriously": Venet, *A Strong-Minded Woman*, 129.

p. 247   "the severest labor of my life": ibid., 116.

p. 247   "kitchens-within-kitchens to turn out little dabs of soup": Baker, *Cyclone in Calico*, 199.

p. 248   "Lift your dresses. There's no one but us women here.": ibid., 205.

p. 252   "I do not deserve any better treatment": Letter from John Logan to Mary Logan, January 20, 1865, quoted in Ecelbarger, *Black Jack Logan*, 216.

p. 253   "small, dilapidated and forlorn" and "vile place": Hight, *History of the Fifty-Eighth Regiment*, 441.

p. 255   "It would amuse you to See the Negroes": Howe, *Home Letters*, 319.

p. 255   "sneaking Yankee" and "ruthless invader": Letter from William Sherman to Ellen Sherman, December 25, 1864, quoted in Simpson and Berlin, *Sherman's Civil War*, 778.

p. 256   "lone chimney stacks, 'Sherman's Sentinels,' told of homes laid in ashes": E.F. Andrews, "Across the Track of Sherman's Army" (*Appleton's Magazine* 11:3 (1908), 308).

p. 256   "the honor is all yours" to "I suppose it will be safe": Letter from Abraham Lincoln to William Sherman, December 26, 1864, in Official Records, Series I, Volume XLIV, 809.

p. 257   "I cannot say I grieve for him as I did Willy": Letter from William Sherman to Ellen Sherman, December 31, 1865, quoted in Simpson and Berlin, *Sherman's Civil War*, 785.

p. 257   "an almost criminal dislike to the negro": Letter from Henry Halleck to William Sherman, December 30, 1864, in Official Records, Series I, Volume XLIV, 836.

p. 257   "as a set of pariahs, almost without rights": Letter from Salmon Chase to William Sherman, January 2, 1865, quoted in Simpson and Berlin, *Sherman's Civil War*, 795, n1.

p. 258   "clogging my roads, and eating up our subsistence": Letter from William Sherman to Salmon Chase, January 11, 1865, quoted in Simpson and Berlin, *Sherman's Civil War*, 794.

p. 258   "But the nigger? Why, in God's name, can't sensible men" to "I profess to be the best kind of friend to Sambo": Telegram from William Sherman to Henry Halleck, January 12, 1865, in Official Records, Series I, Volume XLVII, Part II, 36–37.

p. 258   "pure & unalloyed by the taint of parasitic flattery" to "I am right & wont Change": Letter from William Sherman to Ellen Sherman, January 15, 1865, quoted in Simpson and Berlin, *Sherman's Civil War*, 797–798.

p. 258   "people have prejudices which must be regarded": Telegram from William Sherman to Ulysses S. Grant, December 31, 1864, in Official Records, Series I, Volume XLIV, 841.

p. 259   "The question is settled: negro soldiers will fight": Trudeau, *Like Men of War*, 349.

p. 259   "Charities from the North are given to rank secesh women": Rufus Saxton, diary entry of January 9, 1865, quoted in Byrne, "'Uncle Billy' Sherman," 110.

p. 261   "that cock-and-bull story of my turning back negroes": Telegram from William Sherman to Henry Halleck, January 12, 1865, in Official Records, Series I, Volume XLVII, Part II, 36.

p. 261   "I would prefer to live by ourselves": Report of meeting of Edwin Stanton and William Sherman with ministers and church officers, January 12, 1865, in Official Records, Series I, Volume XLVII, Part II, 40.

p. 262   "We have confidence in General Sherman": ibid., 41.

p. 262   "The way we can best take care of ourselves is to have land": ibid., 39.

p. 263   "I would prefer much to colonize the negroes on lands": Telegram from William Sherman to Lorenzo Thomas, April 12, 1864, in Official Records, Series III, Volume IV, 225.

CHAPTER 14—FIRE AND SWORD

The Carolinas campaign has attracted less of the attention given to the March to the Sea, though in many ways it was more destructive and eventful to the collapse of the Confederacy. One good overview of the campaign is John G. Barrett, *Sherman's March Through the Carolinas*, while a darker view is offered by Jacqueline Glass Campbell, *When Sherman Marched North from the Sea: Resistance on the Confederate Home Front* (Chapel Hill: Univ. of North Carolina Press, 2003). The still-controversial annihilation of Columbia, South Carolina, has attracted little scholarship, but useful places to start are Marion Brunson Lucas, *Sherman and the Burning of Columbia* (College Station: Texas A&M Univ. Press, 1976), and Michael C. Garber Jr., "Reminiscences of the Burning of Columbia, South Carolina" (*Indiana Magazine of History* 11:4 (1915), 285–300).

Sherman's campaign of destruction in the Carolinas was the logical end of his policy of "hard war," with which the general is virtually synonymous today. Some analyses of his methods as they apply to this stage of the war include John G. Barrett, "Sherman and Total War in the Carolinas" (*The North Carolina Historical Review* 37:3 (1960), 367–381); John Bennett Walters, "General William T. Sherman and Total War"(*The Journal of Southern History* 14:4 (1948), 447–480); and David B. Chesebrough, "'There Goes Your Damn Gospel Shop!' The Churches and Clergy as Victims of Sherman's March Through South Carolina" (*The South Carolina Historical Magazine* 92:1 (1991), 15–33). Previously cited works on the same subject include Debra Reddin Van Tuyll, "Scalawags and Scoundrels? The Moral and Legal Dimensions of Sherman's Last Campaigns," and Mark Grimsley, *The Hard Hand of War: Union Military Policy Toward Southern Civilians, 1861–1865.*

Several written accounts of enlisted men and officers provide a useful view of the Carolinas campaign, among them S.H.M. Byers, *With Fire and Sword* (New York: Neale, 1911), and Clement Eaton, "Diary of an Officer in Sherman's Army Marching Through the Carolinas" (*The Journal of Southern History* 9:2 (1943), 238–254). Other sources were David P. Conyngham, *Sherman's March Through the South: Sketches and Incidents of the Campaign*; Jacob D. Cox, *The March to the Sea—Franklin and Nashville* (New York: Charles Scribner's Sons, 1913); F.Y. Hedley, *Marching Through Georgia: Pen-Pictures of Every-Day Life in General Sherman's Army, from the Beginning of the Atlanta Campaign Until the Close of the War*; George Ward Nichols, *The Story of the Great March, from the Diary of a Staff Officer*; Adin B. Underwood, *The Three Years' Service of the Thirty-Third Mass. Infantry Regiment, 1862–1865*; and William B. Hazen, *A Narrative of Military Service.*

The journals of John Hight, in the *History of the Fifty-Eighth Regiment of Indiana Volunteer Infantry*, and Charles Wills, in *Army Life of an Illinois Soldier: The Letters and Diary of Charles W. Wills*, were the basis for their respective stories. The narrative of John Logan follows from his personal papers and reports and correspondence in the Official Records, as well as his biographies: George Francis Dawson, *Life and Services of Gen. John A. Logan, Soldier and Statesman*; Gary Ecelbarger, *Black Jack Logan: An Extraordinary Life in Peace and War*; James P. Jones, *Black Jack: John A. Logan and Southern Illinois in the Civil War Era*; Mary A. Logan, *Reminiscences of a Soldier's Wife: An Autobiography*; and Byron Andrews, *A Biography of General John A. Logan, with an Account of His Public Services in Peace and in War.*

General views of Sherman's strategy in the western theater are detailed in the Official Records, Series I, Volume XLVII, Parts I and II, and in the following: Henry Hitchcock, *Marching with Sherman*; Herman Hattaway and Archer Jones, *How the North Won: A Military History of the Civil War*; and Steven E. Woodworth, *Nothing but Victory: The Army of the Tennessee, 1861–1865.* The ground-level perspective of soldiers in the campaign derives in part from Joseph T. Glatthaar, *The March to the Sea and Beyond: Sherman's Troops in the Savannah and Carolinas Campaigns.*

SELECTED REFERENCES:

p. 265   "Hell hole of secession": Jones, *Black Jack*, 246.

p. 268   "made an abolitionist of him": Hitchcock, *Marching with Sherman*, 250.

p. 268   "He impresses one as a man of talent": Hight, *History of the Fifty-Eighth Regiment*, 453.

p. 269   "The rebels are now reaping the just reward": ibid., 474.

p. 269   "It makes one's blood boil to see the evidences": Nichols, *Story of the Great March*, 101.

p. 269   "We saw but few people, in our march to-day": Hight, *History of the Fifty-Eighth Regiment*, 463.

p. 270   "At the very time orders are issued to destroy tents": ibid., 484.

p. 271   "foolish and unreasonable" and "Is the man crazy?": ibid., 483.

p. 271   "promptness, precision, and soldiery bearing" and "In these respects they out-shine"; ibid., 477.

p. 272   "many of them are going to the dogs" to "May God send it soon": ibid., 466–468.

p. 273   "with mahogany furniture of the best quality": Wills, *Army Life*, 339.

p. 273   "a school of porpoise which looked just like a drove of hogs": ibid., 336.

p. 273   "I never saw so much destruction of property before": ibid., 342.

p. 274   "filled with flames and pitch-black smoke": Nichols, *Story of the Great March*, 153.

p. 274   "The men of this army surprise me every day": Wills, *Army Life*, 345.

p. 275   "As we went along the streets a mob of people gathered": Byers, *With Fire and Sword*, 153–154.

p. 276   "the boys loaded themselves with what they wanted": Wills, *Army Life*, 350.

CHAPTER 15—TO RALEIGH

The Official Records provide a comprehensive account of the movements of Sherman's western armies through the Carolinas during 1865, specifically Series I, Volume XLVII, Parts I and II, for their voluminous field reports and correspondence. For additional information, some of it based on the same sources, John Barrett wrote extensively and well about Sherman's campaigning through the Carolinas, and several of his works have informed the material in this chapter, among them "Sherman's March Through North Carolina" (*The North Carolina Historical Review* 42:2 (1965), 192–207) and *Sherman's March Through the Carolinas*.

For the Battle of Bentonville specifically, this book drew from Mark L. Bradley, *Last Stand in the Carolinas: The Battle of Bentonville* (Campbell, Calif.: Savas Woodbury Pub., 1996), and Charles E. Belknap, "Bentonville: What a Bummer Knows About It" (Military Legion of the Loyal Order of the United States, Commandery of the District of Columbia, War Papers, vol. 12., read at meeting on January 4, 1893), among other previously cited works: Joseph T. Glatthaar, *The March to the Sea and Beyond: Sherman's Troops in the Savannah and Carolinas Campaigns*; Steven E. Woodworth, *Nothing but Victory: The Army of the Tennessee, 1861–1865*; John F. Marszalek, *Sherman: A Soldier's Passion for Order*; and Herman Hattaway and Archer Jones, *How the North Won: A Military History of the Civil War*.

The actions of the 82nd Illinois and the leadership of Edward Salomon in particular were key to the outcome at Bentonville. Some of this story is detailed in David Gleicher, "From Jewish Immigrant to Union General in Under Ten Years" (*Chicago Jewish*

History 15:2 (1992)); Eric Benjaminson, "A Regiment of Immigrants: The 82nd Illinois Volunteer Infantry and the Letters of Captain Rudolph Mueller"; Joseph R. Reinhart, ed. *Yankee Dutchmen Under Fire: Civil War Letters from the 82nd Infantry*; and Mark A. Dluger, "A Regimental Community: The Men of the 82nd Illinois Infantry Before, During, and After the American Civil War." Some of Salomon's military commendations are described in Simon Wolf, "The American Jew as Soldier and Patriot" (*Publications of the American Jewish Historical Society* 3 (1895), 21–40).

Many of the authors and soldiers who wrote accounts of the fighting in the Carolinas had been with Sherman's forces since Georgia, and continued to describe the campaign in all its victory and excess. These include David P. Conyngham, *Sherman's March Through the South: Sketches and Incidents of the Campaign*; Jacob D. Cox, *The March to the Sea—Franklin and Nashville*; Adin B. Underwood, *The Three Years' Service of the Thirty-Third Mass. Infantry Regiment, 1862–1865*; Theodore F. Upson, *With Sherman to the Sea*; F.Y. Hedley, *Marching Through Georgia: Pen-Pictures of Every-Day Life in General Sherman's Army, from the Beginning of the Atlanta Campaign Until the Close of the War*; George Ward Nichols, *The Story of the Great March, from the Diary of a Staff Officer*; Alexander G. Downing, *Downing's Civil War Diary, August 15, 1861–July 31, 1865*; Clement Eaton, "Diary of an Officer in Sherman's Army Marching Through the Carolinas"; and William B. Hazen, *A Narrative of Military Service*.

Several of the main characters' journals and other writings continue to illuminate the progress of Sherman's men through North Carolina, among them John J. Hight, *History of the Fifty-Eighth Regiment of Indiana Volunteer Infantry*; Charles W. Wills, *Army Life of an Illinois Soldier: The Letters and Diary of Charles W. Wills*; and *Slavery in the Clover Bottoms: John McCline's Narrative of His Life During Slavery and the Civil War*. Noah Andre Trudeau's *Like Men of War: Black Troops in the Civil War, 1862–1865* and John David Smith's *Black Soldiers in Blue: African American Troops in the Civil War Era* provide useful context about the assault on Fort Fisher and related actions involving African American troops.

Information on Mother Bickerdyke's activities in 1865 is somewhat scattered, and has been drawn from a variety of primary and secondary sources, among them Mary Livermore, *My Story of the War*; Florence Shaw Kellogg, *Mother Bickerdyke as I Knew Her* (Chicago: Unity, 1907); Nina Brown Baker, *Cyclone in Calico*; Julia A. Houghton Chase, *Mary A. Bickerdyke, "Mother"*; and Margaret B. Davis, *Mother Bickerdyke: Her Life and Labors for the Relief of Our Soldiers; Sketches of Battle Scenes and Incidents of the Sanitary Service*. Her work also appears in the Mary Ann Bickerdyke Papers in the Library of Congress.

John Logan's own story is conveyed in the Official Records, as well as in several biographies: James P. Jones, *Black Jack: John A. Logan and Southern Illinois in the Civil War Era*; Mary A. Logan, *Reminiscences of a Soldier's Wife: An Autobiography;* George Francis Dawson, *Life and Services of Gen. John A. Logan, Soldier and Statesman*; Gary Ecelbarger, *Black Jack Logan: An Extraordinary Life in Peace and War*; and Charles Wolcott Balestier, *James G. Blaine: A Sketch of His Life, with a Brief Record of the Life of John A. Logan*.

SELECTED REFERENCES:

p. 284 "Our army has taken on the character of bandits" to "deeds and misdeeds": Letter from Rudolph Mueller to Friedrich Hecker, March 12, 1865, quoted in Reinhart, *Yankee Dutchmen*, 178.

p. 287 "the *great* man saved the rest of the army": Letter from Rudolph Mueller to Friedrich Hecker, April 2, 1865, quoted in Reinhart, *Yankee Dutchmen*, 186.

p. 289 "We are coming out of the wilderness, thank God": Hight, *History of the Fifty-Eighth Regiment*, 502.

p. 290 "They are splendidly equipped, and march in good order": ibid.

p. 291 "There is now nobody between us and the rebels": ibid., 505.

p. 292 "had worn their clothing pretty much to tatters": Underwood, *Three Years' Service*, 286.

p. 293 "slaveholders' rebellion": Hight, *History of the Fifty-Eighth Regiment*, 507.

p. 293 "There has been quite a moral reformation in the army": ibid., 512.

p. 293 "I ascended the high pulpit": ibid., 516.

p. 295 "The whole four years seems to me more like a dream": Wills, *Army Life*, 371.

p. 296 "The army is crazy for vengeance": ibid.

p. 296 "The troops are in a blaze of excitement": Woodworth, *Nothing but Victory*, 636.

p. 299 "On way to Washington. Short of rations.": Telegram from John Logan to Mary Ann Bickerdyke, May 1865, quoted in Chase, *Mary A. Bickerdyke, "Mother,"* 78.

p. 301 "16,000 men" and "not a cracker in the city": Telegram from Mary Ann Bickerdyke to Henry Bellows, May 1865, quoted in Chase, *Mary A. Bickerdyke, "Mother,"* 79.

p. 302 "I don't wonder Sherman calls you one of his best generals"; ibid., 80.

CHAPTER 16—THE GRAND REVIEW

The Grand Review of the Armies was extensively covered in the Northern press, and appears as a climax of the story in soldiers' diaries and journals. Many of these sources were mentioned in the Introduction, among them the "General News" column of *The New York Times* for May 24 and 25, 1865; F.Y. Hedley, *Marching Through Georgia: Pen-Pictures of Every-Day Life in General Sherman's Army, from the Beginning of the Atlanta Campaign Until the Close of the War*; and George Ward Nichols, *The Story of the Great March, from the Diary of a Staff Officer*. Modern sources also provide valuable context, including Ann McShea, "Hazleton Soldiers in the Civil War Marched on After Lee's Surrender"; Reid D. Ross, "Civil War Grand Review"; "Sherman's March, May 24, 1865: The Grand Review and the End of the Great March" (To The Sound of the Guns: Civil War Artillery, Battlefields and Historical Markers, accessed at https://markerhunter .wordpress.com/2015/05/24/shermans-march-may-24-1865); and William Stroock, "The Grand Review of 1865."

William Sherman faced challenges before the Grand Review in the face of attempts by Edwin Stanton and abolitionist newspapers to cast him as a pariah for his first, abortive peace proposal with Joseph Johnston. Some of this history is documented in Steven E. Woodworth, *Nothing but Victory: The Army of the Tennessee, 1861–1865*; Brooks D. Simpson and Jean V. Berlin, eds., *Sherman's Civil War: Selected Correspondence of William*

T. Sherman, 1860–1865; John F. Marszalek, *Sherman: A Soldier's Passion for Order*; and Michael Fellman, *Citizen Sherman: A Life of William Tecumseh Sherman*. The general also devotes some effort toward explaining his failed proposal in his own *Memoirs*, vol. 2, his justifications supported by evidence from the Official Records.

The procession of John Logan and Mary Ann Bickerdyke at the head of the Army of the Tennessee is attested by numerous sources, and described in somewhat fragmentary form in the references above and in their respective biographies: for Logan, James P. Jones, *Black Jack: John A. Logan and Southern Illinois in the Civil War Era*; George Francis Dawson, *Life and Services of Gen. John A. Logan, Soldier and Statesman*; and Gary Ecelbarger, *Black Jack Logan: An Extraordinary Life in Peace and War*. For Bickerdyke, Nina Brown Baker, *Cyclone in Calico*; Florence Shaw Kellogg, *Mother Bickerdyke as I Knew Her*; Julia A. Houghton Chase, *Mary A. Bickerdyke, "Mother"*; and Margaret B. Davis, *Mother Bickerdyke: Her Life and Labors for the Relief of Our Soldiers; Sketches of Battle Scenes and Incidents of the Sanitary Service*. These sources—along with Logan's and Bickerdyke's various papers in the Library of Congress—also provide copious information on their careers after the war.

The life of Charles Wills after the war is somewhat murky, and his *Army Life of an Illinois Soldier: The Letters and Diary of Charles W. Wills* only offers a bare hint. A few more facts are offered by J.N. Reece, Report of the Adjutant General for the State of Illinois, vol. 5, 1861–1866 (Springfield, Ill.: Phillips Brothers State Printers, 1901), and Wills's pension records in the National Archives. The 1880 United States Census record for Iberia, Louisiana, adds more detail, as does the article "Death of Major Charles W. Wills" in the *New Orleans Times-Picayune* for March 25, 1883.

The postwar saga of the 82nd Illinois continues for many decades in Mark A. Dluger's definitive and exhaustive dissertation, "A Regimental Community: The Men of the 82nd Illinois Infantry Before, During, and After the American Civil War." Salomon's later life is covered in that source, along with David Gleicher, "From Jewish Immigrant to Union General in Under Ten Years," and *Biographical Sketches of the Leading Men of Chicago*. Sabine Hecker's excellent *Friedrich Hecker: Two Lives for Liberty* details the colonel's life and achievements in the years after his active service, as does the collection of Friedrich Hecker Papers at the State Historical Society of Missouri, most of them written in English instead of German after the war. For Rudolph Mueller's star-crossed final years, this chapter draws from Joseph R. Reinhart, ed., *Yankee Dutchmen Under Fire: Civil War Letters from the 82nd Infantry*; and Eric Benjaminson, "A Regiment of Immigrants: The 82nd Illinois Volunteer Infantry and the Letters of Captain Rudolph Mueller."

John McCline's long postwar life is somewhat opaque, though Jan Furman's description of it in *Slavery in the Clover Bottoms: John McCline's Narrative of His Life During Slavery and the Civil War* illuminates part of it, as does Herbert Hagerman's own introduction to McCline's narrative, in the same volume. Beyond that, McCline appears in decennial U.S. census records in states from Michigan to New Mexico, and briefly in city directories of St. Louis and Chicago in the late 19th century. Other information can be gleaned from the Territorial Archives of New Mexico for Governor Hagerman (1906–1907) at the New Mexico Records Center and Archives in Santa Fe. Background on the prominent role played by black troops in the last year of the war derives from Noah Andre Trudeau, *Like Men of War*, and John David Smith, *Black Soldiers in Blue*.

John Hight's own story ends abruptly after his unit's mustering out in the *History of the Fifty-Eighth Regiment of Indiana Volunteer Infantry*, but several supplementary sources offer details on how he spent his years after the Civil War and his life generally. These include Theophilus A. Wylie, *Indiana University: Its History from 1820, When Founded, to 1890* (Indianapolis: William B. Burford, 1890, 207–208); the 1880 United States Census for Cincinnati, Hamilton County, Ohio; and the obituary "Death of John J. Hight" in the *Cincinnati Gazette* for December 22, 1886.

Related information on the Christian revival of war veterans, of which Hight was a significant part, is featured in Steven E. Woodworth, "Religious Revivals During the Civil War" (*Encyclopedia Virginia*; Virginia Foundation for the Humanities, May 4, 2017, accessed at www.EncyclopediaVirginia.org/Religious_Revivals_During_the_Civil _War); Gardiner H. Shattuck Jr., "Revivals in the Camp" (*Christianity Today* 33 (1992); accessed at www.christianitytoday.com/history/issues/issue-33/revivals-in-camp.html); Robert J. Miller, *Both Prayed to the Same God: Religion and Faith in the American Civil War* (Lanham, Md: Rowman & Littlefield, 2007); and Steven E. Woodworth, *While God Is Marching On: The Religious World of Civil War Soldiers* (Lawrence: University Press of Kansas, 2001).

Primary and secondary sources on the life and accomplishments of Mary Livermore are many, and include testimonials from those who admired her as well as critiques from those who disapproved of her ideas. This chapter is drawn from some of the better-known sources, notably Livermore herself. Her *My Story of the War: A Woman's Narrative of Four Years Personal Experience* is useful in describing her work (and that of Mary Ann Bickerdyke) up to the end of the conflict. For the years following, *The Story of My Life, or The Sunshine and Shadow of Seventy Years*, is essential, as are her countless articles in *The New Covenant*, *Woman's Journal* and other publications. Perhaps the clearest distillation of her views comes in "Cooperative Womanhood in the State" (*North American Review* 153:418 (1891), 283–295), an influential treatise on the role of women in postwar America and the possibilities for their future collective advancement. Other sources that describe her importance include Wendy Hamand Venet, *A Strong-Minded Woman: The Life of Mary A. Livermore*; Patricia M. Shields, "Mary Livermore: A Legacy of Caring and Cooperative Womanhood in Service to the State" (from *Outstanding Women in Public Administration: Leaders, Mentors, and Pioneers*, eds. Claire L. Felbinger and Wendy A. Haynes. Armonk, N.Y.: M.E. Sharpe, 2004); and Sarah Edwards Henshaw, *Our Branch and Its Tributaries*.

SELECTED REFERENCES:

p. 306   "admit my folly in embracing in a Military convention": Letter from William Sherman to Edwin Stanton, April 25, 1865, quoted in Report of the Joint Committee on the Conduct of the War (38th Congress, Second Session, 1865), 18.

p. 306   "mean, scheming, vindictive politician": Carl Schurz, *Reminiscences of Carl Schurz, 1863–1869*, vol. 3 (London: John Murray, 1909), 118.

p. 306–07 "Vandal Sherman" and "though in disgrace he is untamed": Letter from William Sherman to John Rawlins, May 19, 1865, quoted in Simpson and Berlin, *Sherman's Civil War*, 902.

p. 307 "the sight was simply magnificent": Sherman, *Memoirs*, vol. 2, 377.

p. 309 "If you won't allow a man to vote because he has black skin": Ecelbarger, *Black Jack Logan*, 246.

p. 309 "the most memorable night of my life": ibid., 282.

p. 310 "he has a backbone like the Brooklyn Bridge" and "the Black Eagle of Illinois": ibid., 294–295.

p. 313 "Whatever she wants is right, and what she says will be the truth": Chase, *Mary A. Bickerdyke, 'Mother'*: 86.

p. 313 "I have almost a dread of being a citizen": Wills, *Army Life*, 370.

p. 314 "No more finding the enemy driving in his skirmishers": ibid., 373.

p. 316 "to receive the plaudits and praises of the entire Northwest": Dluger, "A Regimental Community," 374.

p. 317–18 "songs, hat swinging, scarf waving, wiping of tears" and "uninterrupted drone of jubilation": Letter from Friedrich Hecker to Wilhelm Rapp, June 2, 1873, quoted in Freitag, *Two Lives for Liberty*, 332–333.

p. 318 "What would I do there? Perhaps become a subject": Freitag, *Two Lives for Liberty*, 322.

p. 319 "good fortune for the country": Letter from Rudolph Mueller to Friedrich Hecker, May 27, 1865, quoted in Reinhart, *Yankee Dutchmen*, 192.

p. 323 "The hypocrite is unmasked": Hight, *History of the Fifty-Eighth Regiment*, 538.

p. 325 "Not only did these women broaden in their views": Livermore, "Cooperative Womanhood," 286.

p. 327 "insane and vulgar greed for riches": Livermore, *Story of My Life*, 685.

p. 327 "If she can't convince, she at least commands respect": Venet, *A Strong-Minded Woman*, 185.

EPILOGUE—THE FIRES TO COME

The postwar paper trail for William Sherman, as general-in-chief of the U.S. Army for fourteen years, is lengthy and accessible. Despite the voluminous record, however, the general's autonomy was limited by the president and Congress and most of his stances and attitudes are better revealed in his private letters of the time. The public and personal records are preserved in the William T. Sherman Papers in the Library of Congress and in limited form in reference works such as *Home Letters of General Sherman*, M.A. DeWolfe Howe, ed., and in the general's own *Memoirs*, vol. 2.

A slew of biographies on the general have been published in recent years, though the best still remain Michael Fellman's *Citizen Sherman: A Life of William Tecumseh Sherman* and John F. Marszalek's *Sherman: A Soldier's Passion for Order*, each written from a decidedly different perspective. Other worthy biographies include Robert L. O'Connell's *Fierce Patriot: The Tangled Lives of William Tecumseh Sherman*, B.H. Liddell Hart's now-dated but still valuable *Sherman: Soldier, Realist, American* (Boston: Da Capo Press,

1929, reprint ed. 1993), and, for the latest scholarship, James Lee McDonough's *William Tecumseh Sherman: In the Service of My Country, a Life* (New York: W.W. Norton, 2016).

Accounts of Sherman's various battles with Congress are revealed in the *Congressional Globe*, especially for the 41st Congress (1869–1871), which met during his first years as general-in-chief. Sherman's victory tour of the South is well described in John F. Marszalek, "Celebrity in Dixie: Sherman Tours the South, 1879" (*Georgia Historical Quarterly* 66:3 (1982), 368–383), while Sherman's own "Old Shady, with a Moral" (*North American Review* 147:383 (1888), 361–368) lays out his views of the dangers of a resurgent and unapologetic post-Confederate South. For a perspective on the legacy of the March to the Sea and the Atlanta and Carolinas campaigns, Anne Sarah Rubin's *Through the Heart of Dixie: Sherman's March and American Memory* (Chapel Hill: Univ. of North Carolina Press, 2014) discusses the popular legacy of William Sherman's "hard war" and his continuing resonance as a controversial historical figure. The most damning portraits of Sherman and his invasion, of course, have been written by Southerners: Mary Chesnut, *A Diary from Dixie* (New York: Appleton, 1906); Spencer B. King Jr., ed., "Fanny Cohen's Journal of Sherman's Occupation of Savannah" (*Georgia Historical Quarterly* 41:4 (1957), 407–416); James Robertson, ed., *The Diary of Dolly Lunt Burge* (Athens: Univ. of Georgia Press, 1962); and Margaret Mitchell, *Gone with the Wind* (New York: Macmillan, 1936), among many similar critical and disparaging descriptions of the general's campaigns in Georgia and the Carolinas.

Finally, though it refers to the March to the Sea only tangentially, director Ross McElwee's failed-romantic-quest documentary *Sherman's March* (First Run Features, 1986) offers poignant views of the modern landscape formerly devastated by Sherman's forces, along with thoughtful musings on the paradox of the general's prewar love for the South and his wartime destruction of it.

SELECTED REFERENCES:

p. 330   "simply ridiculous": Fellman, *Citizen Sherman*, 292.

p. 331   "wooden-legged and one-armed men": Remarks of John Logan, "Reduction of the Army," March 10, 1870, quoted in *Congressional Globe*, Appendix, 41st Congress, Second Session, 153.

p. 333   "what the Union armies conquered in war . . . the South conquered in politics": Letter from William Sherman to John Sherman, quoted in Fellman, *Citizen Sherman*, 408.

p. 333   "the Republican party which gave the negro the vote, must make that vote good": ibid.

p. 333   "despotic severity": Sherman, "Old Shady," 364.

p. 333   "the everlasting principles of human nature": ibid., 368.

p. 334   "I say to the South, let the negro vote" and "The Northern people will not long tolerate": ibid., 366.

p. 334   "Otherwise, so sure as there is a God in Heaven": ibid.

SOURCES

INTRODUCTION: TWO ARMIES IN WASHINGTON

Byers, S.H.M. *With Fire and Sword*. New York: Neale, 1911.

"General News." *The New York Times*, May 24 and May 25, 1865, 1.

Hazen, William B. *A Narrative of Military Service*. Boston: Ticknor, 1885.

Hedley, F.Y. *Marching Through Georgia: Pen-Pictures of Every-Day Life in General Sherman's Army, from the Beginning of the Atlanta Campaign Until the Close of the War*. Chicago: Donohue, Henneberry, 1890.

McShea, Ann. "Hazleton Soldiers in the Civil War Marched on After Lee's Surrender." *The Standard-Speaker*, December 20, 2015.

Ross, Reid D. "Civil War Grand Review." *America's Civil War Magazine*, December 9, 2015. Accessed at www.historynet.com/civil-war-grand-review.htm.

"Sherman's March, May 24, 1865: The Grand Review and the End of the Great March." To The Sound of the Guns: Civil War Artillery, Battlefields and Historical Markers, May 24, 2015. Accessed at https://markerhunter.wordpress.com/2015/05/24 /shermans-march-may-24-1865.

Stroock, William. "The Grand Review of 1865." Warfare History Network, March 27, 2017. Accessed at http://warfarehistorynetwork.com/daily/civil-war/the-grand-review-of-1865/.

Woodworth, Steven E. *Nothing but Victory: The Army of the Tennessee, 1861–1865*. New York: Knopf, 2005.

CHAPTER 1: THE WESTERN EDGE

Benjaminson, Eric. "A Regiment of Immigrants: The 82nd Illinois Volunteer Infantry and the Letters of Captain Rudolph Mueller." *Journal of the Illinois State Historical Society* 94:2 (2001).

Bergquist, James M. "People and Politics in Transition: The Illinois Germans, 1850–1860," from *Ethnic Voters and the Election of Lincoln*, Frederick C. Luebke, ed. Lincoln: University of Nebraska Press, 1971.

Biles, Roger. *Illinois: A History of the Land and Its People*. DeKalb: Northern Illinois University Press, 2005.

Davis, James E. *Frontier Illinois*. Bloomington: Indiana University Press, 1998.

Freitag, Sabine. *Friedrich Hecker: Two Lives for Liberty*. St. Louis: St. Louis Mercantile Library, 2006.

Hansen, Harry, ed. *Illinois: A Descriptive and Historical Guide*. New York: Hastings House, 1939.

Hubbard, Mark, ed. *Illinois's War: The Civil War in Documents*. Athens: Ohio University Press, 2013.

Karamanski, Theodore J. *Rally 'Round the Flag: Chicago and the Civil War*. Lanham, Md.: Rowman & Littlefield, 2006.

Kaufmann, Wilhelm. *The Germans in the American Civil War*. Carlisle, Pa.: John Kallmann, Pubs., 1999.

Koerner, Gustave. *Memoirs: 1809–1896*, Vol. 2. Cedar Rapids, Iowa: Torch Press, 1909.

Levine, Bruce. *The Spirit of 1848: German Immigrants, Labor Conflict, and the Coming of the Civil War*. Chicago: University of Illinois Press, 1992.

Livermore, Mary A. *My Story of the War: A Woman's Narrative of Four Years Personal Experience*. Hartford, Conn.: A.D. Worthington, 1889.

Livermore, Mary A. *The Story of My Life, or The Sunshine and Shadow of Seventy Years*. Hartford, Conn.: A.D. Worthington, 1897.

Mahin, Dean B. *The Blessed Place of Freedom: Europeans in Civil War America*. Dulles, Va.: Brassey's, 2002.

McGerr, Michael E. *The Decline of Popular Politics: The American North, 1865–1928*. New York: Oxford University Press, 1988.

Power, Richard Lyle. *Planting Corn Belt Culture: The Impress of the Upland Southerner and the Yankee in the Old Northwest*. Indianapolis: Indiana Historical Society, 1953.

Ray, P. Orman. *The Convention That Nominated Lincoln*. Chicago: University of Chicago Press, 1906.

Reinhart, Joseph R., ed. *Yankee Dutchmen Under Fire: Civil War Letters from the 82nd Infantry*. Kent, Ohio: Kent State University Press, 2013.

Schick, Susanne Martha. "'For God, Mac, and Country': The Political Worlds of Midwestern Germans During the Civil War Era." Ph.D. dissertation, University of Illinois at Urbana-Champaign, 1994.

Smith, Donnal V. "The Influence of the Foreign-Born of the Northwest in the Election of 1860," from *Ethnic Voters and the Election of Lincoln*, Frederick C. Luebke, ed. Lincoln: University of Nebraska Press, 1971.

Trautman, Frederic. "Eight Weeks on a St. Clair County Farm in 1851: Letters by a Young German." *Journal of the Illinois State Historical Society* 75:3 (1982).

Venet, Wendy Hamand. *A Strong-Minded Woman: The Life of Mary A. Livermore.* Amherst: University of Massachusetts Press, 2005.

CHAPTER 2: TIP OF THE SWORD

Baker, Nina Brown. *Cyclone in Calico.* Boston: Little, Brown, 1952.

Biles, Roger. *Illinois: A History of the Land and Its People.* DeKalb: Northern Illinois University Press, 2005.

Chase, Julia A. Houghton. *Mary A. Bickerdyke, "Mother."* Lawrence, Kans.: Journal Publishing, 1896.

Denney, Robert E. *The Distaff Civil War.* Bloomington, Ind.: Trafford, 2002.

Duerkes, Wayne N. "I for One Am Ready to Do My Part: The Initial Motivations That Inspired Men from Northern Illinois to Enlist in the U.S. Army, 1861–1862." *Journal of the Illinois State Historical Society* 105:4 (2012).

Ecelbarger, Gary. *Black Jack Logan: An Extraordinary Life in Peace and War.* Guilford, Conn.: Lyons Press, 2005.

Girardi, Robert I. "Illinois' First Response to the Civil War." *Journal of the Illinois State Historical Society* 105:2–3 (2012).

Harper, Judith E. *Women During the Civil War: An Encyclopedia.* London: Routledge, 2003.

Hicken, Victor. *Illinois in the Civil War.* Champaign: Univ. of Illinois Press, 1966.

Hubbard, Mark, ed. *Illinois's War: The Civil War in Documents.* Athens: Ohio Univ. Press, 2013.

Jones, James Pickett. *Black Jack: John A. Logan and Southern Illinois in the Civil War Era.* Tallahassee: Florida State University, 1967.

Jones, Stanley L. "Agrarian Radicalism in Illinois' Constitutional Convention of 1862." *Journal of the Illinois State Historical Society* 48:3 (1955).

Karamanski, Theodore J. *Rally 'Round the Flag: Chicago and the Civil War.* Lanham, Md.: Rowman & Littlefield, 2006.

King, William C. and W.P. Derby. *Campfire Sketches and Battle-Field Echoes of 61–5.* Springfield, Mass.: King, Richardson, 1889.

Koerner, Gustave. *Memoirs: 1809–1896,* Vol. 2. Cedar Rapids, Iowa: Torch Press, 1909.

Litvin, Martin, *The Young Mary: Early Years of Mother Bickerdyke, America's Florence Nightingale, and Patron Saint of Kansas.* Galesburg, Ill.: Log City Books, 1976.

Logan, Mary A. *Reminiscences of a Soldier's Wife: An Autobiography.* New York: Charles Scribner's Sons, 1913.

Morris, W.S., L.D. Hartwell, and J.B. Kuykendall, *History 31st Regiment Illinois Volunteers.* Evansville, Ind.: Keller Print. and Pub., 1902.

Murray, R. Smith. "Mother Bickerdyke: The Indomitable Nurse." *Chattanooga Times Free Press,* May 4, 2014. www.timesfreepress.com/news/opinion/columns/story/2014/may/04 /mother-bickerdyke-the-indomitable-nurse/138965/.

Paludan, Philip Shaw. *"A People's Contest": The Union and Civil War, 1861–1865.* New York: Harper & Row, 1988.

Power, Richard Lyle. *Planting Corn Belt Culture: The Impress of the Upland Southerner and the Yankee in the Old Northwest*. Indianapolis: Indiana Historical Society, 1953.

Simon, John Y. Foreword to W.S. Morris, L.D. Hartwell, and J.B. Kuykendall, *History 31st Regiment Illinois Volunteers*. Evansville, Ind.: Keller Print. and Pub., 1902; reprint Carbondale: Southern Illinois Univ. Press, 1998.

Young, Agatha. *The Women and the Crisis: Women of the North in the Civil War*. New York: McDowell, Obolensky, 1959.

CHAPTER 3: ECHOES OF CHICKAMAUGA

Bierce, Ambrose. "A Little of Chickamauga." *San Francisco Examiner*, April 24, 1898.

Bower, Stephen E. "The Theology of the Battlefield: William Tecumseh Sherman and the U.S. Civil War." *The Journal of Military History* 64:4 (2000), 1005–1034.

Cimprich, John. *Slavery's End in Tennessee, 1861–1865*. Tuscaloosa: Univ. of Alabama Press, 1985.

Cornish, Dudley Taylor. *The Sable Arm: Black Troops in the Union Army, 1861–1865*. Lawrence: Univ. Press of Kansas, 1956.

Cozzens, Peter. *This Terrible Sound: The Battle of Chickamauga*. Chicago: Univ. of Illinois Press, 1992.

Culp, Michael. "The Formation of Kalamazoo's Own 13th Michigan Infantry." *Michigan Live*, October 16, 2011, accessed at mlive.com.

Fellman, Michael. *Citizen Sherman: A Life of William Tecumseh Sherman*. New York: Random House, 1994.

Fredriksen, John C. *Civil War Almanac*. New York: Checkmark Books, 2008.

Furman, Jan, ed. *Slavery in the Clover Bottoms: John McCline's Narrative of His Life During Slavery and the Civil War*. Knoxville: Univ. of Tennessee Press, 1998.

Grimsley, Mark. *The Hard Hand of War: Union Military Policy Toward Southern Civilians, 1861–1865*. New York: Cambridge University Press, 1995.

Hattaway, Herman and Archer Jones. *How the North Won: A Military History of the Civil War*. Chicago: Univ. of Illinois Press, 1991.

Hight, John J. *History of the Fifty-Eighth Regiment of Indiana Volunteer Infantry*. Princeton, N.J.: Press of the Clarion, 1895.

Lovett, Bobby L. "The Negro in Tennessee, 1861–1866: A Socio-Military History of the Civil War Era." Ph.D. dissertation, University of Arkansas, 1969.

Marszalek, John F. *Sherman: A Soldier's Passion for Order*. New York: Free Press-Macmillan, 1993.

O'Connell, Robert L. *Fierce Patriot: The Tangled Lives of William Tecumseh Sherman*. New York: Random House, 2014.

Sherman, William T. *The Memoirs of William T. Sherman*, vol. 1. New York: D. Appleton, 1886.

Simpson, Brooks D. and Jean V. Berlin, eds. *Sherman's Civil War: Selected Correspondence of William T. Sherman, 1860–1865*. Chapel Hill: Univ. of North Carolina Press, 1999.

Swedberg, Claire E., ed. *Three Years with the 92d Illinois: The Civil War Diary of John M. King*. Mechanicsburg, Penn.: Stackpole Books, 1999.

Van Tuyll, Debra Reddin. "Scalawags and Scoundrels? The Moral and Legal Dimensions of Sherman's Last Campaigns." *Studies in Popular Culture* 22:2 (1999), 33–45.

Walters, John Bennett. "General William T. Sherman and Total War." *The Journal of Southern History* 14:4 (1948), 447–480.

Westwood, Howard C. "Grant's Role in Beginning Black Soldiery." *Illinois Historical Journal* 79:3 (1986), 197–212.

Woodworth, Steven F. *Nothing but Victory: The Army of the Tennessee, 1861–1865.* New York: Knopf, 2005.

CHAPTER 4: THREE VIEWS OF CHATTANOOGA

Barnett, James. "Willich's Thirty-Second Indiana Volunteers." *Cincinnati Historical Society Bulletin* 37 (1979).

Benjaminson, Eric. "A Regiment of Immigrants: The 82nd Illinois Volunteer Infantry and the Letters of Captain Rudolph Mueller." *Journal of the Illinois State Historical Society* 94:2 (2001).

Braeutigam, Friedrich August. "Civil War Diary of Friedrich August Braeutigam." *The Palatine Immigrant* 14:4 (1989–1990).

Burton, William L. *Melting Pot Soldiers: The Union's Ethnic Regiments.* Ames: Iowa State Univ. Press, 1988.

Burton, William L. "'Title Deed to America': Union Ethnic Regiments in the Civil War." *Proceedings of the American Philosophical Society* 124:6 (1980).

Cooling, B. Franklin. "A People's War: Partisan Conflict in Tennessee and Kentucky" from *Confederates, Unionists, and Violence on the Confederate Home Front,* ed. Daniel E. Sutherland. Fayetteville: Univ. of Arkansas Press, 1999.

Cozzens, Peter. *The Shipwreck of Their Hopes: The Battles for Chattanooga.* Chicago: Univ. of Illinois Press, 1994.

Dluger, Mark A. "A Regimental Community: The Men of the 82nd Illinois Infantry Before, During, and After the American Civil War." Ph.D. dissertation, Loyola University Chicago, 2009.

Freitag, Sabine. *Friedrich Hecker: Two Lives for Liberty.* St. Louis: St. Louis Mercantile Library, 2006.

Graham, David. "A Fight for a Principle: The 24th Illinois Volunteer Infantry Regiment." *Journal of the Illinois State Historical Society* 104:1/2 (2011).

Hight, John J. *History of the Fifty-Eighth Regiment of Indiana Volunteer Infantry.* Princeton, N.J.: Press of the Clarion, 1895.

Kaufmann, Wilhelm. *The Germans in the American Civil War.* Carlisle, Pa.: John Kallmann, 1999.

Keller, Christian B. *Chancellorsville and the Germans: Nativism, Ethnicity, and Civil War Memory.* New York: Fordham Univ. Press, 2007.

Koerner, Gustave. *Memoirs: 1809–1896,* Vol. 2. Cedar Rapids, Iowa: Torch Press, 1909.

Mahin, Dean B. *The Blessed Place of Freedom: Europeans in Civil War America.* Dulles, Va.: Brassey's, 2002.

McDonough, James Lee. *Chattanooga—A Death Grip on the Confederacy.* Knoxville: Univ. of Tennessee Press, 1984.

Orendorff, H.H., Armstrong, G.M., et al. *Reminiscences of the Civil War: From Diaries of Members of the 103rd Illinois Volunteer Infantry.* Chicago: J.F. Leaming, 1904.

Reinhart, Joseph R., ed. *Yankee Dutchmen Under Fire: Civil War Letters from the 82nd Infantry.* Kent, Ohio: Kent State University Press, 2013.

Schurz, Carl. *The Reminiscences of Carl Schurz: Volume 3, 1863–1869.* New York: McClure, 1908.

Swedberg, Claire E., ed. *Three Years with the 92d Illinois: The Civil War Diary of John M. King.* Mechanicsburg, Penn.: Stackpole Books, 1999.

Villard, Oswald Garrison. "The 'Latin Peasants' of Belleville, Illinois." *Journal of the Illinois State Historical Society* 35:1 (1942).

Wagner, William. *History of the 24th Illinois Volunteer Infantry Regiment.* Chicago: Illinois Staats Zeitung, 1864.

Wills, Charles W. *Army Life of an Illinois Soldier: The Letters and Diary of Charles W. Wills.* Toronto: Globe Printing, 1906.

Woodworth, Steven E. *Nothing but Victory: The Army of the Tennessee, 1861–1865.* New York: Knopf, 2005.

Woodworth, Steven E. *Six Armies in Tennessee: The Chickamauga and Chattanooga Campaigns.* Lincoln: Univ. of Nebraska Press, 1998.

CHAPTER 5: HEROES IN THE FIELD

Attie, Rejean. "'A Swindling Concern': The United States Sanitary Commission and the Northern Female Public, 1861–1865." Ph.D. dissertation, Columbia University, 1987.

Baker, Nina Brown. *Cyclone in Calico.* Boston: Little, Brown, 1952.

Brockett, L.P., and Mary C. Vaughan. *Women's Work in the Civil War: A Record of Heroism, Patriotism and Patience.* Chicago: Zeigler, McCurdy, 1867.

Chicago Sanitary Commission. *History of the North-Western Soldiers' Fair.* Chicago: Dunlop, Sewell & Spalding, 1864.

Giesberg, Judith Ann. *Civil War Sisterhood: The U.S. Sanitary Commission and Women's Politics in Transition.* Boston: Northeastern Univ. Press, 2000.

Henshaw, Sarah Edwards. *Our Branch and Its Tributaries; Being a History of the Work of the Northwestern Sanitary Commission and Its Auxiliaries, During the War of the Rebellion.* Chicago: Alfred L. Sewell, 1868.

Hoge, Jane. *The Boys in Blue; or, Heroes of the "Rank and File."* New York: E.B. Treat, 1867.

Holland, Mary Gardner. *Our Army Nurses: Stories from Women in the Civil War.* Roseville, Minn.: Edinborough Press, 1998.

Holzer, Harold. "America's Second Declaration of Independence: Lincoln's Emancipation Proclamation." HistoryNet, Nov. 8. 2012. www.historynet.com/americas-second-declaration-of-independence.htm.

Karamanski, Theodore J. *Rally 'Round the Flag: Chicago and the Civil War.* Lanham, Md.: Rowman & Littlefield, 2006.

Livermore, Mary A. *My Story of the War: A Woman's Narrative of Four Years Personal Experience.* Hartford, Conn.: A.D. Worthington, 1889.

Livermore, Mary A. *The Story of My Life, or The Sunshine and Shadow of Seventy Years.* Hartford, Conn.: A.D. Worthington, 1897.

Schultz, Jane E. *Women at the Front: Hospital Workers in Civil War America.* Chapel Hill: Univ. of North Carolina Press, 2004.

Silber, Nina. *Daughters of the Union: Northern Women Fight the Civil War.* Cambridge, Mass.: Harvard Univ. Press, 2005.

Stillé, Charles J. *History of the United States Sanitary Commission, Being the General Report of Its Work During the War of the Rebellion.* Philadelphia: J.B. Lippincott, 1866.

Thompson, William Y. "Sanitary Fairs of the Civil War." *Civil War History* 4:1 (1958).

Tise, Pam. "A Fragile Legacy: The Contributions of Women in the United States Sanitary Commission to the United States Administrative State." M.P.A. thesis, Texas State University-San Marcos, 2013.

Venet, Wendy Hamand. *A Strong-Minded Woman: The Life of Mary A. Livermore.* Amherst: University of Massachusetts Press, 2005.

Young, Agatha. *The Women and the Crisis: Women of the North in the Civil War.* New York: McDowell, Obolensky, 1959.

CHAPTER 6: DAMN YOUR OFFICERS

Andrew, Byron. *A Biography of General John A. Logan, with an Account of His Public Services in Peace and in War.* New York: H.S. Goodspeed, 1884.

Baker, Nina Brown. *Cyclone in Calico.* Boston: Little, Brown, 1952.

Chase, Julia A. Houghton. *Mary A. Bickerdyke, "Mother."* Lawrence, Kans.: Journal Publishing House, 1896.

Davis, Margaret B. *Mother Bickerdyke: Her Life and Labors for the Relief of Our Soldiers; Sketches of Battle Scenes and Incidents of the Sanitary Service.* San Francisco: A.T. Dewey, 1886.

Ecelbarger, Gary. *Black Jack Logan: An Extraordinary Life in Peace and War.* Guilford, Conn.: Lyons Press, 2005.

Giesberg, Judith Ann. *Civil War Sisterhood: The U.S. Sanitary Commission and Women's Politics in Transition.* Boston: Northeastern Univ. Press, 2000.

Hess, Earl J. *Kennesaw Mountain: Sherman, Johnston, and the Atlanta Campaign.* Chapel Hill: Univ. of North Carolina Press, 2013.

Hubbard, Mark, ed. *Illinois's War: The Civil War in Documents.* Athens: Ohio Univ. Press, 2013.

Jones, James Pickett. *Black Jack: John A. Logan and Southern Illinois in the Civil War Era.* Tallahassee: Florida State University, 1967.

Kennett, Lee. *Marching Through Georgia: The Story of Soldiers and Civilians During Sherman's Campaign.* New York: HarperPerennial, 1996.

Logan, Mary A. *Reminiscences of a Soldier's Wife: An Autobiography.* New York: Charles Scribner's Sons, 1913.

Marszalek, John F. *Sherman: A Soldier's Passion for Order.* New York: Free Press-Macmillan, 1993.

McCarley, J. Britt. *The Atlanta and Savannah Campaigns, 1864.* Washington, D.C.: Center of Military History, U.S. Army, 2014.

Porter, Mary H. *Eliza Chappell Porter: A Memoir.* Chicago: Fleming H. Revell, 1892.

Schultz, Jane E., ed. *Women at the Front: Hospital Workers in Civil War America.* Chapel Hill: Univ. of North Carolina Press, 2004.

Secrist, Philip L. *The Battle of Resaca: Atlanta Campaign, 1864.* Macon, Ga.: Mercer Univ. Press, 2010.

Shanks, William F.G. *Personal Recollections of Distinguished Generals.* New York: Harper & Brothers, 1866.

Silber, Nina. *Daughters of the Union: Northern Women Fight the Civil War.* Cambridge, Mass.: Harvard Univ. Press, 2005.

Vermilya, Daniel J. *The Battle of Kennesaw Mountain.* Charleston, S.C.: The History Press, 2014.

Young, Agatha. *The Women and the Crisis: Women of the North in the Civil War.* New York: McDowell, Obolensky, 1959.

CHAPTER 7: THE WHEEL

Andrew, Byron. *A Biography of General John A. Logan, with an Account of His Public Services in Peace and in War.* New York: H.S. Goodspeed, 1884.

Bonds, Russell S. *War Like the Thunderbolt: The Battle and Burning of Atlanta.* Yardley, Penn.: Westholme, 2009.

Castel, Albert. *Decision in the West: The Atlanta Campaign of 1864.* Lawrence: Univ. Press of Kansas, 1992.

Cornish, Dudley Taylor. *The Sable Arm: Black Troops in the Union Army, 1861–1865.* Lawrence: Univ. Press of Kansas, 1956.

Cox, Jacob D. *Atlanta: Campaigns of the Civil War IX.* New York: Charles Scribner's Sons, 1882.

Davis, Stephen. "A Very Barbarous Mode of Carrying on War: Sherman's Artillery Bombardment of Atlanta, July 20–August 24, 1864." *The Georgia Historical Quarterly* 79:1 (1995).

Dawson, George Francis. *Life and Services of Gen. John A. Logan, Soldier and Statesman.* New York: Belford, Clarke, 1887.

Ecelbarger, Gary. *Black Jack Logan: An Extraordinary Life in Peace and War.* Guilford, Conn.: Lyons Press, 2005.

Ecelbarger, Gary. *The Day Dixie Died: The Battle of Atlanta.* New York: St. Martin's Press, 2010.

Furman, Jan, ed. *Slavery in the Clover Bottoms: John McCline's Narrative of His Life During Slavery and the Civil War.* Knoxville: Univ. of Tennessee Press, 1998.

Jones, James Pickett. *Black Jack: John A. Logan and Southern Illinois in the Civil War Era.* Tallahassee: Florida State University, 1967.

Kime, Marlin G. "Sherman's Gordian Knot: Logistical Problems in the Atlanta Campaign." *The Georgia Historical Quarterly* 70:1 (1986).

McCarley, J. Britt. *The Atlanta and Savannah Campaigns, 1864.* Washington, D.C.: Center of Military History, U.S. Army, 2014.

Orendorff, H.H., Armstrong, G.M., et al. *Reminiscences of the Civil War: From Diaries of Members of the 103rd Illinois Volunteer Infantry.* Chicago: J.F. Leaming, 1904.

Sarris, Jonathan D. "Anatomy of an Atrocity: The Madden Branch Massacre and Guerrilla Warfare in North Georgia, 1861–1865." *The Georgia Historical Quarterly* 77:4 (1993).

The War of the Rebellion: A Compilation of the Official Records of the Union and Confederate Armies. Series 1, Volume 38, Parts 2 and 3. Washington, D.C.: Govt. Printing Office, 1891.

Wills, Charles W. *Army Life of an Illinois Soldier: The Letters and Diary of Charles W. Wills.* Toronto: Globe Printing, 1906.

Woodworth, Steven E. *Nothing but Victory: The Army of the Tennessee, 1861–1865.* New York: Knopf, 2005.

Wortman, Marc. *The Bonfire: The Siege and Burning of Atlanta.* New York: PublicAffairs, 2009.

CHAPTER 8: THE ANVIL

Athearn, Robert G. "An Indiana Doctor Marches with Sherman: The Diary of James Comfort Patten." *Indiana Magazine of History* 49:4 (1953).

SOURCES

Attie, Rejean. "'A Swindling Concern': The United States Sanitary Commission and the Northern Female Public, 1861–1865." Ph.D. dissertation. Columbia University, 1987.

Bailey, Anne. J. *The Chessboard of War: Sherman and Hood in the Autumn Campaigns of 1864*. Lincoln: Univ. of Nebraska Press, 2000.

Baker, Nina Brown. *Cyclone in Calico*. Boston: Little, Brown, 1952.

Benjaminson, Eric. "A Regiment of Immigrants: The 82nd Illinois Volunteer Infantry and the Letters of Captain Rudolph Mueller." *Journal of the Illinois State Historical Society* 94:2 (2001).

Bonds, Russell S. *War Like the Thunderbolt: The Battle and Burning of Atlanta*. Yardley, Penn.: Westholme, 2009.

Castel, Albert. *Decision in the West: The Atlanta Campaign of 1864*. Lawrence: Univ. Press of Kansas, 1992.

Davis, Stephen. "A Very Barbarous Mode of Carrying on War: Sherman's Artillery Bombardment of Atlanta, July 20–August 24, 1864." *The Georgia Historical Quarterly* 79:1 (1995).

Dluger, Mark A. "A Regimental Community: The Men of the 82nd Illinois Infantry Before, During, and After the American Civil War." Ph.D. dissertation, Loyola University Chicago, 2009.

Foote, Shelby. *The Civil War: A Narrative, Red River to Appomattox*. New York: Vintage, 1974.

Freitag, Sabine. *Friedrich Hecker: Two Lives for Liberty*. St. Louis: St. Louis Mercantile Library, 2006.

Gleicher, David. "From Jewish Immigrant to Union General in Under Ten Years." *Chicago Jewish History* 15:2 (1992).

Grimsley, Mark. *The Hard Hand of War: Union Military Policy Toward Southern Civilians, 1861–1865*. New York: Cambridge University Press, 1995.

Hight, John J. *History of the Fifty-Eighth Regiment of Indiana Volunteer Infantry*. Princeton, N.J.: Press of the Clarion, 1895.

Kaufmann, Wilhelm. *The Germans in the American Civil War*. Carlisle, Pa.: John Kallmann, 1999.

Kennett, Lee. *Marching Through Georgia: The Story of Soldiers and Civilians During Sherman's Campaign*. New York: HarperPerennial, 1996.

Marszalek, John F. *Sherman: A Soldier's Passion for Order*. New York: Free Press-Macmillan, 1993.

McCarley, J. Britt. *The Atlanta and Savannah Campaigns, 1864*. Washington, D.C.: Center of Military History, U.S. Army, 2014.

Moss, Lemuel. *Annals of the United States Christian Commission*. Philadelphia: J.B. Lippincott, 1868.

Reinhart, Joseph R., ed. *Yankee Dutchmen Under Fire: Civil War Letters from the 82nd Infantry*. Kent, Ohio: Kent State University Press, 2013.

Sherman, William T. *The Memoirs of William T. Sherman*, vol. 2. New York: D. Appleton, 1886.

Simpson, Brooks D. and Jean V. Berlin, eds. *Sherman's Civil War: Selected Correspondence of William T. Sherman, 1860–1865*. Chapel Hill: Univ. of North Carolina Press, 1999.

Trudeau, Noah Andre. *Southern Storm: Sherman's March to the Sea*. New York: HarperCollins, 2008.

The War of the Rebellion: A Compilation of the Official Records of the Union and Confederate Armies. Series 1, Volume 38, Parts 2 and 3. Washington, D.C.: Govt. Printing Office, 1891.

Woodworth, Steven E. *Nothing but Victory: The Army of the Tennessee, 1861–1865.* New York: Knopf, 2005.

Wortman, Marc. *The Bonfire: The Siege and Burning of Atlanta.* New York: PublicAffairs, 2009.

CHAPTER 9: SHADOWY TERRITORY

Andrew, Byron. *A Biography of General John A. Logan, with an Account of His Public Services in Peace and in War.* New York: H.S. Goodspeed, 1884.

Attie, Jeanie. *Patriotic Toil: Northern Women and the American Civil War.* Ithaca, N.Y.: Cornell Univ. Press, 1998.

Attie, Rejean. "'A Swindling Concern': The United States Sanitary Commission and the Northern Female Public, 1861–1865." Ph.D. dissertation. Columbia University, 1987.

Bailey, Anne. J. *The Chessboard of War: Sherman and Hood in the Autumn Campaigns of 1864.* Lincoln: Univ. of Nebraska Press, 2000.

Baker, Nina Brown. *Cyclone in Calico.* Boston: Little, Brown, 1952.

Chase, Julia A. Houghton. *Mary A. Bickerdyke, "Mother."* Lawrence, Kans.: Journal Publishing House, 1896.

Davis, Margaret B. *Mother Bickerdyke: Her Life and Labors for the Relief of Our Soldiers; Sketches of Battle Scenes and Incidents of the Sanitary Service.* San Francisco: A.T. Dewey, 1886.

Dawson, George Francis. *Life and Services of Gen. John A. Logan, Soldier and Statesman.* New York: Belford, Clarke, 1887.

Ecelbarger, Gary. *Black Jack Logan: An Extraordinary Life in Peace and War.* Guilford, Conn.: Lyons Press, 2005.

Giesberg, Judith Ann. *Civil War Sisterhood: The U.S. Sanitary Commission and Women's Politics in Transition.* Boston: Northeastern Univ. Press, 2000.

Grimsley, Mark. *The Hard Hand of War: Union Military Policy Toward Southern Civilians, 1861–1865.* New York: Cambridge University Press, 1995.

Henshaw, Sarah Edwards. *Our Branch and Its Tributaries; Being a History of the Work of the Northwestern Sanitary Commission and Its Auxiliaries, During the War of the Rebellion.* Chicago: Alfred L. Sewell, 1868.

Hitchcock, Henry. *Marching with Sherman.* New Haven, Conn.: Yale Univ. Press, 1927.

Hoge, Jane. *The Boys in Blue; or, Heroes of the "Rank and File."* New York: E.B. Treat, 1867.

Jones, James Pickett. *Black Jack: John A. Logan and Southern Illinois in the Civil War Era.* Tallahassee: Florida State University, 1967.

Kennett, Lee. *Marching Through Georgia: The Story of Soldiers and Civilians During Sherman's Campaign.* New York: HarperPerennial, 1996.

Livermore, Mary A. *My Story of the War: A Woman's Narrative of Four Years Personal Experience.* Hartford, Conn.: A.D. Worthington, 1889.

Logan, Mary A. *Reminiscences of a Soldier's Wife: An Autobiography.* New York: Charles Scribner's Sons, 1913.

Marszalek, John F. *Sherman: A Soldier's Passion for Order.* New York: Free Press-Macmillan, 1993.

McCarley, J. Britt. *The Atlanta and Savannah Campaigns, 1864.* Washington, D.C.: Center of Military History, U.S. Army, 2014.

Moss, Lemuel. *Annals of the United States Christian Commission.* Philadelphia: J.B. Lippincott, 1868.

Patton, William W. "The Sanitary Commission in the Army." *The Sanitary Reporter* 2:17 (Jan. 15, 1865), 129–130.

Porter, Mary H. *Eliza Chappell Porter: A Memoir.* Chicago: Fleming H. Revell, 1892.

Silber, Nina. *Daughters of the Union: Northern Women Fight the Civil War.* Cambridge, Mass.: Harvard Univ. Press, 2005.

Simpson, Brooks D. and Jean V. Berlin, eds. *Sherman's Civil War: Selected Correspondence of William T. Sherman, 1860–1865.* Chapel Hill: Univ. of North Carolina Press, 1999.

Trudeau, Noah Andre. *Southern Storm: Sherman's March to the Sea.* New York: HarperCollins, 2008.

Venet, Wendy Hamand. *A Strong-Minded Woman: The Life of Mary A. Livermore.* Amherst: University of Massachusetts Press, 2005.

Woodworth, Steven E. *Nothing but Victory: The Army of the Tennessee, 1861–1865.* New York: Knopf, 2005.

Wortman, Marc. *The Bonfire: The Siege and Burning of Atlanta.* New York: PublicAffairs, 2009.

CHAPTER 10: COMRADES IN DIRT

Benjaminson, Eric. "A Regiment of Immigrants: The 82nd Illinois Volunteer Infantry and the Letters of Captain Rudolph Mueller." *Journal of the Illinois State Historical Society* 94:2 (2001).

Bonner, James C. "Sherman at Milledgeville in 1864." *The Journal of Southern History* 22:3 (1956), 273–291.

Brockman Jr., Charles J., ed. "The John Van Duser Diary of Sherman's March from Atlanta to Hilton Head." *The Georgia Historical Quarterly* 53:2 (1969), 220–240.

Connolly, James A. *Three Years in the Army of the Cumberland: The Letters and Diary of James A. Connolly*, Paul M. Angle, ed. Bloomington: Indiana Univ. Press, 1959.

Conyngham, David P. *Sherman's March Through the South: Sketches and Incidents of the Campaign.* New York: Sheldon and Company, 1865.

Davis, Burke. *Sherman's March.* New York: Random House, 1980.

De Laubenfels, D.J. "Where Sherman Passed By," *Geographical Review* 47:3 (1957), 381–395.

Dluger, Mark A. "A Regimental Community: The Men of the 82nd Illinois Infantry Before, During, and After the American Civil War." Ph.D. dissertation, Loyola University Chicago, 2009.

Drago, Edmund L. "How Sherman's March Through Georgia Affected the Slaves." *The Georgia Historical Quarterly* 57:3 (1973), 361–375.

Emberton, Carole. "A Hungry Belly and Freedom." Accessed at We're History, November 25, 2014, werehistory.org/hungry-belly-and-freedom/.

Escott, Paul D. "The Context of Freedom: Georgia's Slaves During the Civil War." *The Georgia Historical Quarterly* 58:1 (1974), 79–104.

Force, Manning Ferguson. "From Atlanta to Savannah: The Civil War Journal of Manning F. Force, November 15, 1864–January 3, 1865." *The Georgia Historical Quarterly* 91:2 (2007), 185–205.

Freitag, Sabine. *Friedrich Hecker: Two Lives for Liberty.* St. Louis: St. Louis Mercantile Library, 2006.

Furman, Jan, ed. *Slavery in the Clover Bottoms: John McCline's Narrative of His Life During Slavery and the Civil War.* Knoxville: Univ. of Tennessee Press, 1998.

Glatthaar, Joseph T. *The March to the Sea and Beyond: Sherman's Troops in the Savannah and Carolinas Campaigns.* New York: New York Univ. Press, 1985.

Grimsley, Mark. *The Hard Hand of War: Union Military Policy Toward Southern Civilians, 1861–1865.* New York: Cambridge University Press, 1995.

Guthrie, James M. *Camp-Fires of the Afro-American, or, The Colored Man as a Patriot.* Philadelphia: Afro-American Publishing, 1899.

Hight, John J. *History of the Fifty-Eighth Regiment of Indiana Volunteer Infantry.* Princeton, N.J.: Press of the Clarion, 1895.

Hitchcock, Henry. *Marching with Sherman.* New Haven, Conn.: Yale Univ. Press, 1927.

Hughes Jr., Nathaniel Cheairs, and Gordon D. Whitney. *Jefferson Davis in Blue: The Life of Sherman's Relentless Warrior.* Baton Rouge: Louisiana State Univ. Press, 2002.

Jones, James P. "General Jeff C. Davis, U.S.A. and Sherman's Georgia Campaign." *The Georgia Historical Quarterly* 47:3 (1963), 231–248.

Kennett, Lee. *Marching Through Georgia: The Story of Soldiers and Civilians During Sherman's Campaign.* New York: HarperPerennial, 1996.

Kerr, Charles D. "From Atlanta to Raleigh," in *Glimpses of the Nation's Struggle.* St. Paul, Minn.: St. Paul Book and Stationery Company, 1887.

Levine, Bruce. *The Fall of the House of Dixie: The Civil War and the Social Revolution That Transformed the South.* New York: Random House, 2013.

Marszalek, John F. *Sherman: A Soldier's Passion for Order.* New York: Free Press-Macmillan, 1993.

McCarley, J. Britt. *The Atlanta and Savannah Campaigns, 1864.* Washington, D.C.: Center of Military History, U.S. Army, 2014.

Mohr, Clarence L. "Before Sherman: Georgia Blacks and the Union War Effort," *The Journal of Southern History* 45:3 (1979), 331–352.

Nichols, George Ward. *The Story of the Great March, from the Diary of a Staff Officer.* New York: Harper & Brothers, 1865.

Poe, Orlando M., Chief Engineer, Military Division of the Mississippi. Letter to Richard Delafield, Chief of Engineers, U.S. Army. October 8, 1865.

Reinhart, Joseph R., ed. *Yankee Dutchmen Under Fire: Civil War Letters from the 82nd Infantry.* Kent, Ohio: Kent State University Press, 2013.

"Sherman's March: Journal of an Eye-Witness." *The New York Times*, December 23, 1864.

Trudeau, Noah Andre. *Southern Storm: Sherman's March to the Sea.* New York: HarperCollins, 2008.

CHAPTER 11: ALL AROUND THEM LIGHT AS DAY

Ambrose, D. Leib. *History of the Seventh Regiment Illinois Volunteer Infantry.* Springfield, Ill.: Illinois Journal Company, 1868.

Ash, Stephen V. "Poor Whites in the Occupied South." *The Journal of Southern History* 57:1 (1991), 39–62.

Bailey, Anne. J. *The Chessboard of War: Sherman and Hood in the Autumn Campaigns of 1864.* Lincoln: Univ. of Nebraska Press, 2000.

Brockman Jr., Charles J., ed. "The John Van Duser Diary of Sherman's March from Atlanta to Hilton Head." *The Georgia Historical Quarterly* 53:2 (1969), 220–240.

SOURCES

Connolly, James A. *Three Years in the Army of the Cumberland: The Letters and Diary of James A. Connolly*, Paul M. Angle, ed. Bloomington: Indiana Univ. Press, 1959.

Conyngham, David P. *Sherman's March Through the South: Sketches and Incidents of the Campaign.* New York: Sheldon, 1865.

Downing, Alexander G. *Downing's Civil War Diary, August 15, 1861–July 31, 1865*, ed. Olynthus B. Clark. Des Moines, Iowa.: The Historical Department of Iowa, 1916.

Drago, Edmund L. "How Sherman's March Through Georgia Affected the Slaves." *The Georgia Historical Quarterly* 57:3 (1973), 361–375.

Escott, Paul D. "The Context of Freedom: Georgia's Slaves During the Civil War." *The Georgia Historical Quarterly* 58:1 (1974), 79–104.

Fellman, Michael. *Citizen Sherman: A Life of William Tecumseh Sherman*. New York: Random House, 1994.

Glatthaar, Joseph T. *The March to the Sea and Beyond: Sherman's Troops in the Savannah and Carolinas Campaigns*. New York: New York Univ. Press, 1985.

Hedley, F.Y. *Marching Through Georgia: Pen-Pictures of Every-Day Life in General Sherman's Army, from the Beginning of the Atlanta Campaign Until the Close of the War.* Chicago: Donohue, Henneberry, 1890.

Hitchcock, Henry. *Marching with Sherman*. New Haven, Conn.: Yale Univ. Press, 1927.

Jamison, Matthew H. *Recollections of Pioneer and Army Life*. Kansas City, Mo.: Hudson Press, 1911.

Kennett, Lee. *Marching Through Georgia: The Story of Soldiers and Civilians During Sherman's Campaign*. New York: HarperPerennial, 1996.

Kerr, Charles D. "From Atlanta to Raleigh," in *Glimpses of the Nation's Struggle*. St. Paul, Minn.: St. Paul Book and Stationery, 1887.

Marszalek, John F. *Sherman: A Soldier's Passion for Order*. New York: Free Press-Macmillan, 1993.

Martin, Samuel J. *Kill-Cavalry: The Life of Union General Hugh Judson Kilpatrick*. Mechanicsburg, Pa.: Stackpole Books, 2000.

Mohr, Clarence L. "Before Sherman: Georgia Blacks and the Union War Effort," *The Journal of Southern History* 45:3 (1979), 331–352.

Nichols, George Ward. *The Story of the Great March, from the Diary of a Staff Officer*. New York: Harper & Brothers, 1865.

Schwabe, F. Edward, Jr. *The March to the Sea: The Operational Role of Sherman's Right Wing.* Newport, R.I.: Naval War College, 1986.

Sharland, George. *Knapsack Notes of General Sherman's Grand Campaign Through the Empire State of the South*. Springfield, Ill.: Johnson & Bradford, 1865.

"Sherman's March: Journal of an Eye-Witness." *The New York Times*, December 23, 1864.

Sherman, William T. *The Memoirs of William T. Sherman*, vol. 2. New York: D. Appleton, 1886.

Trudeau, Noah Andre. *Southern Storm: Sherman's March to the Sea*. New York: HarperCollins, 2008.

Underwood, Adin B. *The Three Years' Service of the Thirty-Third Mass. Infantry Regiment, 1862–1865*. Boston: A. Williams, 1881.

Upson, Theodore F. *With Sherman to the Sea*. Baton Rouge: Louisiana Univ. Press, 1943.

Van Tuyll, Debra Reddin. "Scalawags and Scoundrels? The Moral and Legal Dimensions of Sherman's Last Campaigns." *Studies in Popular Culture* 22:2 (1999), 33–45.

Wills, Charles W. *Army Life of an Illinois Soldier: The Letters and Diary of Charles W. Wills.* Toronto: Globe Printing, 1906.

Woodworth, Steven E. *Nothing but Victory: The Army of the Tennessee, 1861–1865.* New York: Knopf, 2005.

CHAPTER 12: YELL LIKE THE DEVIL

Athearn, Robert G. "An Indiana Doctor Marches with Sherman: The Diary of James Comfort Patten." *Indiana Magazine of History* 49:4 (1953).

Bailey, Anne. J. *The Chessboard of War: Sherman and Hood in the Autumn Campaigns of 1864.* Lincoln: Univ. of Nebraska Press, 2000.

Benjaminson, Eric. "A Regiment of Immigrants: The 82nd Illinois Volunteer Infantry and the Letters of Captain Rudolph Mueller." *Journal of the Illinois State Historical Society* 94:2 (2001).

Brockman Jr., Charles J., ed. "The John Van Duser Diary of Sherman's March from Atlanta to Hilton Head." *The Georgia Historical Quarterly* 53:2 (1969), 220–240.

Connolly, James A. *Three Years in the Army of the Cumberland: The Letters and Diary of James A. Connolly,* Paul M. Angle, ed. Bloomington: Indiana Univ. Press, 1959.

Conyngham, David P. *Sherman's March Through the South: Sketches and Incidents of the Campaign.* New York: Sheldon, 1865.

Dluger, Mark A. "A Regimental Community: The Men of the 82nd Illinois Infantry Before, During, and After the American Civil War." Ph.D. dissertation, Loyola University Chicago, 2009.

Furman, Jan, ed. *Slavery in the Clover Bottoms: John McCline's Narrative of His Life During Slavery and the Civil War.* Knoxville: Univ. of Tennessee Press, 1998.

Glatthaar, Joseph T. *The March to the Sea and Beyond: Sherman's Troops in the Savannah and Carolinas Campaigns.* New York: New York Univ. Press, 1985.

Hazen, William B. *A Narrative of Military Service.* Boston: Ticknor, 1885.

Hight, John J. *History of the Fifty-Eighth Regiment of Indiana Volunteer Infantry.* Princeton, N.J.: Press of the Clarion, 1895.

Hitchcock, Henry. *Marching with Sherman.* New Haven, Conn.: Yale Univ. Press, 1927.

Hughes, Nathaniel Cheairs, Jr., and Gordon D. Whitney. *Jefferson Davis in Blue: The Life of Sherman's Relentless Warrior.* Baton Rouge: Louisiana State Univ. Press, 2002.

Jamison, Matthew H. *Recollections of Pioneer and Army Life.* Kansas City, Mo.: Hudson Press, 1911.

Jones, James P. "General Jeff C. Davis, U.S.A. and Sherman's Georgia Campaign." *The Georgia Historical Quarterly* 47:3 (1963), 231–248.

Kennett, Lee. *Marching Through Georgia: The Story of Soldiers and Civilians During Sherman's Campaign.* New York: HarperPerennial, 1996.

Kerr, Charles D. "From Atlanta to Raleigh," in *Glimpses of the Nation's Struggle.* St. Paul, Minn.: St. Paul Book and Stationery, 1887.

Marszalek, John F. *Sherman: A Soldier's Passion for Order.* New York: Free Press-Macmillan, 1993.

McCarley, J. Britt. *The Atlanta and Savannah Campaigns, 1864.* Washington, D.C.: Center of Military History, U.S. Army, 2014.

Nichols, George Ward. *The Story of the Great March, from the Diary of a Staff Officer.* New York: Harper & Brothers, 1865.

Reinhart, Joseph R., ed. *Yankee Dutchmen Under Fire: Civil War Letters from the 82nd Infantry.* Kent, Ohio: Kent State University Press, 2013.

Schwabe, F. Edward, Jr. *The March to the Sea: The Operational Role of Sherman's Right Wing.* Newport, R.I.: Naval War College, 1986.

Sharland, George. *Knapsack Notes of General Sherman's Grand Campaign Through the Empire State of the South.* Springfield, Ill.: Johnson & Bradford, 1865.

"Sherman's March: Journal of an Eye-Witness." *The New York Times*, December 23, 1864.

Sherman, William T. *The Memoirs of William T. Sherman*, vols. 1 and 2. New York: D. Appleton and Company, 1886.

Sherman, William T. "Old Shady, with a Moral." *North American Review* 147:383 (1888), 361–368.

Strong, William E. "The Capture of Fort McAllister, December 13, 1864." *The Georgia Historical Quarterly* 88:3 (2004), 406–421.

Trudeau, Noah Andre. *Southern Storm: Sherman's March to the Sea.* New York: HarperCollins, 2008.

The War of the Rebellion: A Compilation of the Official Records of the Union and Confederate Armies. Series 1, Volume 44, Part 1. Washington, D.C.: Govt. Printing Office, 1891.

Woodworth, Steven E. *Nothing but Victory: The Army of the Tennessee, 1861–1865.* New York: Knopf, 2005.

CHAPTER 13: SENTINELS

Bailey, Anne. J. *The Chessboard of War: Sherman and Hood in the Autumn Campaigns of 1864.* Lincoln: Univ. of Nebraska Press, 2000.

Baker, Nina Brown. *Cyclone in Calico.* Boston: Little, Brown, 1952.

Barrett, John G. *Sherman's March Through the Carolinas.* Chapel Hill: Univ. of North Carolina Press, 1956.

Byrne, William A. "'Uncle Billy' Sherman Comes to Town: The Free Winter of Black Savannah." *The Georgia Historical Quarterly* 79:1 (1995), 91–116.

Campbell, Jacqueline Glass. *When Sherman Marched North from the Sea: Resistance on the Confederate Home Front.* Chapel Hill: Univ. of North Carolina Press, 2003.

Chase, Julia A. Houghton. *Mary A. Bickerdyke, "Mother."* Lawrence, Kans.: Journal Publishing House, 1896.

Davis, Margaret B. *Mother Bickerdyke: Her Life and Labors for the Relief of Our Soldiers; Sketches of Battle Scenes and Incidents of the Sanitary Service.* San Francisco: A.T. Dewey, 1886.

Dawson, George Francis. *Life and Services of Gen. John A. Logan, Soldier and Statesman.* New York: Belford, Clarke, 1887.

Drago, Edmund L. "How Sherman's March Through Georgia Affected the Slaves." *The Georgia Historical Quarterly* 57:3 (1973), 361–375.

Dyer, John P. "Northern Relief for Savannah During Sherman's Occupation." *The Journal of Southern History* 19:4 (1953), 457–472.

Ecelbarger, Gary. *Black Jack Logan: An Extraordinary Life in Peace and War.* Guilford, Conn.: Lyons Press, 2005.

Fellman, Michael. *Citizen Sherman: A Life of William Tecumseh Sherman.* New York: Random House, 1994.

Giesberg, Judith Ann. *Civil War Sisterhood: The U.S. Sanitary Commission and Women's Politics in Transition*. Boston: Northeastern Univ. Press, 2000.

Glatthaar, Joseph T. *The March to the Sea and Beyond: Sherman's Troops in the Savannah and Carolinas Campaigns*. New York: New York Univ. Press, 1985.

Grant, Ulysses S. *Personal Memoirs of Ulysses S. Grant.*, vol. 2. New York: Charles L. Webster, 1886.

Grimsley, Mark. *The Hard Hand of War: Union Military Policy Toward Southern Civilians, 1861–1865*. New York: Cambridge University Press, 1995.

Henshaw, Sarah Edwards. *Our Branch and Its Tributaries; Being a History of the Work of the North-western Sanitary Commission and Its Auxiliaries, During the War of the Rebellion*. Chicago: Alfred L. Sewell, 1868.

Hight, John J. *History of the Fifty-Eighth Regiment of Indiana Volunteer Infantry*. Princeton, N.J.: Press of the Clarion, 1895.

Hitchcock, Henry. *Marching with Sherman*. New Haven, Conn.: Yale Univ. Press, 1927.

Hoge, Jane. *The Boys in Blue; or, Heroes of the "Rank and File."* New York: E.B. Treat, 1867.

Hughes Jr., Nathaniel Cheairs and Gordon D. Whitney. *Jefferson Davis in Blue: The Life of Sherman's Relentless Warrior*. Baton Rouge: Louisiana State Univ. Press, 2002.

Jones, James P. *Black Jack: John A. Logan and Southern Illinois in the Civil War Era*. Tallahassee: Florida State University, 1967.

Jones, James P. "General Jeff C. Davis, U.S.A. and Sherman's Georgia Campaign." *The Georgia Historical Quarterly* 47:3 (1963), 231–248.

Kennett, Lee. *Marching Through Georgia: The Story of Soldiers and Civilians During Sherman's Campaign*. New York: HarperPerennial, 1996.

Levine, Bruce. *The Fall of the House of Dixie: The Civil War and the Social Revolution That Transformed the South*. New York: Random House, 2013.

Livermore, Mary A. *My Story of the War: A Woman's Narrative of Four Years Personal Experience*. Hartford, Conn.: A.D. Worthington, 1889.

Logan, Mary A. *Reminiscences of a Soldier's Wife: An Autobiography*. New York: Charles Scribner's Sons, 1913.

Marszalek, John F. *Sherman: A Soldier's Passion for Order*. New York: Free Press-Macmillan, 1993.

Martin, Samuel J. *Kill-Cavalry: The Life of Union General Hugh Judson Kilpatrick*. Mechanicsburg, Pa.: Stackpole Books, 2000.

Nichols, George Ward. *The Story of the Great March, from the Diary of a Staff Officer*. New York: Harper & Brothers, 1865.

Penningroth, Dylan. "Slavery, Freedom, and Social Claims to Property Among African Americans in Liberty County, Georgia, 1850–1880." *The Journal of American History* 84:2 (1997), 405–435.

Rogers, George A., and R.F. Saunders. "The Scourge of Sherman's Men in Liberty County, Georgia." *The Georgia Historical Quarterly* 60:4 (1976), 356–369.

Rubin, Anne Sarah. *Through the Heart of Dixie: Sherman's March and American Memory*. Chapel Hill: Univ. of North Carolina Press, 2014.

Simpson, Brooks D. and Jean V. Berlin, eds. *Sherman's Civil War: Selected Correspondence of William T. Sherman, 1860–1865*. Chapel Hill: Univ. of North Carolina Press, 1999.

Smith, John David, ed. *Black Soldiers in Blue: African American Troops in the Civil War Era*. Chapel Hill: Univ. of North Carolina Press, 2002.

Tise, Pam. "A Fragile Legacy: The Contributions of Women in the United States Sanitary Commission to the United States Administrative State." M.P.A. thesis, Texas State University–San Marcos, 2013.

Trudeau, Noah Andre. *Like Men of War: Black Troops in the Civil War, 1862–1865*. New York: Little, Brown, 1998.

Trudeau, Noah Andre. *Southern Storm: Sherman's March to the Sea*. New York: HarperCollins, 2008.

Van Tuyll, Debra Reddin. "Scalawags and Scoundrels? The Moral and Legal Dimensions of Sherman's Last Campaigns." *Studies in Popular Culture* 22:2 (1999), 33–45.

Venet, Wendy Hamand. *A Strong-Minded Woman: The Life of Mary A. Livermore*. Amherst: University of Massachusetts Press, 2005.

The War of the Rebellion: A Compilation of the Official Records of the Union and Confederate Armies. Series 1, Volume 47, Part 2. Washington, D.C.: Govt. Printing Office, 1891.

Weintraub, Stanley. *General Sherman's Christmas: Savannah, 1864*. New York: HarperCollins, 2009.

Westwood, Howard C. "Sherman Marched: And Proclaimed 'Land for the Landless.'" *The South Carolina Historical Magazine* 79:1 (1984), 33–50.

Wittenmyer, Annie. *Under the Guns: A Woman's Reminiscences of the Civil War*. Boston: E.B. Stillings, 1895.

CHAPTER 14: FIRE AND SWORD

Barrett, John G. "Sherman and Total War in the Carolinas." *The North Carolina Historical Review* 37:3 (1960), 367–381.

Barrett, John G. *Sherman's March Through the Carolinas*. Chapel Hill: Univ. of North Carolina Press, 1956.

Byers, S.H.M. *With Fire and Sword*. New York: Neale, 1911.

Campbell, Jacqueline Glass. *When Sherman Marched North from the Sea: Resistance on the Confederate Home Front*. Chapel Hill: Univ. of North Carolina Press, 2003.

Chesebrough, David B. "'There Goes Your Damn Gospel Shop!' The Churches and Clergy as Victims of Sherman's March Through South Carolina." *The South Carolina Historical Magazine* 92:1 (1991), 15–33.

Conyngham, David P. *Sherman's March Through the South: Sketches and Incidents of the Campaign*. New York: Sheldon and Company, 1865.

Cox, Jacob D. *The March to the Sea—Franklin and Nashville*. New York: Charles Scribner's Sons, 1913.

Dawson, George Francis. *Life and Services of Gen. John A. Logan, Soldier and Statesman*. New York: Belford, Clarke, 1887.

Eaton, Clement. "Diary of an Officer in Sherman's Army Marching Through the Carolinas." *The Journal of Southern History* 9:2 (1943), 238–254.

Ecelbarger, Gary. *Black Jack Logan: An Extraordinary Life in Peace and War*. Guilford, Conn.: Lyons Press, 2005.

Garber, Michael C., Jr. "Reminiscences of the Burning of Columbia, South Carolina." *Indiana Magazine of History* 11:4 (1915), 285–300.

Glatthaar, Joseph T. *The March to the Sea and Beyond: Sherman's Troops in the Savannah and Carolinas Campaigns*. New York: New York Univ. Press, 1985.

Grimsley, Mark. *The Hard Hand of War: Union Military Policy Toward Southern Civilians, 1861–1865*. New York: Cambridge University Press, 1995.

Hattaway, Herman and Archer Jones. *How the North Won: A Military History of the Civil War*. Chicago: Univ. of Illinois Press, 1991.

Hazen, William B. *A Narrative of Military Service*. Boston: Ticknor, 1885.

Hedley, F.Y. *Marching Through Georgia: Pen-Pictures of Every-Day Life in General Sherman's Army, from the Beginning of the Atlanta Campaign Until the Close of the War*. Chicago: Donohue, Henneberry, 1890.

Hight, John J. *History of the Fifty-Eighth Regiment of Indiana Volunteer Infantry*. Princeton, N.J.: Press of the Clarion, 1895.

Jones, James P. *Black Jack: John A. Logan and Southern Illinois in the Civil War Era*. Tallahassee: Florida State University, 1967.

Logan, Mary A. *Reminiscences of a Soldier's Wife: An Autobiography*. New York: Charles Scribner's Sons, 1913.

Lucas, Marion Brunson. *Sherman and the Burning of Columbia*. College Station: Texas A&M Univ. Press, 1976.

Nichols, George Ward. *The Story of the Great March, from the Diary of a Staff Officer*. New York: Harper & Brothers, 1865.

Underwood, Adin B. *The Three Years' Service of the Thirty-Third Mass. Infantry Regiment, 1862– 1865*. Boston: A. Williams, 1881.

Van Tuyll, Debra Reddin. "Scalawags and Scoundrels? The Moral and Legal Dimensions of Sherman's Last Campaigns." *Studies in Popular Culture* 22:2 (1999), 33–45.

Walters, John Bennett. "General William T. Sherman and Total War." *The Journal of Southern History* 14:4 (1948), 447–480.

Wills, Charles W. *Army Life of an Illinois Soldier: The Letters and Diary of Charles W. Wills*. Toronto: Globe Printing, 1906.

Woodworth, Steven E. *Nothing but Victory: The Army of the Tennessee, 1861–1865*. New York: Knopf, 2005.

CHAPTER 15: TO RALEIGH

Baker, Nina Brown. *Cyclone in Calico*. Boston: Little, Brown, 1952.

Barrett, John G. *Sherman's March Through the Carolinas*. Chapel Hill: Univ. of North Carolina Press, 1956.

Barrett, John G. "Sherman's March Through North Carolina." *The North Carolina Historical Review* 42:2 (1965). 192–207.

Belknap, Charles E. "Bentonville: What a Bummer Knows About It." Military Legion of the Loyal Order of the United States, Commandery of the District of Columbia, War Papers, vol. 12. Read at meeting on January 4, 1893.

Benjaminson, Eric. "A Regiment of Immigrants: The 82nd Illinois Volunteer Infantry and the Letters of Captain Rudolph Mueller." *Journal of the Illinois State Historical Society* 94:2 (2001).

SOURCES

Bradley, Mark L. *Last Stand in the Carolinas: The Battle of Bentonville.* Campbell, Calif.: Savas Woodbury, 1996.

Chase, Julia A. Houghton. *Mary A. Bickerdyke, "Mother."* Lawrence, Kans.: Journal Publishing House, 1896.

Conyngham, David P. *Sherman's March Through the South: Sketches and Incidents of the Campaign.* New York: Sheldon, 1865.

Cox, Jacob D. *The March to the Sea—Franklin and Nashville.* New York: Charles Scribner's Sons, 1913.

Davis, Margaret B. *Mother Bickerdyke: Her Life and Labors for the Relief of Our Soldiers; Sketches of Battle Scenes and Incidents of the Sanitary Service.* San Francisco: A.T. Dewey, 1886.

Dawson, George Francis. *Life and Services of Gen. John A. Logan, Soldier and Statesman.* New York: Belford, Clarke, 1887.

Dluger, Mark A. "A Regimental Community: The Men of the 82nd Illinois Infantry Before, During, and After the American Civil War." Ph.D. dissertation, Loyola University Chicago, 2009.

Downing, Alexander G. *Downing's Civil War Diary, August 15, 1861–July 31, 1865,* ed. Olynthus B. Clark. Des Moines, Iowa: The Historical Department of Iowa, 1916.

Eaton, Clement. "Diary of an Officer in Sherman's Army Marching Through the Carolinas." *The Journal of Southern History* 9:2 (1943), 238–254.

Ecelbarger, Gary. *Black Jack Logan: An Extraordinary Life in Peace and War.* Guilford, Conn.: Lyons Press, 2005.

Furman, Jan, ed. *Slavery in the Clover Bottoms: John McCline's Narrative of His Life During Slavery and the Civil War.* Knoxville: Univ. of Tennessee Press, 1998.

Glatthaar, Joseph T. *The March to the Sea and Beyond: Sherman's Troops in the Savannah and Carolinas Campaigns.* New York: New York Univ. Press, 1985.

Gleicher, David. "From Jewish Immigrant to Union General in Under Ten Years." *Chicago Jewish History* 15:2 (1992).

Grimsley, Mark. *The Hard Hand of War: Union Military Policy Toward Southern Civilians, 1861–1865.* New York: Cambridge University Press, 1995.

Hattaway, Herman and Archer Jones. *How the North Won: A Military History of the Civil War.* Chicago: Univ. of Illinois Press, 1991.

Hazen, William B. *A Narrative of Military Service.* Boston: Ticknor, 1885.

Hedley, F.Y. *Marching Through Georgia: Pen-Pictures of Every-Day Life in General Sherman's Army, from the Beginning of the Atlanta Campaign Until the Close of the War.* Chicago: Donohue, Henneberry, 1890.

Hight, John J. *History of the Fifty-Eighth Regiment of Indiana Volunteer Infantry.* Princeton, N.J.: Press of the Clarion, 1895.

Jones, James P. *Black Jack: John A. Logan and Southern Illinois in the Civil War Era.* Tallahassee: Florida State University, 1967.

Kellogg, Florence Shaw. *Mother Bickerdyke as I Knew Her.* Chicago: Unity, 1907.

Logan, Mary A. *Reminiscences of a Soldier's Wife: An Autobiography.* New York: Charles Scribner's Sons, 1913.

Marszalek, John F. *Sherman: A Soldier's Passion for Order.* New York: Free Press-Macmillan, 1993.

Nichols, George Ward. *The Story of the Great March, from the Diary of a Staff Officer.* New York: Harper & Brothers, 1865.

Reinhart, Joseph R., ed. *Yankee Dutchmen Under Fire: Civil War Letters from the 82nd Infantry.* Kent, Ohio: Kent State University Press, 2013.

Trudeau, Noah Andre. *Like Men of War: Black Troops in the Civil War, 1862–1865.* New York: Little, Brown, 1998.

Underwood, Adin B. *The Three Years' Service of the Thirty-Third Mass. Infantry Regiment, 1862–1865.* Boston: A. Williams, 1881.

Wills, Charles W. *Army Life of an Illinois Soldier: The Letters and Diary of Charles W. Wills.* Toronto: Globe Printing Co., 1906.

Woodworth, Steven E. *Nothing but Victory: The Army of the Tennessee, 1861–1865.* New York: Knopf, 2005.

CHAPTER 16: THE GRAND REVIEW

1880 United States Census. Cincinnati, Hamilton County, Ohio, 80.

Baker, Nina Brown. *Cyclone in Calico.* Boston: Little, Brown, 1952.

Benjaminson, Eric. "A Regiment of Immigrants: The 82nd Illinois Volunteer Infantry and the Letters of Captain Rudolph Mueller." *Journal of the Illinois State Historical Society* 94:2 (2001).

Biographical Sketches of the Leading Men of Chicago. Chicago: Wilson & St. Clair, 1901. 390.

Chase, Julia A. Houghton. *Mary A. Bickerdyke, "Mother."* Lawrence, Kans.: Journal Publishing House, 1896.

Davis, Margaret B. *Mother Bickerdyke: Her Life and Labors for the Relief of Our Soldiers; Sketches of Battle Scenes and Incidents of the Sanitary Service.* San Francisco: A.T. Dewey, 1886.

Dawson, George Francis. *Life and Services of Gen. John A. Logan, Soldier and Statesman.* New York: Belford, Clarke, 1887.

"Death of John J. Hight." *Cincinnati Gazette.* December 22, 1886.

"Death of Major Charles W. Wills." *New Orleans Times-Picayune.* March 25, 1883. 4.

Dluger, Mark A. "A Regimental Community: The Men of the 82nd Illinois Infantry Before, During, and After the American Civil War." Ph.D. dissertation, Loyola University Chicago, 2009.

Ecelbarger, Gary. *Black Jack Logan: An Extraordinary Life in Peace and War.* Guilford, Conn.: Lyons Press, 2005.

Fellman, Michael. *Citizen Sherman: A Life of William Tecumseh Sherman.* New York: Random House, 1994.

Freitag, Sabine. *Friedrich Hecker: Two Lives for Liberty.* St. Louis: St. Louis Mercantile Library, 2006.

Furman, Jan, ed. *Slavery in the Clover Bottoms: John McCline's Narrative of His Life During Slavery and the Civil War.* Knoxville: Univ. of Tennessee Press, 1998.

"General News." *The New York Times,* May 24 and May 25, 1865, 1.

Glatthaar, Joseph T. *The March to the Sea and Beyond: Sherman's Troops in the Savannah and Carolinas Campaigns.* New York: New York Univ. Press, 1985.

Gleicher, David. "From Jewish Immigrant to Union General in Under Ten Years." *Chicago Jewish History* 15:2 (1992).

SOURCES

Hedley, F.Y. *Marching Through Georgia: Pen-Pictures of Every-Day Life in General Sherman's Army, from the Beginning of the Atlanta Campaign Until the Close of the War.* Chicago: Donohue, Henneberry, 1890.

Henshaw, Sarah Edwards. *Our Branch and Its Tributaries; Being a History of the Work of the Northwestern Sanitary Commission and Its Auxiliaries, During the War of the Rebellion.* Chicago: Alfred L. Sewell, 1868.

Hight, John J. *History of the Fifty-Eighth Regiment of Indiana Volunteer Infantry.* Princeton, N.J.: Press of the Clarion, 1895.

Jones, James P. *Black Jack: John A. Logan and Southern Illinois in the Civil War Era.* Tallahassee: Florida State University, 1967.

Kellogg, Florence Shaw. *Mother Bickerdyke as I Knew Her.* Chicago: Unity, 1907.

Livermore, Mary A. "Cooperative Womanhood in the State." *North American Review* 153:418 (1891), 283–295.

Livermore, Mary A. *My Story of the War: A Woman's Narrative of Four Years Personal Experience.* Hartford, Conn.: A.D. Worthington, 1889.

Livermore, Mary A. *The Story of My Life, or The Sunshine and Shadow of Seventy Years.* Hartford, Conn.: A.D. Worthington, 1897.

Logan, Mary A. *Reminiscences of a Soldier's Wife: An Autobiography.* New York: Charles Scribner's Sons, 1913.

Marszalek, John F. *Sherman: A Soldier's Passion for Order.* New York: Free Press-Macmillan, 1993.

McShea, Ann. "Hazleton Soldiers in the Civil War Marched on After Lee's Surrender." *The Standard-Speaker,* December 20, 2015.

Nichols, George Ward. *The Story of the Great March, from the Diary of a Staff Officer.* New York: Harper & Brothers, 1865.

Reece, J.N. Report of the Adjutant General for the State of Illinois, vol. 5, 1861–1866. Springfield, Ill.: Phillips Brothers State Printers, 1901.

Reinhart, Joseph R., ed. *Yankee Dutchmen Under Fire: Civil War Letters from the 82nd Infantry.* Kent, Ohio: Kent State University Press, 2013.

Ross, Reid D. "Civil War Grand Review." *America's Civil War Magazine,* December 9, 2015. Accessed at www.historynet.com/civil-war-grand-review.htm.

Shattuck Jr., Gardiner H. "Revivals in the Camp" *Christianity Today* 33 (1992). Accessed at www .christianitytoday.com/history/issues/issue-33/revivals-in-camp.html.

"Sherman's March, May 24, 1865: The Grand Review and the End of the Great March." To The Sound of the Guns: Civil War Artillery, Battlefields and Historical Markers, May 24, 2015. Accessed at https://markerhunter.wordpress.com/2015/05/24 /shermans-march-may-24-1865.

Shields, Patricia M. "Mary Livermore: A Legacy of Caring and Cooperative Womanhood in Service to the State." From *Outstanding Women in Public Administration: Leaders, Mentors, and Pioneers,* eds. Claire L. Felbinger and Wendy A. Haynes. Armonk, N.Y.: M.E. Sharpe, 2004.

Simpson, Brooks D. and Jean V. Berlin, eds. *Sherman's Civil War: Selected Correspondence of William T. Sherman, 1860–1865.* Chapel Hill: Univ. of North Carolina Press, 1999.

Stroock, William. "The Grand Review of 1865." Warfare History Network, March 27, 2017. Accessed at http://warfarehistorynetwork.com/daily/civil-war/the-grand-review-of-1865/.

Trudeau, Noah Andre. *Like Men of War: Black Troops in the Civil War, 1862–1865*. New York: Little, Brown, 1998.

Venet, Wendy Hamand. *A Strong-Minded Woman: The Life of Mary A. Livermore*. Amherst: University of Massachusetts Press, 2005.

Wills, Charles W. *Army Life of an Illinois Soldier: The Letters and Diary of Charles W. Wills*. Toronto: Globe Printing, 1906.

Woodworth, Steven E. *Nothing but Victory: The Army of the Tennessee, 1861–1865*. New York: Knopf, 2005.

Wylie, Theophilus A. *Indiana University: Its History from 1820, When Founded, to 1890*. Indianapolis: William B. Burford, 1890. 207–208.

EPILOGUE: THE FIRES TO COME

Fellman, Michael. *Citizen Sherman: A Life of William Tecumseh Sherman*. New York: Random House, 1994.

Marszalek, John F. *Sherman: A Soldier's Passion for Order*. New York: Free Press-Macmillan, 1993.

O'Connell, Robert L. *Fierce Patriot: The Tangled Lives of William Tecumseh Sherman*. New York: Random House, 2014.

Rubin, Anne Sarah. *Through the Heart of Dixie: Sherman's March and American Memory*. Chapel Hill: Univ. of North Carolina Press, 2014.

Sherman, William T. *The Memoirs of William T. Sherman*, vols. 1 and 2. New York: D. Appleton, 1886.

Sherman, William T. "Old Shady, with a Moral." *North American Review* 147:383 (1888), 361–368.

Simpson, Brooks D. and Jean V. Berlin, eds. *Sherman's Civil War: Selected Correspondence of William T. Sherman, 1860–1865*. Chapel Hill: Univ. of North Carolina Press, 1999.

Walters, John Bennett. "General William T. Sherman and Total War." *The Journal of Southern History* 14:4 (1948), 447–480.

ACKNOWLEDGMENTS

would most like to thank my wife Teresa for all her help in reviewing this book, reading through the chapters, offering incisive thoughts and comments, and discussing them with me in detail—and for providing much love, support, and daily inspiration. Also invaluable was my editor Jessica Case, who helped to streamline the book's ideas and hone its narrative, and guided it to a successful conclusion with keen insights, thoughtful revisions, and constructive feedback. Also at Pegagus, I'd like to thank Maria Fernandez, Shayna Sobol, and Daniel O'Connor. And of course, I could not have gotten this project off the ground without the ongoing efforts of my manager Adam Chromy, whose lengthy discussions with me about the book's premise and trenchant review of early chapters were critical to the process, and kept me focused on the core elements of this historical saga.

The staff and assistants at several historical libraries also supported me in my research, among them the librarians at the Library of Congress, for the assorted collections and manuscripts pertaining to figures such as John Logan, Mary Ann Bickerdyke, and William Sherman, as well as the staff at the Prints and Photographs Division. Also essential were the research assistants in the National Archives, who aided me in my inquiry into the compiled military service records and pension records of certain key figures in the book, as well as information pertaining to the actions of relevant units from regiments to corps in Sherman's armies. I found other institutional support through the Research Center at the Chicago History Museum, the Illinois State Archives, the Abraham Lincoln Presidential Library, Illinois State Historical Library, Washingtoniana Collection at the District of Columbia Public Library, Historical Society of Washington, D.C., and New Mexico State University–Rio Grande Historical Collections.

I would also like to thank my friends for their support and forbearance through the process, and especially Clara Stemwedel for helping me secure several critical dissertations and research sources that proved key to uncovering the full scope of the story. Finally, thanks as always to my parents and other family members, who have always been there for me and continue to offer their strength, encouragement and great affection. This book is also written in memory of James Osten and Georgetta and Harold Dickey, who supported my writing with much love and enthusiasm, and whose legacy continues to inspire us all.

ILLUSTRATION CREDITS

All maps by the author. © 2018 J. D. Dickey.

All images are public domain unless otherwise stated.

Figure 1: From *Harper's Weekly*, May 19, 1860.

Figures 2, 6, 7, 14, 17, 18, 19, 25, 26, 27, 31, 37, 39, 41, 42, 48, 51, 52, 54, 56, and 58: Courtesy of the Library of Congress.

Figures 3 and 4: From Brockett, L.P., and Mary C. Vaughan. *Women's Work in the Civil War: A Record of Heroism, Patriotism and Patience.* Chicago: Zeigler, McCurdy & Co., 1867.

Figure 5: From Livermore, Mary A. *My Story of the War: A Woman's Narrative of Four Years Personal Experience.* Hartford, Conn.: A.D. Worthington and Company, 1889.

Figures 8 and 55: Courtesy of the New Mexico State University Library, Archives and Special Collections.

Figure 10: From Wills, Charles W. *Army Life of an Illinois Soldier: The Letters and Diary of Charles W. Wills.* Toronto, Ont.: Globe Printing Co., 1906.

Figures 11, 12, 13, 15, 20, 22, 28, 29, 30, 32, 36, 45, 46, and 49: Courtesy of the National Archives and Records Administration.

Figure 21: From *Harper's Weekly*, April 2, 1864.

Figures 24 and 53: Courtesy of the Washington State Archives, Portraits of State Governors.

Figure 33: From *Harper's Weekly*, January 7, 1865.

Figures 34, 35, 38, and 47: From Nichols, George Ward. *The Story of the Great March, from the Diary of a Staff Officer."* New York: Harper & Brothers, 1865.

Figure 40: From *Frank Leslie's Illustrated Magazine*, March 18, 1865.

Figure 43: Courtesy of the St. Louis Mercantile Library.

Figure 44: From *Harper's Weekly*, April 6, 1865.

Figure 50: From *Harper's Weekly*, June 10, 1865.

Figure 59: Courtesy of the Chicago Historical Society.

INDEX